Piracy and the Making of the
Spanish Pacific World

THE EARLY MODERN AMERICAS

Peter C. Mancall, Series Editor

Volumes in the series explore neglected aspects of
early modern history in the western hemisphere.
Interdisciplinary in character, and with a special
emphasis on the Atlantic World from 1450 to 1850,
the series is published in partnership with the
USC-Huntington Early Modern Studies Institute.

PIRACY AND THE MAKING OF THE SPANISH PACIFIC WORLD

Kristie Patricia Flannery

PENN

UNIVERSITY OF PENNSYLVANIA PRESS

PHILADELPHIA

Published by
University of Pennsylvania Press
Philadelphia, Pennsylvania 19104-4112
www.upenn.edu/pennpress

Printed in the United States of America on acid-free paper
10 9 8 7 6 5 4 3 2 1

Hardcover ISBN: 978-1-5128-2574-9
eBook ISBN: 978-1-5128-2575-6

A Cataloging-in-Publication record is available
from the Library of Congress

For Alex, Oliver, and Leila

CONTENTS

Maritime Violence and Imperial Formation

An Introduction

A Spanish frigate, a Chinese junk, and fifteen prahus built by skilled native craftsmen carrying roughly eighty Spaniards and hundreds of heavily tattooed Visayan warriors between them sailed into Manila Bay in May of 1570. This hybrid fleet altered the future of the Philippine islands and the course of global history. Some five years earlier, the Spaniards had established an outpost at Cebu in the Visayan islands in the middle of the archipelago. Cebu's Rajah Tupas brokered an alliance with Miguel López de Legazpi, the first Spanish governor of the Philippines. Legazpi agreed to make peace with Tupas and war on his enemies, a mutually beneficial arrangement sealed by *casicasi*, a blood-mixing ceremony that signified a union between equals. Together, Legazpi and Tupas's fighting men raided coastal villages throughout the central Philippines, seizing captives and whatever other items of value they could lay their hands on. Legazpi eventually learned about Rajah Soliman's wealthy kingdom of May Nila on the big northern island of Luzon, and he set his sights on sending his men and their Indigenous allies to attack it. The Hispano-Visayan fleet's arrival in May Nila led to a tense few days of message swapping and meetings before a bloody battle broke out. The invaders overwhelmed Soliman's fortified kingdom and burned it to the ground. The Spanish claimed the land for their king and founded the capital of their Asian empire above its smoldering ashes.[1]

Popular accounts of this dramatic opening act of the Spanish empire in the Philippines tell a different version of this story, one that erases Tupas and the tattooed Visayans entirely. Take, for example, the Gerilya collective's new mural in Manila's busy Lagusnilad underpass. The spectacular painting visually narrates the past five centuries of the city's history in the artists' signature comic book style. Its first scene portrays idyllic May Nila, whose name means "the place of the water lilies" in Tagalog, before Europeans arrived. The proud elder Soliman sits on a golden throne in the center of the image, surrounded by handsome men and women adorned with gold jewelry. His subjects trade with Chinese merchants in the background. The mural's next scene (Figure 1) shows the Spaniards' rampageous arrival and the destruction of this peaceful and prosperous polity. The invaders come from the sea. White men wearing heavy armor and riding on horseback swarm out of tall European sailing ships and onto the shore brandishing harquebuses and swords. A Catholic friar raises a cross above his head, blessing their holy war against the idolatrous locals. On the beach in the foreground, armed land defenders clasping round shields and *kampilans* (swords) are ready to fight to protect their kin as other warriors load shot into *lantaka* (cannon) aimed at the enemy's boats. Raging red flames surround the picture. The mural traces the proud history of Filipino rebellion against empire from this first bloody encounter on the beach in the sixteenth century through to the Ilustrados and the Katipunan's late nineteenth- and early twentieth-century campaigns against the Spanish and then the U.S. occupying forces.[2] Public celebrations of resistance against empire are exciting, especially for those of us who come from settler colonial societies that continue to lionize conquistador ancestors while silencing Indigenous peoples and their collective dispossession and defiance. Yet this romantic interpretation of Philippines history—one that pitches foreigners against Filipinos in a brutal struggle over sovereignty—distorts the truth about the history of the Spanish empire in the islands.

Piracy and the Making of the Spanish Pacific World is a book about Spanish colonial rule in the Philippines in the long eighteenth century, but it makes sense to start here, at the beginning. Contrasting two distinct visions of Spain's Asian empire at the moments of its birth underscores how dominant interpretations of the history of the Spanish conquest and colonization of the islands omit Indigenous peoples whose actions fail to fulfill modern, nationalist ideals of the rebellious anti-colonial Filipino subject, who is epitomized by the Philippines' national hero José Rizal. The Manila-born and Spain-educated medical doctor, writer, artist, and activist advocated for imperial reform and eventually for Philippines independence. The Spanish colonial government sentenced him to be executed in 1896 as punishment for the crimes of rebellion and sedition.[3] The compacts that the original inhabitants of the Philippines brokered with Spanish conquistadors to wage war in the

Figure 1. Spanish conquistadors pour out of tall sailing ships onto the beach defended by brave land defenders in Gerilya's "Masigasig na Maynila" (2020). Photograph by Fung Yu.

1560s and 1570s continued to characterize and sustain colonial rule in the centuries that followed. This study centers on the hybrid Hispano-Filipino armadas and militias that mobilized in the archipelago to fight against the empire's enemies. It examines how these heavily Indigenous militarized forces were organized, assesses what they achieved, and analyzes the matrix of factors that led individuals and communities to join or support them. These forgotten Indigenous navies and armies are key to explaining how empire was forged in the Philippines from below.

Spain's Asian empire strikes historians as a paradox. On the surface, the Philippines seems like an impossible colony. Archipelagos are notoriously difficult to rule, and vast distances separated this one from centers of Spanish imperial power in the Americas and Europe.[4] The journey from Madrid to Manila involved crossing the Atlantic Ocean to the port city of Vera Cruz in present-day Mexico, traveling overland to Mexico City and on to Acapulco, and then across the Pacific Ocean aboard a galleon. This dangerous journey took roughly two years to complete. Spaniards—a socio-racial group that included men and women born in Spain, in the Americas, and in the Philippines—were always a minority in the islands, even in the capital. Moreover, the Spanish colony was surrounded by rival Asian states and jealous European imperial powers that wanted to destroy it and that attacked time and again. Indigenous communities and Chinese migrants and their descendants within the Philippines repeatedly revolted against colonial rule. And yet Spain's Asian empire was resilient, surviving repeated insurgencies, wars, natural disasters, and, in the early nineteenth century, the monarchical crisis triggered by Napoleon's invasion of the Iberian Peninsula that led to the collapse of the Spanish empire in the Americas. Spanish colonial rule in the Philippines would not end until 1898, some 330 years after Legazpi met Tupas, when the government of the United States of America purchased the islands as part of a peace treaty that ended the Spanish-American War.

The narratives that historians have offered up to explain the longevity of the Spanish empire in the Philippines are lacking in their explanatory power. Many contend that violence and coercion alone permitted colonial power to take root in the islands. The Filipino historian Renato Constantino, for example, claimed that the first Spaniards in the islands tortured Indigenous leaders' wives and daughters until they consented to empire.[5] Others have argued that Catholic missionaries were the glue that held empire together, or have singled out the Spanish colonial government's effective economic reforms as the primary cause of the colonial project's long-term success.[6]

Charting a new course, this study analyzes the Spanish empire in the Philippines through the lens of maritime violence, developing a revisionist view of colonial rule that centers Indigenous agency.

Spain's Asian empire was forged in a sea of piracy. Three waves of maritime violence plagued the early modern Philippines. The first wave comprised the colossal Chinese pirate fleets that boomed amid the chaos of China's turbulent Ming-Qing transition in the seventeenth century. Large-scale Chinese piracy peaked in 1661, when Zheng Zhilong conquered Taiwan and threatened to invade Manila. It declined in the 1680s when the Qing consolidated power, captured the Taiwan pirates' nest, and asserted its authority over China's maritime borders. What Manileños called Moro piracy surged in the first half of the eighteenth century, becoming the second major wave of maritime violence to wash over the Philippines. Pirates from the Islamic maritime states in the Southern Philippine islands and across the Sulu Sea raided ships and coastal villages in Mindanao, the Visayas, and Southern Luzon with the predictable regularity of the monsoon. As these sea-robbers carried off thousands of people each year as captives, they turned into the single greatest threat to the survival of Spanish rule in the archipelago. The third wave of maritime violence hit Manila with the force of a tsunami in 1762 when a joint British Royal Navy and East India Company force invaded and occupied the city. British pirates forced a reckoning with the fragility of Spanish rule in the islands when they took control of the walled capital and raised the Union Jack above Manila's Fort Santiago. All of these adversaries came from the sea to pillage people and other riches. Spanish colonial officials and the disparate communities that bore the brunt of maritime violence in the Philippines lumped these enemies together as pirates. Who was named a pirate in the Spanish Pacific much depended on who was doing the naming.[7]

This book's central argument is that piracy defined evolving relationships between the Spanish colonial government and the Catholic Church, Indigenous peoples, and Chinese migrants and their descendants in the early modern Philippines. The Chinese, whom the Spaniards called *Sangleyes*, were the largest migrant population in the islands during centuries of Spanish colonial rule. Sea raiding gave rise to a Catholic anti-piracy politics and praxis that saw colonial officials and militant missionaries broker agreements with local Indigenous and Chinese communities to wage war against pirates. Additionally, the specter of maritime violence pushed the Crown to pursue diplomatic solutions to piracy and enter into alliances with sovereign Asian rulers. Recent scholarship on the Spanish and other empires in the Americas has emphasized the centrality of negotiation and pacts to colonial rule.[8] In the case of the Philippines, piracy and anti-piracy provided the fundamental framework for making and remaking the colonial bargain, and comprehending this phenomenon is key to challenging "the more rigid definitions of colonial power that see it stemming only from the top down, and of colonialism as a mere exercise in domination by force."[9]

Catholic anti-piracy lent legitimacy to the Spanish empire in the Philippines in the eyes of communities that sought protection from sea-robbers. It also strengthened empire against external and internal shocks. This book illustrates how the state effectively utilized the systems, resources, and traditions it codeveloped to confront pirates to resist the incursions of sea-robbers as well as to suppress Chinese and Indigenous revolts against empire. This analysis advances the findings of recent studies of piracy in other premodern world regions that have highlighted the multifaceted ways that maritime violence functioned to strengthen Europe's overseas colonies, complicating earlier interpretations of pirates as radical visionaries that undermined early modern empires, social hierarchies, racist and sexist ideologies, and slavery and the slave trade.[10]

This book steers piracy studies into new waters by illuminating how maritime violence shaped the colonial politics of belonging in the Philippines. It demonstrates that shifting piracy threats determined which Indigenous and migrant communities would be integrated into the Spanish empire as vassals, and which groups would be othered and subject to segregation, expulsion, and even mass executions. Piracy had a profound impact on the experiences of Chinese sojourners, migrants, and their descendants in the islands, and the transformation of maritime violence caused major changes in the clergy and colonial officials' attitudes toward and treatment of this section of colonial society. Ann Laura Stoler observed that racism in colonial contexts "is often seen as a virtually built-in and natural product" of the encounter between the European colonizer and the colonized subject.[11] In the historiography of the colonial Philippines, the assumed inevitability and invariability of anti-Chinese racism has prevented scholars from grappling with enormous variations in the character and intensity of anti-Chinese views over time, and the actions they inspired. Interrogating the archipelago's colonial history through the lens of piracy brings to light the intertwined histories of Indigenous and Chinese peoples in the Philippines, disrupting the prevailing tendency to study these groups apart in distinct historiographical silos.[12]

The term *Indigenous* is used in this book to refer to the peoples who were native to the Philippines and other territories in the Pacific and Atlantic worlds that Spain claimed to rule. European imperial expansion created the concept of Indigeneity, which Mary Louise Pratt describes as a "historically constructed relationship between subjects who inhabit a place and subjects who arrive(d) there uninvited from elsewhere. . . . Put succinctly, no one is Indigenous until somebody else shows up."[13] The Spanish word *indio* is almost as old as the Spanish empire itself. Christopher Columbus and his shipmates designated the men and women whom they encountered in the Caribbean as indios because they briefly mistakenly believed that they had made landfall in India. But indio meant Indigenous in the Spanish empire from this time onward, long after Columbus's geographical error was corrected. Spaniards lumped together in the "indio" category the many ethnolinguistic groups that they encountered in the Philippines, including Tagalogs, Pampangans, Ilocanos, and Cebuanos, along with the diverse Indigenous peoples that they came into contact with across the Americas. Indio became a legal category of subjecthood in the Spanish empire defined in a body of "Indian" law that was developed to both exploit and protect these vulnerable vassals of the Crown. The legal protections that the empire afforded Indigenous peoples, which encompassed prohibitions on their enslavement, influenced peoples' decisions to self-identify as indios or Indigenous in their dealings with colonial bureaucracies and the Crown.[14] In the early modern Philippines, men and women sometimes adopted hyphenated identities such as *indio-tagalo* that simultaneously marked their indigeneity and their membership in a distinct nation or ethnolinguistic group.[15] I use the identifiers indio and Indigenous in this book to respectfully acknowledge how the people that I write about identified themselves. Today, the term *indio* is increasingly regarded as derogatory in many Spanish-speaking countries. Indigenous is considered a relatively neutral term, however its use in the contemporary Philippines context is complicated.[16]

What it means to be Indigenous in the Philippines today is markedly different from what it meant to be Indigenous in the islands hundreds of years ago. Indigenous peoples in the Philippines, who currently account for roughly 10 percent of the country's population, belong to more than one hundred major ethnolinguistic Indigenous groups, the largest being the Lumads of Mindanao and the Igorots of Luzon's Cordillera Central. Like Indigenous peoples in other parts of the world, they are marginalized and threatened by displacement and violence. Significantly, Indigenous peoples in the contemporary Philippines are regarded as the descendants of the women and men who successfully evaded Spanish and U.S. colonial rule. Both the Spanish and U.S. colonial administrations distinguished these groups from Catholics in the archipelago, with the Spanish labeling them as *infieles* (infidels or pagans) and the Americans designating them "non-Christian tribes." Remarkably, opposing empire in the past has come to define indigeneity in the present, rendering the Indigenous Filipino who was loyal to empire an ontological impossibility.[17]

The Philippines Before and After the Spanish Conquest

There are more than seven thousand islands in the Philippines archipelago, which is conventionally divided into three parts: the big northern island of Luzon, the large southern island of Mindanao, and the Visayan group of islands lying between them. The Philippines are volcanic islands featuring fertile green valleys between soaring mountain ranges. Population density was low and political authority was decentralized in the islands in the middle of the sixteenth century, before Legazpi arrived. The basic unit of political and social organization was the *barangay*, which took its name from the outrigger canoes that plied the archipelago's blue waters. Each barangay was headed by a *datu* (chief) and included between thirty and one hundred families whose members were connected through blood ties and ritual kinship. Maritime raiding influenced all aspects of life in the islands, especially in low-lying coastal regions. Islanders fortified their villages and developed boats and weapons that enabled warriors to move speedily across the sea to assault enemy ships and settlements and to seize useful resources, especially human captives. In this world at war, islanders venerated the bravest fighting men.[18]

Before the beginning of the Spanish conquest, the Philippines were already a highly connected archipelago situated in the geographic middle of maritime Asia. This world region, shown in Map 1, stretched north from the Philippines to Japan and Korea and south to the Maluku Islands and Java (in present-day Indonesia).[19] To the east lay the Ayutthaya kingdom (centered in present-day Thailand) and the colossal kingdom of China. During the reign of the Ming dynasty, China's population more than doubled from approximately 60 million in the late fourteenth century to 150 million by 1600, dwarfing the population of any other state in the region. Maritime Asia was characterized by contested sovereignties and geopolitical rivalries, yet China was so large that its policies, its prosperity, and its crises reverberated through-out the region.[20] Long-distance trading networks connected upland and lowland communities in the Philippines to each other and to farther flung polities across seas. Islam arrived in the islands via intra-Asian trade, but it was not the dominant religious tradition. Religious plurality prevailed when the first Catholic missionaries came calling.[21]

Iberian dreams of conquering Asia sowed the seeds of Spanish overseas expansion. At the end of the fifteenth century the Catholic monarchs—King Ferdinand II of Aragon and his wife, Queen Isabella of Castille—invested in Columbus's voyage to discover a sea route to the so-called Spice Islands (the Maluku Islands). The monarchs were eager to acquire cloves, nutmeg, and pepper; commodities that would make them rich in this life. Desiring salva-tion in the next, they believed that backing the God-ordained mission to spread Catholicism to distant lands would also save their souls. After Colum-bus accidentally discovered Caribbean islands and the American continent during his voyage to Asia, the Crown's campaigns to conquer Atlantic and Pacific colonies advanced as interconnected enterprises that unfurled in uni-son.[22] Ferdinand Magellan, a Portuguese navigator in the service of the Span-ish monarchy, reached the Philippine islands in 1521, where he was killed by Datu Lapu Lapu and his men.[23] That same year, an army of Spanish soldiers led by Hernan Cortés and their Indigenous Tlaxcalan allies conquered the great Mexica city of Tenochtitlan. The Spaniards tore down the towering templo mayor and built new palaces and churches above its sturdy founda-tions, transforming Mexico City into a center of Spanish colonial power.[24]

As the sixteenth century progressed, hybrid Spanish and Indigenous mil-itary forces waged wars of conquest that expanded Spanish rule deeper into the Americas. Black auxiliaries, Tlaxcalans, and Cholulans joined the in-vasions of Mayan lands in southern Mexico and Central America. In 1533, Spanish conquistadors and their Indigenous allies captured Cuzco, the capital of the Incan empire nestled high in the Andes, before seizing Quito (1534), Bogotá (1538), and Potosí at the foot of the great silver mountain (1545). Spanish and Native American forces then pushed into Mapuche ter-ritory in present-day Chile and into the lands controlled by the Chichime-cas in northern Mexico.[25] These campaigns coincided with multiple Spanish transpacific expeditions to explore and conquer maritime Asia.[26] Legazpi's was the first of these ventures to succeed in establishing an outpost in the Philippine islands at Cebu and to find the crucial return maritime route to Mexico. He relocated the capital of Spain's nascent Asian empire to Manila

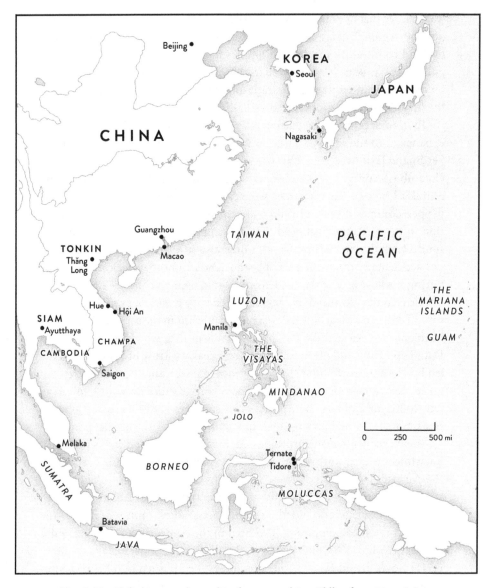

Map 1. The Philippines are located in the geographic middle of maritime Asia, which facilitated the development of long-distance trading networks that linked the archipelago to other islands and littoral zones in the western Pacific Ocean region.

to take advantage of its protected bay and established trade with Chinese merchants.

The Spanish conquest transformed the Philippine islands. Manila became a bustling port city and the center of imperial power in the archipelago. Galleon ships sailed between Manila and Acapulco almost every year from the late sixteenth century until the outbreak of Mexican wars for independence in the early nineteenth century. Scholars have called Manila the birthplace of globalization because the city created a direct maritime connection between Asia and the Americas for the first time in human history. For 250 years, the great ships brought silver, soldiers, and friars to Manila and returned to America brimming with commodities sourced from across maritime Asia. The trade's transformative impact on material culture and the history of capitalism has been the subject of sustained scholarly inquiry over several generations.[27] The commerce attracted merchants and settlers from across the planet who gave Manila a cosmopolitan flair. The Manila-born Jesuit priest and scholar Pedro Murillo Velarde described the city in 1749 as "a universal mission, equal to all the other missions of the world, for gathered here are people from all of the universe."[28] Manila's Fort Santiago was connected to the thick walls that wrapped around the urban center's Intramuros (within-the-walls) zone. The cannon that lined fort and city walls were ready to bombard pirates that dared sail into Manila Bay, or the city's Chinese residents if they rose up in rebellion against the Spanish governor. The most important government and ecclesiastical buildings stood inside Intramuros. Manila boasted multiple churches, convents, and chapels because the city was the headquarters for the Catholic missionary orders in the archipelago. The five major missionary orders that were active in the islands had all established a presence there by 1606, including the Augustinians, the Augustinian Recollects, the Discalced Franciscans, the Jesuits, and the Dominicans.[29]

The cosmopolitan colonial capital was not the only place in the Philippines that was changed by colonialism. Over time, the Spanish colonial government and missionary orders oversaw the construction of a network of presidios and fortified churches across the archipelago that facilitated the protection and exploitation of Indigenous Filipinos. In the Philippines context, protection was primarily understood as defense against pirate raids. In Manila and its hinterland, as well as in frontier zones, colonialism intruded into Indigenous people's lives in the form of the extraction of resources, primarily through the payment of the head tax known as tribute, and through the performance of tributary labor. Missionaries used many strategies to convert Indigenous and Chinese people in the islands to Catholicism, including a program of relocating barangays from ancestral lands to villages in proximity to churches, which was known as *reducción*. Native and Chinese communities that embraced the faith of the conquistadors made Catholicism their own, incorporating aspects of pre-Hispanic, animistic, and Chinese traditions into Catholic devotions.[30]

Colonial power is never total. Spanish authority in the Philippines was geographically uneven and extra-state and anti-state zones persisted across the islands. The Spanish colonial government was unable to dominate high-altitude zones. Hispano-Filipino military expeditions mounted in the seventeenth and eighteenth centuries failed to conquer the communities that inhabited the highest reaches of the Cordillera.[31] Nicolas de la Cruz Bagay and Pedro Murillo Velarde's 1734 map of the Philippine islands identified multiple locations along Luzon's mountain ranges where Igorot, Calinga, and Negros "gentiles" lived beyond the reach of colonial officials and missionaries.[32] These peoples were the descendants of the women and men who fled to these zones of refuge to escape colonialism. Hispano-Filipino armadas and militias also failed to subdue the Islamic South, or the sea, which became sanctuaries for people fleeing empire. Early modern Spaniards in the Philippines saw their grasp on the colony as tenuous even in Manila. Generations of Spanish governors were anxious that foreign pirate invaders coming from the sea or disgruntled Chinese and Indigenous Filipinos would destroy Spanish sovereignty in the islands.

Core Concepts and Methods

Three conceptual and methodological strategies have shaped this study's design and key conclusions. Inspired by a rich corpus of scholarship on popular allegiance to Spain in colonial Latin America, the first of these consists of looking for loyalty to empire from the bottom up.[33] Loyalty is broadly defined as individual and collective support for the Spanish Crown and its representatives in the islands, including the clergy. Such support manifested in a range of actions, the most conspicuous of which was enlisting in the hybrid colonial ground and naval forces that attacked the empire's enemies. *Piracy and the Making of the Spanish Pacific World* shows that the reasons for fidelity to empire were multiple and complex and were informed by calculated assessments and reassessments of personal and group interests. This view of loyalty opposes the racist characterization of Indigenous and Black people who supported the Crown as ignorant or naive "victims of manipulation," which is a thread that runs through the nationalist historiographies of the Philippines as well as postcolonial Latin American republics.[34] As David Sartorius noted, scholarship on "patriotism and political allegiance usually target nation states, while dismissing pro-colonial affinities as the misfires of historical subjects acting against their interests: dupes, victims, collaborators."[35] This book's approach stands in stark contrast to the resistance-as-method that dominates the literature on the Philippines' colonial past. Scholars' decisions to prioritize recovering and celebrating rebellion against colonial rule, from subtle, everyday acts of resistance to all-out armed insurrections, has come at the cost of ignoring or burying evidence of subaltern support for the Spanish empire in the islands.

The second methodological strategy is spatial. This study adopts an amphibious approach, interrogating the connections between terrestrial and aqueous spaces, and breaking down false barriers between them.[36] It locates the early modern Philippines within two overlapping transoceanic worlds: the global Spanish empire and maritime Asia. Each chapter begins with the arrival or departure of ships, underscoring the archipelago's ties to ports and polities within and across imperial borders. It is attuned to the plural and sometimes contradictory ways that people living in the islands imagined and interacted with the Catholic Church and with Spain, its monarchs, and its large, polycentric and transoceanic imperial bureaucracy. It also considers how the islands' diverse inhabitants thought about and experienced historical developments, from those that took place close to home to those that happened far away, and in the past as well as in the present. The global turn in early modern studies has influenced this approach, but the archive also gestures and pulls in these geographical directions. This spatial method represents a departure from studies that focus on events within the Philippines proto-nation state's borders, and from transoceanic frameworks that tend to locate the archipelago as either part of Asia or part of the Spanish empire, but rarely both.[37]

This study's third methodological strategy is archival. It relies heavily on primary source materials that are preserved in the archives of the Catholic Church and Catholic missionary orders that were active in the Philippines and the archives of imperial Spain's transoceanic bureaucracy. It analyzes a range of materials within this expansive archive of empire, including printed chronicles or histories of Spanish colonial rule in the Philippines that were written and published in the seventeenth and eighteenth centuries, and unpublished manuscripts such as maps, letters, reports, census records, petitions, poems, peace treaties, and declarations of war. The English translations of this predominately Spanish-language trove that appear in this book are my own, unless indicated otherwise. Historians face multiple challenges in accessing and interpreting this archive. It is dispersed across physical and digital collections in multiple countries, including the Archivo General de Indias in Seville, the Archivo General de la Nación in Mexico City, the National Archives of the Philippines in Manila, the British Library in London, and the Newberry and Lilly Libraries in the United States of America. Such decentralization requires travel time, funding, and visas that continue to be difficult for scholars from the Philippines and Latin America to obtain, reproducing the inequities that structure this history from its infancy. The generally limited indexation of these collections necessitates a "deep-dive" approach to exploring historical records. The only way to know the contents of boxes upon boxes of manuscripts is the slow and dusty practice of opening and reading files that tend to be organized chronologically. The necessarily immersive approach allowed me to gauge the clergy's and colonial officials' perceptions and experiences of empire and how these shifted over time. Through this process, piracy generated documentary soundings that were too loud to ignore.

Empire's archive was produced largely by elite Spanish men. This study mines documents composed by successive Spanish governors of the Philippines and members of Manila's Audiencia, which together made up the Spanish colonial government in the islands, and others crafted by bishops and the heads of Catholic missionary orders in the archipelago, along with their respective scribes and secretaries. Less important Spaniards, such as priests stationed at small frontier presidios and the captains of ships that patrolled watery borderlands, also authored materials that became part of this archive. Heeding Ann Laura Stoler's advice, I explored "the grain with care and read along it first" with attention to these colonists' evolving impressions of piracy and colonial rule. Interrogating empire's archive requires being aware of its makers' agendas and biases. These historical actors consciously brought an archive into being that served the empire's interests, advancing its goals to conquer and colonize or exploit and convert Indigenous people and

Chinese migrants in the Philippines. They were also invested in presenting idealized versions of themselves, and they crafted narratives designed to gain rewards and avoid punishments.[38] Paying attention to the discord and tension between these multiple agents of empire that emerges in colonial documents elucidates that colonizers were plural and heterogeneous rather than homogeneous or totalizing. Critics have pointed out that Emma Blair and James Robertson's fifty-five volume collection of primary sources pertaining to the history of Spanish rule of the Philippines—translated or summarized in English for easy North American consumption—similarly served the United States of America's empire in the Philippines.[39] The U.S. government backed this ambitious research project in the first decade of the twentieth century with the goal of developing and making available the knowledge that Yankee colonial administrators required to govern the unfamiliar Filipinos. The state was also invested in highlighting Spanish abuses in the islands to legitimize the allegedly "just, humane, [and] civilizing government" that the United States imposed on Filipinos down the barrel of a gun.[40] It is smart to be wary of scholarship that relies too heavily on this volume to interrogate the history of Spain's Asian empire, but it remains a valuable resource to historians and teachers when it is read with the degree of suspicion and skepticism that empire's archive demands.

Above all, I endeavor to recover Indigenous and Chinese peoples' voices, actions, and ideologies from colonial records. In most cases their traces survive in texts authored by Spanish elites. The rare Indigenous and Chinese migrant testimonies that survive in the archive are mediated by translators and scribes, including the passionate letters that the rebel leader Diego Silang addressed to Indigenous communities in Ilocos during the Seven Years' War, and Chinese community leaders' petitions to the government to halt their forced exile from the colony in the aftermath of this conflict. Even if the archive is riddled with lies and part-truths, engaging with a broad range of materials and a plethora of voices allows us to draw conclusions about what happened in the past and why. In the Philippines, the problem of the intentional silencing and erasure of subalterns in empire's archive are compounded by the archive's destruction and degradation. Natural disasters and wars, from eighteenth-century conflicts to World War II, resulted in countless colonial records being stolen or obliterated.[41] This study attempts to construct meaning from a mosaic of extant fragments of information, triangulating from multiple data points to recover forgotten and marginalized lives and ideas, while respecting the limits of what can be known.

Book Organization

This book is organized chronologically, elucidating how piracy impacted Spanish colonial rule in the Philippines and its evolution over time. Chapter 1 examines Moro piracy in Philippine borderlands. It analyzes trends in pirate raiding and how this crisis was conceptualized, highlighting how toxic Spanish ideas about Muslims and Islam that were developed in the Mediterranean world influenced Spanish interpretations of raiding in the Philippines as a religious crisis. The chapter considers the colonial government's strategies for defeating Moro piracy in the first half of the eighteenth century, which included forming alliances with the sovereign rulers of neighboring sultanates, including the Sulu Sultan Azim ud-Din, and brokering pacts with the Crown's Indigenous vassals to mobilize hybrid Hispano-Filipino armadas into holy war against mutual pirate enemies. It shows that Catholic anti-piracy campaigns increased demands on Indigenous labor that could intensify tensions between Indigenous communities and the Spanish colonial government, and at times this exploded into violent, anti-colonial rebellions. Yet on the whole, anti-piracy coalitions tended to strengthen imperial legitimacy in regions that bore the brunt of raiding.

Shifting focus from the borderlands to Manila, Chapter 2 examines how shifting piracy threats impacted Chinese sojourners and settlers and their descendants in the city and its hinterland. The seventeenth-century rise of massive Chinese pirate fleets that threatened to invade Manila produced a cycle of genocidal violence targeting this migrant community in the capital of Spain's Asian empire. Fears of pirate invasions sparked Chinese massacres in 1603, 1639, and 1662, with at least fifteen thousand Chinese men killed in each of these bloody episodes. This chapter argues that the subsequent suppression of large-scale Chinese pirate fleets terminated this mass-killing cycle. The holy war against Moro piracy created new opportunities for the Chinese to support Catholic anti-piracy campaigns in the first half of the eighteenth century, which facilitated the Sangleyes' integration into the Catholic republic of Manila as faithful vassals.

Chapters 3 and 4 focus on the British invasion and occupation of Manila, which occurred in 1762–1764, at the height of the global Seven Years' War. The invaders were a multiethnic British Royal Navy and East India Company force dispatched from Madras (Chennai)—men who were pirates in the eyes of Manileños. Chapter 3 revisits the history of the first six months of the invasion. The British expected that oppressed Indigenous Filipinos would welcome them as liberators, but during the siege of the capital they faced a fierce local opposition. Yet the invaders seized Manila and temporarily forced the Spanish colonial government into exile outside of the capital, which sparked Chinese rebellions and a massive Indigenous revolt against Spanish empire that spread across much of Luzon. The exiled Spanish government and friars worked with Indigenous and Chinese mestizo elites to mobilize a massive loyalist army that fought and eventually won a two-front war against the British and the local insurgents. Chapter 4 analyzes who fought in this army and why, and explains how it was able to restore Spanish colonial rule. In the face of this crisis, the colonial state and its allies successfully harnessed anti-piracy traditions and resources to secure Spanish sovereignty.

Chapter 5 considers the colonial government's efforts to strengthen empire in the wake of the British occupation of Manila and the revolts that left it reeling. The British invasion rapidly and drastically altered the status of Sangleyes in the Philippines. The Chinese were collectively scapegoated for the war, and Spain's king ordered the expulsion of all China-born migrants from the Philippine islands. The chapter reconstructs the two-stage expulsion process that involved victims being forcibly relocated from their homes across the archipelago to a market hall turned internment camp in Manila, and then forced to board ships that ostensibly delivered them to China. This chapter recovers the strategies that Chinese migrants used to resist forced migration, while also drawing attention to the crucial ways in which Indigenous peoples, Chinese mestizos, multiethnic merchants, and the clergy collaborated with the colonial government to carry out this violent policy.

In the 1770s the threats that British and Moro pirates posed to Spain's Asian empire led the Crown and its agents in the Philippines to pursue a new military alliance with the Nabob Haidar Ali, the ruler of the Indian state of Mysore and a sworn enemy of the British. The epilogue examines the embassy that Manila sent to Mysore in 1776 to finalize this treaty. Spain's first attempt to form a compact with a South Asian state sheds light on how maritime violence continued to push the Spanish to broker alliances in Asia at the dawn of the Age of Revolutions.

Overall, this analysis of the entangled history of piracy and empire in the Spanish Pacific offers readers a richer understanding of the dynamics of colonial rule in the Philippines. As the first serious, sustained, and archive-based study of subaltern loyalty to Spain in the archipelago, it complicates the widely accepted narrative that Indigenous peoples as well as Chinese migrants and their descendants in the islands were everywhere and always rebelling against empire, either in subtle, coded ways or in all-out revolts.[42] Comprehending how and why maritime violence led diverse communities to form alliances with colonial officials and missionaries across an extended period of time explains the puzzling longevity of Spanish colonial rule in the Pacific.

What this case study reveals about colonialism in the Philippines matters beyond the archipelago's fluid borders. *Piracy and the Making of the Spanish Pacific World* offers insight into piracy's impact on the trajectory of globalization and European imperial expansion in maritime Asia, contributing to a growing interdisciplinary literature on maritime violence and the making of the modern world. In addition, the book engages with ongoing debates in the historiography of the global Spanish empire. Shining a spotlight on hybrid Hispano-Filipino armadas and militias disrupts the enduring myth that Spain ruled a global empire "without a standing army, or much use of force."[43] This study upholds recent scholarship's emphasis on the centrality of bargaining and negotiation to colonial rule, introducing a novel cast of mobile and multilingual intermediaries that will feel familiar to historians of colonial Latin America.[44] Yet it also emphasizes that regional developments shaped the colonial bargains that were struck in the Philippines, contributing to the distinctiveness of colonialism in the Spanish Pacific. The following pages make an argument for more connected histories of colonial Latin Asia and colonial Latin America, while demonstrating that we cannot comprehend Philippines history without an eye on the archipelago's entanglement in maritime Asia.

The Spanish empire, like all European empires, classified colonial subjects along the lines of race, social status, and religion. Colonial othering has long afterlives. The politics of exclusion that piracy fostered in the early modern Philippines did not disappear with the dissolution of Spanish colonial rule in the islands. The legacies of empire and Catholic anti-piracy include continued discrimination and violence against Muslims in the Philippines, who have been subject to massacres, extrajudicial killings, and displacement.[45] Moreover, colonial Manila was a laboratory for experiments in state strategies of exploiting, surveilling, and segregating people of the Chinese diaspora and other "others" that influenced discriminatory exclusionary policies adopted by states across the Pacific world in the nineteenth and twentieth centuries.[46] Spain's Asian empire nurtured Sinophobic discourses, including the narrative that the rulers of China were hell-bent on invading

Pacific islands, and that the diasporic Chinese were a dangerous fifth column that was ready to support the motherland in the coming war. Such anxieties persist to this day and continue to contribute to prejudice against Chinese migrants and their descendants beyond the Philippines, as well as the escalating militarization of the Pacific. Confronting the colonial roots of modern racist anxieties may give us the knowledge and courage to think critically about and challenge them.

CHAPTER 1

_____

Muslim Pirates and Holy War
in Philippine Borderlands

Twenty-five large long boats flying brightly colored silk banners and streamers appeared on the watery horizon offshore from Palompong as the sun set
on a warm June evening in 1754. Clanging cymbals and drumbeats that kept
hundreds of oarsmen rowing in a steady rhythm became louder as the flotilla neared the shore. This instantly recognizable *Moro* (Muslim) pirate fleet
had come to the Visayas in the central Philippines from the Sulu Zone in the
south to steal silver, pigs, and people. In "great confusion and fear," Palompong's villagers and their Jesuit priest took refuge in the pueblo's fortified
stone church and prepared for a long siege. More than one thousand pirates
landed on the beach and attacked at daybreak the following morning. They
set fire to the sacristy, dug trenches around the church, and began pounding
the building with a barrage of artillery and arrows. The scared and exhausted
people inside united to resist their enemy. Women pumped water out of the
well to extinguish the flames licking the roof and huddled over fires making
bullets. Men protected the high walls, returning fire at the invaders from the
watchtower. Rocks and iron relentlessly rained down on the church for five
days and nights before the pirates torched Palompong's houses and crops and
abandoned the village, leaving its white beach bloodstained and strewn with
their dead.[1]

Spanish colonial rule in Philippine borderlands was forged in maritime
violence. Raiding, which was called *mangayaw* from Luzon to Mindanao,
structured life in the islands for centuries before and after the first Spaniards
set foot in the islands, and its impact on empire was profound.[2] The first half
of the eighteenth century witnessed an unprecedented surge in raiding, and
attacks like the siege of Palompong became more frequent, more geograph-

ically widespread, and more devastating. Colonial officials and missionaries in this era regarded Moro piracy as the single biggest threat to the Spanish empire's survival in Asia; this was a crisis that combined the catastrophe of sea-robbers carrying off entire villages as slaves with the emergency that was the spread of Islam. Moro piracy came to dwarf Spanish concerns about the potentially treacherous Chinese living among them and the rival European empires that were jostling for control of Pacific islands and sea-lanes, even after the British captured a galleon ship in 1743. The alarm that Islamic piracy sounds in the archive drowns out talk around these lesser threats. The galleons that plied the Pacific between Cavite and Acapulco have received far more attention from historians than the fast-moving, shallow-bottomed prahus that carried sea-robbers between islands.[3] Yet these raiding fleets had a far greater impact on relations between the Hispanic monarchy and island polities, and thus on the limits and possibilities of Spain's Asian empire.

This chapter elucidates how Moro piracy shaped Spanish colonial rule in the Philippines, particularly beyond Manila. It begins by exploring how the Spanish conceptualized Moro piracy in the archipelago, linking Spanish perceptions of Muslim maritime violence in Asia to the long and global history of anti-Islamic politics in the larger Iberian world. The chapter then analyzes the Spanish colonial government's strategies for combatting Moro piracy in the first half of the eighteenth century, which centered on brokering agreements with the Crown's Indigenous Catholic vassals as well as with the sovereign Muslim leaders of neighboring sultanates that mobilized men and boats into military campaigns against mutual pirate enemies. Negotiation was central to empire-building in a watery world at war. Revealing the complex dynamics of transcultural diplomacy and holy war, this chapter analyzes the anti-piracy partnership that the Spanish colonial government struck with the sultan of Sulu Azim ud-Din in the 1740s. Then, it examines the massive, semi-autonomous Hispano-Filipino naval forces that were mobilized against Moro pirates to defeat them with brute force, focusing on the 1754 campaign. These were the largest Indigenous navies mobilized anywhere in the Spanish empire, and perhaps anywhere in the wider world at this time.

Catholic anti-piracy in Philippine borderlands highlights the fragility of empire, as well as its potency. The network of presidios and fortified churches that provided platforms for pursuing anti-piracy diplomacy and war strongly influenced how Indigenous peoples encountered and experienced Spanish colonial rule. The escalating war against sea-robbers increased demands on

Indigenous labor, contributing to tension between local communities and the Crown's representatives on the ground that at times exploded into anti-colonial rebellions. Yet on the whole, anti-piracy coalitions tended to strengthen imperial legitimacy in regions that bore the brunt of raiding.

Previous studies of the "Moro wars" in the early modern Philippines are divided into two camps. One comprises scholars who laud the feats of European "warrior" priests against Moro enslavers, and the other celebrates Moro pirates as brave anti-colonial heroes who successfully resisted Spanish incursions into their ancestral lands and seas.[4] Charting a new course, this analysis centers on the diverse Indigenous peoples who bargained and collaborated with the Spanish Crown and its representatives in the islands, giving rise to joint Hispano-Filipino military campaigns. Looking at empire through the lens of piracy sheds light on why islanders who once "had neither lords nor kings, and every pueblo, even the tiniest ones, [were] republics unto themselves," elected time and again to support the Spanish empire.[5]

Anti-Islamic Politics in the Global Spanish Empire

Anti-Islamic politics and Iberian imperial expansion were entwined from the beginning. The burning desire to destroy Dar al Islam—the lands where Muslims were free to practice their religion—inspired Europe's first violent campaigns to conquer and colonize countries beyond the continent. Spaniards were among the authors of medieval Europe's first toxic anti-Islamic polemics, including lurid biographies of the Prophet Mohammed and fake histories of Islam's origins and doctrines.[6] They cultivated spurious stories of Muslims raping, torturing, and slaughtering Christians in the Holy Land that inspired Pope Urban and European monarchs to send Catholic armies to conquer Jerusalem at the end of the eleventh century. Islamophobia infused the launch of the Spanish conquest of the new world at the end of the fifteenth century. Christopher Columbus's expedition to Asia in 1492 chased hot on the heels of Spain's 1491 military defeat of the Emirate of Granada, the last surviving Islamic state in the Iberian Peninsula. Spain's Catholics interpreted this victory as the triumphant finale of the *reconquista*, their centuries-long holy war to expel Muslims from Iberia. The Niña, the Pinta, and the Santa María prepared for sail as Catholics turned Granada's mosques into cathedrals and forced the city's Muslim residents to convert to their religion. Defeating the Moros, the term that the Spanish used to designate Muslims in the Mediterranean world, established the precedent of territorial conquest and settlement in Spain that made imperial expansion across the ocean conceivable, as well as legally and morally justifiable. It sparked a religious fervor for bold campaigns to convert more of the world's population to Catholicism.[7]

The twin conquests of Islamic Spain and the Indies blended in important ways in the sixteenth century. Conquistadors likened the Indigenous peoples they encountered in the Americas to Muslims. They used the word Moro to label the people of central Mexico and the Andes, and they described their sacred buildings as mosques. Santiago Matamoros—the moor-slayer— became the patron saint of Spain and the personification of the Spanish conquest of the New World. Iberian Catholics believed that miraculous apparitions of Santiago, one of Christ's twelve apostles, intervened in battles to deliver them victories from Granada to Peru, linking wars of conquest across the globe.[8] Images of Santiago on horseback trampling over turbaned Moros and naked Indigenous people were carved and painted on the walls of churches and castles, and also appeared in theatre and dance performances across the Americas.[9] When Spaniards went to Southeast Asia, they took the moor-slayer with them. Conquistadors dedicated the main fort in Manila to Santiago, linking the Philippines to Iberian and American conquests.

Islam arrived in the Philippines hundreds of years before Christianity. Muslim merchants and holy men had introduced their faith to the archipelago by the thirteenth century. Yet Islam was not the dominant religion in the pre-Hispanic Philippines, and the diverse peoples who inhabited the islands recognized a range of *anitos* (spirits), including ancestors, celestial bodies, and sacred animals.[10] But when the first Spaniards arrived in Manila in the sixteenth century, they encountered Muslims practicing circumcision according to Islamic law and giving their children names in the Islamic tradition.[11] Spaniards labeled Muslims in the Philippines as "Moros," too.[12] Early modern Europeans lumped the planet's Muslims together. The Czech Jesuit Mathias Tanner's illustrated collection of biographies of Jesuit martyrs, for example, visually homogenized diverse Muslims as Ottoman Turks.[13] The volume depicted Christian-killing Muslims in North Africa, India, and Southeast Asia all wearing the stereotypical Turk's turbans and bushy beards, and wielding their distinctive curved swords, which are shown in Figure 2. As Geraldine Heng observed, "the streaming of diverse Muslims—whatever their geographic origins, national provenance, ethnoracial/tribal grouping, or linguistic community—into a corporate entity by virtue of religion alone suggests an extraordinary ability on the part of the Latin West to grant an essence-imparting power to Islam, a power to convert a quintessential identity that horizontally flattens out other identity attributes."[14] Colonial officials in Manila regarded the worlds' Muslims as not only alike, but politically united in their efforts to destroy Christendom. Melchior Davalos, a fiscal and oidor in Manila's Audiencia in the 1580s, informed King Philip II that the Muslims of the "Malaca, Goa, Calicud, Ormus" and "Samatra, Java, and Bornei" were aided by the "Turks, Mamelukes, Moors from Tunez [Tunis], and Moors who were driven away from Granada at the time of the Catholic kings."[15] Maritime Asia was conceptualized as an extension of the Mediterranean's religious borderlands in the Iberian imagination.

The hysterical intolerance of Islam resulted in systemic prejudice and violence against Muslims across the global Spanish empire.[16] Anti-Muslim violence included forced conversions to Catholicism and forced migration. In 1609, King Philip III of Spain expelled several hundred thousand *moriscos* (Muslims who had converted to Catholicism and their descendants) from the Iberian Peninsula. Islam was effectively prohibited in the territories over which Spain claimed to rule. It became a crime for the king's vassals to use names in the Islamic tradition or to speak or write in the Arabic language. The Spanish Inquisition investigated and harshly punished cases of Catholic converts practicing Islam after their baptisms.[17] In 1643, for example, the Inquisition's delegates in Manila arrested the Tidore-born Alexo de Castro after his wife, his daughter, and an enslaved woman in their household charged that he was a crypto, or secret, Muslim. The women alleged that Castro was performing Islamic prayers in their home and was in contact with Muslims from Ternate. These accusations led Castro to be transported as a prisoner to Mexico City, where the Inquisition investigated the case and ultimately sentenced him to exile from the Philippines.[18] The Spanish doctrine of *limpieza de sangre* held that Muslim ancestry stained or polluted blood. Catholics with Muslim ancestors faced discrimination and were excluded from joining the clergy or holding government posts.[19] Crucially, the Crown also upheld that it was lawful for Christians to enslave Muslims in the Spanish empire, incentivizing subjects to make Muslims captives and profit from their unfreedom.[20]

Anti-Islamic politics profoundly shaped how the Spanish conceptualized maritime raiding in the Philippines. In the eyes of colonial officials and friars in the archipelago, raiding was an Islamic phenomenon. Muslims became synonymous with pirates, even though *mangayaw* was never the exclusive

Figure 2. Illustrations depicting Muslims murdering Jesuit missionaries, including Mauritius Serpius in Africa, c. 1678 (top left), Franciscus Ribeirus in Africa, c. 1633 (top right), Alphonsys de Castro in the Molukus, c. 1558 (bottom left), and Vicentuius Alvarus in India, c. 1606 (bottom right). Tanner, *Societas Jesu*, 182, 188, 226, 227. Courtesy of the John Carter Brown Library.

domain of any one sect. Raiding to seize useful resources including food, weapons, and especially human captives defined political economies and cultures in the islands. At the outset of the Spanish conquest of the Philippines, approximately 1.5 million people lived in Luzon and the Visayas.[21] Population density was generally low, and political authority was decentralized. The basic unit of political and social organization was the barangay, named after the outrigger canoe that carried raiders across the sea. Each barangay included between thirty and one hundred families that were connected through blood ties and ritual kinship, and was headed by a chief known as a *datu* in the Visayas and *maginoo* in Tagalog. In Mindanao datus recognized the authority of regionally powerful sultans. Datus led armed bands of sailor-warriors in raids against enemy towns and boats. A datu's longevity as leader was often determined by the success of the raids they led and by their capacity to defend their followers against enemy raids.

Mangayaw meant that barangays were fortified. Communities developed and acquired weapons including cannon to protect themselves from attacks. Coast-dwellers constructed large, shallow-bottomed boats that could transport hundreds of warriors hundreds of miles, moving fast across the sea to flee or pursue their foes. Islanders venerated the bravest fighting men. In the Visayas, war heroes covered their bodies from head to toe in tattoos that archived their exploits.[22] Crucially, raiding compelled barangays to build coalitions to wage war against their enemies.[23] Powerful datus and sultans in the Philippines sent tributary missions to China's Ming emperors as early as 1373 in pursuit of weapons to arm their raiding fleets.[24] Piracy cultivated an openness to alliances with outsiders that would eventually help the Spanish to establish a foothold in the islands and gradually expand their influence.

Raiding plagued the Spanish empire in the Philippines from its earliest days. In the early seventeenth century, the missionary Diego Bobadilla wrote that Moro pirates "infest the seas, seizing so many of our boats, robbing pueblos, burning them, sacking churches . . . tearing [sacred images] into pieces and insulting them, and capturing such a quantity of Christian indios, that it breaks the heart to say it."[25] Raiding patterns changed over time. The first half of the eighteenth century witnessed an unprecedented surge in pirate attacks across the archipelago.[26] The large and heavily armed Moro pirate fleets that attacked Hispano-Filipino communities in the 1740s and 1750s often comprised between forty and fifty double-decked long-oared boats known as prahus and three thousand sailor-warriors.[27] These armadas originated from different corners of the Sulu Zone that stretched west from

Mindanao across the Sulu Sea to the northeastern coasts of Borneo, and south across the Celebes Sea to the large Indonesian island of Sulawesi.[28] Powerful sultans in the region usually sponsored the fleets. Studies of piracy in the early modern world have emphasized the multiethnic character of pirate captains and crews. Moro pirate fleets comprised men of many nations.[29] Malay or Southeast Asian men from various islands accounted for the majority of sailor-warriors in pirate fleets, but European "renegades" and Chinese men were also present on board.[30] Spaniards homogenized all of these pirates as Moros or Muslims.

In 1754 Manila's archbishop reported that Moro pirates had seized twelve thousand captives from the Philippines over the previous decade, most of whom were Catholic, tribute-paying Indigenous vassals of the king of Spain.[31] Slavery was not new to the Philippines. Scholars have emphasized the complexity of the institutions of slavery and servitude that operated in these societies before and after the establishment of Spanish colonial rule. There were multiple pathways into enslavement in the islands. In addition to being enslaved in raids, men, women, and children could also be born into slavery, or could temporarily become slaves to repay debts. It was not unusual for a person to move in and out of slavery in their lifetimes.[32] However, the rapid increase in the number of people being enslaved in maritime assaults was reaching crisis levels in this period. The majority of people taken captive in raids would have been absorbed into their captors' economies and societies. Slaves were an essential source of maritime, agricultural, and reproductive labor in the Sulu Zone. Male captives were often forced to work as galley slaves, rowing prahus in voyages that could last for months on end. They were also put to work diving for pearls and harvesting the *tripang* (sea cucumber) that their enslavers sold to Chinese and European merchants. Enslaved women were frequently put to work as domestic servants and market sellers, and some became the concubines of datus.[33] Other captives were sold or bartered into the Southeast Asian slave trade. Jolo, the island in the geographical center of the Sulu Zone, developed a thriving slave market by the mid-eighteenth century that facilitated the trafficking of Filipino slaves to farther flung port cities, including Batavia, the capital of the Dutch East Indies.[34]

The eighteenth-century raiding boom had multiple causes. In 1718, Hispano-Filipino forces reoccupied the presidio at Zamboanga in Western Mindanao for the first time in fifty years. They had abandoned this outpost in 1662 when the Chinese pirate Koxinga blockaded Manila, prompting the

governor to recall to the capital all soldiers and ships that were stationed in
the borderlands. The eighteenth-century renewal of the Spanish empire's
aggressive expansion into the Sulu Zone triggered a violent, defensive response from the region's datus and their followers.[35] Cesar Majul argued
that Islam functioned as a cohesive ideology that united diverse Islamic polities in the islands in a *jihad* (holy war) against the bellicose Catholic empire.[36] The region's deepening entanglement in the capitalist world economy
also contributed to the raiding crisis. The marked increase in raiding corre-
sponded with growing numbers of British and other European merchants visiting the Sulu Zone to buy tripang and other "exotic" agricultural products
that they could sell profitably in Chinese ports. Sultans sought more and more
slaves to meet the merchant-driven growth in demand for agricultural labor.[37]
Natural disasters, including earthquakes and volcanos, could also push communities into raiding.[38]

Regardless of its causes, colonial officials and friars in the Philippines were
convinced that Moro piracy could destroy Spain's Asian empire. Raids
drained the royal treasury and crippled the colonial economy. Tribute payments plummeted in lowland areas where piracy emptied towns of people.
For example, between 1750 and 1757, the number of tribute payers in the
Visayan town of Kalibo almost halved from 1,174 to 549. In the northern
Mindanao town of Butuan, they plummeted from 800 to 130 in the same
period.[39] Missionaries reminded Spanish governors in Manila that they had
a duty to defend the king's native vassals and their property, and that the
failure to deliver this protection would undermine the empire's legitimacy.
An Augustinian friar with a global vision of empire urged the Philippines
governor to take note of royal decrees that ordered colonial officials in Paraguay to "use all means possible" to protect the Guaraní from Portuguese sla-
vers.[40] It made sense to him that laws protecting Indigenous people from
enslavement in the Americas applied to Indigenous populations in the Philippines, too.

Even Manila was considered vulnerable to pirate raids. It was conceivable to the Spanish that Moros could conquer Mindoro, an island located only
eighty kilometers from the city, and use it as a base to lay siege to and even
conquer the capital.[41] Moreover, Spaniards understood the expansion of Moro
piracy to be tantamount to the expansion of Islam. In an age in which "religious unity constituted national unity," the spread of Islam could feasibly
undermine Spanish sovereignty in the islands.[42] It was widely held that
Muslims, the sworn enemies of Christians, could never be loyal subjects of a

Catholic monarch, or peaceful neighbors. The gravity of this threat led Jesuits to urge the Crown to abandon its Mariana Islands missions and redirect
resources to the conquest of the Muslim territories in the Sulu Zone.[43]

The need to reign in Moro raiding in the islands shaped the form of Spanish colonial rule in Philippine borderlands. Catholic anti-piracy gave rise to
a network of presidios and fortified churches that stretched across the islands.
Map 2 presents a snapshot of this archipelagic defense system in the mid-
eighteenth century, at which time it incorporated twenty-nine presidios.[44]
Each of these forts boasted a complement of fighting men and artillery. Presidios were strategically located to defend Indigenous communities against
raids. Some defended towns against attacks mounted by mountain-dwelling
"infidels" who lived beyond the effective reach of Spanish jurisdiction, but
most aimed to protect populations against Moro pirates. Coastal presidios
were located to block pirate fleets' preferred maritime routes into the Visayas
and Luzon and served as bases for Hispano-Filipino fleets to hunt pirates and
sustain their own raiding expeditions. Presidios also provided refuge for
people fleeing raids.[45] Additionally, fighting men attached to presidios were
routinely mobilized to put down Indigenous revolts against empire.

Presidios in the Philippine islands were hybrid Hispano-Filipinos institutions. Most were defended by soldiers who belonged to the two branches
of the colonial government's standing army in the islands: the Spanish infantry, whose members were mostly Mexican convict soldiers, and the Pampangan infantry, which recruited Indigenous Pampangans. Fighting men
from communities near presidios supplemented this colonial army. Some presidios, including four in the Calamianes to the west of the Visayas, were exclusively defended by local Indigenous forces.[46] Frontier pueblos were akin
to "a sleeping army"; their populations were armed, skilled at warfare, and
ready to fight when the need arose.[47]

The physical form of presidios reflected European and Southeast Asian
styles of architecture and modes of warfare. Many adopted elements of the
pre-Hispanic garrison and early-warning defense systems that were inno-
vated in the archipelago to protect coastal communities from raiding.[48] Lin-
capan's small presidio was little more than a soldiers' camp at the peak of a
steep hill. This natural fortification allowed watchers to spot approaching
enemy fleets, in addition to offering some protection to lowlanders fleeing
Moro raids.[49] Other presidios incorporated features promoted by Europe's
leading military engineers, including bastions built into the corners of their
defensive walls. The largest presidios in the islands were similar to major forts

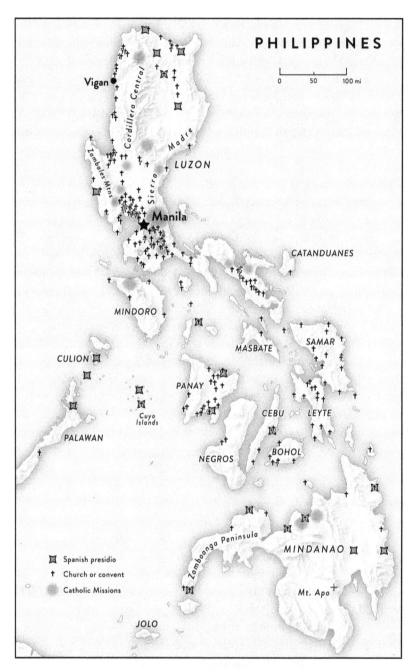

PHILIPPINES

Vigan

Cordillera Central

Zambales Mtns

Sierra Madre

LUZON

Manila

CATANDUANES

MINDORO

MASBATE

SAMAR

CULION

PANAY

CEBU   LEYTE

Cuyo Islands

PALAWAN

NEGROS

BOHOL

Zamboanga Peninsula

MINDANAO

Mt. Apo

JOLO

0   50   100 mi

☒ Spanish presidio
† Church or convent
   Catholic Missions

Map 2. This map shows the location of Spanish presidios, Catholic churches and convents, and Catholic missions in the Philippines in the mid-eighteenth century.

constructed in other parts of the global Spanish empire, including at Acapulco and San Juan de Ulúa at Veracruz.[50] Zamboanga's presidio dedicated to Nuestra Señora del Pilar was the biggest outside of Luzon. Pedro de San Cristobal, the procurador of the Jesuits in the Philippines, described it as "a most necessary barrier against this *morisma* . . . [and] the total defense of these *christiandades* (Christian lands)."[51] Some three hundred soldiers permanently guarded this outpost. Pedro Murillo Velarde and Nicolás de la Cruz Bagay's 1734 map of the Philippines (Figure 3) included an illustration of this mega presidio that shows the sizable town that grew up around it.[52] Zamboanga's appearance on a map made by a Tagalog engraver and a criollo Manileño Jesuit highlights its importance to eighteenth-century Filipinos, including those who had never set foot in Mindanao.

Religious and military functions and aspirations melded in presidio and fortress churches. Like Catholic churches, presidios were named after Catholic saints, and several were dedicated to Santiago the moor-slayer. Large presidios incorporated their own chapels, and the hefty Zamboanga presidio boasted a chapel, a Jesuit church, and a Jesuit-run college. Most smaller presidios had a chaplain who served fighting men and surrounding communities. Presidio-stationed priests' responsibilities extended far beyond prayer and the pastoral care of fighting men. They played key roles in constructing and maintaining the empire's defensive network, primarily by acting as intermediaries between the Crown and the colonial government and local Indigenous communities and by negotiating their respective contributions of labor and other resources to support fortified outposts.[53] Missionaries might have been the only Spaniards or Europeans whom some islanders ever laid eyes on. The clergy effectively stepped in to fill the gaps created by a minimal colonial administration and scarce Spanish population in the islands, leading the historian Roberto Blanco Andrés to describe them as "friar-civil servants."[54] Studies highlighting friars' important contributions to Catholic anti-piracy campaigns in Philippine borderlands, however, have understated the vital contributions of Indigenous elites, who were known as the *principalia*. Indigenous go-betweens were also crucial to facilitating defensive and offensive alliances between the state and Indigenous communities on the frontier.

Proximity to presidios and fortified churches impacted how empire intruded into Indigenous lives. The colonial government had several mechanisms for squeezing labor and other resources from the Crown's vassals in the Philippines in the eighteenth century, with tribute and the *polo* being the

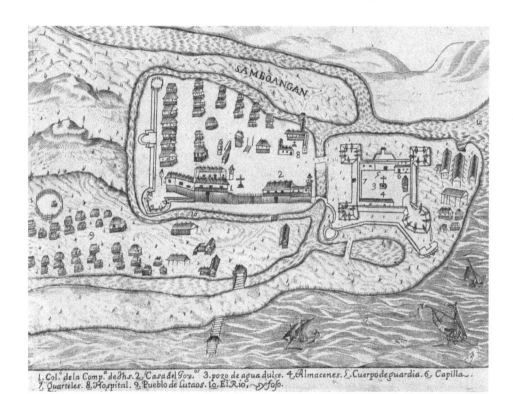

SAMBOANGAN

1. Col.ª de la Comp.ª de Jhs. 2. Casa del Gov.ᵒʳ 3. pozo de agua dulce. 4. Almacenes. 5. Cuerpo de guardia. 6. Capilla. 7. Quarteles. 8. Hospital. 9. Pueblo de Lutaos. 10. El Rio, ⌐y foso.

Figure 3. This detailed vista of Zamboanga appeared as a vignette in Pedro Murillo Velarde and Nicolás de la Cruz Bagay's 1734 map of the Philippines. Murillo Velarde and Bagay, *Carta hydrographica*. Library of Congress, https://www.loc.gov/item/2021668467/. See also Biblioteca Nacional de España, MSS/19217(H.11V-12R), 112.

most important. The tribute was an annual head tax payable in silver or in kind in designated locally produced products such as *palay* (prehusked rice) and coconut oil. The polo was a tributary labor draft that saw Indigenous men complete stints of labor for the colonial government for minimal pay and rice rations. Polo labor often supported the war against Moro pirates, with polo workers cutting down trees and transporting timber that would be used in naval and presidio construction.[55] The *repartimiento* or the *bandala* system that obliged Indigenous communities to sell goods to *encomenderos* and the colonial government at fixed, below-market prices was another tool that the colonial government used to extract resources from this population. The principalia, who were exempt from the polo and paying tribute, facilitated these systems on the ground.

The Spanish colonial government and missionaries expected that Indigenous communities that were close to churches and presidios would live as Catholics. Men, women, and children were required to learn the basic tenets of the Catholic faith, to confess their sins to a priest, and to attend mass and receive the sacrament of the eucharist at least once each year. They were obligated to baptize their children, to marry in the church, and be buried in the church's sacred grounds. Missionaries strived to suppress non-Catholic beliefs and rituals in the islands. Friars encouraged their flocks to abandon traditions like penis piercing, and to have sex only within marriage.[56] Filipinos living near forts and fortress churches made Catholicism and Catholic anti-piracy their own. Cults grew up around revered local images of Jesus Christ and his mother that had connections to sacred trees and wells, reflecting the religious syncretism that defined Catholicism across the Iberian world.[57] Sean McEnroe suggests that in frontier regions of the Spanish empire, Indigenous peoples were often "at liberty to enter or withdraw from the areas under colonial authority."[58] Numerous Indigenous peoples in the Philippines proved this to be true when they fled to upland mountainous zones that lay beyond Spanish control, and the reach of the Church.

Moro Diplomacy

Maritime Asia was a multipolar world. Historians have highlighted the prevalence of interimperial and transcultural alliance-making across the region in the eighteenth century as European empires and Asian states vied for partners in trade and war.[59] Agents of the Spanish empire in the Philippines

used presidios as platforms to broker military alliances with the sovereign
rulers of Islamic sultanates that aimed to contain maritime violence in the
archipelagic borderlands. Piracy spurned unlikely friendships. Remarkably,
Islamophobia did not stop the Spanish from entering into partnerships with
Muslims. However, the Spaniards' intense dislike and fear of Islam inflected
Moro diplomacy, as the Spanish pushed for Muslim rulers to agree to treaties
with provisions for Catholic missionaries to tour and work in their jurisdictions. As Cesar Majul noted, "the ultimate Spanish objective of integrating
Muslims into the colonial body politic, that is, through their conquest, was
never abandoned."[60]

After reoccupying Zamboanga in 1718, the Spanish brokered an alliance
with Muhummad Jafar Sadiq Manamir, the sultan of Tamontaca, whose seat
of power was in central Mindanao. The sultan and his army came to the aid
of Hispano-Filipino forces at Zamboanga when they were under siege by
Moro pirates in 1721, ensuring that the presidio remained in Spanish hands.
Governor Valdés Tamón returned the favor in 1733 when he dispatched
one hundred Spanish soldiers and more than three thousand Indigenous
fighting men from Bohol to assist the sultan of Tamontaca in a war against
the sultan of Malinog. The Spanish continued to supply cannon, shot, and
gunpowder to the sultan of Tamontaca throughout the 1730s.[61] This experience led other regional rulers to recognize the benefits of a Spanish alliance. Ambassadors from other sultanates went to Manila with hopes of
striking similarly advantageous compacts. Representatives from Bayúg and
Manaláo in Mindanao, for example, arrived in the Spanish capital bearing
invitations for Catholic friars to evangelize in their respective kingdoms.[62]
These sultans embraced conversion diplomacy, understanding that promises
of increasing the islands' Catholic population would capture the Spaniards'
attention and resources.[63]

Moro diplomacy was so common in this period that Muslim ambassadors became a staple of colonial theatre. Diplomats were standard characters in the komedyas or Moro Moro plays depicting wars between Muslims
and Christians that were performed across the Philippines.[64] The Spanish colonial government also pursued diplomacy with Asian rulers beyond the
Philippines in a bid to get piracy under control. Governor Valdés Tamón
strengthened relations with Borneo's rulers, reaching an agreement to sell
gunpowder to the kingdom in return for access to its copper, which was necessary for founding artillery.[65] Spanish colonial officials also sought out
partnerships with other European colonies to suppress Islamic piracy in

the region. In the 1750s, Spanish governors in Manila asked the Dutch in Batavia to prohibit the trafficking of Indigenous Filipino slaves who were victims of raiding into the Dutch East Indies.[66]

Examining the alliance that the Spanish struck with the sultan of Sulu Mohammad Azim ud-Din illuminates the dynamics of Moro diplomacy in the mid-eighteenth century and its impact on empire in the Philippines. Azim ud-Din was well prepared to rule a powerful Islamic kingdom in this turbulent region when he became the sultan of Sulu in 1735. Centered on the island of Jolo, a major center of trade connecting Pacific and Indian Ocean worlds, the sultanate was one of the richest in Sulu Zone. Azim ud-Din had studied Arabic, Malay, and Islam "with the Arabs of the *extramuros* of Batavia" in his youth.[67] Growing up in Jolo's royal court, he had met ambassadors from neighboring kingdoms, including Spaniards from Manila, and he had visited China on a diplomatic mission.[68] In the first year of his reign, Azim ud-Din sought an alliance with the Spanish that would consolidate his rule and strengthen his kingdom's influence. He dispatched representatives to the Spanish presidio at Zamboanga who succeeded in obtaining permission to send an embassy to Manila. Two years later, in 1737, the sultan's ambassadors sat down with Valdés Tamón in Manila's royal palace and brokered the terms of the "Treaty of Peace and Friendship." As this was an agreement between kings, Spain's Philip V added his signature to the document that bore the sultan's seal in 1742.[69]

The Spanish hoped that the alliance with Azin ud-Din would curb the increasingly devastating Moro pirate raids. The treaty formally ended hostilities between Spain and the Sulu sultanate, with Azim ud-Din committing to withdrawing support for attacks on the king's subjects. To reverse the impact of previous raids, the sultan also agreed to liberate Christian Filipino slaves and return sacred objects in his kingdom that had been stolen from Catholic communities.[70] The treaty was a mutual defense pact. The parties agreed to unite against any enemy who attacked either kingdom. In addition, the treaty established free trade between the two powers. Although the treaty itself was silent on religion, conversion was a central theme in the talks that framed and facilitated the development of this partnership. In 1744, Philip V wrote a letter to the sultan in which he "urgently" requested that Jesuit missionaries be welcomed into Jolo and provided with land to build a church.[71] The monarch made it clear that closing the door to Jesuits would jeopardize the new Sulu-Spanish alliance. Azim ud-Din agreed to accept missionaries on the condition that the Spanish government in Manila honor him with a gift of six thousand silver pesos and twelve *piculs* each of gunpowder, nails, and iron, resources that he claimed were necessary to fight pirates.[72] Juan de Arechederra, the Caracas-born Dominican friar and bishop of the Philippines province of Nueva Segovia, was the interim governor of the colony who agreed to this concession.

The treaty brought mixed results for the Spanish. On the one hand, Azim ud-Din freed few Christian slaves, and the missionaries whom he permitted to enter Jolo found few converts. The two Jesuits who arrived on the island in May 1748 were disappointed that they were forced to reside within the sultan's walled palace compound. This may have been necessary for their protection as local elites protested their presence, but it made preaching impossible.[73] On the other hand, Azim ud-Din delivered on his promise to support Spanish military campaigns against their mutual enemies. Spanish colonial officials held the people they called *tirones* (Orang Tedong or Tirun) responsible for many of the slave-raiding attacks carried out in the Philippines at this time.[74] At least a thousand fighting men from Jolo joined the Hispano-Filipino fleet's attacks on the tirones on the northeastern coast of Borneo in 1746 and 1747.[75] Arechederra publicly praised the "heroic" sultan for his support: he was a "true friend of the Spaniards."[76]

The alliance took an interesting turn in January of 1749 when Azim ud-Din unexpectedly arrived in Manila with a retinue of seventy people in tow, including members of his family, court officials, servants, and enslaved people.[77] The sultan informed Arechederra that he had fled Jolo after narrowly surviving an assassination attempt coordinated by his brother Bantilan, who had seized the throne in a coup. Crafting a narrative that found sympathy with the bishop-governor, Azim ud-Din explained that his kindness toward Catholic missionaries had caused the revolt. The sultan asked Arechederra for asylum and military support to restore him to power by force. The governor was keen to offer both. Arechederra agreed to provide ships and soldiers to back Azim ud-Din in a military campaign, but only if the sultan converted to Catholicism. Arechederra embraced this opportunity to suppress Moro raiding and Islam in the Sulu Zone; objectives that were not easily disentangled.

Manila staged a spectacular celebration to officially welcome Azim ud-Din to the capital a week after he sailed into Manila Bay. The festivities mimicked the extravagant ceremonies that cities across the Spanish Empire staged to formally receive archbishops, governors, and viceroys.[78] A grand parade escorted the sultan from his temporary residence in the suburb of

Binondo to the Spanish governor's royal palace in the heart of the walled city. Arechederra led the procession riding in a gleaming carriage pulled by six horses. Almost three thousand Indigenous and mestizo militiamen marched behind him in a display of the Spanish colony's military might. Many wore armor and were armed with lances, pikes, and bows and arrows. Manila's grand stone churches, convents, and two-story shops and houses were handsomely decorated for the occasion. The parade passed under painted triumphal arches and swathes of damask in amaranth and sunset hues that evoked a "a flaming Spring."[79] The sound of choral music and the loud hum of the thirty thousand–strong crowd that lined the streets to watch the festivities filled the air. In the main plaza in front of the governor's palace, the militiamen joined the Indigenous Pampangan regiment in a salute to the governor and his guest of honor. Inside, elite Manileños dressed in their finest silks and jewels lined up to greet the sultan.

Azim ud-Din's transition from a Muslim sultan to a Catholic king commenced in the weeks that followed these festivities. Conversion entailed the sultan renouncing Islam and devoting time to studying the key tenets of the Catholic religion in preparation for being baptized. Arechederra assigned two Jesuits to provide the sultan with religious instruction.[80] Baptism is a Catholic ritual that involves a priest pouring blessed water over a person's head or submerging the person in water to cleanse them of original sin. It is also an initiation ceremony that makes a person a member of the Catholic Church. The sultan had to abandon his concubines. Azim ud-Din also shaved his beard, which Arechederra identified as "one of the principal markers of religion in his sect."[81] He removed his turban and started dressing in the style of the Spaniards of Manila. In the early modern world, conversion was understood as a physical as well as spiritual metamorphosis.

In the islands, and particularly within the colony's "friarocracy," Azim ud-Din's conversion to Catholicism and the government's promise to support a military intervention to return him to the throne in Jolo were controversial and contested developments. Across the Iberian world, Spaniards and Portuguese suspected that Muslims faked conversions to Christianity, and they were convinced that converts continued to clandestinely practice Islam after their baptisms.[82] The missionaries who had known Azim ud-Din in Jolo did not trust him. They advised Arechederra that the sultan was a devout and learned Muslim. He was "not only a *pandita*, which corresponds to a bishop in his false sect—but a *pandita* of the *panditas* and teacher to them all."[83] The archbishop of Manila—the Franciscan friar Pedro Martínez de Arizala—

suggested in a series of letters to Arechederra that the sultan wanted to convert only because it was politically convenient to do so. Moreover, he claimed Azim ud-Din was insufficiently prepared to be baptized. His study of Catholicism was rushed and was compromised by a reliance on interpreters who were "indios or *secular*" (priests who did not belong to a missionary order), all "rough or barbaric, and lacking knowledge of these matters."[84] Martínez urged Arechederra to slow down, as "time is the great discoverer of the secrets of the soul."[85]

The Archbishop's prejudice against Asians and Muslims evidently influenced his discomfort with the alliance. He criticized the "excessive pomp" of the sultan's entry into Manila, which he described as inappropriate for a man who was an "indio, and a Moro."[86] Furthermore, the Archbishop thought that Spain's long history of conflict with Muslims in the Mediterranean should discourage any dealings with Muslims. He brought up Spain's failed efforts to convert the moriscos to Catholicism, reminding Arechederra that "although this community of converts showed all signs of studying Christian doctrine with great zeal," they never truly embraced this faith, and ultimately "there was no other remedy than expelling them from the Kingdom."[87] Like many of his contemporaries, Martínez looked to the Maghreb to make sense of maritime Asia.[88]

Arechederra tried to win Martínez's support, responding to his case against Azim ud-Din's baptism and the military pact in a series of letters. The governor justified treating Azim ud-Din as a sovereign, stating that although the sultan is "an indio mohometano, he is a KING and is recognized as such by our Majesty the KING of Spain."[89] He also marshaled vague historical precedents of powerful Muslims including "an ambassador of Tunisia" who converted to Catholicism in the Mediterranean world that vindicated Azim ud-Din's baptism.

When he accepted that he would not gain Martínez's approval, Arechederra found another way to proceed with his grand plans and do Moro diplomacy on his terms. In April the governor convened a council of theologians to weigh in on Azim ud-Din's conversion.[90] He appointed to the council fourteen heavy-hitting regular clergymen from the major religious orders active in the Philippines: the Dominicans, the Franciscans, the Augustinians, the Augustinian Recollects, and the Jesuits. These men were the heads of their respective orders in the islands, and the principals and professors at Manila's two universities: the Dominican University of Santo Tomás and the Jesuit College of San Ignacio. The special council held a two-day-long inquiry into the sultan's preparedness for baptism. Azim ud-Din attended part of this meeting, where he was interrogated by council members via an interpreter. The friars asked the sultan to recite several Catholic prayers including the Ave Maria and the creed in Latin, which he was able to do. They were impressed by Azim ud-Din's ability to provide the "correct" answers to simple and complex questions about Catholic beliefs, such as "How many wives can a Catholic have?" and "What is the Holy Trinity?" The council also posed questions to the sultan about Islam, and most of its members were satisfied when he conceded that the religion was "full of errors."[91]

Moro piracy came to bear on the theological council's deliberations when they considered a priest's dramatic account of being captured by the tirones in 1745 and subsequently rescued by Azim ud-Din.[92] Conveying the horrors of the Sulu middle passage, Fray Valdepeñas testified that he almost died during his captivity. The friar's pirate captors kept him naked and fed him little more than salt water and *sagu* during the voyage across the Tirones Sea, making him very sick and dangerously thin. Valdepeñas believed that Azim ud-Din had saved his life. When the sultan learned that pirates had picked up a "padre of the Christians of Manila," he dispatched a battalion of soldiers and slaves to rescue Valdepeñas and bring him back to Jolo. Valdepeñas was moved by the tenderness and respect that Azim ud-Din had shown him when he arrived on the island. The sultan made sure that the friar was served nourishing meals. He ordered a Chinese barber from the city's *pariancillo* to cut Valdepeñas's hair. He also gave the friar new clothes, initially offering fine embroidered silk pieces from his own wardrobe until a simple *sarampuri* robe was made, which was the cloth that the Franciscans typically wore in the Philippines. Valdepeñas insisted that the sultan's kindness and generosity toward a Catholic priest was proof that he had been touched by "some light of the true religion," and was thus prepared for baptism. Valdepeñas also made excuses for Azim ud-Din's failure to free enslaved Christians in his kingdom. He explained that the sultan did not have the authority to manumit slaves that his subjects had legitimately obtained, but he praised Azim ud-Din for his promises to free any enslaved person who ran away from their enslaver and sought refuge in his palace.[93]

On the weight of this evidence, the council ruled that the sultan was ready to "receive the holy waters of baptism," although Azim ud-Din's Jesuit catechists abstained from the vote.[94] Arechederra made arrangements for the sultan to be baptized in Pangasinan in a church located within his own diocese of Nueva Segovia. Azim ud-Din donned Spanish-style clothing—a bright red, cochineal-dyed cape, a silver sword, and a hat full of fine feathers—for this ritual.[95] Baptism endowed the sultan with a new name and title: he became *King Fernando Primero, Rey de Jolo* (King Fernando the First, King of Jolo). This name reveals Arechederra's high hopes for Azim ud-Din's conversion. Fernando was the name of the Spanish monarch who had reigned over the defeat of the last Islamic kingdom in the Iberian Peninsula at the end of the fifteenth century, and the governor hoped that Azim ud-Din would be the sovereign who would usher in the conquest of Islamic Asia.

The Spanish colonial government pushed ahead with plans to restore Azim ud-Din to his throne after his baptism. The Marques Francisco José de Ovando threw his support behind this initiative when he arrived in the islands in July of 1750 to take up the post of governor of the Philippines. Ovando organized an armada that planned to transport Azim ud-Din to the island of Basilan, which lies just off the coast of Zamboanga. Hispano-Filipino forces planned to unite with the sultan's loyal fighting men at this rendezvous point, from where they would attack and reconquer Jolo. The armada set sail in 1751. However, the plan went awry and was abruptly terminated during the fleet's stopover in Zamboanga after Indigenous Filipinos loyal to the Spanish revealed that the sultan was plotting against the empire. Azim ud-Din had written two letters to the sultan of Mindanao from the presidio. In the first letter, written in Spanish, Azim ud-Din encouraged the other sultan to cooperate with the Catholic forces. A second letter was written in jawi and was purported to be a translation of the Spanish text.[96] Yet when Thomas Álvarez, the presidio governor's interpreter, and Benito Gaspar, an Indigenous man from Lutao in Misamis Occidental, translated this text, they found otherwise.[97] According to these men, Azim ud-Din had tried to issue a warning to the Mindanao ruler in the second jawi letter. He had explained that he was writing "under pressure, being under foreign dominion, and I am compelled to obey whatever they tell me to do, and I have to say what they tell me to say."[98] The letter prompted Spanish officials to search Azim ud-Din's boat. Sailors emptied his luggage chests and tore furniture apart, and found twelve *krises* (daggars) sewn inside two pillows, and enough muskets and "every [other] sort of weapon" to arm more than two hundred men.[99] The search also turned up a Koran and six other Arabic books, which were considered proof that Azim ud-Din was continuing to practice Islam. Meanwhile, there was no trace of the bible or any of the Catholic relics and sacred images that Azim ud-Din had been gifted in Manila. The image of San Francisco Xavier inlaid in precious stones on a gold chain that the president of the Audienica had placed around the sultan's neck on the occasion of his farewell was missing. Azim ud-Din was outed as a traitor.

The sum of evidence persuaded presidio officials that Azim ud-Din had fabricated the coup and the "false civil war" in Jolo as part of an elaborate scheme to lure the Spanish into the Sulu sultanate and destroy them.[100] They were sure that Azim ud-Din, with the backing of his brother Bantilan and the neighboring sultan of Mindanao, was preparing to seize Zamboanga in a surprise attack, and planned to use the fort to advance the Muslims' *reconquista* of the Philippines. Colonial officials never scoffed at Azim ud-Din's aspirations to "make himself master" of the entire archipelago. The sultan and his son were taken back to Manila, this time as prisoners. They were locked up in a house in Intramuros and placed under armed guard.

The Spanish continued to pursue Moro diplomacy after the sultan's humiliating betrayal of the Spanish. Governor Ovando unsuccessfully attempted to negotiate a prisoner exchange with Jolo, offering to swap Azim ud-Din for the many Christian captives that were allegedly harbored on the island.[101] Ovando worried that Azim ud-Din's imprisonment would incite other Islamic maritime states to attack Manila. He feared that the "Turks of Mecca" would support Bantilan, making the Moro pirates an even more formidable enemy. In the face of these threats, Ovando sent an embassy to Borneo to strengthen ties with the kingdom in 1752.[102] The governor claimed that the mission was a triumph. Borneo ceded Paragua and the small island of Balaba, which were ideal sites for future presidios, to the Spaniards in return for the Spanish agreeing to respect Borneo's sovereignty. Borneo promised to release Christian captives without ransom, although no slaves were returned immediately. Manila and Borneo also agreed to a mutual defense pact: "they promised to be friends of our friends, and enemies of our enemies . . . and as a principal article of this alliance, to not give any aid to Jolo in the war."[103]

Manila's enthusiasm for scaling up the war against Moro piracy was magnified in the aftermath of Azim ud-Din's treasonous betrayal. Archbishop Martínez was a loud proponent of total war against Moro pirates. In 1754 he penned a "brief address that proves that the only way to liberate the islands of piracy and the most serious harm caused every year by the neighboring Moros is continuous war against their homes and lands without considering any peace treaty or ceasefires or exchanges of letters."[104] Martínez saw no alternative for dealing with these "sworn and irreconcilable enemy of Christians."[105] Ovando agreed at this point that "war would be more useful than peace."[106]

Waging Holy War Against Moro Pirates

A huge Hispano-Filipino armada mobilized against Moro pirates in 1754 after the alliance with Azim ud-Din fell apart.[107] Contemporaries called this maritime force the "*armada de los pintados.*" The term "pintados" can be translated as "painted" or "tattooed," and in the Philippines it referred to the Indigenous people of the Visayas who traditionally filled the anti-piracy fleets. Visayan warriors had been heavily tattooed when they first encountered Europeans in the sixteenth century, and although these body markings were rare in the eighteenth century, the term pintados stuck.[108] The mid-eighteenth-century hybrid armada incorporated fighting men and boats from across the archipelago, including fleets dispatched from Manila, soldiers and ships attached to presidios, and the semiautonomous Indigenous marine forces from southern Luzon, the Visayas, and northern Mindanao, the regions that bore the brunt of Moro pirate raiding attacks. Catholic priests were conspicuous and important actors in this naval campaign, with Governor Ovando appointing the Jesuit missionary Joseph Ducos its commander in 1754.[109] Previous studies that centered on soldier-priests in the war let Indigenous fighting men fade into the background as the passive followers of these heroic religious leaders.[110] Using the 1754 campaign as a case study, the final section of this chapter mines the colonial archive to recover Indigenous people's paths into these armed forces that made Spain's Asian empire possible. Borrowing methods from the rich historiography of Black and Indigenous participation in colonial Latin America's militias, it complicates the argument that subalterns were forced or coerced into the Spanish empire's war against Moro pirates.

In public, Governor Ovando proclaimed that the hybrid Catholic armada would destroy the Islamic south. The fleet would "capture or kill" all Moros and "banish them from the world."[111] Ovando's private orders to military officials articulated the more modest goals of rescuing Christian captives, securing the presidios at Iligan and Zamboanga, and destroying as many Moro prahus and pueblos as possible to permanently weaken the enemy.[112] Ovando was cognizant of the limits of Spanish power in the Philippines. In a letter to the king, he recalled how Governor Sebastián Hurtado de Corcuera had captured the Sulu citadel at Jolo with only "600 Spaniards and 1000 Indigenous warriors" in 1638.[113] Ovando knew that it was impossible to repeat this victory more than a century later. Jolo and other Moro settlements were well defended with large, modern fortifications, heavy artillery, and trained fighting men equipped with firearms.[114] From May to September of 1754, the composite Hispano-Filipino navy divided into smaller fleets that patrolled the coasts of northern Mindanao in an attempt to block the routes of the pirate flotillas heading north into the Visayas for the raiding season. They came to the aid of Christian towns under siege and engaged the enemy in bloody battles at sea and on land. Hispano-Filipino forces also made landfall and attacked enemy towns in Mindanao, setting fire to houses, crops, and boats. This could be categorized as an environcidal war, as fighting men destroyed the environmental infrastructure that sustained rural populations.[115] The Catholic forces frequently found villages empty of people. Captain Cesár Falliet, the Swiss mercenary who commanded the armada for part of the 1754 campaign, remarked that Moros could "move a city as easily as we can move a boat."[116] Southeast Asians avoided mass death and destruction in war through flight. For local rulers, the principal aim of warfare was to preserve and increase their total number of followers. Sacrificing lives to secure a small territory was seen as highly irrational.[117]

War caused massive destruction and displacement across the coastal central and Southern Philippines, with Mindanao bearing the brunt of the carnage. Moro raiding parties razed the northeastern Mindanao towns of Surigao, Higaquet, and Pahuntungan, leaving no trace of their churches or other buildings, or of the two thousand people who had inhabited them and who had either been enslaved or killed by their foes.[118] The rival forces used brutal violence against each other. After Moro pirates murdered the Recollect friar Joseph de la Virgen del Niño Perdido, they sliced his corpse into tiny pieces. During a September battle in Misamis in northern Mindanao, the Catholic maestre de campo Malabohoc boarded a Moro boat and slit the throats of the one hundred or so men who were on board.[119] Ferocity was common among combatants on both sides of this ruthless war.

Pampangans were prominent in the 1754 anti-piracy campaign. Spanish accounts of the conflict highlight and valorize Pampangan soldiers, such as the *alférez* (sublieutenant) Marino Pedro de Guevara, who led an *armadilla* (little armada or fleet) into battle, and the infantryman Lorenzo de Jesus, who died defending the empire.[120] By this time Pampangans had earned a reputation as the Indigenous conquistadors of Spain's Asian Empire, comparable to the Tlaxcalans of New Spain.[121] The roots of the Hispano-Pampangan partnership can be traced back to 1594, when Pampangans defended Manila against the invading Chinese pirate navy led by Limahong.[122] Almost a decade later, in 1603, Pampangans and Spaniards joined forces to wage war against the Chinese who revolted in Manila. Pampangan soldiers were permanently stationed in Manila to defend the capital in the aftermath of this conflict.[123] These native fighting men participated alongside Spanish and Mexican soldiers in the conquests of Taiwan and the Mariana Islands in the seventeenth century.[124] In the first half of the eighteenth century, the Hispano-Pampangan partnership was largely an alliance against Moro piracy. Pampangan infantry companies permanently guarded most of the presidios that were strategically scattered across the Philippines and the Mariana Islands.[125] Moreover, Pampangan fighting men were routinely deployed to put down Indigenous uprisings in the Philippines, including the Tagalog revolt that broke out in central Luzon in 1745.[126]

The Pampangan alliance with the Spanish "endured not because of some mystical affinity" between them or because the Pampangans had been made dependent on the Spanish, but rather because the people of these two nations had carved out sophisticated economic, political, cultural, and social bonds to confront the challenges of a specific historical situation.[127] Pampangan loyalty to Spain was not unshakable, and Pampangans rebelled against empire, too. Francisco Maniago, a member of the Pampangan principalia, led a major revolt in Pampanga in 1660 and 1661, when thousands of Indigenous people protested the exploitation of polo workers.[128] At the time the Spanish in the Philippines were at war with the Dutch, which intensified the colonial government's demand for fighting men and other workers that were required to build and maintain a growing naval fleet. Throughout the history of the Spanish empire in the Philippines, such exploitation prompted countless Pampangan families to flee lowland settlements for the mountains to escape their obligations to the colonial state.[129] Yet individual and collective acts of resistance did not undermine the Pampangans' reputation as loyal vassals who could be relied on to defend the empire.

The majority of Pampangan fighting men who went to war in 1754 were soldiers who were integrated into the standing armies stationed at presidios. Previous studies have argued that these native soldiers were forced to enlist in the military as a means to repay debts, or they did so to avoid arduous tributary labor obligations which could include the grueling work of cutting down trees and transporting heavy logs from hillsides to shipyards for naval construction.[130] It is true that the distinction between soldiers and polo workers blurred at times. Half of the Pampangan infantrymen deployed at the Cavite fort in 1739, for example, were laboring as sawyers in the port's shipyards, which is the kind of work that was associated with tributary labor.[131]

There is also clear archival evidence that some Pampangan men were forcibly recruited to the 1754 anti-piracy campaign. The government rounded up "vagrant" Pampangans in Pampanga as well as in Manila and Cavite and pressed them into the armada.[132] "Vagrancy" was an umbrella category for many behaviors that were deemed socially unacceptable, including being unemployed, untethered to a barangay or unregistered to pay tribute, publicly drunk, or engaged in theft and petty crime.[133]

Proof of coercion, however, needs to be balanced with evidence of other factors that encouraged individual Pampangan fighting men and their communities to choose to join and support the war against Moro pirates. It is not a stretch to argue that the patriotic politics of Catholic anti-piracy inspired subalterns to become soldiers of God in the holy war against Muslim enemy others. This ideology infused the Pampangan public sphere. Priests in the province preached about the Moro wars from the pulpit. Pampangan elders passed down oral histories that celebrated their kin's heroic feats on watery battlefields.[134] Komedya or Moro Moro plays celebrated Pampangan valor in the ongoing war. These plays were performed in Christian pueblos across the Philippines. They recreated mythical and historic battles between Muslims and Christians that took place in the Mediterranean world as well as in the archipelago. One of the earliest komedyas performed in Manila dramatized Governor Corcuera's seventeenth-century victory over Sultan Corralat, a campaign in which Pampangan fighting men had played a central role. Isaac Donoso suggested that Spanish elites promoted such dramas to "strengthen the authority of the official power in the Iberian Christian Kingdoms."[135] Surely Pampangans too had a vested interest in promoting historical narratives that celebrated their bravery, military prowess, and loyalty to kings and queens of Spain. Patriotic theater could have stirred pro-war feelings and inspired young men to enlist in anti-piracy campaigns.[136]

There is no doubt that Pampangan elites benefited significantly from multigenerational alliances with the Spanish. The Pampangan principalia, like other Indigenous elites in the Philippines and the global Spanish empire, were exempt from paying tribute and performing the polo. The Crown extended these privileges to military officials. Felipe Álvaro, a *natural* (Native) and principal of Lubao pueblo, petitioned the king to confirm his appointment to the position of *maestre de campo de las tropas milicianas* and the privileges that he was entitled to by virtue of this appointment, which included exemptions from tribute and polo labor. Álvaro requested that several of his family members also be exempted from these same obligations, including his brothers Tomás and Miguel, and his wife, Antonia Buñga Clara, and their children. When a fiscal in the Council of the Indies assessed Álvaro's petition, the bureaucrat noted that the "governors of those islands" commonly conceded such privileges to Pampangan principales.[137]

Bargaining for privileges was a continuous process between the colonial government and Indigenous elites. In 1754, Pampangan military officials petitioned the colonial government for the right of Pampangan soldiers to be honored with burials in Manila's royal chapel. This church stood within the walled city—the symbolic center of Spanish power in maritime Asia—and was one of the most opulent and important religious buildings in Manila.[138] The Spanish governor of the Philippines and the members of Manila's Audiencia attended mass in the royal chapel, which was also the burial place of Spanish and Mexican soldiers who perished in the islands. Pampangan soldiers clearly believed that they had earned the right to be interred here too. The government rejected the Pampangan's petition on this occasion, reinforcing the unequal status of Indigenous and Spanish soldiers, which was also reflected in the Indigenous soldiers' lower rates of pay. Pampangans earned on average less than half the salary paid to Spanish infantrymen.[139] Collaboration and cooperation did not mean equality between Spaniards and Indigenous people in the islands. War was not incompatible with colonial difference.

What the spotlight on Pampangan soldiers has obscured is other Indigenous peoples' participation in colonial military forces. Although the exact numbers of Indigenous soldiers who were deployed in the 1754 anti-piracy campaign is unknown, colonial records clearly show that Visayans and other Indigenous fighting men outnumbered others in the campaign. Cesár Falliet estimated that 500 "indios" from Bohol and Iligan joined the campaign with their own boats and military officials.[140] Published and unpublished accounts of battles that occurred that season identify at least eleven pueblos in southern Luzon, the Visayas, and northern Mindanao that contributed soldiers and ships to the Hispano-Filipino armada.[141]

Outside of Manila and Pampanga, the recruitment of Indigenous soldiers to the Moro wars was a decentralized process coordinated by the native principalia, local colonial officials, and Catholic missionaries that drew on long-standing traditions of mobilizing men into battle in the islands. The anthropologist Lee Junker has shown that "regionally powerful paramount chiefs . . . could quickly raise large-scale fighting forces through vertically and horizontally ramifying ties of clientage and alliance."[142] Priests and *alcalde mayores* bargained directly with datus to send their followers and boats into battle against mutual enemies. Combining to fight against common enemies potentially benefited all parties involved. Indigenous communities secured access to resources that made them more able to repel the raids that were carrying away kin as slaves, and to stage offensive attacks on their foes. The Spanish colonial government gained bodies on the ground and on the water that were needed to reign in attacks on presidios and shipping. Missionaries stood to gain Catholic converts.

Catholic priests were uniquely placed to act as coalition-builders uniting Indigenous communities and the Spanish colonial government in the war against Moro pirates. They were multilingual and generally fluent in the languages of the communities in which they were embedded. Missionaries gained the trust of local communities through living among them and waging war with them for many years. It also helped that priests had access to the firearms, artillery, and ammunition that coastal Filipino communities wanted to better defend themselves. The clergy were also regarded as intermediaries between people and God, or the sacred and the profane. Their "semi-divine" status further enhanced their perceived trustworthiness and authority in Philippine borderlands.[143]

The dispersed archives of Spain's Asian empire contain scattered evidence of ad hoc, pueblo-level negotiations over Hispano-Filipino military mobilizations. A Jesuit account of the 1754 campaign reveals that several datus and principales from the "mountain gentile" communities in upland Mindanao attended a Jesuit-sponsored war strategy meeting in the field in June that year. The missionaries and the datus agreed to a temporary alliance that led to the non-Christian mountain-dwellers and Iliganos from the presidio and town on the northern coast of Mindanao carrying out joint attacks on Moro settlements in the region.[144] Similar short-term military partnerships were brokered in the Visayas. In February of 1747, for example, the Spanish government in Manila granted a license to the "naturales" of the town of Guiuan in Samar to send five hundred armed men into battle against the Moros.[145] The formation of short-term alliances shows the agile Spanish empire in action. Spain's delegates in the Philippines negotiated with diverse Indigenous communities to build cross-cultural military partnerships that were responsive to mutual challenges.

The Spanish also established more official and enduring anti-piracy compacts with Indigenous communities. The maestre de campo Don Pedro Tamparong and Don Ygnacio Cavilin, who were Indigenous principales at the northern Mindanao presidio towns of Iligan and Dapitan, respectively, negotiated a contract with the colonial government in the 1750s. Tamparong and Cavilin committed to mobilizing a naval force consisting of five hundred men and two larger boats known as *galeras,* in addition to another twenty-four smaller, lighter, and faster boats that would patrol the coasts of northern Mindanao for an eight-month season each year.[146] The captains of this Indigenous armada were drawn from the ranks of the principalia, and all of its sailor-warriors were native fighting men. This Indigenous navy was unparalleled in the Iberian Atlantic world. The colonial government for its part supplied the fleet with costly and difficult-to-obtain muskets, cannon, and shot, in addition to paying the salaries of the armada's officials and sailor warriors and providing their rice rations.[147] The Jesuit priest Padre Ducos facilitated the development of this partnership, although it was premised on the longstanding, intergenerational alliance between the Spanish colonial government and communities that had grown around the presidios at Iligan and Dapitan. Pedro Tamparong's ancestor Basilio Virtudes Tamparong collaborated with Jesuit missionaries to fight Moro pirates and convert the people of northern Mindanao to Catholicism in the late 1710s.[148] He rose to the rank of maestre de campo and general of the Indigenous soldiers at the Iligan fort.[149] Spain's King Charles III formally approved the compact with Tamparong and Cavilin in August 1760.[150] The Council of the Indies, an advisory board that counseled the Crown on all matters arising from ruling Spain's vast overseas empire, expressed concern that such a large naval force was to be "placed in the hands of the principales datus" of Iligan and Bohol. Arming Indigenous people was always a risky strategy. Despite "the fidelity with which the governor says [the datus] serve" the Crown, the council cautioned that there was still a risk that they could revolt and turn the government-provided arsenal against the empire. But ultimately, the council recognized that colonial officials in the far-away colony had a far better grasp of the local situation than they themselves ever would, and they trusted the missionaries' and colonial officials' judgment on this matter.

Forging anti-piracy alliances in the Philippines was a process that transformed Indigenous people into vassals of the Spanish monarch. Compacts to fight Moro pirates determined the details of tribute that members of a community would transfer to the monarchy. The act of paying tribute was more than an economic exchange; it was regarded by the Spanish as an act of submission that conferred vassal status on tribute-payers. Alliance-making developed a vocabulary of vassalage in communities on the periphery of

Spain's Asian empire. Datus deployed the language and tropes that were appropriate of loyal vassals addressing their monarch in formal correspondence with the king of Spain. Pedro Tamparong emphasized that he served the king with "fidelity and love" and promised to "defend his Majesty's kingdom always."[151] Oona Paredes contends that Filipinos who entered into military coalitions with the Crown saw themselves as *sacupes* rather than vassals. This Southeast Asian concept evoked an egalitarian relationship between "one thing as being part of a larger group of things." William Henry Scott presents a slightly different definition of *hacup*—a cognate of sacup—as "any inclusive group, but especially one supportive of a person on whom they were dependent, like children of their parents or slaves of their masters."[152] This interpretation suggests that there was more meaningful overlap between the Filipino concepts of belonging and the meaning of vassalage in the Hispanic monarchy. Vassalage in the global Spanish empire was also conceptualized as a paternal relationship between a fatherly king and his children or dependents.[153]

Borderlands Indigenous communities participated in the 1754 campaign against Moro pirates for multiple compelling reasons, and chief among them was the desire to rescue captive kin. It was common for religious orders to ransom priests who were seized by Moros in the Philippines, making payments to their captors to secure their release.[154] In contrast, Filipino captives were more likely to be freed by Hispano-Filipino forces during attacks on Moro ships and settlements without money or other goods changing hands.[155] Enslaved people often liberated themselves, jumping into the sea and swimming toward friendly armadas as they approached.[156] An unpublished Jesuit account of the 1754 pirate war claims that Hispano-Filipino forces rescued five hundred Christian captives that year, the majority of whom were Indigenous. The account lists the names, sex, and towns of origin of three hundred Filipino liberated slaves, noting that the identities of the rest were lost in the confusion of war.[157] Roughly even numbers of males and females were rescued. The redeemed captives came from diverse parts of the Philippines, reflecting the broad geographic scope of Moro raiding in the mid-eighteenth century (see Table 1). Three quarters of the redeemed captives were adults. Many women were rescued with small children in tow. Thomasa Barabara, a woman who had been captured in a raid on Sorsogon in southern Luzon, was rescued with her two-month-old baby boy, whom she had given birth to aboard a Moro slave ship.[158] Some captives were seized and subsequently rescued as part of larger family groups. Ignacio Calimpong and his wife Maria

Michaela were rescued with their fourteen-year-old daughter Francisca Dom-
inga, their three-year-old daughter Maria Ignacia, and their two-year-old
son Juan Alejo. This family were among the 117 people who had been captured in a raid on Balooy in Mindanao. Rescued Filipino captives were allowed to return to their home communities.

Historians have been oddly reluctant to acknowledge the trauma that
women and men experienced during raids and once they were taken captive.
James Francis Warren, for example, suggested that enslaved people put to
work in raiding fleets, manacled and "compelled to row for long stretches—
ten, twelve, even fourteen hours at a time" gained "the possibility of a better
way of life, exchanging discomfort and servitude for the opportunity of
skilled local work, adventure, and social advancement as a slave raider."[159]
This sympathetic view of slavery in maritime Asia is grounded in the assumption that Visayans and other islanders in the Philippines regarded being a tribute-paying vassal of the Spanish Crown as a worse fate than being
enslaved and trafficked far from home. The great lengths that communities
went to protect themselves from maritime raids challenges this premise. Although Filipino captives mostly remain silent in the archive, it does not take
a great imaginative leap to fathom the terror and grief that these victims of
trafficking experienced. Sadness and despair characterize the few testimonies from enslaved Southeast Asians that were recorded in this era. Wange
Hendrik Richard van Bali, a man who was born enslaved on the Indonesian
island of Flores in the second half of the eighteenth century, was bought and
sold and transported across the archipelago by Asian and Dutch merchants
in multiple transactions. When as an adult van Bali finally returned to the
village where he was born and raised, he described how he "saw it and became sad, not able to speak out of sorrow, and looked at it in melancholy."[160]
Sitting with such emotive ties to place and kin, and the anguish of forced
separation from family and country, must be central to our attempts to make
sense of popular support for Spanish anti-piracy in the Philippines.

Indigenous solider warriors in the armadas de los pintados often knew
the enslaved peoples that they rescued. Liberated captives largely came from
the same regions as the fighting men who rescued them. The captives who
swam up to Hispano-Filipino vessels were initially regarded with suspicion
and treated as potential spies. Crews bound their feet and hands together with
rope or chains until their identity could be verified by kin in the Catholic
fleets. For example, in 1752, an unnamed runaway captive who swam to a boat
in the Hispano-Filipino armada claimed that he had an uncle in the fleet.

Table 1. Captives redeemed in the 1754 anti-piracy campaign by place of origin

Town	Island	Region	Number of liberated captives
Albay	Luzon	Bicol	2
Macalaya	Luzon	Bicol	4
Maripipi	Luzon	Bicol	3
Sorsogon	Luzon	Bicol	82
Buracan	Luzon	Camarines Sur	4
Balooy	Mindanao	Mindanao	117
Lubungán	Mindanao	Mindanao	1
Sambuang (Zamoboanga)	Mindanao	Mindanao	5
Tugauan	Mindanao	Mindanao	8
Caraga	Mindanao	Mindanao (north)	2
Hingoog (Gingoog)	Mindanao	Mindanao (north)	1
Abac (Capul)	Capul	Visayas	2
Aclan (Aklan)	Panay	Visayas	7
Bacon (Bacong)	Negros	Visayas	2
Bogobong	Mindoro	Visayas	7
Capul	Capul	Visayas	1
Catbalogan	Samar	Visayas	3
Guivan	Samar	Visayas	1
Iloylo	Panay	Visayas	1
Lalabiton	Samar	Visayas	7
Leyte	Leyte	Visayas	11
Liloan	Cebu	Visayas	2
Masbate	Masbate	Visayas	1
Romblon	Romblon	Visayas	1
Tanhay	Cebu	Visayas	9
Tiaco	Tiaco	Visayas	1
Vsigan	Panay	Visayas	2
Dolan	*Not identified*		1
Dumugan (Dumugsan)	Negros	Visayas	1
Dungan	*Not identified*		1
Hibaloc	*Not identified*		1
Lactaan [Mactan?]	Island adjacent to Cebu	Visayas	3
Maet	*Not identified*		1
Unknown			1
Total			296

The man was freed after his uncle was located and corroborated his identity.[161] Personal ties to the victims of Moro slavery compelled individuals to fight with the Spanish rather than against them.

The Philippines borderlands were not the only region in the global Spanish empire that suffered the scourge of slave-raiding. Incessant raids gave rise to militarized Indigenous-Spanish coalitions in the Americas, too. In mid-eighteenth century Commanchería (present-day New Mexico and West Texas in the United States of America), Commanche and Ute slave-raiding promoted the formation of military coalitions between missionaries and Apache communities that were vulnerable to these attacks.[162] Missionaries in the Philippines compared the archipelago to the South American province of Paraguay, where Jesuits armed the Guaraní to fight against Brazilian *bandeirante* who hunted and enslaved them.[163] Convent libraries in the Philippines would have held copies of theological treatises like the Paraguay-based Jesuit Diego de Boroa's work that justified making war to protect the king's Indigenous vassals. Boroa asserted that "it is licit, just, and holy to kill the one who attacks the innocent, defending him or her when he or she would otherwise be defenseless."[164] Philippines missionaries would have also read hagiographic literature celebrating the soldier-priests who were martyred in these American borderlands, and perhaps modeled themselves in their image.[165]

Beyond rescuing captive kin, there were significant material incentives for Indigenous peoples in the Philippines to wage war on Moro pirates. Hispano-Filipino forces enslaved Muslim people that they took as prizes in battle, contrary to the long-held view that Christian Filipinos did not have slaves.[166] As noted earlier in this chapter, the enslavement of Muslims in a just war was legal in the global Spanish empire. Manila's Junta de Guerra ruled in 1741 that the Indigenous men who participated in anti-piracy campaigns could "enslave some of the enemy Moros they seize."[167] A rare surviving ledger that the Manila notary Domingo Cortés de Arquiza used to record all of the transactions that he processed in 1755 reveals that several Moro slaves were bought and sold in the cosmopolitan capital that year.[168] Phelipe de Silva, a *Malabar* or South Asian man, sold the twelve-year-old enslaved boy whom he called Adonis for eighty pesos to Francisca Caugue, a *mestiza de Sangley* living in Santa Cruz. The notary described Adonis as having dark skin and a scar above his left eye and declared that he was a "legitimate captive of the Malay nation."[169] Given the timing of this transaction, it is highly likely that Adonis was captured in the 1754 campaign, or his enslavers tried to pass him off as someone who was to make this transaction legal and acceptable.

The men who went to war in 1754 came home "enriched with loot."[170] An inventory of treasures seized from the enemy that year reveals that the bulk of prizes were textiles, including rolls of damask and clothing, such as "a cape of iridescent purple *pequin* . . . adorned with a silk braid."[171] These textiles were most likely of Chinese origin. Indigenous elites held on to a large portion of such luxury goods that were taken in battle. Yet it was customary for datus to grant sailor-warriors a share of what was plundered, in addition to the modest salary and rice, salt, and tobacco rations that monarchs often provided them during stints of military service.[172] Filipino and Spanish military traditions recognized that it was crucial to reward fighting men "who leave their lands and homes to work and to shed blood, or die for their country, for their law, and for their King."[173]

Datus were also known to reward their followers' successes in battle with relief from tribute. Sailor-warriors could also defer redeeming earned material rewards for their military service. Junker explains that "Philippine chiefs were generally obligated to fulfill any reasonable requests for assistance" that their followers made, including food provisions when crops failed, and contributions toward bride payments.[174] The Spanish Crown's decisions about the distribution of war booty reflected local war customs. Its compact with Don Pedro Tamparong permitted sailor-warriors to keep "what they can use in war," such as weapons and boats.[175] In 1741, the colonial government in Manila determined that "to motivate the natives" to enlist in the anti-piracy campaign, proclamations should be published promising them that they could keep what they seized from Moro enemies in battle.[176] These announcements would have been read out in public places to ensure their wide dissemination.

For datus, wealth accrued in war reinforced their authority both within their communities and in wider regional networks. Datus were not strictly hereditary positions. Although the sons of datus were expected to become datus, followers were free to choose their leaders and could leave their town and go live under another datu if they wished. Datus regularly gifted luxury items or prestige goods like the textiles described above to neighboring chiefs as a strategy of strengthening horizontal alliances, and to their followers to reinforce patron-client ties. In the Visayas and in Mindanao, datu status was strongly linked to military prowess. The Visayan epics that were often sung before an armada went into battle lionized the heroic feats of datus and warriors, and celebrated the great numbers of slaves and other treasures they seized. Battlefield exploits were also a means of social mobility for nonelites. Men who killed enemies in battle in the Visayas wore special red clothing that marked their strength and bravery. Victories on the battlefield sometimes created opportunities for fighting men to become datus themselves.[177]

Spanish monarchs also issued rewards to Indigenous vassals for exceptional contributions to the holy war against Moro pirates. In 1725, the Crown awarded a stipend of six pesos per month to Basilio Virtudes Tamparong in recognition of his efforts to facilitate the conversion of hundreds of "mountain people" to Catholicism.[178] Tamparong had also escorted a Spanish ambassador to Mindanao, paying for ten soldiers to protect the diplomat during this journey. The clergy facilitated the circulation of Filipino petitions for rewards to the king and Council of the Indies in Spain. Padre Pedro José de Sisa, a Jesuit missionary based in Iligan, was instrumental to the Crown's decision to reward Tamparong. He prepared the petition in accordance with the established conventions of this genre and ensured that this physical file made its way to the Royal Palace in Manila and eventually to the Royal Court in Spain.

Culture and faith should not be underestimated as factors that encouraged Indigenous support the colonial government's war against Moro pirates. Raiding and revenge raiding were deeply spiritual experiences in the Philippines before and during the Spanish colonial period. All combat was understood as a spiritual confrontation, and the person or group with the greatest quantity of "soul stuff" or spiritual potency prevailed. There was a multitude of mechanisms for enhancing soul stuff, including using talismans, weapons like the kris that were endowed with supernatural powers, and various rituals including fasting.[179] Visayan informants told the Jesuit missionary Francisco Ignacio Alcina in the mid-seventeenth century that warriors traditionally launched warships into the sea by rolling them over a captive seized in war; "they squeezed him and left him like a tortilla," in the friar's words. This sacrifice to the gods ensured that that the ship and the sailor-warriors that it carried would be "feared by enemies and brave in making captives."[180] In time, prayers and petitions to Catholic saints blended with these pre-Hispanic traditions in many parts of the islands.

"He who goes to sea learns how to pray" was a popular saying in early modern Spain.[181] The presence of priests aboard the *galleras* named for

Catholic saints, including the *San Felipe* and the *Santo Niño*, ensured that shipboard life in the armada de los pintados was punctuated by prayers and invocations, just as it was in Spanish ships that sailed in other seas. The willingness of priests to take up arms and fight alongside their communities would have surely persuaded some Catholic soldiers to join the holy war. Accounts of Hispano-Filipino anti-piracy campaigns are colored with miracles: heavenly interventions in battles that favored Catholics over the Islamic pirates. Survivors of the Moro pirate siege of Palompong recounted that a group of villagers who were ambushed by pirates were extraordinarily immune to the bullets that rained down on them. They attributed this miracle to the Jesuit saint Francisco Xavier, "who defended his children, so that none could be wounded."[182] Catholic relics, usually fragments of a deceased holy person's bone or hair, or pieces of clothing that they had worn or touched, accompanied priests and their flocks into combat to protect them from injury and death. Such spiritually potent Catholic sacred objects were compatible with local beliefs in the supernatural power of *anting anting* (amulets) that could protect people from harm.[183] Accounts of talismans and war miracles circulated in print and oral storytelling, reinforcing the seductive idea that God looked kindly on men who risked their lives to fight the Catholic empire's Islamic enemies.[184]

Coercion was undeniably a factor in the recruitment of Indigenous men to anti-piracy fleets. Spanish colonial officials did use threats and violence to mobilize Indigenous people to fight in the holy war. Indigenous and mestizo elites who failed to support anti-piracy campaigns were sometimes punished by Spanish colonial officials. For example, Pedro Orthuño de Leon, the alcalde mayor of Iloilo, staged a surprise nighttime military drill in 1723 to prepare local militiamen to defend the town and presidio against an enemy attack. Orthuño was furious when "less than one hundred men of all nations" responded to the alarm and reported for duty. He arrested four men—the leaders of the local militias and the cabezas de barangay—and sent them to Manila to be punished for failing in their duty to rally troops.[185] An anonymous mid-eighteenth-century critique of the Spanish empire that was written in the Philippines complained that Visayans were conscripted as oarsmen into the royal navy for three months at a time without being paid.[186]

Intensifying midcentury military campaigns led to increased demands on Indigenous labor. In addition to filling boats with fighting men, communities were expected to contribute other resources to the war effort, including rice, wood, and boats. In 1744, these mounting pressures contributed to the outbreak of an anti-colonial revolt in Bohol, an island in the Visayas that supplied large numbers of soldiers and ships to anti-piracy campaigns. The revolt started as a heated dispute between the Jesuit missionary Gaspar Benito Morales and locals in the town called Inabanga over the price that the cleric was charging for a Catholic burial. Locals killed Morales, and the brother-and-sister duo Francisco and Gracia Dagohoy led an angry group of villagers into the mountains, where they would be free of the friars. The Dagohoy's rebellion grew. People in Hagna executed another Jesuit priest who had ordered them to cut down trees and transport the heavy planks of wood to the beach to build a boat.[187] Masses of sailor-warriors and their families joined the maroons after they returned to their pueblos following a stint at sea fighting pirates and found their families impoverished by tribute payments that had been imposed even on women in their absence, contrary to custom and practice.[188] The demands of war eroded the colonial bargain in Bohol.

Pedro de Estrada, the provincial of the Jesuits, was convinced that the Bohol revolt ultimately aimed to overthrow the Spanish. The rebels "only want liberty, and to be able to make themselves lords of all the island without any submission to a Catholic king, and they think they can easily achieve this by killing all the priests."[189] Estrada feared that the revolt would become general and that colonial rule across the Visayas would collapse. The Jesuits and their remaining Indigenous allies responded to the uprising with terror. They executed two men who were accused of killing a priest, and then placed their severed heads and hands in public places across the islands, and burned the rest of their bodies to ashes and threw them into the sea. Local officials deemed this brutality necessary because "if these natives are not terrorized with an example, we should worry that the entire province will revolt."[190] Missionaries recruited Indigenous fighting men to torch Alcabuceo, the village in Talibon that was a rebel safe haven. The Jesuits requested that the colonial government in Manila send soldiers to quash the rebellion, but a war council in the capital decided that the state could not afford to divert resources away from the anti-piracy campaign to reconquer former vassals hiding out in the mountains of Bohol. The rebels and their descendants remained in the mountains until the rebellion was finally put down by Hispano-Filipino forces in 1827. The outbreak of the Bohol uprising serves as an important reminder that war did not always strengthen bonds between the state, the church, and Indigenous communities in the Philippines. Yet the pressing need to resist pirate raids may have prevented more people from joining the Dagohoys in their pursuit to live without empire.

Conclusion

Spanish colonial officials and missionaries in the Philippines were anxious that Moro piracy would end Spanish sovereignty in the archipelago in the first half of the eighteenth century. This was an era in which, in the words of one historian, devastating sea raids on coastal communities formed "a pattern of tragedy so recurrent as to become almost tedious."[191] Moro piracy was a double-barreled threat. It combined the calamity of pirates destroying villages—burning crops, homes, and churches, and taking entire towns captive—with the specter of the spread of Islam. The real and imagined dangers of pirate raids led the colonial government to funnel valuable resources into efforts to destroy this enemy. The fact that Moro pirates were enslaving one thousand baptized Indigenous Filipinos and the occasional Catholic priest every year added a sense of urgency to this objective. This chapter leaves little doubt that the Spanish would have annihilated Muslim sea-robbers if they had been powerful enough to do so, but the Islamic maritime polities in the southern Philippines and the Sulu Zone were not easily defeated. As Frederick Cooper observed, "empires perpetuated violence because they were strong and because they were weak."[192]

Moro piracy fundamentally shaped the evolution of Spain's Asian empire. The indominable sea-robbers forced the Spanish Crown and its representatives in the islands—colonial government officials and missionaries—to pursue partnerships with sultans, datus, and the principalia to build new forts, fortified churches, and huge hybrid Hispano-Filipino naval fleets that waged war on their mutual pirate enemies. War was not only a function of empire but a process that brought it into being. Interrogating the ideologies and practices of Catholic anti-piracy in the contested Philippine borderlands complicates the persistent myth that Spanish conquistadors imposed empire on islanders who had little say in the matter. Recovering the dynamics of anti-piracy treaty-making and alliance formation highlights the centrality of negotiation to Spain's Asian empire, and the extent to which it was forged from below. Raiding and counterraiding drew islanders into coalitions with the Spanish Crown to ensure their individual and collective survival, if not their prosperity. Catholic priests and the Indigenous elites were important go-betweens in alliance formation, but they were ultimately able only to broker compacts that served a community's interests. The desire to protect kin from raids, and to rescue those who had been stolen away into slavery, were compelling reasons to seek out Spanish support. The Dagahoy revolt illustrates that the escalating war against pirates put pressure on Indigenous communities that could blow up into rebellions. More often, however, anti-piracy alliances strengthened imperial legitimacy in the archipelagic borderlands.

CHAPTER 2

Sea-Robbers and Sangleyes in the Catholic Republic of Manila

Only two years after conquistadors conquered Soliman's kingdom of May Ni-la, pirates almost destroyed the settlement they built above its smoldering ashes. The Teochew sea-robber Lin Feng (林鳳), whom the Spanish called Limahong (林阿鳳), sailed into Manila Bay in November of 1574 with a fleet of one hundred ships and several thousand men. Limahong headed one of maritime Asia's last massive mid-sixteenth century pirate fleets. He steered it toward the Philippines to evade the Ming court's anti-piracy patrols and to capture the Spaniard's famed riches. Clad in bamboo helmets and armed with cutlasses and daggers, the pirate fleet's fighting men swarmed and sacked Manila. They set fire to its wooden buildings, burning most of them to the ground, and they slit the throats of anyone who was not quick or clever enough to flee. The Spanish rebuilt and refortified after the pirates retreated, but Limahong returned months later. His fleet formed a crescent in the bay in front of the city before hundreds of men disembarked and attacked. This time they were unable to defeat the Spanish and Mexican soldiers and settlers and their Indigenous allies who had amassed to defend Manila. The pirates withdrew and established a rival outpost 175 kilometers to the northwest at Lingayen, where they kidnapped local datus to ransom for provisions.[1] Hispano-Filipino forces cooperated with the Ming navy to destroy this pirates' nest in 1575, but Limahong's ghost would haunt the Philippines long after the pirate's death, shaping Sino-Spanish relations in the islands for centuries to come.

Manila's large Chinese population set it apart from other urban centers in the global Spanish empire. In the long seventeenth century, the numbers of Chinese migrants and their descendants in and around the capital fluctuated between ten thousand and forty thousand, dwarfing the capital's Spanish population. Many early moderns considered the Chinese to be Spain's essential partners in the conquest and colonization of the Philippines. Nonetheless, a debate over whether the Chinese posed a fundamental threat to the Spanish colony, and whether and under what conditions they should be permitted to live within its borders, persisted throughout the long period of Spanish colonial rule in the islands, albeit with varying degrees of urgency.

The scholarship on Sino-Spanish interactions in Manila has expanded in recent years. The literature is divided between studies that portray Sino-Spanish relations as idyllically tolerant, and others that emphasize the conflict and violence that characterized their *convivencia* (living together). Both camps tend to mute the significant changes that occurred over time.[2] This chapter shows that Sino-Spanish relations were more like a pendulum swinging between these extremes. Major shifts in the nature of piracy in maritime Asia transformed how powerful Spaniards in Manila perceived Sangleyes and in turn altered the policies that the Crown and the colonial government conceived of and implemented to control this large and diverse cohort. Embracing Catholicism was key to Chinese migrants and their descendants' success in securing privileges in the Philippines, including rights to reside in and move about the Spanish colony, but piracy impacted how Church and government officials interpreted and responded to Chinese migrants' religious conversions. War and violence on the indomitable seas that surrounded the islands shaped what was possible on shore.

This chapter introduces Manila's diverse Chinese migrant population. It develops a chronological analysis of the laws and policies that the Spanish Crown and its delegates in the Philippines adopted to attempt to manage this segment of colonial society from the late sixteenth century until the eve of the 1762 British invasion of Manila. It argues that the explosion of massive Chinese pirate syndicates during China's turbulent Ming-Qing transition triggered mass killings of the Chinese in Manila and its hinterland in 1603, 1639, and 1662. An estimated fifty thousand Chinese men were murdered in these three state-sponsored killing sprees. Successive Spanish governors of the Philippines in this era regarded the Chinese living among them as a fifth column that was willing and able to assist the Chinese pirates who they believed were planning to attack Manila, and time and again, they embraced genocidal slaughter to thwart the pirate threat. This cycle of massacres disappeared in the late seventeenth century as the Qing state consolidated its authority in China and its maritime regions and brutally suppressed large-scale Chinese piratical organizations. The subsequent rise of slave-raiding Moro piracy in the Sulu Zone created new opportunities for Chinese migrants and Chinese mestizos to be integrated into the Catholic republic of Manila as Christian vassals of the Spanish Crown.

The rich and growing historiography of the Chinese diaspora in the Americas has emphasized the ways in which Chinese migrants functioned as "others" against which the imperial and national identities that excluded them were formed.[3] Yet in the case of the Philippines in the first half of the eighteenth century, the othering of Moro pirates facilitated Chinese assimilation into the transoceanic imperial Spanish nation. Nation-bounded histories of the Philippines have blind spots. The connections between piracy and the politics of belonging in colonial Manila become visible only when we zoom out from the cosmopolis and consider historical patterns and processes across the Philippines archipelago and greater maritime Asia. This chapter bridges the separation or siloing of histories of the Chinese diaspora and the histories of Spanish-Indigenous relations in the archipelago that has obscured the extent to which these were entangled and mutually constituted. Moreover, scholarship on the Moro wars has traditionally focused on the borderlands regions of Mindanao and the Visayas. This study breaks new ground by elucidating how colonial anti-piracy politics played out in the capital, where they came to operate as a force of social cohesion.

Recovering migrant agency is central to making sense of the evolving politics of belonging in Spain's Asian empire. Edward Slack accurately observed that previous scholarship has portrayed Chinese migrants as either "inscrutable, parasitic, or opportunistic 'middle-men'; or as victims of Spanish arrogance and brutality with extremely limited agency to either rebel, convert to Catholicism, or return to China."[4] This chapter reads the Spanish empire's archive along and against the grain to push beyond these two-dimensional portrayals of the Chinese in the Philippines to recover how they experienced, navigated, and shaped the colonial government's attitudes and actions toward them. Individual and collective choices and strategies intersected with major political developments in maritime Asia to determine the dynamics of social inclusion and exclusion in early modern Manila.

Managing Multiethnic Manila

The Kingdom of May Nila and other polities across the Philippines were already integrated into intra-Asian trading networks before the first Spanish conquistadors arrived in the islands. The archipelago is mentioned in China's Song dynasty records dating back to the late tenth century, and the Philippines' archeological record shows sustained trade between the archipelago and China from this time onward.[5] Yet the Spanish conquest and the influx of American silver into Manila in the late sixteenth century rapidly transformed the city into a global center of trade that connected multiple world markets, intensifying the traffic of people into and through the city.[6] The silver, silks, and spices that flowed through Manila were accompanied by people from many different parts of the planet. The Dominican missionary Juan Cobo remarked in 1589 that the "diversity of people" in Manila was "immense."[7]

The cosmopolitan capital of Spain's Asian empire was home to Spaniards and other Europeans who were always in the minority. The number of Spaniards in Manila—a socioracial category that encompassed men and women born in the Iberian Peninsula, the Americas, and the Philippines—never exceeded 4,000 at any time from the sixteenth to the eighteenth centuries.[8] Newcomers from New Spain, many of whom were convict-soldiers, were also an important and visible part of the urban population. On average, 156 soldiers traveled from Mexico to Manila each year in the seventeenth century, falling to an average of 87 from 1765 to 1811.[9] The Philippines' Indigenous population was hit hard by the Spanish conquest. The estimated number of Indigenous people living in Manila and its hinterland declined from approximately 43,000 in 1565 to 32,000 in 1700. The combination of diseases that Europeans introduced into the islands and the conquistadors' exploitation of Indigenous labor devastated the native population.[10] It recovered in the eighteenth century, reaching an estimated 70,000 by 1800.[11] The diverse men and women that Spaniards called *extranjeros* (foreigners) included other non-Spanish Europeans, including the Irish and French, sojourners and settlers from East Asia including Japan, and merchants and migrants from Southeast Asian kingdoms such as Ternate, in addition to Africans, Armenians, *malabares*, and other peoples from the Indian subcontinent.[12]

The Chinese were by far the largest group of foreigners present in Manila for as long as the Spanish empire existed in the islands. The capital's fluctuating Chinese population rose to up to ten times the number of Spaniards in the colony.[13] Chinese migration to the Philippines was part of a larger pattern of outward migration from China into maritime Asia. Large Chinese communities developed in port cities across the region, including in Nagasaki, the bustling Japanese center of maritime trade, and in Batavia (Jakarta), which served as the headquarters of the Dutch East India Company in Asia.[14] Scholars have described Chinese migrants and their descendants as a diaspora, which Lok Siu defined as "a collectivity of people who share a common history of dispersal from a homeland (real and imagined) and emplacement elsewhere, and who maintain a sense of connection to both places, as well as with their geographically dispersed co-ethnics."[15] This category is useful, with the caveat that migrants and their descendants' real and imagined connections to China varied greatly among this massive and multifarious collective and over the passage of time.

Almost all Chinese sojourners and settlers in the Philippines were male. Chinese women stayed home, and men who went abroad often found new wives and sexual partners where they settled.[16] The majority of these male immigrants were Hokkien speakers from the southern region of Fujian known as Minnan.[17] Seventeenth-century archives shed little light on Chinese migrants' villages or cities of origin. Government censuses of the Chinese in the Philippines conducted in 1769 and 1779 revealed that more than 80 percent of Chinese migrants who were present in the islands in these years came from three southern Fujian counties: Jianjiang and Tong'an in Quanzhou and Longxi in Zhangzhou. At the height of Chinese migration to the Philippines in the nineteenth century, more than 90 percent of migrants still came from Minnan.[18]

Multiple factors contributed to the great early modern waves of male migration from southeastern China to Manila. Fujian's rugged, mountainous terrain limited opportunities for agriculture, pushing men to leave the communities that raised them. Shipbuilding and long-distance trade dominated the region's maritime economy, and its port cities were major gateways for trade to the Nanyang, as Southeast Asia was known in China, predisposing its population to migration across the sea.[19] The violence and disruption of the civil war that swept across China in the seventeenth century also prompted decisions to leave. Chinese fiction idealized Southeast Asian kingdoms as places of alternative possibility in this era of turmoil. Chen Chen's 1664 novel *The Sequel to the Water Margin* (水滸後 傳) depicted Siam as a "haven for outlaws and refugees."[20] Manila and its riches possibly occupied a similar status in the Chinese migrant imagination. Migration was not an easy feat. The

Ming and Qing states sought to strictly control maritime trade and travel. Those who went to Nanyang often did so illegally and were liable to be punished if they returned to China.[21]

The Spanish colonial government used the word Sangley to refer to Chinese migrants in the Philippines. Historians believe that this homogenizing term is a transliteration of a Hokkien word, possibly *sionglai* (常来), meaning "frequent visitors," or from *shengli* (生理), meaning trade. Sangley was not strictly a pejorative word. The most accurate English translation of Sangley is "Chinese," meaning a person who is a native of China. Chinese migrants and their descendants in the Philippines adopted the term Sangley to describe themselves in their dealings with the colonial government and the Crown. Only rarely was Sangley interchangeable with *chino* in the Philippines context. "Chino" was a broad signifier in the islands that could refer to natives of China and an array of polities across East Asia and Southeast Asia, including people from Japan and Java. Spaniards sometimes referred to Indigenous Filipinos as indios chinos in the Philippines, but this hyphenated identification was more commonly used in Mexico and the Americas.[22] Given the ambiguity of the chino category, Spanish laws regulating the presence and actions of Chinese migrants more often referred to Sangleyes.[23]

The Chinese migrants who settled in Manila frequently established families in and around the capital. Manileños labeled the offspring of male Chinese migrants and their archipelago-born wives as mestizos or mestizos de Sangley. Chinese migrants often married Chinese mestiza women whose mothers were Indigenous Filipinas and whose fathers or other male ancestors had migrated to the Philippines from China. The soldier and notary Diego de Rueda y Mendoza's 1625 account of the Manila wedding of his baptized Chinese migrant friend and the friend's mestiza de Sangley bride illustrates that Chinese weddings could be elaborate, transcultural, and joyous affairs. Rueda delighted in watching musicians and a crowd holding colorful banners accompany the bride to the church where her Catholic marriage ceremony was held. He admired her beautiful silk and damask layered dress, and her "very costly and elegant" headdress. After the church service, the newlyweds' Spanish and Chinese friends and relatives gathered for a feast to celebrate their union. Rueda enjoyed the Chinese play that was staged to entertain the guests.[24] Previous studies of the rise of a distinct Chinese mestizo identity tend to overstate the extent to which Sangleyes and mestizos de Sangleyes were separate identities and communities before the mid-eighteenth century.[25]

An enduring myth about early modern Chinese migration to the Philippines is that all Sangleyes were wealthy merchants. Antonio de Morga, an early chronicler of the Philippines who lived in Manila from 1594 to 1604 and served as an *oidor* (judge) in its Audiencia, divided Sangleyes into two groups: wealthy merchants, and "poor and greedy" workers.[26] This is a simplistic binary, but it underscores that there were many more Chinese in the city and its hinterland than those who came to trade luxury commodities for precious metals. The Tagalog engraver Nicolás de la Cruz Bagay's 1734 engraving of four Chinese men echoed Morga's categories (Figure 4). The two men on the left show the trappings of wealth. The man labelled "Christian" dons a Spanish-style hat above the long hair that falls across his shoulders, and he wears a silk coat, stockings, and shoes. The non-Christian *"gentil principal"* (well-to-do gentile) beside him also wears shoes and stockings beneath a long silk shirt. His hair is pulled back into a queue under a conical hat, and he grasps a fan in one hand and a full money bag in the other. The two men on the right, both barefoot, come from the ranks of the poor. One, a boatman, carries rope and a pole that was used to navigate small boats through the crowded bay, and the other, a fisherman, holds his catch beside him.

Sangleyes held an array of occupations in and around the capital. The Chinese fed Manileños. Juan Cobo noted that there were "innumerable" Chinese fishermen in the city. Sangley fishmongers, butchers, and gardeners brought their produce to the city's markets. Chinese bakers made bread using wheat imported from China. Manila's houses, convents, churches, and forts were built by Sangley stonemasons, carpenters, and laborers. Chinese artisans carved and painted the religious statues that were revered in homes and chapels and were exported across the Pacific. Skilled and unskilled workers labored in the shipyards of Cavite where the great galleons were built, and they toiled in the sweltering ironworks where the cannon and artillery that defended the empire were forged.[27] Morga confessed that "the truth is that without these Sangleyes, it would be impossible to sustain this city."[28] Such comments from high-ranking government officials have influenced historians' assessments of Chinese migrants as co-colonists to the Spanish in the Philippines.[29]

Sustained Spanish efforts to spread Catholicism among Manila's Sangleyes gave rise to Chinese Catholic communities in the city. King Philip II nominated the Dominican missionaries who first arrived in Manila in 1587 to take charge of the mission to the Chinese in the capital. By 1588, the order had established a modest church in the Parián, Manila's Chinese district.

Figure 4. This engraving was one of the vignettes depicting the diverse peoples of the Philippine islands that framed Nicolás de la Cruz Bagay and Pedro Murillo Velarde's 1734 map of the archipelago. Murillo Velarde and Bagay, *Carta hydrographica*. Library of Congress, https://www.loc.gov/item/2021668467/.

Chinese architects and builders must have assisted in the design and construction of the first wooden Catholic church dedicated to the biblical three kings that was built in the Parián in 1617, as contemporaries noted that it resembled a Chinese temple. This church burned down in 1639 and was reconstructed in stone.[30] Hundreds of Chinese migrants were being baptized in these Parián churches every year in the late sixteenth and early seventeenth centuries. As the previous chapter noted, the Catholic ritual of baptism involved an ordained priest pouring water over the forehead of a new convert and anointing them with oil, a ceremony that was understood to erase a person's sins and admit them to the community of Catholics. Baptism usually followed a period of instruction in the core tenets of the Catholic faith, but priests also performed the ritual for Chinese men in Manila who were gravely ill and close to death, regardless of their religious education.[31]

It was common for Chinese converts to Catholicism to undergo a physical transformation at their baptism, with men often cutting off the long, plaited ponytails known as queues. Spaniards interpreted queue cutting as evidence of a new convert's commitment to Catholicism because they knew that this act would be interpreted as a symbol of Ming loyalism and a rejection of Qing authority in China and punished harshly if the convert returned to the country of their birth. As Diego de Rueda—the wedding guest—noted, for the Sangleyes, "cutting their hair is taken as an infamous rejection of their kingdom, land, and obedience to the [Chinese] king, so they were not allowed to return to their kingdom."[32] Notably, Chinese migrants and their children sometimes adopted new Christian names at their baptism. When Matheo Giang San and Ynes Lamanis baptized their infant daughter in 1621, they gave her the name of her *padrina* (godmother) Joana Joanio. One 36-year-old Chinese migrant was baptized in the Three Kings parish church in 1632 as Pedro de Mendiola, taking the name of his sergeant major *padrino* (godfather).[33] These naming practices could obscure a person's Chinese heritage in parish records and should caution historians against relying on names to determine ethnic identities or origins.

Chinese Catholic culture flourished in the first century of Spanish colonial rule in Manila. During Holy Week in 1589, Sangleyes processed solemnly through Manila's streets carrying candles and banners bearing Catholic images. Juan Cobo claimed that this admirable "display of devotion" proved wrong those critics who contended that the Chinese or their souls were "so inaccessible" to the friars and God.[34] Some forty years later, Diego de Rueda observed that the Parián's Catholic residents had "placed images of Our Lady in every street, and a cross or other religious image on each lamp."[35] During the annual Catholic feast of Our Lady of the Rosary, Chinese guilds built elaborate altars decorated with flowers and cut paper that they dedicated to the Mother of God. Yet despite these outward demonstrations of Christian devotion, among some Spanish elites there was a persistent suspicion of the sincerity or authenticity of Chinese Catholicism. This anxiety manifest in what is now known as the Chinese rites controversy, which embroiled Catholic intellectuals in the Philippines and around the world in an extended debate over the extent to which Chinese beliefs and traditions, and particularly rituals associated with filial piety and devotions to ancestor spirits, were compatible with fundamental Catholic beliefs.[36] Spanish concerns that Sangleyes were practicing idolatry manifest on the ground in Manila in multiple ways, including in priests and government officials' efforts to study and police Chinese good-luck rituals associated with gambling, as well as funerary and mourning traditions.[37]

Campaigns to convert Sangleyes in Manila were connected to Spanish aspirations to spread Catholicism in China, which was home to approximately two hundred thousand Catholics at the end of the seventeenth century.[38] The generations of mostly European-born missionaries who traveled to China maintained ties with their counterparts in the Philippines. China's Catholic population fell in the early eighteenth century as Catholics faced persecution under the Qing and the Catholic Church became less tolerant of rituals that honored ancestor sprits. However, the missionary desire to evangelize in China persisted and influenced the clergy's and the Spanish colonial government's treatment of the Chinese in the Philippines. Religious concerns profoundly shaped the contours of Spanish imperial expansion at the local and global levels.

Neither the Spanish awareness that empire in the Philippines seemed to rely on the Chinese nor the Spanish desire to save Chinese souls rendered these migrants' presence consistently welcome or inevitable. The "Chinese question," to borrow May Ngai's concept, which was essentially whether Sangleyes posed a threat to the Spanish colony and whether they should be permitted within its borders, was hotly debated among the Church and government officials across the Philippines, Mexico, and Spain.[39] Some of the arguments that were voiced in favor of restricting or entirely eradicating the Chinese from the Philippines remained surprisingly consistent across the seventeenth and eighteenth centuries. Counterintuitively, the enemies of the Sangleyes accused them of damaging the city's political economy. They complained that the Chinese dominated commerce and skilled trades and the profits that flowed from these activities, leaving Spaniards and Indigenous Filipinos impoverished. They alleged that the Sangleyes also injured the political economy of souls, spreading usury, sodomy, and non-Christian beliefs among Indigenous neophytes as though these sinful behaviors and heresies were contagious diseases. Some singled out poor and propertyless Chinese workers as being especially troublesome and undesirable members of colonial society. The Dominican friar Plácido de Angulo complained that China exported the very worst of her population to Manila: migrants were "of the lowest esteem and importance in that whole kingdom, because almost all of them are fishermen, seditious men, runaways, criminals, dangerous people; those who go to other lands in search of riches that they are unable to find in theirs."[40] But the gravest allegation that Manileños made against Sangleyes was that they were a fifth column that was willing and able to support Chinese invasions of the capital, be they backed by China's emperor or renegade Chinese pirates. It was this fear that most threatened the security of the Chinese in the Spanish colony.

The Spanish experimented with various strategies that aimed to simultaneously exploit the benefits that Sangleyes provided to their Asian empire, while limiting the serious risks that they posed to its survival. Restricting the overall size of the Philippines' Chinese population was a popular tool for achieving this delicate balance. In 1603, King Philip III decreed that no more than three thousand Chinese could reside in the colony. King Philip IV doubled this limit two decades later.[41] No comparable caps were placed on other non-Spanish ethnic groups anywhere else in the empire. As was often the case in empires, there was a gap between law and practice. The estimated twenty-six thousand Chinese who were present in Manila in 1621 proved that colonial officials disregarded the Crown's Chinese population controls.[42]

It is well known that the Spanish colonial government in Manila attempted to segregate Sangleyes from the rest of the city's population. The Parián and the Chinese licensing system were the core components of the government's segregation strategy over many generations. Inspired by Spain's historic Jewish and Muslim ghettos, Governor Gonzalo Ronquillo de Peñalosa established the Parián in 1581. It quickly evolved from a single building consisting of shops and living spaces for Chinese merchants to a crowded Chinese neighborhood. By 1603, the district contained four hundred shops and an estimated eight thousand Chinese residents. Laws mandated that Sangleyes sleep inside of the Parián and imposed tough penalties on those who spent the night elsewhere, including the confiscation of property and four years of hard labor aboard royal galleys. The Parián moved back and forth across the Pasig river several times before the mid-seventeenth century, when it settled in its permanent position behind Intramuros. This site lacked direct access to Manila Bay, which theoretically allowed it to be cut off from the ocean and from China in the case of a rebellion.[43] The Chinese quarter stood within firing range of the heavy artillery that was mounted on the high walls of Fort Santiago. In stark contrast to fortifications erected in other Spanish port cities that were designed to defend the king's vassals from the attacks of pirates and other foreign invaders, Manila's defenses were constructed to protect the city from the enemy within.[44]

The Chinese licensing system also forced Sangleyes to live apart. From 1610 onward, the colonial government required all Sangleyes to buy a license that granted them permission to disembark in Manila, to reside in the city between the annual *ferias* (trading fairs), and to work in a trade. A 1721 royal order reiterated that it was illegal for a "chino" to leave his or her house without one of these licenses.[45] Some licenses operated like internal passports and afforded Sangleyes restricted rights to leave the Parián. For example, the fisherman Samyong and his four *compañeros* paid eighty pesos for a collective license to build and operate a fish farm oustide of the city in 1636.[46] Two decades later, José Suyco and Domingo Sunco each paid six pesos for licenses keep shops and sell wine in Santa Cruz, one of Manila's Chinese neighborhoods.[47] In 1745, thirty-year-old Ong Juco, a native of Leongque, purchased a license that authorized him to visit the Manila neighborhoods of the Estacada and Santa Cruz, and to travel up and down the Pasig from the coast to Lake Taal, and as far as the island of Mindoro eighty miles south of the capital. The license imposed a curfew on Ong Juco, ordering him to return to the Parián every night within an hour after the bells for evening prayers tolled, or to sleep aboard his boat. If he violated these rules and the segregation regime they upheld, Ong Juco faced banishment from the city after a period of forced labor in the royal shipyards of Cavite.[48] Chinese licenses were a lucrative business that generated substantial income streams for both the royal treasury and the individuals who rented the monopoly on license distribution. Both Spanish and Chinese men held this monopoly at different times.[49] In 1644, Chinese licenses generated 113,668 pesos for the colonial government, equal to almost 20 percent of its total income.[50] In the mid-eighteenth century, they added approximately 25,000 pesos a year to the colonial treasury.[51]

Although the Crown granted some exemptions, Chinese migrants were generally prohibited from having weapons in their homes or on their person. Chinese boats were also banned from carrying firearms.[52] Restricting access to weapons clearly aimed to minimize the risk of an armed rebellion and war against empire. It is also true that swords and other weapons functioned as symbols of prestige and power in the early modern world. Some historians have noted that laws restricting Black, Indigenous, and Chinese people's rights to bear arms in the Spanish empire were rooted in their symbolic meaning, and Spaniards' desires to strengthen a socio-racial colonial hierarchy that situated them at the top.[53]

It would be a mistake to cynically interpret sustained, state-supported efforts to convert Chinese migrants in Manila to Catholicism as being driven by the government's desire to control this population. There was, however, a prevailing assumption among global Spaniards that Catholic faith and identity were entwined with loyalty to the Spanish Crown, and conversion campaigns were a means to shore up support for empire from below.[54]

Chinese Pirates and Chinese Genocide: A Seventeenth-Century Cycle of Violence

The layered strategies that the Spanish colonial government adopted to control Sangleyes failed to achieve their main goal of preventing major violent clashes from erupting between Chinese migrants and Spanish and Indigenous communities in Manila. Chinese massacres occurred in the capital and across Luzon in 1603, 1639, and 1662. These mass killings can be described as genocidal because at the moment they occurred, the state and its army of executioners sought to eliminate the Sangleyes entirely.[55] Contemporaries estimated that at least fifteen thousand Chinese men were murdered in each of these grisly episodes. Early modern Spanish sources were prone to hyperbole, and it is possible that recorded death tolls were inflated. But what is astounding is that the archive evoked death on an immense scale. Death overwhelmed the senses. In 1639, the Augustinian missionary Casimiri Díaz wrote that for months after the killings it was impossible to drink the water that flowed through the rivers of Luzon, for they were "corrupted with the foul-smelling stink of death."[56]

Historians have struggled to adequately explain this cycle of massacres and its disappearance. Previous studies attributed the mass killings to deep, underlying tensions between the Spanish and the Chinese in Manila. Juan Gil pointed to a vague "socio-cultural clash" that occurs between peoples from different cultures living in proximity, one that is exacerbated when they occupy different social ranks: the conquerors and the conquered.[57] In a similar vein, Birgit Tremml-Werner pointed to unsolved social conflicts between the Chinese and the rest of colonial society. In Tremml-Werner's analysis, the "numerical imbalance" between the Spanish and the Chinese strained their living together. Spanish discrimination against the larger Chinese population fed the Sangleyes' seething resentment that exploded into rebellions, which in turn prompted violent reprisals from colonial authorities.[58] Additionally, Tremml-Werner and others have suggested that ecological and economic crises, including poor harvests and famines, and the failure of the galleon to arrive in Manila, could ignite ordinarily tense Sino-Spanish relations into periodic explosions of mass anti-Chinese violence.[59] Yet these interpretations fall short of explaining why this cycle of extreme violence abruptly ended in the mid-seventeenth century.[60] There were no mass killings of Chinese in the Philippines after 1662. Reinterpreting Chinese massacres through the lens of piracy reveals that major shifts in the real character of maritime violence in Philippine waters impacted the fate and fortunes of the people of the diaspora in the Spanish colony.

The arrival of Fujianese dignitaries in Manila in May of 1603, thirty years after Limahong's attack, triggered the first Chinese genocide in the city. Fujian's governor sent the assistant magistrate of the port of Haicheng to meet with the leaders of the Spanish, a trip he made accompanied by more than one hundred men. In Manila, the Ming official informed the Spanish governor Pedro Bravo de Acuña that he had come to explore the Cavite's fabled gold mountains. Acuña was sure that this Southeast Asian El Dorado story was a ruse to mask the true reason for the mandarins' visit: to plan for a Chinese invasion.

Tensions were already running high between the Spanish and the Chinese. Only a decade earlier, in 1593, the then Philippines governor Gómez Pérez Dasmariñas had forced 250 Chinese rowers to take him to the Moluccas. These forced maritime workers had mutinied, murdered Desmariñas, and escaped with the ship.[61] The visiting officials' activities gave the Spanish the impression that they were settling in to Manila for the long haul. They began to the administer justice in the Parián in elaborate public ceremonies that saw them parade through the Chinese quarter on horseback surrounded by guards of archers and men carrying the banners and tablets that symbolized their authority, and the canes that they used to flog their countrymen who they found guilty of various crimes.[62] Acuña was convinced that the visitors intended to plant seeds of sedition among Manila's Sangleyes in preparation for the arrival of an invading Chinese fleet big enough to carry 100,000 men. He dreaded that Manila's Sangleyes would join forces with their countrymen when enemy warships weighed anchor in Manila Bay.

The governor began to prepare the city to fight a two-front war against the awaited invaders from across the ocean and against the sea of Chinese who resided in the capital. Acuña ordered workers to demolish buildings that stood too close to the defensive walls of Intramuros and to deepen the ditches that encircled them. Conspicuous preparations for battle in turn set resident Sangleyes on edge. Convinced that the Spanish were going to attack them, the Chinese revolted. On the third of October, some twelve thousand Sangley "rebels" gathered on the northern bank of the Pasig river. Fighting broke out in the neighborhoods of Quiapo and Tondo between the Chinese rebels and Hispano-Filipino forces loyal to the colonial government, including Spaniards, Mexicans, Pampangans, Tagalogs, and Japanese fighting men. The loyalists burned the Parián to the ground. The Chinese attacked Intramuros but were forced to retreat. Hispano-Filipino forces hunted down and slaughtered Sangleyes as they fled, without any effort to distinguish or protect baptized Chinese.[63] Original Spanish and Chinese sources claim that between fifteen thousand and thirty thousand Chinese were killed that year. Few Sangleyes remained in Manila in the wake of the killing spree.[64]

The Spanish colonial government did not wait long before attempting to encourage Chinese traders to return to Manila in the aftermath of the slaughter. The Audiencia sent a modest diplomatic mission to Macao with letters for the Portuguese administration there, as well as for Chinese officials in Fujian and Guangdong, that presented a version of events that was favorable to Spaniards.[65] It also made an effort to return the victims' property to their families in Fujian to make amends. The Ming court investigated the massacre and finally blamed Fujianese dignitaries and their party for causing the tragedy. Ultimately, the Ming had little sympathy for migrants who had abandoned China and their filial ties.[66] Manila's Sangley population recovered quickly, with more than six thousand Chinese arriving in the city in 1606.[67]

Piracy in maritime Asia underwent a major transformation in the decades that followed Manila's first Chinese massacre. Petty piracy had long been endemic in China's maritime frontier, particularly in coastal Fujian. Maritime workers moved easily between legal work and piracy as fishermen and

sailors frequently joined small, ad hoc bands of opportunistic sea-robbers as
a means of survival in hard times.[68] One Qing scholar-official observed that
there were so many pirates along China's coast that "the boats of wicked
scoundrels are like froth floating on the sea."[69] Yet the chaos of the Ming-
Qing transition contributed to the dramatic rise in large-scale raiding carried out by massive and complex pirate federations. China was thrown into
a bloody civil war after the Manchu-led Qing captured Beijing in 1644, which
drove the Ming emperor to commit suicide. Ming loyalists and the Qing and
their supporters fought for control of the kingdom. Wars and revolts coincided with famine and natural disasters that disrupted life in almost all of
China. Coastal communities were most affected by the huge pirate syndicates
exploiting the war-induced anarchy to expand their influence across the
ocean. The Anhai-based Zheng family headed the biggest and most powerful of China's professional piracy organizations in this era. It controlled an
estimated 90 percent of all shipping in maritime East Asia, far exceeding the
size of the Dutch East India Company's operations (the VOC).[70]

The Zheng frightened the Spanish in Manila. In 1639, Manileños feared
that the Chinese pirate they called Iquan (Zheng Zhilong, 鄭芝龍), the patri-
arch of the Zheng family, was readying to invade their city. Zheng Zhilong
was a product of globalizing maritime Asia. He was born in Fujian, like most
of Manila's resident Sangleyes. In his youth he went to Macao, where he
learned Portuguese, was baptized, and eventually married a Japanese
woman. In the late 1620s, his pirate fleet carried out raids in Guangzhou
and Zhangzhou prefectures, gaining grassroots support by attacking the
rich and sharing treasure with the poor.[71] He later turned into an agent of
the Ming and used his navy to crush rival pirate organizations, becoming so
powerful that a Qing official described him as "a whale swallowing up the
sea."[72] In Manila, rumors of his coming invasion coincided with Spain's loss
of its colony on the Isla Formosa (Taiwan) to the Dutch, which left the Philippines more vulnerable to foreign attacks.[73] Stories spread that the pirate
was sailing up and down the coasts of Luzon enticing Sangleyes to join his
campaign to conquer the Philippines. Manila's Chinese bakeries were central to this conspiracy. Rumors swirled that the Sangleyes were going to
launch an attack on Intramuros from within its Chinese-run *panaderías*,
while Iquan captured the silver-laden galleon ship that was en route to Luzon from Mexico.[74] History added weight to this conspiracy: the pirate and
the resident Sangleyes allegedly wanted to avenge the deaths of their kin who
were killed in the turn-of-the-century genocide.

The Spanish colonial government treated talk of the Zheng invasion seriously. In the beginning of 1639, it hanged six Chinese migrants found guilty of building battle-ready vessels on the Pangasinan coast, presumably in preparation for the coming pirate war.[75] Then in late November a major Chinese rebellion broke out in Calamba, a town on the southwestern banks of Laguna de Bay. Spanish Governor Sebastián Hurtado de Corcuera had forced six thousand Sangleyes to relocate to this locale to cultivate rice and other crops. Many sickened and died in the harsh working conditions, and the angry survivors revolted. They murdered Laguna's alcalde mayor, set fire to the town, and marched on Manila armed with sickles and lances.[76] There is no hard evidence that an expected pirate invasion inspired this peasant rebellion. But the rebels had almost certainly encountered the rumors of the Zheng fleet, and it is definitely possible that the peasants anticipated or at least hoped that Iquan would assist them in their struggle against the Spanish. What is clear is that Spanish colonial officials perceived the Chinese uprising to be linked to a pirate invasion, and it was this imagined connection that precipitated another Chinese genocide.

Battles broke out between Sangleyes and Hispano-Filipino forces in Manila and surrounding regions in late November of 1639 and continued through to January of the following year. The governor ordered alcaldes mayores across Luzon to round up and kill Sangleyes in their respective districts, which resulted in the murders of an estimated twenty-two thousand people.[77] There was no effort to distinguish baptized Sangleyes from their countrymen, or to spare them from the slaughter. In the midst of a pirate crisis, Chinese baptisms were meaningless in the eyes of the state. Turmoil in China prevented Ming officials from responding to the genocidal attack on its overseas subjects, contributing to the lack of Chinese sources documenting the massacres.

The only extant Chinese testimony of the mass killings is Juan Ynbin's unpublished eyewitness account, and it gives a harrowing sense of the magnitude of the slaughter. Ynbin was a baptized stonemason working on the construction of a church at Caysasay when the genocide began. He described being rounded up with other Chinese men in the town and briefly imprisoned in a fort, where a priest visited him and listened to his final confession. Soldiers then led Ynbin to a beach to be executed with his hands tied behind his back. Bodies of dead men were strewn across the sand. Ynbin was forced to kneel among the corpses on the bloodstained shore as an Indigenous man brought a machete down hard across the back of his neck. He survived the severe injury that he sustained, which some of his contemporaries regarded as a miracle. Augustinian missionaries recorded Ynbin's testimony as part of an inquiry into his miraculous survival, which they attributed to the intervention of the Virgin of Caysasay.[78] Even in the immediate aftermath of this slaughter, these missionaries acknowledged the redeemable nature of Chinese migrants, and their potential to be integrated into the Catholic republic of Manila.

Although Zheng Zhilong never attacked Manila, his piratical empire continued to expand in the 1640s and 1650s. In the early 1660s his eldest son, Zheng Chenggong, who was more commonly known in the West as Koxinga (a name derived from his honorific title, 国姓爷), inherited control of the Zheng organization. Koxinga conquered the Dutch colony in Taiwan in January of 1662 with a formidable force of four hundred ships and twenty-five thousand men under his command.[79] Emboldened by this victory, the pirate leader sent the Italian Dominican friar Victorio Riccio as his ambassador to Manila in May that year, with demands that the Spaniards pay him tribute.[80] The Spanish Audiencia "resolved to die a thousand times rather than consent to such humiliation," and once again began to prepare for a war against Chinese pirates.[81] The rich hid their wealth. The government tore down several churches and the San Lázaro Hospital de los Naturales so the pirate army could not use these buildings as strongholds to attack Intramuros, and recalled ships and soldiers from Zamboanga and other presidios across the Philippines archipelago to reinforce the capital's defenses. The withdrawal from Zamboanga is the clearest indication that at this moment, the state perceived Chinese pirates to be a greater threat to Spanish rule over the Philippines than the *piratas moros* of the Sulu Zone.[82]

Thirty-year-old rumors about an alliance between Chinese bakers and pirates were resurrected in the nervous city. It was said that the bakers were planning to sneak into the homes of Spaniards and slit their throats as they slept, clearing a path for the pirate offensive.[83] Equally dangerous fake news spread that the Spanish colonial government was preparing to kill all of the Chinese. A Dominican friar overheard "common people . . . telling the Sangleyes that they were to have their heads cut off, as if they were men already sentenced to death."[84] The threat of a Chinese pirate invasion pushed the government into another genocidal slaughter. Battles broke out on the twenty-fifth of May. Hispano-Filipino forces bombarded the Parián with artillery and between eight thousand and nine thousand Chinese attacked the walls enclosing Intramuros. Thousands of Sangleyes were killed in the battle, and hundreds drowned as they tried to swim across the Pasig to safety. In the weeks that followed, the army and militias loyal to the Spanish hunted down the Sangleyes who had retreated into the hills of Sagar and Antipolo. The government ordered the Sangleyes to return to the Parián. Soldiers decapitated those who refused. Many who complied were deported to Taiwan on ten dangerously overcrowded sampans each carrying up to thirteen hundred men as a spiteful "tribute" to Koxinga.[85] This massacre ushered in an unprecedented collapse of junk trade. Only two ships from China arrived in Manila in 1663. Trade and human traffic between China and Manila boomed again in the 1680s.[86]

The shocking genocidal mass killings of Sangleyes in 1603, 1639, and 1662 stand in stark contrast with the typical colonial government responses to rebellions and conspiracies to revolt that erupted in American cities in the same period. On the other side of the great Pacific Ocean, colonial officials generally met rumored and real uprisings against their governments with investigations that sought to identify and discipline their ringleaders only. Accused rebel leaders were usually put on trial before they were punished. In early seventeenth-century Mexico City, for example, amid a wave of anti-Black hysteria, the Audiencia oversaw the arrests and executions of twenty-eight Afro-Mexican men and seven Afro-Mexican women after an investigation found the group guilty of plotting to overthrow the government, massacre Spanish men, and install a Black king. Colonial officials ensured that their deaths were a gruesome public spectacle. They ordered the group to hang until they took their last breaths in front of a large crowd in the Plaza Mayor, and then placed their mutilated corpses on public display as a macabre warning to others who dared cross the Crown.[87] In the Isthmus of Panama, another part of the empire plagued by piracy, the colonial government backed the capture, torture, and execution of *cimarrones*—enslaved people who had run away and sought freedom in the forests—without trials.[88] These killings were brutal, but they never reached the extreme scale of the Chinese massacres in the Philippines.

Major shifts in piracy in maritime East Asia explain the end of this uniquely Filipino cycle of mass killings. Koxinga's death in January 1663 put an end to the Zheng family's plans to invade the Philippines and hearkened the rapid decline of professional piracy in China. The Qing state successfully suppressed large-scale Chinese piracy. It gradually regained control of China's maritime borders by cutting off contact between mainland China and the hub of pirate operations in Taiwan, which effectively starved the pirates of resources. The Shunzhi emperor prohibited coastal and overseas trade in 1652. In the early 1660s, the Kangzi emperor brutally enforced this ban with his infamous scorched earth policy. Qing government soldiers forced entire communities to abandon the coast and relocate thirty kilometers inland, torching villages to prevent people from returning. Any person they caught trespassing in evacuated zones was put to death, as were the pirates who fell into the state's hands.[89] The Qing conquered the weakened pirate kingdom in Taiwan in 1683. Large pirate conglomerates did not remerge in China until the late eighteenth century. The suppression of Chinese piracy directly impacted Spanish attitudes toward the Chinese in the Philippines and created new pathways toward social inclusion.

Sino-Spanish Relations After Chinese Piracy:
Expulsions and Conversions

Sino-Spanish relations underwent a substantial transformation in the final decades of the seventeenth century and the first half of the eighteenth century. While some powerful Spanish voices in Manila continued to lobby the Crown for an Asian empire free of Sangleyes, they were marginalized by others that grew more tolerant and accommodating of Chinese migrants and their descendants. Spanish laws and policies introduced to manage the "Chinese problem" on the ground increasingly distinguished non-Christian infidels from baptized Chinese migrants and people of Chinese descent, and carved out a space for the latter within the social and cultural world of the Catholic capital.

    Victorio Riccio became a fervent advocate of Chinese expulsion following his stint as a mediator between Koxinga and the colonial government. Riccio's letter to King Charles II warning that a Chinese uprising in the capital could destroy Spanish sovereignty in the islands prompted the monarch to order the expulsion of Chinese "infidels" from the Philippines in November of 1686. The edict's distinction between baptized and unbaptized Chinese migrants implicitly acknowledged that those who embraced the faith of the Spaniards could forge a life in the colony as vassals.[90] When the expulsion order arrived in Manila, colonial officials did little to enforce it. The government's inaction was consistent with its restrained response to a Chinese conspiracy that year. A group of Chinese men murdered the Chinese official who managed Chinese licenses, fueling rumors that the homicide was part of a larger conspiracy that would see Chinese bakers lace bread with broken glass to kill Spaniards. The government arrested and executed eleven men involved with this plot, displaying their dismembered body parts along the Pasig River.[91] But unlike in 1603, 1639, and 1662, this conspiracy did not lead to mass killings, which is indicative of just how much anti-Chinese attitudes and anxieties had shifted in Manila.

Governor Gabriel de Curucelaegui y Arriola and Manila's Audiencia sought the king's permission to delay the expulsion of unbaptized Chinese in 1688.[92] Without challenging the rationale for expulsion, he explained that it was inconvenient, if not impossible, for a forced migration operation to happen very quickly. For one thing, Chinese economic interests were so entangled with those of the Spaniards and Indigenous peoples in Manila that all parties needed extra time to resolve their debts and settle accounts before the Chinese were ejected from the city. The government also needed time to gather more boats to transport deportees across the sea: there simply were not enough ships, sailors, and pilots in Manila to deport so many people. He appealed to the king's grace to not force boats to set sail to China with more passengers than they could safely carry or without an adequate crew, which would put people's lives at risk.[93] In a report to the Crown the following year the governor inflated the numbers of Chinese migrants that he claimed to have expelled. He cited forcing 1,197 Chinese to leave Manila by ship that year. This tally, however, included 861 men who came to the city to trade and who departed at the end of the feria, or the trading season, most of whom would have always intended to leave. The remaining 331 exiled Sangleyes were rounded up from the Parián and Extramuros and were probably poor men whom the government deemed troublesome.[94] Without the support of Manila's officials, there was little the king could do to expel non-Christian Chinese from the Philippines.

Chinese voices made powerful arguments against expulsion that spoke to the crux of the Chinese question. The *cabezas* (headmen) of Manila's twenty-four Chinese *gremios* (guilds) asked the king to abandon expulsion all together.[95] Their petition to the monarch methodically listed the ways that the Philippines would suffer if the Chinese were banished from the colony. In addition to making predictable points about how the loss of Chinese labor and the income generated by Chinese licenses would injure the economy, they presented a fascinating, novel argument about how political change in China and corresponding shifts in piracy in the region altered the risks that Sangleyes posed to Spanish sovereignty in the archipelago. The cabezas acknowledged that the Chinese had risen up against the Spanish in the past when China was in chaos and "there were tyrants in her coastal lands and pirates in her seas."[96] Yet the "tartars" (the term the Spanish used to refer to the Manchu Qing dynasty) had "relentlessly harassed and weakened" these tyrants and pirates and now dominated China. Now "all the Sangleyes are dominated by the tartars," they reasoned, and "it is not possible that they could stage an uprising in these islands."[97] Regional geopolitics mattered when it came to the status of the Chinese in Spain's Asian empire.

Additionally, Chinese community leaders made the potent point that Manila's Sangleyes were essential to the colony's defense against pirates and other enemies. They noted that although the Spanish relied on Pampangan and Merdican men to be soldiers, it was Chinese workers who equipped these fighting men for battle. Skilled Sangley sword makers and ironsmiths crafted weapons for the colonial military. Sangley tailors and milliners made their uniforms and hats, and Sangley fishermen, as well as "potato-men" and "chicken-men," ensured the soldiers were fed. Put simply, without the Chinese, there was no army.[98] This letter reflected a major development in the conceptualization of the Chinese in this colonial society. Rather than pirate-collaborators, Sangleyes were now essential partners in Spain's war against sea-robbers and other foes. Shifting perceptions had a real impact on migrant lives in the capital. The colonial government increased its surveillance of Sangleyes. It conducted censuses of Manila's Chinese population in 1689 and 1690, an exercise that captured the names, occupations, place of residences, and religions of hundreds of Sangleyes in the capital. The Crown also made concessions in response to these persuasive pro-Chinese arguments. A royal decree issued in 1696 permitted up to six thousand Chinese "infidels" to be present in Manila.[99]

The Chinese question continued to be debated in Manila in the eighteenth century. Anti-Chinese Manileños, including archbishops, kept up pressure on the Crown to more tightly control Sangleyes in the Philippines.[100] In 1732, the Crown responded with instructions for Manila's Audiencia and the Ecclesiastic Council to form a committee to review and report on the best strategies to manage this potentially dangerous population. Committee member and Manila's *alguacil mayor* Don Joséf de Memije y Quirós advocated for a prohibition on Sangleyes marrying in the Philippines so that "in a very short time we can liberate the provinces of them."[101] Interestingly, Memije reasoned that events in China legitimized his proposal. The emperor's recent death had led to a surge in the state persecution of Christians:

"they have demolished churches and expelled the missionaries," he pointed out. For Memije, this signaled that it was no longer necessary for the Spanish to tiptoe around Chinese expulsion to avoid upsetting the Qing court and undermining the Church's activities in China.

But Memije was an outlier. The majority of junta members were satisfied with the status quo. Ecclesiastic Council delegates ridiculed the suggestion that the Chinese harmed Catholicism in the islands. They reasoned that the Chinese were not evangelists; they evoked anecdotal evidence that the Indigenous Filipinos were worshiping the Virgin Mary rather than Chinese dragons to prove their point.[102] Governor Valdés Tamón also defended Sangley settlers. He observed that there was "very little difference" between Chinese merchants and merchants from "other republics of the world," who shared a common goal of making money. Furthermore, the governor emphasized that "many Sangleyes have true knowledge of our holy religion," and it would be wrong to expel Christians to heathen China.[103] As the previous chapter noted, Valdés oversaw the expansion of the Spanish presidio network into the Sulu Zone and the intensification of war against Moro pirates. The holy war between Christians and Muslims defined his understanding of Spanish colonial rule in Asia and allowed him to conceptualize Chinese migrants as being allies in this struggle. The Islamic pirate other cleared a path for the Chinese to enter the Catholic republic.

Expulsion remained on the Crown's agenda, and Manila continued to resist enforcing it. King Philip V decreed "the total expulsion and extermination of infidel Sangleyes" from the Philippines in 1744.[104] This expulsion order maintained the distinction between baptized and unbaptized Chinese migrants and permitted the later to remain indefinitely in the Spanish colony. In fact, the 1744 decree instructed the colonial government to ensure that baptized Sangleyes did not "escape" to China, where they would be tempted to apostatize, or renounce their Catholic faith. Philip V acknowledged that expelling non-Christians would hurt the colonial economy, entailing the loss of up to twenty-five thousand pesos that were generated by the sale of Chinese licenses alone. He reasoned that this was a reasonable price to pay for religious purity.

Not even the discovery of another Sangley plot against Manila pushed the colonial government to round up and deport unbaptized Chinese migrants in accordance with the Crown's orders. On the first Wednesday in June that year, Don Bartolome Chamqua, the *cabecilla principal* of the Sangleyes, informed Spanish colonial officials that six hundred Chinese from the Parián, the nearby town of Samal, and Angono in Laguna de Bay were conspiring to attack Manila that Saturday.[105] It was rumored that the rebels were planning to enter Intramuros at dawn disguised as dockworkers, and they would begin slaughtering Spaniards when the church bells across the metropolis tolled noon. The government immediately appointed Don Francisco Costilla Borroto, Manila's *alcalde del crimen* and the commissioner in charge of the Sangley expulsion, to investigate the conspiracy.[106] The plot was particularly alarming because it coincided with a major Indigenous revolt that had spread across much of central and southern Luzon. Pueblos around Lake Taal to the south of the capital, and Pampangan towns in the north, had risen up against the Augustinian, Dominican, and Jesuit friars, whom they accused of illegally seizing and occupying ancestral lands. Mobs were tearing down buildings that friars had erected on contested lands and beat drums to scare their valuable cattle stock into the mountains, and armed bands blockaded roads and rivers. Violent clashes were breaking out between the native rebels and loyalist soldiers, including at least one hundred Pampangan troops who mobilized to put down the uprising by force.[107]

Even in the context of widespread social unrest, a Chinese conspiracy did not drive the government to indiscriminately slaughter thousands of people. Costilla's inquiry led to a spate of arrests, including of at least 160 people in Cavite and the fishing village of Angono in Pangasinan. Unbaptized and baptized migrants as well as Philippines-born Chinese mestizos, including women, were among the arrested, which suggests that the boundaries between Sangleyes and mestizos de Sangley were still porous. Costilla did discriminate, however, on the basis of wealth. His inquiry targeted poor Chinese migrants and people of Chinese descent, and especially maritime workers and their families. The men arrested in Angono were mostly shrimp fishermen who slept in sparsely furnished *camaríns* and *camaríncilos* (huts and shacks). In Manila, Juan Yongco was identified as the "principal engine" of the rebellion.[108] The forty-one-year old was a native of Tayteng in China and a baptized Christian. He lived in the Estacada with his mestiza wife Francisca del Rosario and their young son. Yongco supported his family by making regular voyages to the Visayas, either as a sailor or as a petty merchant, and he ran a small shop out of his home.[109] Yongco's neighbor Maria Monica, a widowed mestiza de Sangley, testified that he was so poor "he does not even have enough to eat."[110] The notary who prepared an inventory of Yongco's confiscated belongings remarked that most of his worldly possessions, which included clothes and textiles as well as several Chinese books, paper, and an inkwell, were "unusable because they are old and battered."[111] Yongco and others who were arrested during Costilla's inquiry were jailed in the dank dungeons of Fort Santiago for as long as six months until the investigation was finalized in January of 1746.

Costilla's inquiry concluded that there was no conspiracy. The then governor, José de Ovando, dismissed the "so-called" and "imagined uprising" as the work of a few "irrelevant and dissonant voices."[112] Only one Chinese migrant—Lou Jayco—was deported to China as a result of Costilla's investigation. Jayco, a Parián resident, had been found in possession of a crudely drawn map of Intramuros. Colonial officials initially feared that this was evidence of a meticulously planned attack on the capital, but soon came to see it as the artwork of a deranged man. The Audiencia's report noted that Lou Jayco "has lost his sanity, and wanders around day and night . . . making everyone laugh, and it is public and notorious that . . . he is entirely crazy."[113]

The colonial government continued to expel relatively small numbers of Chinese men from Manila in the early 1750s, although a precise count is difficult to ascertain. José Arévalo Tiongsay, the baptized Chinese migrant who rented the exclusive right to sell Chinese licenses in Manila at this time, sought government compensation for the expulsion of 856 Sangleyes between 1750 and 1752. According to Tiongsay, these deportees were shipwreck survivors and members of the urban proletariat—barbers, shopkeepers, cooks, fishermen, and others "without trades"—and his profits suffered as a result of their forced migration.[114] The government accused Tiongsay of exaggerating deportations. They pointed out that the government's records documented a steady flow of almost five thousand Chinese people arriving in Manila in this period. Moreover, Tiongsay had paid to print four thousand Chinese licenses in Manila in 1750 and double this number in 1752, which would not have made financial sense if there was not a market for licenses. Manila's archbishop Pedro de la Santísima Trinidad's complaints to the Crown about the government's "lukewarm" enforcement of expulsion substantiates the Audiencia's evidence that it had largely abandoned mass deportations.[115] The king and the Council of the Indies were frustrated by the Manila government's failure to cleanse the colony of non-Christian Chinese and continued to put pressure on Manila to ramp up removals of "infidels."

Sangley expulsion morphed into a program of Sangley conversion in the middle of the decade. Governor Pedro Manuel de Arandía Santisteban signed off on a report on the progress of Chinese deportations in 1756 that revealed a surge of Chinese baptisms in the capital. This document claimed that 2,070

Sangleyes were forcibly removed from the Philippines but provided frustratingly few details about these deportations, and it is likely that this number was merely a count of Chinese people ordinarily departing Manila for ports across maritime Asia.[116] It also stated that 3,413 baptized Chinese resided in the Philippines, which must have been a conservative count. Almost two-thirds of this population lived in Manila, including in the Parián, Tondo, and Extramuros. Extraordinarily, more than half of these residents had converted to Catholicism in 1756.[117] Arandía described baptized "Christian Sangleyes who presently exist in or are found in these islands" as "vassals of your majesty," showing that conversion to Catholicism was a mechanism through which migrants transformed from "others" to royal subjects.

Arandía's report on Chinese conversions says little about how and where the neophytes were baptized, and there are no extant accounts of Sangley baptism ceremonies in this period. These might have been private rituals conducted quietly in the cool, candlelit darkness of the city's stone churches. What is striking is that the elaborate mass baptisms of Indigenous converts that were staged in Manila during his governorship were imagined as the baptisms of Chinese descendants. When Franciscan missionaries coordinated an official public ceremony celebrating the baptism of eleven Igorot men in Manila in January of 1756, the Indigenous converts were said to be the "descendants of the many Chinos who took refuge in the mountains" during the previous century's Chinese revolts and massacres.[118]

The notion that the Igorots had Chinese ancestors was widespread in Manila. Fray Juan de la Concepción's multivolume *General History of the Philippines* told that Limahong's soldiers and sailors had fled to the cordillera, "and those who dispersed are the Igorots who live in the Kingay mountains."[119] Missionaries accompanied the Igorot converts to the capital, where they were greeted as honored guests. The governor formally welcomed them into the Royal Palace's Room of the Kings, where the new converts swore an oath of loyalty to the Crown in front of the monarch's portrait. They were then baptized in the church of Our Lady of the Candelaria in the suburb of Dilao. The most powerful men in the colony stood in as godfathers, including the alguacil mayor Joseph de Memije and the regidor Santiago de Orendaín. Reflecting the view that baptism involved a physical as well as a spiritual transformation, the men arrived to the church "in their native dress," and left with gifts of Spanish pants and shirts. This baptism ceremony can be read as an act of reconciliation in which the Sangleyes of Manila as well as the descendants of the Chinese pirates who had once attempted to destroy the Catholic republic were welcomed into the body politic.

Attempting to recover the meaning of conversion to Chinese migrants who volunteered to be baptized is difficult when we have to rely on Spanish sources. Until recently, scholars have argued that Chinese and other migrants in the Philippines converted to Catholicism "for convenience."[120] Despite the rich scholarship on religious mestizaje in the Americas, researchers have been reluctant to see this process in the Philippines context, particularly where the Chinese are concerned.[121] It is true that conversion offered real material rewards to Asian migrants and other non-Catholic foreigners in Manila. The colonial government granted ten-year exemptions from tribute to Sangleyes after their baptisms, and in rare cases it offered a monthly stipend to new converts.[122] Becoming Catholic was also necessary for migrants to gain the right to reside, travel through, and marry in this colonial society. However, recognizing the material benefits of conversion should not eliminate faith as a factor that drove individuals' decisions to be baptized.

Rich archival evidence reveals that the people of the Chinese diaspora made Catholicism their own in Manila and its hinterland. Costilla's 1745 investigation into the Chinese uprising, for example, documented objects of Catholic devotion among the possessions of arrested Sangleyes. Notaries listed two rosaries, one of which contained a gold reliquary, in addition to a wooden crucifix and picture cards depicting several different saints among Ventura Quinco's confiscated belongings.[123] Juan Yongco owned an image of Our Lady of Binalbagan, the santo who was venerated in Negros where the mariner visited frequently.[124] Several of the Chinese fishermen arrested in Angono in relation to the conspiracy were baptized, and two had large, colorful, painted images of Our Lady of Caysasay displayed in their modest homes.[125] This wooden image of Jesus's mother Mary was renowned for saving Juan Imbin's life after he was severely injured in the 1639 mass killings of the Chinese, and she became an unofficial patron saint of Chinese and Chinese mestizos in the Philippines in the aftermath of the massacre.[126] The Augustinian missionary Fray María de Castro's account of the Chinese Caysasay shrine in 1790 attests to her large following of devotees. Castro was unimpressed by the cave that housed the shrine, which was "very dark, and sad, and so humid." He also thought that the image itself was not particularly beautiful, having "one eye bigger than the other." The shrine's walls were covered with folkish paintings depicting miracles attributed to the holy woman. Believers visited the shrine every Saturday to pray the rosary before the image and to touch it. They regularly offered ex votos, masses, candles, alms, and rosaries to the shrine and brought gifts to the Virgin, making the image "very rich" with "jewels of gold, silver, pearls."[127]

The Spanish colonial government was wary of this devotion, suspecting that Sangleyes saw Our Lady of Caysasay as the Chinese goddess Ma-Cho (媽祖), the patron of seafarers. The government issued an edict in 1756 that outlawed candles being lit before likenesses of Ma-Cho and other Chinese idols and prohibited Sangleyes from referring to Our Lady of Casasay as "Má Choú."[128] Surely for many devotees, the lines distinguishing the protectoress of seagoers and the defender of Chinese migrants in the Philippines blurred as the Catholic santo and the Chinese goddess blended into one figure.[129] It would be too simplistic to interpret this overlap as proof that the cult of Caysasay was a "public transcript" crafted to obscure a hidden, secret one—in James C. Scott's words, a "nonhegemonic, contrapuntal, dissident, subversive discourse."[130] Rather, it points to the complex process of religious syncretism. The Philippines' transformation into a majority-Catholic nation did not simply involve locals and the large migrant Chinese population passively adopting the beliefs and rituals that Spanish and Mexican conquistadors imported into the islands. Catholicism in the early modern Philippines was plural and hybrid, incorporating ideas and practices from Catholic Spain and the Americas, as well as from Southeastern China and from the Indigenous cultures that thrived across the archipelago.

Chinese Anti-Piracy and the Moro Wars in Manila

Studies of the Moro wars have glossed over the fact that this conflict saturated Manila's early modern public sphere.[131] The holy war against Islamic pirates was embedded in the city's urban space. The tall city walls that encircled Intramuros stood as a stern reminder that an enemy invasion from the sea was always imminent. Manila's large Fort Santiago, constructed above the ashes of the sixteenth century stronghold of Rajah Suleman, was named for Santiago, "the moor-slayer," the apparition of Saint James who miraculously intervened at the mythical medieval battle between Spaniards and Muslim invaders at Clavijo. A large wood carving of Santiago on horseback decapitating Muslim soldiers trampled under hoof hung above the fort's main entrance, an image that was widely reproduced in art and architecture across the early modern Hispanic world, entangling European and New World conquests.[132] Manila's temporary architecture also evoked the holy war. The painted triumphal arches that were erected in 1743 for the public celebrations surrounding the opening of the new Franciscan temple depicted rocket-shooting Moros flanked by a "ferocious" horned devil.[133] Plays dramatizing the historical and fantastical wars between Muslims and Christians were regularly staged as part of the city's calendar of public Catholic rituals. The "unending Moro wars" were also a dominant theme in Manila's print culture.[134] The city's convent presses printed pamphlets and chronicles that told of violent Moro raids on Philippine pueblos and the heroic feats of past and present Hispano-Filipino forces who valiantly fought against them. Sermons preached from pulpits around the city and its hinterland spread these narratives across the archipelago.[135]

Azim ud-Din's arrival in Manila in January of 1749 escalated the Moro wars' presence in the capital. The spectacular celebration that Governor Arechederra staged to welcome the sultan and his seventy-member entourage into the city in the first days of the new year was described in detail in Chapter 1. The sultan was baptized four months later in the small town of Paniqui in Pampanga, and another major public festival was held in Manila to celebrate. Azim ud-Din entered Manila for the first time as a Catholic with great fanfare. Gun salutes and a flotilla of ships decked out in colorful streamers that blazed above the river greeted the boat that delivered him to Manila. The sultan processed from the beach to Intramuros in a parade that paused at the church of Santo Domingo to collect the sacred image of Our Lady of the Rosary, before moving on to the cathedral, where a solemn thanksgiving mass was said. The celebrations continued with a week-long festival. During the daytime, giant puppets were displayed and bullfights were staged in the plaza, and the sultan awarded prizes to the champions. As darkness fell, the city's night sky was lit up by firework castles and flickering candlelight that illuminated the towers, windows, and balconies of the city's baroque cathedrals and stone buildings. Arechederra described these lights as a "divine fire" that "warmed hearts, beautifying them without consuming them."[136] The scale of the festivities reflected the governments' conviction that Azim ud-Din's conversion marked a crucial stage in the spiritual and military conquest of Jolo, a major victory in Spain's Asian holy war.

Chinese migrants and mestizos joined the celebrations of the sultan's baptism alongside Indigenous Filipinos and Spaniards. The governor's printed account of these festivities, gifted to the monarch to demonstrate the "glory and high power of our King and Lord at the extreme edges of his monarchy," highlighted the diversity of the revelers.[137] People of the Chinese diaspora lined the parade route that the sultan traced into the city. Chinese gremios coordinated their members' contributions to the fiesta.[138] Chinese mestizos from the pueblo of Binondo performed *comedias* during the multiday festivities. Sangley and Chinese mestizo guilds alike organized puppet shows and candlelit carts that carried choirs and bands and were pulled through city streets crowded with dancers. For the governor, the numerous Chinese couples dressed as Spaniards with wigs and Spanish-style three-pointed hats were a highlight of these events. These costumed performers danced with a beautiful lion puppet that they skillfully made to seem alive and as though it was prowling and dashing through a jungle.[139] During the festivities, the governor visited the Sangley and Chinese mestizo principalia in their homes.

In Manila, as in other cities across the global Spanish empire, festivals functioned as "forums where various social groups and individuals negotiated their public image."[140] Carolyn Dean showed that in the seventeenth century, Indigenous Andean elites used a rich symbolic vocabulary to present themselves in Corpus Christi festivals as nobles and victors, a faction that had embraced Catholicism and collaborated with the Spanish to suppress the rebellions of rival Indigenous groups.[141] Similarly, Lisa Voigt has demonstrated that festivals in South American mining towns allowed for the "resignification" of communities excluded from the imagined Spanish and Portuguese nations, including Africans and their descendants.[142] This scholarship challenges the notion that popular participation in fiestas was always pregnant with hidden, subversive meanings and agendas, an assumption that has distorted studies of the colonial carnivalesque in the Philippines.[143] Sangleyes, Chinese mestizos, and other marginalized people in the cosmopolis used fiestas celebrating victory over Islam as a platform to demonstrate their loyalty to the Church and the Crown, which was the foundation of their inclusion in the Catholic republic of Manila.

Manila's 1749 fiestas were a celebration of the Spanish colony's past, present, and future victories over Moro pirates. Through participating in the celebrations of Azim ud-Din's conversion to Christianity, the people of the Chinese diaspora inserted themselves into the holy war epic as allies of Spain in the ongoing war against Islamic sea-robbers. The mid-eighteenth-century celebrations evoked historic Hispano-Filipino victories over Moro pirates and other enemies in several ways. The incorporation of the sacred image of Nuestra Señora del Rosario de "La Naval" referenced the colony's mid-seventeenth-century naval victories over the Protestant Dutch, which were widely attributed to this miraculous carved-ivory statue.[144] Manila's La Naval was also widely regarded as being connected to the Mediterranean image of the mother of God Nuestra Señora del Rosario, who was revered for delivering victory to the Catholic fleet against Islamic forces in the 1571 battle of Lepanto.[145] The eighteenth-century parades echoed Governor Sebastián Hurtado de Corcuera's famous triumphal return to Manila after he defeated the Muslims of Mindanao and Joló in 1638. Hurtado had marched through the capital with nearly two hundred chained Muslim slaves whom the Spanish and their allies had captured in battle. "Friendly indios and Sangleyes" liberated from the sea robbers marched behind the human spoils of war. The procession ended at the cathedral, where the enslaved people were baptized before being gifted to members of the city's ruling Spanish elite.[146] Through these rituals and performances, Sangleyes inserted themselves into the historic anti-piracy campaigns in the archipelago.

The participation of elite Chinese and Chinese mestizos in the holy war extended beyond symbolic gestures with donations of resources to the military campaign. The people of the Chinese diaspora made one major collective contribution and many individual donations to the war against these sea-robbers during two distinct fundraising drives between 1751 and 1754. The Parián's *común de los Sangleyes* donated the large sum of 10,285 pesos to fund the colonial government's holy war in 1753.[147] The Común was an autonomous governing council that comprised the Parián's *cabecilla principal gobernador* (principal head and governor) and other officials, and represented all of the gremios within the Parián. This large donation included silver drawn from the Sangley's *caja de comunidad* (community chest) and money collected from fines and penalties, as well as the forgiveness of outstanding loans that the Común had previously made available to the treasury when its silver reserves were scarce, including a 5,048 peso loan from August 1746. The statement that the Común's cabecilla principal penned to formalize this generous gift deployed the language of Catholic anti-piracy. He explained that this gift to the king was "for the wars and expeditions against the Moros Joloes Tirones Mindanaos and other Mohometanos—our enemies."[148] With this donation, the most powerful Sangleyes of the Parián asserted that they and those they represented belonged to and were committed to defending the Catholic Republic of Manila. Through this donation, the Sangleyes marked themselves as Hispanic patriots. As Fabio López Lázaro observed, the Hispanic patriot "was not limited to a 'European' identity or even a European American one" in the early modern Iberian world. Rather, it was a "global identity co-terminal with the boundaries of the monarchy. Pirates and heretics were its antithetical 'other.'"[149]

In addition to the large collective donation, many Chinese and Chinese mestizos individually responded to the government's requests for help to fight the Moro pirates. In February of 1751, Governor Ovando issued a decree calling on the city's *vecinos* and *moradores* to generously give silver, weapons, and boats for the campaign against the "Joloeses" and "tirones." Some 524 people answered the call.[150] A total of 124, or almost 25 percent of these donors, were Chinese mestizos from Santa Cruz and Binondo. Almost half (254) of the remaining donors were Indigenous Filipinos belonging to the gremios or naturales in Rosario and Tondo. Two Frenchmen and one Armenian also gave to the cause. The donors' disclosed occupations, shown in Table 2, suggest that Chinese mestizo donors were wealthy members of Manila society. Many were artisans. Thirty-six (29 percent) were silversmiths, and twenty-one (17 percent) were sculptors. Others were cobblers, carpenters, scribes, interpreters, and cabezeas de barangays. In 1754, Ovando made a second request for "voluntary and gracious donations of money and arms" to equip the armada heading into war against Moros led by Cesár Falliet.[151] The term "gracious" in this context signified that donations were gifts rather than loans and would not be repaid.[152] A total of 112 men and women responded to the request for assistance over a three-day period. The majority of these donors were Spaniards, but the Chinese cabecilla de los Sangleyes and the Chinese mestizo Matheo de los Angeles also made contributions.

Significantly, Ovando's donation decrees did not specify the quantities of silver that individuals were expected to contribute to the war, and what people ultimately gave varied wildly. Nine members of the gremio of Binondo donated to the anti-piracy campaign 1751. Its *goberadorcillo*, Juan de los Reyes, gave twelve pesos to the cause. The sculptor Luíz Gonzales gave two pesos. Agustín Dionicio, a silversmith, contributed only four tomínes, or half a peso. Three other men in the gremio donated swords and lances in lieu of money.[153] The 1754 donations ranged from 500 pesos to a few tomínes. Approximately 10 percent of donors offered weapons either instead of or in addition to silver coins to the war drive. Matheo de los Angeles, a member of the Chinese mestizo guild of Santa Cruz, donated two swords and a lance in 1751 and eight bayonets and ten pesos in 1754. Carlos Saballa, another gremio member, donated a *canon de arcabuz*. Juan de Dios, an Indigenous farmer from Tondo, donated two lances, one bow, and five arrows to the

Table 2. Analysis Chinese Mestizo's donations to the Moro wars in 1751

Oficio	English translation	Number	Chinese Mestizo donations (%)
Aseytero	Oil producer/ merchant	2	1.61
Barbero	Barber	1	0.81
Bruñidor	Polisher	1	0.81
Cabeza de Barangay	Mayor	9	7.26
Carpintero	Carpenter	2	1.61
Corredor	Broker	3	2.42
Curtidor	Tanner	8	6.45
Dorador	Gilder	2	1.61
Escribiano	Scribe	6	4.84
Escultor	Sculptor	21	16.94
Gobernadorcillo	Mayor	1	0.81
Labrador	Agricultural laborer	2	1.61
Maestro de la escuela	Schoolteacher	1	0.81
Pintor	Painter	3	2.42
Platero	Silversmith	36	29.03
Tabaquero	Tobacco farmer/ seller	1	0.81
Tendero	Shopkeeper	3	2.42
Viajero	Domestic trader	1	0.81
Ynterprete	Interpreter	2	1.61
Zapatero	Cobbler	2	1.61
	illegible	2	1.61
	none	15	12.10
Total		124	

war.[154] The Armenian Juan de Dios Cachíq offered a rifle. The Marques de Monte Castro offered a veritable arsenal to the war against Southeast Asian Muslims in 1745: eight rifles with bayonets attached, four pistols, twelve lances, and twelve cutlasses.[155] Don Calixto de Lecea donated his unnamed Black slave to the campaign.[156] It seems that the act of donating weapons and enslaved men to the anti-piracy armadas would have forged a personal connection between Manileños and the battles that took place far from Manila but firmly within the urban imagination. Entrusting an arcabuz or a dagger to a sailor-warrior who would use it to shoot the enemy or slit his throat was an intimate act.

Ovando's efforts to raise resources to fight Moro pirates in mid-eighteenth-century Manila were distinct from empire-wide campaigns to fund imperial wars.[157] Manila's local initiatives were driven from the governor's palace.

Rather than collecting silver to aid distant armies heading into battle on the other side of the earth, Manileños dug deep into their pockets to assist sailor-warriors from Luzon and neighboring islands to fight a local, familiar enemy. The heterogeneity of donations reinforces that these were voluntary rather than forced. In his study of colonial finances in late eighteenth-century Mexico, Carlos Marichal argues that donations were often coerced contributions to the royal treasury, a type of double taxation for subjects who were required to pay tribute under the law. For Marichal, the proof of coercion lies in the universality of donations. Contributions were collected from "the entire urban and rural population of colonial Mexico," and like other colonial taxes, the value of these donations was specified in government decrees.[158] In contrast, Manileños' donations to the Moro wars were not universal, nor were they either standardized or exacted from all members of colonial society.

Multiple factors influenced Chinese support for Catholic anti-piracy in Manila. Chief among them was the reality that every migrant in Manila who went to sea or was engaged in maritime trade—from ship owners and merchants to captains, sailors, and fishermen—had an interest in the suppression of piracy. Chinese people were among those taken captive by the pirates who roamed the Sulu Zone. Legazpi, the first Spanish governor of the Philippines, met thirty Chinese men enslaved by Filipino Muslims in Mindoro in 1569. He purchased their freedom in exchange for information about China, the Philippines, and their connections across the small sea.[159] In the late seventeenth century, the British pirate William Dampier seized Spanish, Chinese, and Chinese mestizo sailors in his raids in Philippines waters.[160] A Spanish account of the bloody raid on Batad in 1753 notes that Sangleyes, their wives, and their children were among those who were killed in the attack.[161] The Chinese too were vulnerable to Moro piracy, and thus they were invested in destroying it.

A strong, transoceanic Chinese anti-piracy tradition likely strengthened the Sangleyes' support for Manila's campaigns against Moro pirates. Chinese migrants and their descendants were familiar with histories of the pirates they called wokou, a term that translates literally to "dwarf bandits" and was a derogatory term for Japanese pirates. Wokou raided not only boats and port towns but also villages and cities deep in the Chinese interior. Over generations, these pirates developed a reputation for extreme brutality in China. They seized captives for ransom, and they raped, tortured, and murdered their victims. Chinese sources described how the wokou disemboweled, decapitated, and dismembered their victims, desecrating bodies to torment the soul that would have no rest in the afterlife. The terrifying wokou were also portrayed as demons. They were said to croak like frogs when they talked, and they were depicted as having the long, tangled hair and blackened faces of ghosts.[162] A common motif in Chinese artistic representations of pirate attacks was refugees escaping from sea-bandits, carrying their worldly possessions and their children on their backs into the safety of the mountains.[163] This pattern of people fleeing from pirates also inspired Qing poetry. "A Song on Ransom" recounts a pirate attack on a nameless Chinese town where captives were seized, and the poor as well as the rich had to sell all of their possessions to raise the ransom for their kin.[164] Chinese migrants carried this anti-piracy tradition with them to Manila.

The religious or spiritual elements of Manila's holy war against Moro pirates would have been familiar to Chinese migrants and seafarers. In China, the ocean was understood as a "mysterious and hostile space . . . haunted by vengeful ghosts," and it was widely thought that navigating safely across the sea depended on the blessings of deities as much as technical skill.[165] Religion permeated shipboard life on Chinese vessels. Boats were equipped with altars, and everyone on board participated in religious rituals, which included making offerings of money and miniature clothes as gifts to spirits.[166] The goddess Ma-Cho was the most important protector of those who crossed the ocean. In Ma-Cho hagiography preserved in temple paintings, in books illustrated with woodblocks, as well as in oral histories, the goddess defended sailors against sea monsters, storms, and pirates, although pirates, too, sought out her protection.[167] Praying to Catholic saints for divine assistance in naval battles was compatible with Chinese maritime knowledge and traditions.

The politics of patronage were surely factored into decisions to support the Moro wars in Manila. Contributing to the cost of military campaigns against pirates was a way for wealthy Manileños to accumulate political capital. As in other parts of the Spanish empire, financial assistance to the state in crisis situations could reinforce existing advantages and open doors to new partnerships or concessions. Marichal described this as a "fiscal pact" between colonial elites and the crown or state.[168] Chinese support for Spain's holy war in Asia must be analyzed in the specific context of the discrimination that this community confronted in the Philippines. To be a Catholic and loyal vassal of the Spanish monarch, or at least a committed ally of the king, was the basis of the right to live, work, and marry in Manila. For Sangleyes, these basic rights were constantly under threat. Chinese participation in the campaign against Moro pirates was in part a calculated strategy of asserting collective and individual allegiance to the Church and the Crown in order to defend and potentially expand the restricted privileges that they enjoyed in the city.

Conclusion

Tens of thousands of Chinese men—merchants, sailors, farmers, artisans, refugees, and adventurers—farewelled the kingdom where they were born and raised and boarded boats bound for Manila in the two centuries after the Spanish conquest of the city. Many of these migrants settled in the capital of Spain's Asian empire, where they labored, built homes, raised families, and set roots. Spaniards encouraged and celebrated Chinese conversions to Catholicism, and generations of newcomers agreed to be baptized, joining the city's growing multiethnic Catholic congregations and forging vibrant new Catholic traditions in the city and its hinterland. This chapter demonstrated that piracy shaped these migrants' fates and fortunes, ensuring that the history of the people of the Chinese diaspora in the Philippines would be punctuated by moments of extreme violence. How powerful Spaniards conceptualized maritime violence in waters surrounding the archipelago strongly influenced their perceptions of Sangleyes—whether they considered them essential partners in their colonizing project or enemies who threatened to destroy it. These attitudes influenced the colonial government's evolving strategies to exploit and control Chinese migrants, which included segregation, restrictions on migrants' physical mobility and their faith and religious observances, in addition to limits on the number of migrants permitted in the colony, forced migration, and mass killings.

Spaniards were rarely in agreement over the Chinese question, but voices in favor of Sangley integration or exclusion dominated at different times. The Spanish colonial government's well-founded fears of Chinese pirate invasions of Manila sparked three genocidal massacres of Chinese men in the seventeenth century. In these moments of mass killings, Sangley baptisms were rendered meaningless in the eyes of Spaniards, and Chinese Catholics were not spared from death. Murder on a massive scale coincided with the rapid expansion of large-scale Chinese piracy that was nourished by the anarchy of China's midcentury civil war. The conclusion of the war in China and the Qing's subsequent suppression of large-scale Chinese piracy put an end to this uniquely Filipino cycle of violence. From the 1680s to the 1750s, the specter of Chinese pirates destroying Manila was replaced with the specter of slave-raiding Muslim pirates seizing sovereignty in the islands. The intensifying Moro pirate war created new opportunities in the capital for Sangleyes and their descendants to assert their status as loyal Catholic vassals of the Spanish monarch, and claim the corresponding privileges in the archipelago. On the eve of the British invasion of Manila, Sangleyes and Chinese mestizos were united with other Catholic communities in the capital against a common pirate enemy.

Recognizing how regional rhythms of sea-banditry shaped Chinese lives in Manila necessitates zooming out from the Parián and grappling with the city's messy entanglements in maritime Asia during the first disruptive wave of European imperial expansion and globalization. It also requires seeing the heavy presence in Manila of the state-sponsored holy war against Islamic Southeast Asian pirates, a military campaign that was conceived of as part of a global conflict between Catholic polities and Muslims for control of territory, trade, and souls. The dynamics of piracy and Catholic anti-piracy politics defined when and under what circumstances Sangleyes were eligible to be included in the capital of the Catholic Republic of Manila. The arrival of a new pirate enemy in 1762 would shatter the armistace between Spaniards and Sangleyes that was forged in the face of Moro piracy.

CHAPTER 3

_____

The Pirates from Madras

The British Invasion and Occupation of Manila

Thirteen British Royal Navy and East India Company ships that had come from Madras sailed into Manila Bay late in the afternoon of the twenty-third of September in 1762. Soldiers standing guard at Fort Santiago alerted Manuel Antonio Rojo del Rio to the fleet's arrival. Rojo was the archbishop of Manila and the interim governor of the Philippines, making him the highest-ranked ecclesiastical and civil authority in the Spanish colony. He dispatched an officer to greet the fleet and inquire about the reason for its visit, even offering assistance if the ships were in distress. Although rumors of war and tall ship sightings had made their way to Manila in the preceding weeks, the capital was yet to receive official word from Spain that King Charles III had declared war against Britain months earlier. The British responded with a letter informing the archbishop-governor that Spain had joined the colossal global conflict between Britain and its European rivals that would eventually be known as the Seven Years' War. Violent clashes between armed forces had broken out across oceans and continents as burgeoning imperial powers fought for control of trade, territory, and people on a planetary scale. The British had come "to conquer Manila and the Philippine islands, and show the Spaniards that their sovereign's most remote dominions are not secure against the force and power" of the British military.[1] They instructed Rojo to peacefully surrender the colony, or their men and munitions would take it by force. Rojo refused and vowed to fight.

This surprise attack from the sea plunged Manila and much of Luzon into a new and devastating war. The British captured Intramuros after a three-week siege, forcing the Spanish colonial government into exile in the provinces. The conspicuous Spanish defeat in the capital promptly triggered mass

Chinese and Indigenous revolts against the empire that spread across much
of the big island. Spanish colonial officials were forced to raise a large loyalist army to fight a multifront war against the invaders and homegrown insurgents to shore up Spanish sovereignty in the archipelago. The war involved
the total mobilization of this colonial society's resources to destroy opponents.[2] Churches, homes, shops, crops, and entire villages were turned to
ash, and tens of thousands of people were killed, wounded, and displaced.
Examining this conflict in depth reveals the great extent to which the islands'
entanglement in a world of war at sea impacted colonial rule in the Philippines. Local responses to the invasion illuminate the sources of the Spanish
empire's resilience in the Philippines, as well as its acute vulnerabilities.

Beginning with the British forces' siege and capture of Intramuros, this
chapter reconstructs the history of the first six months of the Seven Years'
War in the Philippines, focusing on how ordinary people experienced and
reacted to the conflict that unfolded around them. The British had anticipated
that Indigenous Filipinos—exploited and persecuted by Spain—would welcome them as liberators. Instead, the invaders were confronted by an impassioned local resistance. The British commander General Draper was shocked
by Indigenous soldiers' apparent willingness to die to preserve Spanish sovereignty in the islands at the siege of Manila. He recalled how "Native" fighting men, "although armed chiefly with bows, arrows, and lances . . . advanced
up to the very muzzles of our pieces . . . and died like wild beasts, gnawing
the bayonets."[3] Longstanding Catholic anti-piracy traditions bolstered the colonial government's capacity to combat the invaders. Spanish colonial officials, the clergy, and Indigenous and Chinese mestizo elites worked together
to rally thousands of loyalist troops to the capital's defense in a military
campaign that was widely conceptualized as a holy war. The fact that the
British acted like pirates contributed to the widespread willingness to meet
them in battle.

This chapter also analyzes the organization and aspirations of the rebellions against the Spanish empire that erupted across Luzon in the wake of
the invasion. The British occupation of Intramuros was a catastrophe for the
Spanish, but it struck many Sangleyes and Indigenous people as a rare opportunity to renegotiate their obligations and rights under colonial rule, and
particularly the burden of tribute and the polo, the prevailing system of forced
labor in the colony. Friars in Ilocos in late 1762 witnessed Indigenous leaders
persuade their families and neighbors that "since Castile no longer commands us, as they have been defeated by the English, there is no reason to

pay them tribute." The Ilocanos resolved to form *juntas* (local councils) to prevent the English from taking over, "since they would surely suppress Catholicism." Many of these juntas also committed to abolishing the "many oppressions" and "injustices and humiliations" that the Spanish had intro- duced.[4] Their revolt grew. By the end of the year, communities across mul- tiple provinces, including Pangasinan, Pampanga, and Cagayan in addition to Ilocos had risen up in armed rebellion against the Spanish empire. The insurgents realized the radical potential of Catholic anti-piracy. They wea- ponized the colony's anti-piracy arsenal against the Spanish empire and ap- propriated its rhetoric to legitimize their powerful, popular movement. By March of 1763, where this chapter concludes, the British were struggling to hold on to Manila, and it was the local insurgencies that posed the greatest threat to the restoration of Spanish colonial rule in the Philippines. Chap- ter 4 shifts focus to consider the composition and motivations of the diverse loyalist army that eventually crushed these rebellions along with the British "pirates."

The destruction and dislocation of colonial records in the Philippines was a legacy of the war. The British destroyed and pilfered countless leather-bound books, maps, and manuscripts from convents and government libraries in Manila and its hinterland with the intention of using these materials to guide their future efforts to colonize the Pacific.[5] Yet war also generated a rich ar- chive that this chapter utilizes to interrogate the history of this conflict from below. The handful of existing studies of the British invasion of Manila have treated it as a clash between Spanish and British forces entangled in a European imperial war, rather than an armed struggle that swept up a myr- iad of diverse men and women in a composite archipelagic space.[6] Moreover, they make the mistake of assuming that the fighting men who participated in the British, insurgent, and loyalist armies unquestioningly followed their leaders; their fidelity is overlooked or taken for granted rather than scruti- nized. In contrast, this chapter highlights the extent to which military lead- ers bargained with combatants to secure their support. Despite the global turn in history, the literature on the Seven Years' War continues to margin- alize maritime Asia and to privilege watery and terrestrial battlefields in Europe, North America, and the Atlantic world.[7] In focusing on the war's non-European actors in the Pacific, this study takes inspiration from and ad- vances the growing revisionist historiography of the world's first global war that centers on Black and Indigenous combatants in other parts of the globe.[8] Subaltern fighting men, who were the majority of combatants in the

Philippines and other colonial battlegrounds, determined this war's path and outcomes, and defined the contours of empires in the process.

The Surprise Invasion

Some three thousand men came to Manila with the British fleet. The expedition's origins in Madras (Chennai), an eastern Indian city and British East India Company outpost, made the fighting force "wildly heterogenous."[9] Englishmen were in the minority. Approximately three hundred troops were French and other European soldiers whom the British had taken prisoner at Pondicherry (Puducherry) when they captured the French colony in India after a four-month siege in 1761. Over one thousand fighting men were South Asian soldiers known as *sepoys*. There was a contingent of Africans comprising men who had most likely traveled to Southern India via the Indian Ocean slave trade that thrived between Portuguese Mozambique and Goa. The fleet carried an additional one hundred or so South Asian *lascars* to Manila to perform the heavy labor of war—transporting supplies from ship to shore to battlefield, and burying the dead.[10] The composition of this military force reflected the East India Company's concerns for the security of Madras; it did not want to risk sending too many European troops to the Philippines in case they were needed on the Coromandel Coast.[11]

Manileños saw the invaders as pirates. Like colonial officials and the diverse vassals of the Crown across the global Spanish empire in the eighteenth century, Manileños lumped together the foreigners who attacked ships and coastal settlements from the sea into the pirate category.[12] Some historians have insisted on the importance of legal distinctions between pirates and privateers. They make a clear differentiation between the former, who engaged in unlawful maritime violence, and the latter, who operated within the confines of the law, with the approval of a monarch or other recognized sovereign authority. Yet these differences were imperceptible or irrelevant to most people who were caught up in the chaos of war.[13] For locals, the British invasion almost immediately took the shape of the past century's pirate attacks on the capital and the ongoing sea-robber raids that plagued Catholic communities in Philippine borderlands.

The invaders made landfall on the beach in front of Malate church that stood roughly two kilometers south of Intramuros in September 1762.[14] Taking advantage of the element of surprise in their assault, they hastily began

preparations to lay siege to the walled city of Manila. Laying siege—
surrounding a place with an armed force to defeat those defending it—was
so central to warfare in maritime Asia that the very architecture of Manila
and fortified churches and settlements across the Catholic archipelago were
designed to withstand siege tactics.[15] Soldiers and sailors captured Manila's
gunpowder factory on the first night of the invasion. They torched the Er-
mita church and the church of San Juan in Bagambayan, and they also set
alight the wood and palm houses and shops that spread outward from the
city's thick stone walls. The invaders strategically started these devastating
fires to clear the suburban belt in front of the walled city, eliminating places
that the Spanish could use to launch counterattacks, and opening up a path
to shower the city walls with heavy artillery. The British documented this
path of destruction in a map, shown in Figure 5. The densely populated area
between the landing place on the right and the edge of Intramuros on the
left was flattened. Thick black smoke filled the air as Extramuros burned.
The roaring flames muffled the sounds of shouting and gunfire as locals
covered in sweat and soot rushed to rescue their families and their possessions and flee from the attack.[16]

The pirate invasion plunged Manila into pandemonium. Over the following days the invaders captured a third church, the one dedicated to Santiago
the moor-slayer that stood less than three hundred meters from the fort. British officials ordered four hundred of their fighting men to dig trenches and
build fascines and gabions, cages woven from wicker and filled with sand
and rocks and bundles of wood and sticks tied together that combined into
defensive structures that protected artillerymen and their big guns. Captain William Stevenson, a British military engineer, was surprised that his
men were unable to convince "the natives to assist us (though all means were
used to encourage them to come in) which was a very unfortunate circum-
stance."[17] The black legend of Spanish rule, or the notion that it was particularly depraved and despised by Indigenous people, had led the masterminds
of the Manila expedition in London and in Madras to assume that Filipinos
would eagerly embrace this opportunity to "throw off the Spanish yoke."[18]
They quickly realized that they had been wrong.

Manileños kept the British forces "in continual alarms" as they went about
their war work.[19] Hispano-Filipino units repeatedly carried out small-scale
attacks against the invaders. British records of the siege note that on the
twenty-seventh of September, "some of the seamen straggling from their
quarters . . . alone were murdered by the natives."[20] The following day the

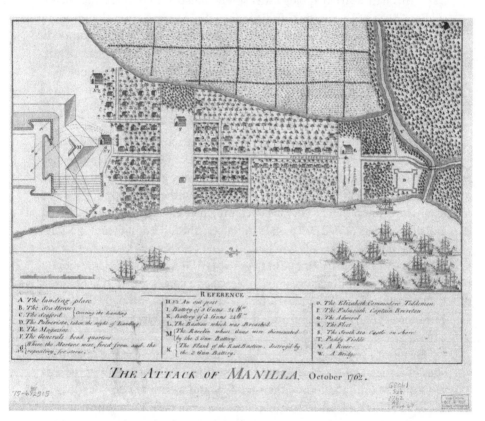

Figure 5. A British map showing the surprise attack on Manila, noting the landing place of the British Royal Navy and East India Company's men, the buildings they destroyed, and where they bombarded the city walls. *The Attack of Manilla, October. 1762.* Library of Congress, https://www.loc.gov/item /75692515/.

British camp received the decapitated torso of one of their own, a "Mr Fryer, maimed in the most inhuman manner." A letter from Archbishop-Governor Rojo was attached to the corpse, blaming the killing on the "ignorance and barbarity of their natives who are utterly unacquainted with the customs of war." This half-hearted apology was surely intended to provoke the enemy soldiers' fears of "barbarous" Indigenous Filipino warriors.[21] The invaders clashed with Hispano-Filipino militias in skirmishes in the neighborhoods surrounding Intramuros, including at Dilao, Parañaque, and Bagambayan. Before dawn on the fourth of October, a contingent of local combatants "surprised the [British] seamen's quarters . . . and killed and wounded a good many of them."[22] In retaliation, the invaders killed some two hundred local fighting men as they retreated from the attack.

October was the height of the wet season in Luzon. Torrential downpours drenched the invading forces in the second week of the war when they began to barrage the city with shells fired from heavy guns mounted on ships anchored in the bay and the towers of captured Catholic churches. For days, explosive cannon shot or "bombs" weighing between fifty and one hundred and fifty pounds rained down on Intramuros. The force of shot and shrapnel colliding into the city walls sent bodies flying into the air.[23] Unrelenting artillery fire was a core technique of siege warfare. It wore down enemy morale and defenses, and ultimately aimed to tear open a hole in the walls of besieged forts and cities, creating a breach for the enemy to pass through. Soldiers in Intramuros returned fire, turning the land below the city walls into killing zones.

Fort Santiago and churches inside of Intramuros were at the same time sites of refuge and the focal point of hostilities. Although many residents evacuated Manila and moved their families and wealth to safer locations in the city's hinterland, others sought protection from the invading army within the walled city as previous generations had done in the face of pirate attacks.[24] One block away from the central plaza, the Church of Santo Domingo filled up with "women, children, and the sick."[25] Some women joined the fight to defend Manila, climbing into the church's elevated choir and its tower to shoot arrows at the invaders.

Thousands of Indigenous fighting men from rural communities outside of Manila began to arrive in the capital as the siege continued, reinforcing the Spanish and Pampangan regiments ordinarily stationed at Fort Santiago and the city's other residents who took up arms to defend the city.[26] On the night of the first of October, Intramuros's churches, convents, and government buildings were temporarily transformed into barracks for more than three thousand mostly Indigenous fighting men from the Bulacan, Tondo, and Pampanga provinces.[27] From this point in the siege onward, Indigenous Filipinos accounted for the majority of those that took up arms to defend Manila. Catholic anti-piracy facilitated the flow of Indigenous fighting men into Intramuros. The deeply rooted tradition of military mobilization of local communities in the face of pirate attacks and other emergency situations made their rapid deployment to the capital possible. Like the Spanish colonial government's recent military campaigns against Moro pirates, the fight against the British assumed the character of a holy war. Priests were prominent in the defense of the city. Missionary orders organized deliveries of cattle and rice from their haciendas to feed the fighting men amassed to defend it. Some militant missionaries joined soldiers shooting at the enemy atop the city walls, while others accompanied the soldiers in prayer.[28] Rojo preached that he had "seen the angel of the Lord, sent forth from the Almighty, to destroy the army of the heretics before their city."[29] The Spanish and their allies reported visions of sacred sky signs during these desperate early days of shelling and close combat. Anchors, palm trees, and crosses appeared in the heavens, reassuring the loyalist Catholic army that God was on their side.[30]

Despite their fervor, the Spanish forces could not hold Intramuros. The invading army breached the walls early in the morning of the sixth of October. They kept up "a constant fire of grape and musketry," making it impossible for the Spanish forces to repair the gaping hole in the city walls.[31] Pablo Ngien, a Dominican friar in Manila that day, estimated that he saw ten thousand people ranging from babies to the elderly flee from the capital after the enemy broke into Intramuros. Refugees whose homes had been destroyed in the invasion and fighting men who had come from the provinces to defend the capital ran away from the carnage.[32] Witnesses watched many Hispano-Filipino soldiers who were determined to escape from the enemy jump from Fort Santiago's walls into the Pasig River, where many were hit by bullets and drowned as they tried to swim to safety.[33]

Archbishop-Governor Rojo walked out of the fort waving the white flag of surrender amid this chaos. He met with British officials and agreed to sign the twelve-point capitulation agreement that they proposed, which presented the conditions for an immediate ceasefire. Rojo consented to handing over Fort Santiago to the British, along with all of the other fortifications, military stores, and ammunition in the Spanish colony. In addition, he agreed to pay the British a hefty ransom of four million silver pesos. Half of this huge sum of money was to be collected immediately from Manila's royal treasury, the missionary orders, and the silver aboard the galleon ship that was due to arrive in Manila any day. The king of Spain was to pay the other half at a later date. In return for this payment, British officials promised to protect Manila from being looted and to allow locals to freely practice their religion and engage in commerce unhindered.[34] Rojo understood this treaty to be a provisional one that would remain in effect until the kings of Spain and England reached an agreement about the fate of Manila and the Philippine islands.[35]

The archbishop-governor had valid reasons to surrender. As he saw it, the British army could not be defeated. The loyalist forces under his command were outgunned and overwhelmed in Intramuros, and they were almost out of food and gunpowder on the day he signed the capitulation agreement.[36] Rojo would have understood that under the conventions of siege warfare, the fate of a captured city was proportionate to the resistance it had mounted, meaning that his refusal to capitulate could lead to a massacre and the maximum loss of life and property.[37] It is clear that attacks on churches weighed heavily on Rojo's decision to call an end to hostilities. "To see my church impoverished, left without a single thing, I fell as though dead," he wrote.[38] The archbishop-governor lived as a pampered prisoner of the British in Intramuros until his death in January 1764.

Rojo's capitulation, however, brought the opposite of peace. Shortly after the capitulation papers were signed, the invading army captured and executed one hundred loyalists who refused to put down their weapons and surrender.[39] Like the more familiar pirates of maritime Asia, the invaders committed shocking acts of violence against the local population, raping countless women and torturing and executing men in gruesome public spectacles. Soldiers hanged one man to die on the tall cross that stood in the patio of the church of San Francisco because he would not reveal where silver was hidden. They hanged another three men on the cathedral's metal gates, leaving their dead bodies to rot in full view to intimidate the locals into submission.[40]

Like all pirates, the invading army turned its energy to pillaging, despite British officials' promises to avoid this. Spanish records indicate that enemy soldiers plundered Manila for at least forty hours straight on the orders of their commanders. General Draper denied that he had given his men instructions or permission to sack the city, but not that it happened. The highest-ranked officials simply had no power to reign in the loot-hungry troops. "All military men know," he explained, "how difficult it is to restrain the impetuosity of troops in the first fury of an assault, especially when composed of such as variety and confusion of people, who differed as much in sentiments and language, as in dress and complexion."[41] Draper conceded that "the inhabitants [of Manila] were undoubtedly great sufferers."[42] With these actions the invaders crushed whatever good will Manileños might have held toward them.

Looters targeted Manila's richly adorned churches. They emptied these sacred buildings of everything that they could carry off, including silver chalices, embroidered textiles, and carved wooden altars. They destroyed the statues of religious figures that were known as *santos*, including Nuestra Señora del Rosario "La Naval," the best-known Marian image in Manila. Enemy troops took La Naval from her sanctuary in the Dominican church and convent in Intramuros and defiled her. They stole her silver crown "studded with precious stones, and destroyed her vestments," decapitated the ivory statue, and tore the arms off the statue of the child Jesus that she held close to her chest.[43] The Spanish elites who documented their experiences of the war in letters and chronicles were more willing to describe in graphic detail the abuse of La Naval than the violence that so many living and breathing women suffered at the hands of enemy soldiers. Testimonies documenting the assault of this sacred image of the mother of God might be understood as a metaphor for the unspeakable brutality that so many women were subjected to.

The invaders also raided homes. The wealthy widow Josepha Agustiana de Larraguiver reported that soldiers robbed her of eight thousand pesos and stole her treasured objects of devotion and trunks full of clothing and jewelry, leaving her "without even a cloak to cover herself."[44] Troops also plundered bodies, "taking from the Indigenous women their bracelets, chains, and other ornaments of gold and silver."[45] Many Manileños tried to protect their property. Rojo estimated that in their efforts to halt the pillaging, three hundred Indigenous people and "the sergeant major of the royal regiment, two captains, two subalterns and about fifty soldiers of the regular troops, and thirty of the commerce militia were killed on our side, and many were wounded."[46] Falliet, the Swiss mercenary and merchant and long-term Manila resident, called the British "barbarous pirates." Describing the sacking of Manila to a friend in Batavia, he wrote that "the city even to its very foundations [was] plundered and robbed, the churches profaned, virgins violated, a thousand sacrileges committed, and so many other abominations as would make even nature blush and which give horror to relate."[47]

In the face of such violence and loss, Rojo's capitulation shocked and infuriated many Spaniards in the Philippines who were certain that the war against the British could be won, or who at least believed that they were duty bound to their God and to their king to try to secure a military victory against the invaders. Simón de Anda y Salazar, a Basque oidor in Manila's Audiencia, condemned Rojo for committing "vile treason."[48] In the first week of October, Manila's Audiencia had taken steps to preserve the Spanish colonial government in exile from the capital if the invaders captured the city. The Audiencia nominated Anda to make the five-hour overland journey from Manila to the pueblo of Bulacan, the capital of Bulacan Province, where he was to reestablish Spanish rule if and when Intramuros was lost. In accordance with these plans, Anda was proclaimed governor and captain general of the Philippines in Bulacan shortly after Rojo surrendered.[49] Anda argued that because Rojo was a prisoner of war, he had no authority to negotiate a treaty with the British, and the deal that he struck was invalid. Anda rallied his fellow Spaniards to maintain a "cruel and destructive war" against the enemy.[50] He was confident in the Indigenous people's "loyal spirit" and the clergy's capacity to "excite them to the defense of the country against the English enemy," even after "the loss of Manila."[51] "If the British want to rule this country," he declared, "their chiefs well know that they have to win it first with force."[52] In the months that followed, Rojo made repeated pleas to the "loyal *naturales* and their *cabezas* of these Philippine Islands" to end their resistance and "avoid offending, or causing any harm whatsoever to our opponents."[53] Yet these calls fell on deaf ears. Rojo effectively abandoned his authority over the diverse loyalist forces who rallied to defend Spanish rule when he gave up Manila to pirate terror.

Empire by Negotiation: British Objectives and Strategy in Manila

To comprehend the British forces' actions in Manila during the Seven Years' War, it is necessary to understand what the men who planned the invasion and occupation of the city hoped that it would achieve. Recent studies have shown that the invasion and occupation were part of Britain's sustained militarized Pacific turn, challenging a more dominant view of the naval campaign as an opportunistic "case of corporate raiding," or little more than a holdup of a silver-rich colony.[54] The British admiral George Anson's 1743 capture of a Spanish galleon ship certainly contributed to the idea of Manila in the British imagination as a city that was dripping with silver and ripe for pillaging, encouraging invasion fantasies across the Anglo world. The mountains of galleon silver that Anson stole were eventually loaded on carts and paraded through London accompanied by sailors, flags, and brass bands in a patriotic celebration of Britannia's power.[55] Although dreams of stealing another spectacular silver haul were at play in the 1760s, the planning that went into the conquest of Manila at the highest levels of British government reveals its intention to use the city as a platform to establish a permanent British presence in the archipelago. The British imagined a new colony in maritime Asia in Spanish Manila's image: a thriving British hub of inter-Asian trade and, in the words of East India Company officials, as a base to launch future attacks on "Spanish provinces in the South Seas, both of South and North America."[56] This long-term vision influenced British strategy in Manila in the 1760s.

The British established a government in Manila in an effort to place colonial rule in Luzon on a firm footing. The Madras-born East India Company official Dawsonne Drake was proclaimed the first (and last) British governor of Manila "and all its dependencies" on the second of November in 1762, in an official ceremony staged outside of the Governor's palace in the main plaza in Intramuros.[57] Four East India Company servants joined Drake as members of the Manila Council, a committee that met frequently to discuss and make decisions about how to rule the new British colony and to win the war against the loyalists.[58] The Council tried to strengthen the British position in Manila through negotiation. It recognized that local Indigenous support was necessary to deliver a victory against the loyalist forces. Accordingly, one of Drake's first tasks as governor was to distribute manifestos written in Spanish and Tagalog that guaranteed that all people who swore loyalty to Britain's King George III would be liberated from servitude and the burden of tribute and would be free to continue to practice Catholicism. The British were confident that these promises would deliver popular support. These manifestos also threatened that "rebels" who refused to submit to British authority would be punished.[59] Drake repeatedly distributed these olive branch messages to the local population throughout the occupation.[60]

The siege proved that the invaders had been overconfident in their expectations of being welcomed by the Filipinos as liberators, but their grasp of colonial politics in the islands was not all wrong. The British understood and attempted to take advantage of the fact that tribute and the polo strained relations between Indigenous peoples and Spanish colonial officials and the clergy. They knew that the people of Bohol were "in rebellion" against the

Spanish and anticipated persuading them to support the war against Anda and the loyalists.[61] They also saw Moro pirates as potential allies and hoped to enter "into a coalition with the Llanon of Maguindanao to secure the conquest of the islands." Merchants and sailors of all nations circulated such valuable political intelligence across the globe.[62]

If anyone welcomed the British as liberators, it was Sultan Azim ud-Din and his son, Prince Mohammed Israel, who were still prisoners of the Spanish in Manila in 1762. During their imprisonment Azim Ud-Din had maintained secret communication with his family in Jolo as well as with British East India Company agents, even signing a trade agreement with the Company in November of 1761.[63] The sultan recognized that an alliance with the British offered an immediate pathway out of captivity, if not a more durable check on Spanish power. During the occupation, the sultan and the Company formalized a mutual defense and trade pact that granted the British the right to "erect Forts or Factories" in Jolo and its dependent territories.[64] A British ship and guards escorted Azim ud-Din and his son to Jolo at their request before the end of the war. The Company "advanced to Prince Israel the sum of 1,000 Dollars" that he was to repay "in the goods of his Country" to kick-start a healthy commercial relationship between the two parties.[65] Although the sultan did not offer much assistance to the war against the loyalists in Luzon, the British-Sulu alliance led the East India Company to set up a short-lived outpost at Balambangan island, situated between Palawan and Sabah. Moro pirates destroyed the British factory in 1775.

A small clique of elite European Manileños became useful agents of the British in the occupied city. Santiago Orendaín, a Manila-born lawyer, provided translation services to the British government. He likely drafted the "olive branch" manifestos that the British distributed to communities in and around the capital. Orendaín also assisted in the surveillance of communities under occupation, drawing up "a list of such persons as have absconded from Manila."[66] The Dublin-born medical doctor Eduardo Wogan, who had lived in Manila for at least a decade when the British invaded, also served the British government as a translator. Francisco Zapata, formerly the *justicia mayor* of Tondo, joined the invaders' army and led British forces into battle against the loyalists.[67] Diego O'Kennedy, another long-term Irish resident of Manila, acted as a liaison between the British government and the local Chinese community. O'Kennedy's influence is apparent in almost all of the British government's extensive dealings with Chinese migrants in the occupied city and its hinterland. He was instrumental in persuading Drake to recruit Chinese instead of Indigenous Filipinos as soldiers, and to create a Chinese cavalry unit attached to the British forces. O'Kennedy claimed that the Chinese were the "properest people to be trusted," in contrast to the "malays or mestezes ... [who] may go to the enemy with horse and arms."[68] He recruited "twenty five good resolute fellows" to be part of the Sangley horseback regiment, "reconnoitered a proper place for stables," and organized the purchase of saddles, bridles, and other equipment for the cavalry. He also negotiated generous salaries to be paid to the Chinese cavalrymen to ensure their compliance with his plans.[69] Chinese go-betweens also contributed to organizing Chinese support for the occupation. Lucas Guatlo, a wealthy Chinese entrepreneur who had rented the lucrative *ramo de vino* (government monopoly on wine) in Bulacan before the war, became captain of the British Sangley regiment. Guatlo was instrumental in recruiting Chinese migrants into this armed unit.[70]

Personal politics drove many of these elite men into British arms. Some of the European traitors had been wronged by the Spanish colonial government before the invasion and embraced the opportunity to get revenge. Orendaín, for example, had been a close advisor to Governor Arandía, a man who made powerful enemies during his 1750s governorship. Arandía infuriated the clergy when he emptied Manila's ecclesiastical prisons, giving liberty to men and women whom ecclesiastical courts had convicted of a host of religious crimes, including prostitution, sodomy, and incest. The governor had offended the Dominicans when he ordered the demolition of several buildings that the religious order owned in Intramuros on the grounds they were damaging the city walls. These scandals made a mockery of the Catholic Church. Moreover, Arandía angered ordinary Manileños when he oversaw the destruction of the *casillas* (modest houses) that Indigenous people had built around the capital. One of the governor's enemies had mocked the government's claim that these structures were "depraved and dangerous to the republic, as though the poor should build sumptuous palaces for their homes."[71] Following Arandía's death in 1759, his successor had Orendaín arrested on charges of embezzling government money. Soldiers had dragged Orendaín out of the Augustinian church where he had sought sanctuary and locked him up in Fort Santiago's prison cells. The new government also punished Orendaín's immediate family members, placing his wife in the Colegio de Santa Potenciana and his daughters in a Jesuit *beaterio,* which were both Catholic institutions for laywomen. Although Rojo freed and dropped charges against Orendaín when he became interim governor of the colony prior to the British invasion, Orendaín's bitterness toward the Spanish endured. In a 1762 letter to the British, Orendaín described war "as an act of vindictive Justice and not only a reparation of honor."[72]

It is likely that Wogan and O'Kennedy also held grudges against powerful Spaniards in Manila. As foreigners, both men had faced harassment at the hands of the Spanish Inquisition and had been forced to answer to accusations of freemasonry in the decade before the British invasion. These Irish migrants may have calculated that collaborating with the British was the best way to guarantee their safety given the track record of Spanish officials doubting their Catholic faith and fidelity to the Crown.[73] Money surely also factored into these men's decisions to support the British. Orendaín's efforts to profit from the invasion are particularly well documented. His attempt to sell the stolen contents of the Augustinian Library to the British for thirty thousand pesos left a long paper trail.[74]

British efforts to gain local support in Manila found the most success with Chinese migrants. Large numbers of Sangley recruits were integrated into the multiethnic British fighting forces in the first months of the occupation. Captain Richard Bishop employed fifty armed Chinese as sentinels in the fort of Cavite.[75] Chinese fighting men were prominent in the British forces that clashed with the loyalists in skirmishes and battles in late 1762. These included a major battle at Pasig in November where the heavily Chinese and South Asian British forces suffered significant loses, and Hispano-Filipino units made off with valuable cannon.[76] Shortly after this engagement, Chinese fighting men supported the British in a long siege of the exiled Spanish government's headquarters in Bulacan. A large Hispano-Catholic army dug in and defended the town for almost twenty nights, but they eventually ran out of gunpowder. Indigenous fighting men fled when they saw that defeat was inevitable, leaving only a handful of Spaniards, including four friars, to fight to the death.[77] Soon after, Anda reestablished his exiled government in the Pampangan town of Bacolor. In addition to soldiering, Chinese men contributed to these British campaigns as guides, helping the invading army to traverse overland roads. Parián shopkeepers sold food to the British, including rice, dried fish, and the locally distilled liquor arak. These provisions were essential to keeping the British army well fed and just a little bit drunk.[78] Yet despite the victory at Bulacan, British gains were limited. The invaders lacked the manpower to hold on to the pueblo, so they burned it down and withdrew to Manila.[79]

Historians cannot dismiss the importance of the assistance that many Sangleyes rendered to the invaders, but it is blatantly wrong to claim that all

Chinese migrants betrayed the Spanish and enthusiastically supported the enemy.[80] British officials in Manila were deeply frustrated by the Chinese who betrayed their confidence. Drake's angry characterization of the people of the diaspora as "the refuse of the Chinese, who fly their own Country," showed his lack of trust in this section of colonial society.[81] In and around Manila, local Chinese responses to the global war were far more complex than previously acknowledged.

The Chinese Rebellion, and the Chinese Massacre

For the multitudes living beyond the capital, the British conquest of Manila signified the end of Spanish rule in Luzon, or at least a severely weakened Spanish colonial state. Subalterns across the big island rebelled against the Spanish in the final months of 1762, forcing the government-in-exile to pivot to fighting a multifront war against British invaders and Chinese and Indigenous insurgents. The pirate invasion of Manila shattered Sino-Spanish relations in Luzon. Seeing hundreds of Chinese men joining the British forces led Anda to suspect all Sangleyes of collaborating with the invaders. In December, rumors reached Anda that at least one thousand Sangleyes had gathered at Guagua, where they were organizing to attack Spanish and Indigenous Catholics on *nochebuena*—the night of the twenty-fourth of December—when the faithful would be attending Christmas Eve church services.[82] The nochebuena plot pitted the Chinese against the Catholic Hispano-Filipino population, marking them as outsiders and enemies of the Catholic colonial polity. It was rumored that the Chinese were going to slit the Spaniards' and Indigenous parishioners' throats and sack and torch their sacred buildings and their homes. This conspiracy was particularly worrying because Guagua was an important trading center situated at the mouth of the Pampanga River that runs from the Sierra Madre mountains into Manila Bay. If the loyalists lost control of this port, it would have been very difficult for them to move troops and supplies through the region to fight against the British forces and other enemies of the state. A successful Chinese strike on Guagua also had the potential to open a pathway for British forces and their allies to march into Pampanga and bring the region under their control.

The exiled government responded swiftly and severely to the nochebuena plot. Unlike the previous decade's rumored Chinese rebellions, the Guagua conspiracy was bona fide. Anda led hundreds of mostly Indigenous fighting men to Guagua to meet the rebels. The loyalist battalions that arrived in the town on the twenty-first of December found hundreds of Chinese troops armed, dug in, and ready for combat. Surely the desire for revenge drove some of the Chinese men to fight at Guagua. The British invasion provoked some Sangleyes to act on long-standing, seething resentments against the Spaniards who had humiliated and extorted them, taxing their pride as well as their pesos. For others, going to Guagua was a matter of survival. The invasion escalated to extreme levels the tension and mistrust between the Chinese and Spaniards and Indigenous communities in Luzon. Each of these groups feared that the others were readying to attack them, and this alarm pushed the Chinese to band together in self-defense and prepare for the coming battle.

Anda claimed that he tried to negotiate a peaceful resolution to the Guagua standoff. He initially offered to pardon Chinese rebels who handed over their weapons and dispersed, returning to their respective villages. Two Augustinian friars attempted to talk the Sangleyes into submission, but their entreaties were met with a barrage of stones and bullets, prompting the loyalist forces to return fire.[83] Reserves of trust ran low on both sides. The Chinese knew that if they surrendered their weapons, they would be unable to protect themselves if Anda went back on his word and attacked. A battle broke out early the next morning and continued until six in the evening. Anda's forces and the Chinese rebels suffered heavy casualties. After a full day of combat, the loyalists finally overwhelmed the Sangleyes and took control of the town as darkness fell. They captured as many rebel survivors as they could and imprisoned them in Bacolor, where Anda's government was temporarily headquartered.[84]

The beleaguered Spanish could not afford to tolerate a Chinese rebellion. Anda and his war council resolved to execute all of the Chinese and Chinese mestizos who were involved in the plot. The governor sent orders to capture and kill the Chinese rebels who had fled from Guagua to the clergy and Indigenous leaders throughout Pampanga, including gobernadorcillos, cabezas de barangay, and principales. At the same time, Anda imposed harsher restrictions on Chinese migrants residing in the Philippines. He prohibited Sangleyes from bearing arms and instructed that any found in possession of weapons should be considered traitors and executed.[85] These new orders made every Chinese person in Pampanga a suspected rebel and at risk of being murdered.

Days after the Guagua engagement, loyalist military officers and local Indigenous leaders oversaw the execution in Bacolor of 181 Chinese men who
were accused of participating in the revolt. Although this was the largest
massacre of Chinese people to occur in the Philippines in the eighteenth
century, it has been erased from historical memory.[86] There was no trial to
investigate or prove the prisoners' culpability, but agents of empire made
an effort to give the slaughter an air of legality. Before the killings began,
Bacolor's gobernadorcillo de naturales, the gobernadorcillo de mestizos,
and a scribe appeared before four companies of Indigenous militias standing at attention in the plaza. The gobernadorcillo de naturales read aloud a
formal proclamation in Spanish and Kapampangan declaring, "this is the
justice ordered by the king our señor, in his royal name and in the name of
the governing Audiencia of these islands, with the consent of the Council of
War, that these chinos, for being traitors to His Majesty and allied with the
British enemy, and traitors to the patria, are condemned to death, and to lose
their estates."[87] This performance of justice signaled that even though the
Union Jack was flying above the Governor's palace in Manila, the Spanish
colonial government remained sovereign and powerful in this place. Indigenous soldiers began the grisly work of killing the captured Chinese men
after this statement was read.

Balthasar Casal, the captain of the king's regiment, wrote down an official account of the executions. Casal neglected to record the murdered men's
names or any other information that could identify them, but his unusually
vivid report reveals the desperate anguish and rage that they experienced in
their final hours on this earth.[88] Armed militiamen took out groups of ten
prisoners from the jail at a time and escorted them to the gallows that had
been hastily put up in the town square.[89] The prisoners resisted. There was a
commotion in the jail after the first thirty men had been hanged. Some prisoners had tossed "handfuls of coins" on the ground to distract or bribe their
jailers. A guard noticed that one prisoner was holding a bolo (machete), and
then realized that he had used it to cut the ropes that had tied other prisoner's hands behind their backs. The unrestrained prisoners were holding
sharpened bamboo poles and were ready to fight for their lives. Militiamen
entered the jail and disarmed the Chinese in a violent struggle and made
sure that the prisoners who staged this rebellion were the next to hang. Another skirmish erupted in the jail after two more hours had passed, and 130
men had been executed. The guards saw that the remaining prisoners had
managed to arm themselves again. Judging it unsafe to enter the jail at this

time, the soldiers climbed up on the building's roof and fired shots at the prisoners below. The militiamen deemed it safe to enter when the prison fell quiet. They found seventeen men dead with bullet wounds. Another twenty men had hanged themselves with nooses crafted from stockings and belts or strips of torn shirts tied to the bars of the cell. They located eleven survivors hiding under the floorboards, lying on the damp earth below the prison, and killed them. All of the prisoners were dead by two o'clock in the afternoon. The massacre victims were denied Catholic burials.

Pampanga remained on high alert after the killings in Bacolor. Anda warned communities to be prepared for surprise Sangley attacks, and encouraged leaders to post sentries along the roads and rivers that led into their towns, and to post guards outside churches when locals gathered for religious services. The maritime invasion of Manila had completely disrupted the *convivencia* that generations of Sangleyes and their descendants had brokered with successive Spanish colonial governments and other local communities in the Philippines.

The Great Indigenous Revolt

Sangleyes were not the only people in Luzon who refused to support Simón de Anda's exiled government and its war against the British. The rumblings of rebellion among Indigenous communities were audible during the siege of Manila. Pangasinan witnessed the first signs of the coming revolt. The coastal province, whose name means "land of salt," sits between Pampanga and the sea.[90] Some fifteen hundred Pangasinense fighting men under the command of Dominican friars had set off toward the besieged city at the beginning of October. Heavy rains made their journey difficult. In some places, the men had to wade across swollen rivers where the water reached above their chests. The friars' failure to provide adequate rice rations added to the troops' exhaustion and discontent. When news of the fall of Manila reached this caravan of militiamen while they were still on their way to the capital, they immediately stopped obeying the friars' orders and abandoned the military campaign, and headed back to their respective villages.[91]

The Augustinian friar Pedro Andrés de Castro y Amuedo remarked that "the loss of Manila was extremely sad for all, [but] for the Pangasinense, it was magnificent."[92] In the friar's eyes, the locals joyfully welcomed Spanish defeat. Castro was the librarian at the Augustinian convent in Intramuros, and he wrote one of the most detailed accounts of the war in Luzon.[93] Rebels multiplied across the province. The head of the Dominican order in Pangasinan, Padre Melendez, was in the provincial capital of Lingayen when he overheard a "conceited and stupid" mestizo loudly shouting in the street "now there is no king, no priest, and no alcalde!" Melendez ordered the man to be punished with fifty lashes, leading to a brutal public display of the Church's sustained power.[94] Joaquín Gamboa was still the alcalde in Pangasinan, but his attempts to collect tribute from local communities at this tense moment sparked mass protests.

A noisy crowd that grew to three thousand people gathered on the third of November outside of the casa municipal building in Binalatongan, which was the largest town in Pangasinan. Melendez and other Dominican friars went there to negotiate with the angry assembly. The crowd was amenable to bargaining. José Magalong, the town's gobernadorcillo, presented a list of demands to the missionaries. The people did not want to pay tribute to the Spanish while the British occupied Manila, and they insisted that whatever tribute they had already paid that year be returned to them. They reasoned that the British might come asking for tribute now they had established themselves in the capital, and they could not afford to be double-taxed, paying tribute to two sovereigns at the same time. Their other demands included that several unpopular colonial officials be fired and replaced, from the despised Alcalde Gamboa to the local schoolmaster. Additionally, the crowd wanted to halt the practice of local men being forced to work as guards in the town's jail, a job that they considered particularly offensive and insufficiently remunerated.[95] Notably, the protestors articulated a commitment to Catholic anti-piracy. They vowed that if the English invaded their province, they would send a strong and well-armed army to halt their advance.[96] Around this time in Laguna, the region around Lake Taal south of Manila, Indigenous people had arrested, whipped, and killed an alcalde. The people accused the colonial official of being "fond of the English" after he ordered them to disarm.[97] The invasion from the sea had thrown colonial society into disarray.

Back in Pangasinan, the crowd at Binalatongan made a deafening roar as they chanted "What is in the paper! What is in the paper and nothing more!"[98] They refused to quiet down or disperse until their written demands were met. At some point that day, the guards protecting the casa municipal arrested and dragged inside of the building a man named Juan de la Cruz Palaris, whom they identified as the leader of the mob. This infuriated the protestors. They shouted even louder and banged their hands and sticks against the building's walls until Palaris was freed. Melendez refused to approve a moratorium on tribute, and the people refused to quit their protest. The crowd's demands would not have fundamentally changed the colonial order if the friars agreed to them. Yet in coming together to loudly dissent, the people showed that they were emboldened by the pirate occupation of Manila. The middle ground had shifted, and the Spaniards realized that they needed to tread carefully as they figured out the limits of their power in this changed colonial world.

The rebellion radiated outward from Binalatongan across Pangasinan. The Spain-born Augustinian friar Pedro Vivar wrote that "what began as a disturbance in one pueblo, grabbed a second, and the two snatched a third, and by the time the news of it spread there was no remedy, because so many had united."[99] Vivar, who was living and preaching in the northern Ilocos pueblo of Batac in 1762, authored another detailed account of the Indigenous revolt that swept across the country. The local bands that joined the insurgency raided weapons and ammunition from fortress churches across the province, turning the colony's anti-piracy weapons stockpiles against the Spanish colonial government. By the beginning of December, only two small Pangasinan towns with Dominican churches—Asingan and Binmaley—remained subordinate to Spanish rule.[100]

Friars continued to bargain for peace with the insurgents. Pedro Ire, the provincial of the Dominicans, organized a conference with Indigenous delegates from pueblos across Pangasinan to try to broker a peaceful solution to the crisis. Catholicism imbued friar diplomacy. The meeting was held in Manaoag, the town that was home to the sanctuary of Our Lady of the Most Holy Rosary of Manaoag, a revered, ivory-carved statue of the Mother of God holding her infant son. The Dominicans declared this sacred image to be the patroness of the loyal forces. The missionaries offered a full Catholic mass in her honor for the delegates at the conference, and when it concluded, they invited the delegates to swear oaths of loyalty to the Spanish government before the image. Through these ceremonies the Dominicans articulated the idea that submission to Spanish colonial rule and submission to God were intricately linked. The priests and the delegates failed to find a mutually agreeable path forward. In early December, Binalatongan's rebels ordered all Spaniards to evacuate the province, exempting only the clergy from expulsion.[101]

The wave of unrest rippled through the neighboring Ilocos Province in the middle of December. On the fourteenth of that month, an angry mob

numbering two thousand armed Indigenous people brandishing weapons—
many stolen from royal anti-piracy fleets—assembled at the alcalde mayor's
residence in Vigan, a populous port city that also served as the provincial
capital and a center of Catholic missionary activity in the region.[102] The crowd
shouted "long live the king of Spain and death to bad government!"[103] Ilocano voices hollered the familiar refrain spouted by crowds of protestors
across the global Spanish empire, an aggressive demand for reforms to the
colonial system articulated from a position of loyal subjecthood.[104] Tribute
was the core grievance that continued to fan the flames of the uprising.
The people of Vigan revolted when Ilocos's Mexican-born alcalde mayor
Antonio Zavala y Uría took steps to commence the annual head tax collection, contrary to Anda's orders to pause tribute in an effort to calm the
masses. As in Binalatongan weeks earlier, the crowd in Vigan called for a
moratorium on the tribute and tributary labor obligations, and they demanded that the alcalde surrender his ceremonial baton and quit. Points of
friction dating back to before the war deepened the divide between colonial
officials and the Crown's Indigenous subjects. Vigeños despised Zavala for
his perceived failure to adequately deal with the epidemic that brought
death to Ilocos in 1756. He was also said to be weak on Moro pirates. There
were accusations in the air that the corrupt alcalde accepted bribes from
Muslim sea-robbers and gave them passports to visit and trade in Ilocos,
which was a ruse for their expeditions to seize and enslave Christians.[105]
Catholic anti-piracy nourished the insurgency in ways that the Spanish colonial government could not have anticipated.

Diego Baltasar Silang y Andaya emerged as the leader of the rebellion in
Ilocos. Silang was born in Vigan to the son of principales. When he was a
young boy, Silang went to live with and work as a servant for a Vigan priest,
which gave him access to a Spanish education in addition to opportunities
to build close relationships with some of the most powerful men in Luzon.
When the British invaded Manila, Silang was married to María Josefa Gabriela Silang, an Indigenous woman who had also been raised in Vigan as a
servant in the home of another priest, Tomás Millán.[106] Diego Silang was employed as a courier for Millán and for Santiago Orendaín, work that required
him to travel frequently between Ilocos and Manila through central Luzon.
Silang was also an *abogadillo* or *apoderadillo*.[107] Vivar explained that these
Indigenous "little lawyers" or "little advocates" rose from the ranks of
the common people to represent them in disputes against the principalia
and Spanish elites. Apoderadillos were part of an ecosystem of grassroots

organizing in the Philippines. They used intimidation and violence to force elites to negotiate with them on a variety of matters and were known to threaten to burn down principales' houses and kill their carabao to push them to comply with the people's wishes. Apoderadillos' authority came from their capacity to effectively mobilize the community, or in Vivar's words, "to make private causes common."[108] They had to be cunning and charismatic to be effective, and attuned to the shifting thoughts and feelings of the polity.

Silang strikes us as a classic Indigenous intermediary.[109] He was trusted and respected by Spaniards and Indigenous peoples alike, and he was capable of operating within and across plural cultural spaces. He was literate and multilingual, and he possessed a rich knowledge of the geography and the complex politics of central Luzon, making him well placed to lead a revolt. As Yanna Yannakakis observed, across the Spanish empire such Indigenous intermediaries "held the colonial order in balance: most often, they defused tensions in colonial society," but on occasion, in moments of crisis, "the pressures were such that they abandoned the middle ground."[110] Diego and Gabriela Silang are celebrated as heroes in the Philippines today. Their likenesses are memorialized in bronze busts and equestrian statues in prominent parks and city streets, as well as on the silver screen.[111] Less is known about Juan de la Cruz Palaris, the apparent leader of the Pangasinan revolt. There are fewer extant primary sources pertaining to Palaris, and the rebellion in Pangasinan has received less attention from scholars in comparison to the Silang revolt. What we do know is that Palaris's contemporaries claimed that before the British invasion, he worked in Manila as a coachman for one of the Audiencia's oidores. Palaris, like Silang, would have had close ties to elite Spaniards and access to knowledge of colonial politics from multiple perspectives.[112] Such networks and information were valuable for leaders of armed struggles.

Historians have traditionally interpreted the rebellions in Pangasinan and Ilocos as two distinct, regionally limited movements, the former headed by Palaris and the latter led initially by Diego Silang and eventually by Gabriela.[113] The archive, however, points to closer connections between these simultaneous revolts. The clergy regarded the people who rose up in rebellion in Binalatongan and Vigan as allies.[114] Melendez observed in January of 1762 that the people of Pangasinan "are united with those of Ilocos," and they were "imitating" each other.[115] Diego Silang was in correspondence with rebels in Pangasinan. He wrote letters addressed to "Francisco de la Cruz," a "captain general" in the newly formed rebel army in that province, requesting that he send Pangasinense fighting men to Bantay to battle against the loyalists.[116] It is possible that Francisco de la Cruz and Juan de la Cruz Palaris were in fact the same person. Furthermore, Diego Silang's contemporaries identified him and many of the insurgents in Ilocos as being Pangasinense, suggesting that Silang spoke the language and had kinship ties to the province. Blood ties deepened the connections between rebels across the region.

Earlier studies of the Indigenous insurgency have glossed over the fact that it spread deep into the Cagayan valley in northeastern Luzon and the upland Sierra Madre ranges, regions where Spanish authority was more precarious.[117] The Cagayan River is the longest in the Philippines. It flows from the Caraballo Mountains in central Luzon to the Babuyan Channel near Aparri, a town on the island's northern coast. The villages along the river's five hundred kilometers were not large, but they were many, and the events set in motion by the pirate invasion of Manila had a dramatic impact on their populations. The people of Ilagan, a pueblo that was also known as San Fernando, revolted in February of 1763, arresting and whipping their gobernadorcillo.[118] Men and women also rose up in rebellion upriver in the town of Tuguegarao. The location of this village, and others that became the sites of major protests and battles discussed in this chapter, are shown in Map 3. The participation of various ethnolinguistic polities in the insurgency across such a large geographical area has led some historians to characterize it as a protonationalist movement, a precursor to José Rizal and the Ilustrados who rallied against Spanish sovereignty in the Philippines in the late nineteenth century.[119] But this analysis does not account for the comparably diverse fighting men who mustered in the loyalist counterrevolutionary army, and who could have just as readily been identified as the ancestors of a conservative Catholic patriotism in the islands.

The Spanish colonial government-in-exile partnered with Dominican missionaries to put down the Cagayan uprising with brute force. Juan Manuel Arza de Urrutia, Pangasinan's alcalde mayor, led a company of two hundred Pampangan soldiers that marched from Bacolor to Cagayan to fight the rebels and end their rebellion. Arza recruited more fighting men as the battalion moved across country. The alcalde and the friars brokered the deployment of an estimated two thousand Cagayanes and another one thousand upland fighting men. The extant sources refer to these mountain dwellers as "Igorots" and "Tinguian," collapsing multiple cultural-linguistic groups into generic categories that make it difficult to identify them more precisely. Although the Spaniards thought of these mountain people as "a cruel and

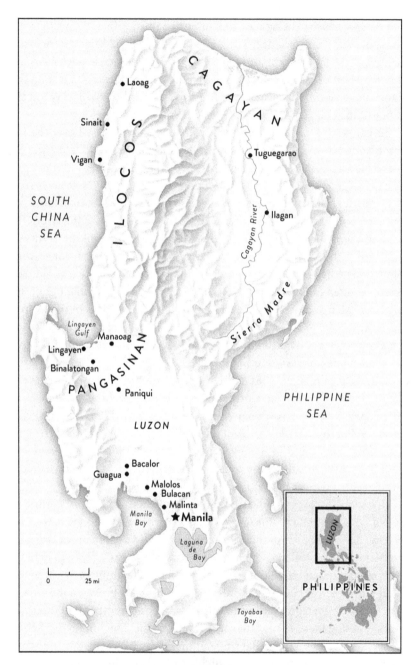

Map 3. This map shows the location of important protests and battles that took place in Luzon in 1763, illustrating the geographic spread of anti-colonial rebellions across the island.

barbarous nation, who eat human flesh and drink human blood," they were eager to forge military alliances with them when it served the empire's needs.[120] This heterogeneous loyalist force defeated the rebels at Tuguegarao. The encounter ended with loyalists dragging rebels out of the church where they had sought refuge. Arza hanged several men that he singled out as the movement's leaders, before withdrawing to fight the war on other fronts.

By the beginning of 1763, the Indigenous rebellions had transitioned into a full-blown anti-colonial war. Many pueblos across Luzon were either fighting or preparing to fight against the loyalist armies that were mobilizing to suppress their revolt with "blood and fire."[121] Major battles between rebel and loyalist armies involved far greater numbers of fighting men than the loyalists' skirmishes with the British forces. In one of the war's largest battles, the two large Catholic armies—one committed to preserving the colonial order, and the other committed to revolutionizing it—clashed at Paniqui on the Agno River in Pangasinan in late February. Both sides suffered heavy casualties, and both sides claimed victory.[122] Insurgents and loyalists alike redirected lifetimes of experience fighting pirates to waging war against their enemies. Rebels drew on intergenerational knowledge of military construction to build fortifications and defensive walls, such as those built between Narvacan and Santa to the south of Vigan using coral and other materials harvested from the sea, and stones brought down from the mountains.[123]

Diego Silang set up a kind of government that mimicked the Spanish colonial administration to organize rebel's war effort and consolidate his leadership. He appointed Cristobel Sales to serve as his *escribiano* (secretary) and recruited several interpreters to manage his correspondence in Spanish, Ilocano, and other languages spoken in Luzon. Silang designated three or four corporals in each pueblo, with many drawn from the ranks of apoderadillos, to strengthen the Silanista presence on the ground.[124] Yet decision-making was distributed across insurgent communities by both necessity and design. Silang's efforts to centralize power in himself and those closest to him were probably less successful than he claimed. Spanish voices also likely exaggerated his authority and the extent to which he was calling the shots.

Negotiation characterized the great Indigenous revolt. The friars who observed the rebellion up close noted its democratic character. The thousands of Indigenous people who had gathered in Vigan at the outset of the rebellion on the fourteenth of December of 1762 had spent the night before they protested in meetings, deliberating over their demands as well as their collective strategies for achieving them.[125] Such assemblies continued to occur

as the insurgency spread from village to village. Silang's apoderadillo supporters traveled from town to town, presenting the case for joining the
revolt to locals. Often they carried letters that Silang had written to the
people, addressing them in their own language.[126] Barangays listened to
what Silang or his representatives had to say to them, and then collectively
decided how to proceed. The collective process meant that entire pueblos
were aligned with or opposed to the revolt at any one time.[127]

Indigenous communities had to weigh up the risk of violence against
them when they were deciding how to respond to the war. Joining the rebellion or the loyalist campaign to suppress it or attempting to remain neutral
all carried a risk of retaliation. Pueblos often made these choices under duress. When the apoderadillo called Caramba from Badoc went to Batac to
recruit the community to the revolt, he allegedly threatened to set the village
on fire if the people refused to support Silang. It was said that the Silanistas
forced their opponents into exile on the uninhabited island of Pingit, leaving
them to survive with only a small rice ration. While it is true that Spaniards
who made such claims were interested in discrediting the revolutionary
movement and its leaders, this kind of threat-making was consistent with
the strategies that apoderadillos used before the war, and they cannot be
shrugged off as imperialist propaganda.[128] As the military historian David
Bell writes, "civil wars are the cruelest of wars. . . . By definition, neither side
recognizes the legitimacy of the other . . . there are no honorable adversaries, only traitors," which contributes to escalating brutality.[129] The insurgency prompted Castro, the Augustinian friar, to confront the centrality of
violence to the Spanish colonial system. He despairingly declared that "only
the fear of our firearms has preserved the colony until now, and not the true
love and loyalty owed to our Catholic and glorious monarch."[130]

Everywhere the insurgency's aims became more radical as the British occupation of Manila dragged on. Early cries for a temporary moratorium on
tribute evolved into the radical demand for tribute abolition as time passed
and the rebels grew in number. Fundamentally, the people who rose up in
rebellion across Luzon sought to abolish the head tax and other core mechanisms through which the colonial state extracted labor and other resources
from their communities. Anti-tribute politics are evident in the rebels' actions
as well as words. In Laoag, mobs broke into the local church and found and
destroyed the registry of tribute payments, which were the records that the
government used to manage the head tax collections over generations.[131]
Pueblos in revolt also wanted to abolish the polo. They condemned mandatory

financial contributions to community chests that ostensibly funded local projects that served the common good, such as purchasing rice to feed villagers when crops failed but that were widely perceived as being a scam that enriched the principalia.[132] They also wanted to axe the *bandala*, the scheme that compelled Indigenous communities to sell the products they produced, such as textiles and cotton, to the colonial government at fixed prices that were well below market rates.[133] Silang echoed common grievances when he repeatedly asserted that this complex system of exploitation impoverished Filipinos. The Spaniards "will let you wear nothing but a loincloth, leaving you only your Christianity," he wrote.[134] Vivar sympathized to a degree, acknowledging that government policies made Indigenous peoples "believe that the Spaniards only want to exploit them."[135] The Philippines insurgency had much in common with the Andean rebellion led by Tupac Amaru two decades later.[136] Like Silang, Tupac Amaru promised his supporters a world in which tribute and forced labor would vanish, a world in which they would be free.

It was not lost on the insurgents that the work that tribute did for empire extended far beyond revenue raising. Anda, a trained lawyer, defended tribute as an important symbolic gesture of fidelity to the Crown, akin to a loyalty oath and other performative acts of submission to the monarchy.[137] Tribute also did heavy lifting in the creation of what historians have called "colonial difference." A head tax on some, tribute strengthened a "sliding scale of inferiority" among imperial subjects that divided colonial society between tributaries, who were Indigenous Filipinos and Chinese migrants and their descendants in the Philippines, and those who were exempt because they were Spaniards and mestizos.[138] Tribute was such a fundamental part of the platform on which Spain's Asian empire stood that abolition threatened to bring it crashing down.

Despite the centrality of tribute to the civil war in Luzon, the armed struggle was more complex than an Indigenous versus Spanish conflict. On some occasions Silang advocated "forming a Christian union between principales and *timawas* (commoners or peasants)," hinting at a pan-Indigenous movement against European empire and settler colonists, or what historians of Latin America have described as a caste war.[139] Yet more frequently, Silang and other leaders of the rebellion pitted the Indigenous common people against the principalia. They condemned Indigenous elites for being complicit in the exploitation of the Indigenous majority and encouraged their followers to seek revenge against these traitors. Silanitas rode into Sinait on horseback shouting, "In God's mercy the time has come to leave our slavery in which the alcaldes mayores and principales have kept us without any concern."[140] Friar Manuel Gutierrez, who replaced Melendez as vicar general of Pangasinan, insisted that Indigenous elites were not part of the insurgency. The rebels "were usually the poorest, the most unknown, the vilest and the lowest of the town. Many of them were known thieves . . . and all were the most vulgar and miserable people."[141]

Discord between peasants and the principalia materialized through numerous confrontations. One of the first things that the people of Ilocos did when they joined the revolt was to set up tribunals in their towns and put the principalia on trial. Benito Estrada, one of Silang's brothers-in-law, oversaw a people's tribunal in Batac, where the timawas forced principales to answer to a litany of crimes. They made local elites pay twenty-peso fines as penalties for their transgressions, and compelled them turn over all of their possessions, including the wives' and daughters' jewelry. The judges—all peasants—then ordered the principales to kneel before them and kiss their hands. Such scenes prompted Vivar to write that "Silang had turned the world upside down, making principales timawas and the timawas principales."[142] Furthermore, in the first months of 1763, Silang put many Ilocano principales under house arrest, moved some to prisons in Vigan, and exiled others to Cagayan, and he ordered his corporals to arrest or kill any who tried to escape.[143] While violence against the principalia clearly attracted supporters to the rebellion, it must have also alienated some factions. Silang must have thought that attacks on the principalia were getting out of hand when he attempted to reign in the violence in March of 1763, disseminating orders that corporals could harm these Indigenous elites only with his prior authorization.[144]

Historians have downplayed the great Indigenous revolt's deeply Catholic character, even though this saturates the archive.[145] The insurgents framed their struggle as a holy war against invading sea-robbers. Appropriating Catholic anti-piracy to lend legitimacy to the movement, Diego Silang repeatedly asserted his commitment to fighting against the British to defend Catholicism in the Philippines, and he called on the people to join his campaign to save the islands for God and the king of Spain.[146] Imitating the language that priests used to talk about their roles as spiritual leaders of communities, Silang described himself as a minister of God and a shepherd protecting his flock. He repeatedly claimed that God himself was responsible for the rebellion; as God was all-powerful, how could it be otherwise? "Not even a leaf on a tree moves unless it is God's will," he reasoned in one of his letters, and this almighty God had chosen Silang to lead this sacred rebellion.[147]

Silang appointed himself *cabo mayor* (major corporal) in his Catholic army, reserving the higher rank of general for the revered image of the Nazarene Christ whose sanctuary was in Sinait. This life-size carved wooden image of Jesus was discovered by a local fisherman in 1620 and was believed to have floated across the ocean to Ilocos from Japan, where Catholics were facing persecution and exile. This image was miraculous. It sweated scented oils and cried salty tears. In 1756, Ilocanos carried the Nazarene to Vigan to end the epidemic that was ravaging the city. The Nazarene conquered this sickness, encouraging more devotees. Pilgrims traveled from across the region to attend the weekly Friday masses at the Nazarene's sanctuary, and brimming crowds participated in the annual celebration of the image's discovery.[148] Silanistas fashioned a scepter and a small golden helmet for the Nazarene Christ—symbols of military and political power—to acknowledge and honor its role in their war. Silang insisted that this image of God was directing the campaign.[149]

The Nazarene was a defining element of Silanista culture. Soldiers in the rebel Catholic army marched into battle under flags bearing the image of the Nazarene Christ or his name.[150] They adopted a uniform of sorts, wearing clothes bearing Catholic symbols and donning rope necklaces that held carved figures of Christ close to their hearts.[151] When loyalist troops captured the sixty-year-old Silanista Antonio de la Cruz in late December of 1762, he was wearing a white cloak emblazoned with a cross. Cruz had multiple items hidden in his clothing, including "a fruit called *ojo de gato* (eye of the cat), a slice of ginger, and a tiny piece of paper stuck to a ball of wax, and some small leaves, and dried betel leaf." Loyalist soldiers suspected that these objects were evidence of some kind of witchcraft or dark magic. Cruz argued that at least some of them had medicinal properties; the ojo de gato and the ginger eased the swelling and pain in his arthritic knees. For Silanistas, some of these items and religious objects would have doubled as talismans that afforded protection, shielding their bodies from the enemy's bullets and arrows. Convictions in such potent objects blended Filipino conceptions of power as a real force that could be physically accumulated in amulets known as anting-anting and European Catholic traditions of miraculous objects, including those that protected fighting men in war.[152]

Catholicism manifest in the spaces of the insurgency. The houses where Diego Silang resided during the war were marked by forms of domestic devotion that were familiar to Ilocanos. Walls were adorned with stamped prints and paintings of saints, and candles that burned on temporary altars filled the rooms with a flickering light and a warm yellow glow that evoked the sacred space of a chapel. The insurgents also practiced Catholic rituals. Silang frequently prayed the rosary, a set of prayers in honor of Mary, the mother of God, and he ordered his troops and other followers to do the same.[153] In early 1763, the rebel leader also urged the people of Ilocos to observe Lent, the forty-day liturgical period leading up to the Catholic festival of Easter that is traditionally devoted to somber self-reflection and self-denial through fasting. Silang encouraged "meditations on the words and sufferings of our Lord Jesus Christ, and prayer for souls in purgatory." He prohibited his followers from gambling on playing cards and cockfighting, getting drunk, or engaging in love affairs during Lent, and he threatened to punish those who indulged.[154] Silang was cultivating God's favor through these collective sacrifices and devotions, seeking divine intervention to protect his army and deliver victory. Like many Indigenous people in the islands, the rebel leader likely also regarded such asceticism in the Lenten season as a means of transferring power to people and to anting-anting.[155]

The revolt's religious elements were not extraordinary in the Philippines or in the larger Iberian and Catholic world in this era. Across the global Spanish empire in the eighteenth century, saints and Catholic symbols assumed central roles in Indigenous revolts against colonial governments. The 1769 Otomí rebellion in the central Mexican Sierra de Tutotepec has interesting parallels to the Philippines' insurgency. The Otomí man Diego Agustín who led this movement claimed to be divine and able to communicate with God. He persuaded his followers to stop paying money to priests and tribute to the king. He instructed them to build a staircase on top of a mountain from where God was going to ascend to earth and revolutionize colonial society, ensuring that Indigenous people would take the place of Spaniards and Spaniards would take the place of Indigenous people. The rebels decorated the staircase with crosses, and they prayed in a temple in front of an altar adorned with images of the Virgin of Guadalupe, sacred obsidian stones said to be the heart of God, and a mask carved from green stone that represented the God of maize.[156] Mexico's viceroy mobilized a military campaign that suppressed this Otomí movement with force. Communities in central Mexico continued to incorporate the Virgin of Guadalupe in armed struggles against empire. The image emerged as an important symbol in Mexico's wars of independence in the early nineteenth century. Armies fighting against empire marched into battle waving flags that bore the image of the Mexican Marian apparition.[157]

Stiff opposition from the clergy posed a serious problem for a Catholic army. Friars in Luzon unilaterally refused to back the Indigenous revolts. In Pangasinan, popular support for the Palaris rebellion began to wane after Spaniards were expelled from the province. Although rebel leaders exempted priests from expulsion, many clergymen chose to abandon the province out of fear, or in protest; they wanted their absence to hurt the revolutionary movement. Diego Silang made serious attempts to win the friars' favor. He was appropriately deferent in letters he addressed to the clergy. In one letter to a friar, for example, Silang described himself "bowing before your feet, like the image of God that you are on earth."[158] When such overtures did not have the desired effects, rebel leaders took steps to isolate the clergy from the people and limit the damage they could cause to the anti-colonial campaign. The rebel leader Pedro Leonardo dispatched orders to towns in rebellion across Ilocos to bring their priests to the convent in his hometown of Narvacan, roughly twenty kilometers south of Vigan, where they could presumably be more easily brought under rebel control.[159] Silang denied issuing this order, labeling it an "entirely cruel trick of the devil.[160] Rebels forced other missionaries to remain in their convents under a kind of house arrest. Pedro Vivar was effectively imprisoned in his parish residence in Batac for the duration of the revolt in 1763 and into 1764. Many captive friars managed to escape their guards and run away to the mountains.[161]

The insurgency's fate was determined in battle. In March of 1763, insurgents and loyalists clashed in Bayambang, a town along the Agno River in Pangasinan. The loyalist forces included a regiment of the Pampangan militia headed by Captain Joseph Manalastas, in addition to fighting men from Ilocos, Cagayan, and Pangasinan, and "a troop of well-armed, clear eyed, and brave native Bataanes" accompanied by their chaplain, Fray Diego Zurita. They found the rebels waiting for them, protected by fortified trenches along the riverbank lined with *lantaka*, the small cannon that Hispano-Filipino armadas carried aboard the ships that chased Moro pirates on the ocean. The loyalists broke through these defenses and defeated the rebels. Shortly afterward, towns in Pangasinan sent representatives to Anda to broker peace.[162] Ilocos remained in revolt. The following chapter examines how the loyalist army was able to strangle and defeat the insurgency later that year.

The British retained control of Intramuros at this time as the anti-colonial war raged across Luzon, but Governor Drake's army struggled to extend its

authority beyond the occupied walled city. The heterogeneous British forces
and the loyalists deployed guerrilla tactics against each other around the capital and its hinterland. Loyalist units attacked the boats that the British had
seized or purchased to explore the island's navigable waterways, killed the
soldiers and crew on board, and sent their bloated bodies floating downriver
to Intramuros.[163] Fighting men loyal to Spain also murdered and decapitated
fighting men in the British forces who strayed from the relative safety of large
groups.[164] British troops continued to assault fortified churches around Manila. Captain Jeremiah Sleigh took the church at Matolos "by storm" after a
two-hour siege in January. Yet Sleigh noted that he did not think that the British could capture and hold any additional territory, "as the country is all in
arms."[165] The British faced increasingly trying circumstances in the Intramuros. The loyalists were blockading the roads and rivers leading into Manila
and were succeeding in starving the invaders of essential supplies. As the
Spanish fiscal of Manila, Leandro de Viana, noted, there was "no beef in the
butcher shop, not even for the English governor."[166] It was difficult for anyone to see how the British could hold out in the walled city for much longer.

Conclusion

Six months after the British captured Intramuros, their grip on the capital
was exceedingly weak. The invaders had found some firm friends among the
occupied population, including Sultan Azim ud-Din and his son, a handful
of traitorous Spaniards and other European Manileños, in addition to many
Sangleyes in and around Manila, and at least some Indigenous rebels beyond
the capital. But these allies were too few to sustain the British occupation
over an extended period of time, or to transform Luzon into a British colony. The fact that the British had followed the pirate playbook—attacking
from the sea, sacking and destroying churches and venerated sacred objects, as well as countless homes—only encouraged people to support the
loyalist campaign to dislodge them from the islands. It was equally clear to
Dawsonne Drake and to Simón de Anda's camps that the days of the British
in Manila were numbered. Drake described how his government and their
soldiers were "besieged by our unjust and unreasonable enemies. Their bar-
barities shocked human nature, murdering in all corners, cutting off and
harassing those that dared to fetch us provisions; so that we were obliged to
send out parties to fight for our subsistence." The invaders were resigned to

defeat. "Continued scenes of this kind . . . tried the patience of the (Manila) Council, who began to look upon themselves as lost to pleasure, interest and the world itself," Drake wrote.[167]

Yet at this juncture, the fate of the anti-colonial revolt that had erupted in the aftermath of Spain's temporary loss of Manila was less certain. One missionary wrote that "we find ourselves deafened and shocked" in the face of the insurgency.[168] These radical anti-colonial movements had absorbed vast numbers of diverse peoples across Luzon, from the salt-making coastal Pangasinense to Ilocanos, Cagayanes, and the Igorots of the mist-covered cordillera. The invasion from the sea had instigated a fundamental shift in relations between Spanish colonial officials and friars and Chinese and Indigenous communities in Luzon, creating conditions where subalterns were emboldened to attempt to reset the colonial bargain, demanding tribute abolition and the termination of forced labor, if not to oust the Spanish entirely. Like rebellions against colonial rule that manifest in other parts of the Iberian world in this era, the insurgency in the Philippines was a profoundly Catholic social movement. Its leaders encouraged Catholic devotions, and their followers marched into battle waving flags that bore Catholic symbols and wearing crosses and other amulets on their bodies to obtain divine protection. Although a shared Catholic faith and the politics of Catholic anti-piracy ultimately strengthened Spanish colonial rule in Luzon, the revolts against empire demonstrate that these ideologies simultaneously provided Indigenous rebels with ready-made frameworks to articulate their values and ideals and organize toward the goal of ending exploitation across ethnolinguistic divides.

Notwithstanding the magnitude of this crisis, Anda continued to have faith in the clergy's power to rally a multiethnic loyalist army to defeat the insurgency in addition to the British invaders and restore Spanish rule and the colonial order. Spain's Asian empire remained capable of mobilizing diverse soldiers and weapons against its challengers. It could claw back territory and tribute-payers despite losing Intramuros and effective control over so much of the region and so many of its people. The following chapter turns to these loyalist forces and recovers the history of their hard-won victory.

CHAPTER 4

The Loyalist Army and the Great War

When the silver-laden *Filipino* galleon arrived in the Philippine islands in March of 1763 on the final leg of its transpacific voyage to Manila, the ship was intercepted by a group of men who delivered the alarming news that the British had conquered Manila. Not only had the Spanish been forced out of Intramuros by foreign invaders, they had also lost control of huge swaths of Luzon to Indigenous insurgents. Simón de Anda y Salazar, one of the Spanish oidores (judges) in Manila's Audiencia, had established a government-in-exile in Pampanga. Militant missionaries and Indigenous and Chinese mestizo community leaders were cooperating with Anda to mobilize a massive loyalist army that was now embroiled in a multifront war against the British invaders and the insurgents. In the small town of Palapag on the island of Samar in the Visayas, the galleon's passengers, who included thirty Augustinian friars, worked with Franciscan missionaries and local people to unload the galleon's treasure. They smuggled at least one and a half million silver pesos over sea and over land to Anda's camp while British Royal Navy vessels kept up their hunt for the coveted ship.[1] In April, after months of searching, the British found the *Filipino* galleon run aground and empty.[2] The huge amount of silver that Spain's King Charles III had sent to Manila to shore up the colony's defenses against Moro sea-robbers was redirected to the war against the new pirate menace in the archipelago.

The hostilities that began with the British invasion of Manila quickly transformed into a total war that upended the lives of communities across much of the large island, resulting in displacement and death on an unprecedented scale. One missionary who survived the war called these "revolutionary times."[3] For the people who lived through this tumultuous period, the immediate future of the Spanish empire in Asia seemed uncertain, and colonial rule came closer to collapse than it ever had in their lifetimes. The wars of 1762–1764 forced men and women across the Philippines to make difficult decisions. Would they throw their lot in with the invaders or the insurgents and seize this chance to destroy or remake the colonial order? Or would they back the loyalist army and join its campaign against the empire's enemies in a bid to restore Spanish rule? Trying to remain autonomous and survive in their own pueblos or in the relative safety of the mountains was another option. Yet all of these choices were risky in the context of a bloody and protracted war. All of the factions embroiled in this conflict—the British, the Spanish and their diverse allies, and the insurgents—showed a readiness to harshly punish and even kill anyone who refused to support them. The people who were swept up in this complex conflict had to make these choices multiple times, and often altered their political and survival strategies as the war progressed and tides turned.

Whereas the previous chapter focused on the rebellions that broke out against Spanish colonial rule, this chapter centers on the multitude who fell in behind the loyalist army and put their lives on the line to defend Spanish sovereignty. The loyalists who waged war against the British and homegrown rebels were arguably the most diverse fighting force that saw action anywhere in the eighteenth-century world. The majority of loyalist fighting men were Indigenous people who belonged to multiple ethnolinguistic groups in the Philippines. The loyalist army also recruited people of the Chinese diaspora, including Chinese mestizos, in addition to Mexicans, Spaniards, and other European and South Asian soldiers who defected from the invading British forces.[4] British officers wrote condescendingly about the army's motley character, and the conspicuous presence of priests in its ranks. One remarked that "they cannot think of the followers of Mr. Anda merit any other name than rabble, as they are composed of Indian vagabonds, robbers, assassins—and a few deserters headed by disorderly and irreligious friars (who contrary to the cannons of the Roman Catholic Church take up arms). . . . Can such troops headed by such leaders deserve any other name?"[5] The loyalist army was also large by early modern standards. Approximately four thousand Indigenous Filipino fighting men came from the provinces to defend Manila with firearms, arrows, lances, and machetes during the siege of the city in the first week of October in 1762.[6] In May the following year, British officers estimated that "12000 people are kept in the pay of Señor Anda."[7] Eyewitnesses estimated that twenty thousand people took part in the battle between loyalist and rebels at Vigan at the end of July. And when the war finally ended in March of 1764, some five thousand soldiers accompanied Anda when he triumphantly marched into Intramuros to formally retake possession of the walled city.[8]

This chapter presents the first in-depth study of the heavily Indigenous loyalist forces that fought against the Spanish empire's adversaries in Luzon during the Seven Years' War. Previous studies of the war in the Philippines have marginalized subaltern loyalists to the point of erasing them. Both Spanish- and English-language scholarship on this conflict have traditionally focused on the personalities and strategies that the European leaders of the rival imperial armed forces pursued when they clashed in the Pacific, overlooking Indigenous and Chinese actors.[9] Following a markedly different path, interpretations of the war developed within the proudly nationalist Philippines historiographical tradition have emphasized recovering and celebrating the great Indigenous revolts.[10] Today monuments across the archipelago memorialize the leaders of these rebellions. A bronze bust of Diego Silang stands in Manila's Rizal Park, and an equestrian statue of Gabriela Silang waving a kampilan high above her head guards Ayala Avenue in Makati City. These heroes are honored as freedom fighters who paid the ultimate price in their armed struggle against colonial rule. In contrast, the thousands of Indigenous troops who died defending empire have been excised from public space and public memory.

Loyalists deserve our attention. In defeating the British and suppressing the massive Indigenous uprising that shook the colony to its core, they laid the foundations for another one and a half centuries of Spanish rule in the islands. This chapter develops a profile of the loyalist army, revealing who joined its ranks and how. It examines the plural factors that pushed and pulled fighting men into its battalions. Galleon silver certainly mattered, incentivizing fighters to join the cause for king and Church. Yet Catholic antipiracy also ensured that the polity was well prepared and willing to combat a new pirate enemy and suppress an Indigenous revolt. The deeply rooted tradition of fighting sea-robbers meant that every town in the Philippines was "a sleeping army."[11] Priests and barangays were armed and ready to fight. Like the colonial society's previous pirate wars, loyalists conceptualized this military campaign as a holy war, providing the army with ideological ammunition. The final section of the chapter considers how and why the loyalists were able to defeat the British army and the Indigenous revolt. It illustrates that bargaining and negotiation continued to play important roles in fostering support for reconstituting Spanish sovereignty in the Philippines from the bottom up, albeit in the context of extreme violence. Diego Silang wrote that the loyalists "finished" their enemies with "blood and fire," coercing masses of unenthusiastic vassals to submit to a system that they resented.[12] It is not a stretch to argue that the key to understanding the longevity and resilience of Spanish rule in the Philippines lies in comprehending how loyalists conceived of the world they inhabited and their places within it, and their corresponding choices and actions in this period of crisis.

Dissecting the Rabble: The Composition of the Loyalist Forces

The enormous and heterogeneous loyalist army that waged war against the British invaders and Indigenous and Chinese insurgents was fundamentally polycentric, absorbing the standing army's battalions, existing colonial militias, and new armed units.[13] Simón de Anda attempted to coordinate and control the army's actions across a large territory. The exiled governor relied on a network of friars, secretaries, translators, and couriers to transmit intelligence and commands between his war council and the various and volatile fronts where the army was deployed. Yet there were limits to Anda's capacity to direct this military campaign, especially as war impeded the circulation of men and information across a large and difficult terrain. The loyalist army effectively comprised many interlinked units that interacted with Anda's government-in-exile, and also among themselves. In 1762 and 1763, priests and Indigenous and Chinese mestizo leaders took charge of recruiting and organizing fighting men at the pueblo level, as they had traditionally done to confront other pirate threats. Most of the armed bands that mobilized in the loyalist army were less formal than the militias that existed across the Spanish empire at this time. In the rush of moving men into war in this emergency situation, soldiers' names and other details that could shed light on their identities and life experiences were generally not recorded. Nonetheless, it is possible to build a composite picture of the loyalist forces from an array of sources found in multiple archives using methods that historians have developed to study armies and militias in colonial Latin America.[14]

There were approximately five hundred priests in the Philippines when the British invaded Manila, and many of them were prominent in the loyalist military campaign.[15] The small Saint John of God missionary order was the only one in the islands that refused to recognize Anda's authority during the war, choosing instead to obey orders handed down by Archbishop Rojo, who had surrendered to the British. Anda condemned these friars for betraying

Spain. He called their decision to supply black cattle from their hacienda to the British a "public act of disloyalty to his Catholic majesty."[16] All of the other religious orders in the Philippines were devoted to winning the two-front war against the British and the insurgent rebels.

Like the better-known militant Jesuit missionaries in Paraguay, priests in the Philippines became soldiers in 1762 and 1763, taking up arms against their enemies. The Augustinian friar Castro y Amuedo's vivid account of the battle between the British and loyalist forces at Bulacan celebrated the heroic efforts of soldier-priests. Castro recalled that Friar Agustín de San Antonio valiantly mounted a horse with his sword in hand and charged at enemy lines, conjuring up an image that evoked the mythical figure of Santiago the moor-slayer.[17] Historians are trained to read accounts like Castro's with skepticism, recognizing that friars had a penchant for producing hagiographic martyrdom narratives that exaggerated the bravery of their fellow missionaries on the battlefield. However, British sources also underscore the clergy's visible participation in battles, leading us to put our agnosticism aside. Dawsonne Drake condemned "the Augustine Friars [who] . . . appeared in arms, contrary to their ecclesiastical functions thereby occasioning the effusion of much human blood."[18] Surely the devout among Luzon's multiethnic society were more willing to go into battle when they could do so alongside priests.

Besides fighting, priests provided logistical support that was essential to raising and sustaining a large army. The religious orders helped to feed troops. The Augustinians, for example, brought cattle and rice from their haciendas to Intramuros to feed soldiers during the siege of the walled city.[19] Franciscan missionaries worked to smuggle huge amounts of silver to Anda, organizing men and boats to transport the contents of the royal treasury from Manila to the first loyalist headquarters at Bacolor.[20] Drawing on their experiences digging trenches and building walls to protect coastal pueblos from Moro pirate attacks, missionaries helped to fortify pueblos facing assaults from the British and local insurgents.[21] They also worked diligently to arm Anda's fighting men. Padre Montero, the parish priest at Lipa, stashed gunpowder in his church for the loyalists.[22] Another priest, Juan Facundo de Acosta, oversaw gunpowder production at the factory that the loyalist army established in exile.[23] Significantly, many of the weapons and munitions that friars turned over to the loyalists came from the Church's anti-piracy stockpiles. In late 1762, the Franciscan Provincial Fray Roque de la Purificación gave Anda forty rifles that he had amassed "all these years to resist the Moros who continually persecute" families living in Franciscan missions.[24] Anda collected another cache of firearms and gunpowder from the Playa Honda Fort. The loyalist army had to cast a wider net for weapons and munitions after a year of fighting. In November of 1763, the governor-in-exile sent Francisco Arburu and Juan Morera to collect firearms and shot from presidios and churches in Leyte and Palapa in the Visayan islands, and to the Camarines and Albay on the southern tip of Luzon.[25]

The *Regimiento del Rey* (King's Regiment), the standing army in the Philippines, was a core component of the loyalist forces that mobilized in 1762–1764. There were approximately 2,400 soldiers in the Regiment distributed across the Philippines when the British invaded.[26] The regiment was formally divided into a Spanish company and a Pampangan company, with Pampangans making up approximately one-third of all soldiers in this colony-wide unit. Two thirds of the regiment's forces were stationed within a twenty-league radius of Intramuros. Colonial nomenclature can be confusing. Very few *peninsulares* or Spain-born men served in the Spanish company. This unit included career soldiers recruited from Manila's creole or Philippines-born population, such as Alexandro Carballo, who enlisted as a twenty-one-year-old cadet in 1757. Indigenous Filipinos and *castas* were officially permitted to enlist in the regiment from 1757 onward, paving the way for men like Joachin Villaseñor, a "mestizo español," and Antonio Latinos, a "mestizo de Armenio," to join as young cadets before the end of that decade.[27] The majority of the men in the Spanish company were born in New Spain.[28] The galleons that arrived in Manila each year were full of Mexican soldiers. Most were *forzados* (convicts) who had been sentenced to complete terms of penal servitude on the frontier of the Spanish Empire for a range of criminal offenses, including vagabondage, robbery, and sexual transgressions. This forced migration across the Pacific was a utilitarian policy that cleansed Mexico's cities and highways of unruly men and boys who disrupted the social order, and it produced cheap soldiers and workers to defend distant colonies.[29]

Although previous studies of Mexican convict soldiers in the Philippines have emphasized that forzados "were engaged in an almost constant mutiny" against the colonial system, Spanish and British sources present compelling evidence that these forced migrants participated in the loyalist campaign in large numbers.[30] Castro praised the four hundred Mexicans who defended Manila's city walls during the siege. The British Captain Jeremiah Sleigh estimated that the loyalist forces that warded off his attack on Matolos in January 1763 numbered four hundred men and included "three priests, an alcalde, and great many *Guachinangoes*," which was the term that the British used to describe these Mexican soldiers.[31] The British shipped "331 Guatchi-nangoe prisoners" from Manila to Madras in February that year when they accepted that the forzados could not be convinced to switch sides and support their government.[32] What happened to them after they were shipped out of Manila is unknown.

As noted above, Indigenous Filipinos accounted for the overwhelming majority of loyalist fighters. Anda singled out the Pampangans as the Spanish empire's staunchest allies. He established his government-in-exile in Bacolor on the basis of Pampangans' renowned fidelity to the Crown. The king of Spain would later issue a royal order acknowledging the "outstanding services of the Indians of the Pampanga Province" during the war.[33] Hundreds of Pampangan troops in the loyalist army had already belonged to the Regimiento del Rey when the war broke out, and many more enlisted during the military campaign. The recruitment of Indigenous soldiers was organized at the local level in pueblos and barangays with strong communal structures. The formation of the Pampangan *Compañia de Alabarderos* (Pikemen Company) in mid-1763 left an archival trail that offers unique insight into local recruitment processes. This military unit was established as a personal bodyguard for Simón de Anda, and it exclusively signed up men who were the firstborn sons of the Pampangan principalia, such as the twenty-five-year-old Don Joseph Cayanan Macaspac, the son of Bacolor principales Don Lucas Cayanan y Doña Manuela Ayang.[34] The gobernadorcillos and cabezas de barangays of sixteen Pampangan pueblos each selected three men to serve in this prestigious company. It illustrates that Indigenous militias reflected the hierarchical character of colonial Philippines society. The Alabarderos soldiers were paid three pesos each month in addition to a rice ration, which was more than what other Indigenous soldiers were paid in other military units.

Pampangans were only one of many ethnolinguistic groups across Luzon and the Visayas that joined the loyalist army. Tagalogs, Cagayanes, Ilocanos, Pangasinense, and other Indigenous fighting men from lowland regions across Luzon as well as from the upland cordillera also went to war to preserve Spanish rule. Captain Don Joseph Manalastas, for example, led his countrymen into battle against rebels in Ilocos in 1763, supported by a "well armed, clear-eyed, and courageous" militia from the neighboring Bataan region. An estimated two thousand "indios" from Bohol island in the Visayas accompanied Miguel Lino de Ezpeleta, the archbishop of Cebú, to Bulacan to join the loyalists.[35] The pueblo-based recruitment model that funneled men to the Alabarderos company was replicated across Luzon and the Visayas. Anda and other regionally powerful colonial officials and priests issued pueblos emotive calls or demands for fighting men. It was up to the town to determine who among them would go to war.[36]

The Catholic clergy recruited parishioners into loyalist militias and directed their activities during the Philippines' Seven Years' War. Shortly after Manila fell, fifteen hundred Indigenous fighters "all armed for war" arrived in Pagsanjan, the capital of the Laguna province that comprised a cluster of Tagalog towns surrounding Lake Taal, fifty kilometers south of Manila.[37] Three Franciscan friars led this militia—Fray Bernardo del Corral, the parish priest at Majayjay, Fray Pedro Gea from Lucban, and Fray Miguel de Victoria of Tayabas.[38] They had come because Nicolás Beaumont y Echauz, the Spanish colonial government's treasurer, was in town with other exiled Spanish colonial officials and the contents of the royal treasury. Beaumont had evacuated over one hundred thousand silver pesos from Manila with the help of a small army of porters, soldiers, boatsmen, and pilots, supported by six horses, sixty carabao, and many boats.[39] Rumors had reached the friars that these Spanish officials were planning to surrender the treasure to the British, and they were determined to use the Franciscan-Tagalog militia to halt this treasonous betrayal. The friars went to the house of Laguna's alcalde mayor, Don Manuel Cano del Monte, and demanded that he hand over the king's silver. Fray Pedro Gea walked into the house with a sword strapped to his belt shouting, "Viva the faith in God and Death to traitors! Viva the king of Spain!" Corral followed closely behind with a shotgun in his hand. The surprised officials tried to persuade the priests that they were not traitors. The priests told them to shut up. Treasurer Beaumont saw that he had little choice but to hand over the keys to the convent where the silver was stored. The Franciscans and the Tagalog militiamen proceeded to relocate the silver to Corral's church and convent at Majayjay the next day, and they fortified the sacred building to protect the treasure.[40]

The friars' spiritual and military training had prepared them well for the war against the British, and corrupt Spanish government officials if it came to that. Corral, a Toledo-born Spaniard, had joined the Franciscan missionary order with dreams of going to China. Perhaps he wished for "martyrdom, a glorious death that the East Asian missions seemed to offer in spades."[41] But the Qing persecution of Christians in China meant that Corral was sent to the Philippines instead, and it was here that he was given his chance to fight and die for Christ.[42] For two decades before the British invasion, Corral had

lived and worked on the Mauban coast in central eastern Luzon, a region that
was "continuously invaded by Moros."[43] He gained military experience fighting pirates that equipped him to confront a new breed of sea-robbers. The
conflict between the Franciscans and exiled colonial officials over control of
the silver was short-lived and can be attributed to the disruption of the invasion that threw the colony into chaos, and these parties were soon collaborating. Corral went on to command a large militia unit from Majayjay and
surrounding Franciscan pueblos that engaged in guerrilla warfare against the
British.[44] He got his hands dirty digging trenches and building forts alongside Indigenous workers, including the elderly and young children. Corral's
Franciscan-Tagalog company blocked supplies from reaching the British occupying army. It marched through Manila's hinterland stealing or setting fire
to enemy boats traveling up and down the river, and it seized cattle that British soldiers had commandeered to kill and eat. The Laguna militias also
went into battle in the town of Guadalupe, killing some English soldiers and
taking others as prisoners.

The Indigenous soldiers who took up arms against Indigenous rebels in
Pangasinan, Ilocos, and Cagayan were mostly native to these provinces, and
the mobilization of fighting men remained locally organized in these regions.
Towns tended to act as blocks in these insurgent provinces, with pueblos or
barangays collectively deciding whether they would support or oppose the
revolt, or to attempt to remain neutral. The residents of the small town of
Asingan in Pangasinan opposed the revolution and remained loyal to the
Spanish colonial government and the Crown throughout the war. Other
towns wavered, assessing and reassessing their position as time passed and
circumstances changed. In the insurgent regions, priests and loyalist Indigenous leaders worked to persuade pueblos to support them and contribute
men to fight for their cause. In July of 1763 for example, Mathias de la Cruz
wrote to communities in Abagatan—the southern region of Ilocos—asking
each pueblo to send a contingent of thirty men to fight against the rebels in
the north, leaving it up to the pueblos to decide whom they would dispatch.
This militia draft mimicked the emergency system that sent men to meet
Moro pirates seen approaching coastal settlements.[45]

The Chinese mestizo militia that joined with the loyalist forces was
crucial to the campaign to restore Spanish sovereignty in Manila and Luzon,
contrary to the recent claim by some historians that this armed body was
"merely window-dressing for status-conscious mestizos."[46] At least four
Chinese mestizo militia units saw action in the war. Its members built and

defended fortifications, including the large fort with trenches and batteries on the Polo River at Tinajeros. Located roughly nine kilometers north of Intramuros, this fort successfully impeded British attempts to push outward from the walled center of Manila into the hinterland, and cut off food and other essential supplies from reaching the invading army's base. Mestizo militias also saw action in combat. Vigan's large Chinese mestizo community, for example, sent fighting men to meet rebels in battle in the city and its hinterland.[47]

In the Chinese mestizo militias we can discern a level of autonomy that characterized the larger loyalist army. Wealthy Chinese mestizos who were respected by powerful Spaniards and the Chinese mestizo community in Manila and its hinterland played key roles in the management of the militia, as well as directing its military activities. Rich mestizos de Sangley funded these units with their personal wealth. Antonio Tuason, the gobernadorcillo of the Binondo mestizos, donated money to pay for their clothing and food.[48] Matheo de Los Angeles headed up the militia unit. Los Angeles had a long history of serving the Crown prior to the war. In the mid-1740s he traveled to Spain to deliver a rare white deer captured in the mountains of Laguna de Bay to King Fernando VI, a gift from the Philippines governor. After returning to Manila in the early 1750s, he set up a home in the multiethnic neighborhood of Santa Cruz, where he found work as an interpreter.[49] As Chapter 2 noted, Los Angeles donated silver and weapons to the Philippines' war against the Moro pirates in 1751.[50] He is a good example of a person whose experience fighting Moros was seamlessly redirected toward a new British enemy.

Despite the faithful service of Chinese mestizo militiamen, Chinese migrants and their families were vulnerable to violence from Spanish colonial officials and the wider colonial community during the war due to fears that they were traitors. The lines separating Chinese migrants and Chinese mestizos blurred in wartime. Sangleyes and their descendants faced increasing surveillance and abuse after the 1762 Christmas conspiracy and the Bacolor massacre, which were discussed in the previous chapter. The archive gestures to other mass Chinese killings during the war. In February of 1763, for example, Anda ordered Manuel de Los Angeles to kill the Chinese in Angat, a pueblo in Bulacan Province.[51] Anda also prohibited Sangleyes from having weapons in their homes or on their person, and ordered local officials to execute any Sangley found in possession of a weapon.[52] Moreover, to restrict Chinese migrants' mobility, Anda issued orders that Sangleyes across Luzon were to present themselves to the *gobernador de naturales* in their villages three times a day, at morning, noon, and sunset, and prescribed a penalty of twenty-five lashes to punish noncompliance. In addition, he ordered Sangl-eyes to obtain written permission from pueblo officials to travel outside of their hometown. Anyone breaking these rules was to be punished with fifty lashes and a six-peso fine.

At the same time as he ramped up repressive restrictions on Chinese mi-grants, Anda refused to accept that their disloyalty to Spain was inevitable. In May of 1763, public notices printed in Spanish and Hanzi and signed by Anda appeared in Santa Cruz, a Manila neighborhood that had a large Chi-nese and Chinese mestizo population. These notices announced a general pardon for Chinese people who remained in the area on the condition that they register their presence and refrain from taking up arms against Span-iards or assisting the invaders in any other way.[53] During the war, British as-sumptions of Chinese disloyalty to the Spanish enabled some to be effective double agents. In mid-1763, British captains began to realize that the "Chi-nese are employed as spies" for the loyalists.[54] Captain Backhouse captured the "Chinese mestizo" Juan de la Cruz in possession of an incriminating com-mission signed by the Spanish general Bustos, and with a "list of soldiers" that he had ostensibly recruited to the cause. Cruz had allegedly escorted a group of ten or twelve Chinese men to a village just outside of Manila who all had commissions from Anda "to act as Spies upon all occasions." Cruz's cooperation with the Spaniards cost him his life. Backhouse insisted on "hanging this villain, and every other Commissary that I can catch," in order to discourage other Chinese from working to undermine the British campaign.[55]

Of course, for Chinese migrants there were alternatives to siding with Anda or Drake. Anecdotal evidence points to many deciding the flee from the Philippines and the dangers that the clash of global empires in Manila posed to them. Some Chinese Manileños profiteered from the invasion with-out backing either imperial power. British officers frequently complained about Chinese shopkeepers in the Parián getting rich from swapping Span-ish silver coins for rupees at unfair exchange rates. Captain Backhouse also accused the Chinese of counterfeiting coins, manufacturing "bad barillas, ru-pees or dollars" that they passed on to soldiers, but "refused to take again the moment after issued from their hands."[56] Self-interest and survival trumped siding with either European empire.

European and South Asian deserters from the British invading forces were a small but very visible contingent in Anda's army. By early 1763, the loyalist army incorporated three ethnically homogeneous infantry companies formed entirely of "English, French, and Malabar" deserters.[57] The twenty-three-year-old Scot "Carlos Murrai" fled to Anda's army in April 1763 and was quickly promoted to corporal in the *Compania Inglesa* (English Company).[58] "Enrrique Willson," a twenty-one-year-old native of Plymouth, joined the company in March 1763 and became a captain by September.[59] "Monsuir Bretaña" led a company of "120 Frenchmen who deserted from the enemy."[60] The French defected en masse to the Spanish camp as soon as they arrived in the Philippines. It was rumored that an entire French garrison stole themselves away from the British camp in the dead of night disguised in women's clothes.[61] In February 1763, Drake was compelled to place his remaining French troops under lock and barrel on prison ships anchored in Manila Bay to prevent more of these highly skilled soldiers from running away and bolstering enemy forces.[62] Castro praised the highly skilled European artillerymen who fought with the loyalists in the May 1763 battle against the British at Malinta. "It was God's wish that one of our artillerymen, a Frenchman, landed a good shot on the enemy's gunpowder barrels that exploded and sent men flying."[63] This disaster forced the enemy to retreat. Several hundred deserters remained in Manila and in the Spanish colonial military forces after the war.[64]

Death and desertion depleted the British forces in Manila. When East India Company officials in Madras began making arrangements to evacuate their army from the Philippines in September 1763, on the first anniversary of the invasion, the Madras Governor George Pigot admitted that "if we receive one half of the number sent it will exceed our expectation."[65] Only eight hundred soldiers remained in the British service by March 1764.[66]

Fighting women remain largely absent from the war's surviving written records, with the significant exception of Gabriela Silang, who replaced her husband Diego as leader of the revolt in Ilocos after his death. It is significant that the Spanish voices that discussed Gabriela's role in the war that they lived through did not convey surprise that a woman had joined or even become a leader in the armed revolt, as this suggests that Gabriela was not exceptional in this regard. As the previous chapter illustrated, some armed women defended Manila in the siege of the city.[67] An Indigenous woman named María Lenor Josepha, a member of the principalia, earned a mythological status for killing Diego Silang. She is celebrated for this deed in the triumphal painting *Alegoría de la defensa de Filipinas por el Alavés don Simón de Anda*.[68] This apocryphal history signifies a more widespread presence of fighting women in the loyalist forces. Indigenous women were visible in anti-colonial movements across the larger Iberian world. Micaela Bastidas, who was married to José Gabriel Tupac Amaru, would become a prominent leader in the Andean revolt that erupted on the other side of the Pacific less than two decades later, for example.[69]

By choice or by force, countless women would have sustained the conflicting military forces that clashed in Luzon through their productive and reproductive labor. Feeding children and animals and taking care of crops fell on women while men were away fighting.[70] The war also impacted women whose families moved them out of war zones and harm's way. Wealthy Spaniards and the principalia in and around Manila and Pangasinan evacuated their wives, mothers, daughters, and sisters, placing them in convents and other safe houses as enemy forces advanced into these zones.[71]

Inspiring the Catholic Army: Motivations to Fight

Reckoning with the diversity of the loyalist forces prompts us to question how so many different people—men and women who spoke different languages and who had very different life experiences—united behind the loyalist cause. Untangling the factors that compelled so many into the loyalist army requires us to deal with what the historian Eric Van Young described as a "testimonial problem."[72] Although the war generated a large and rich archive, it is remarkable how little direct examples there are of individuals clearly articulating their reasons for taking up arms to defend Spanish sovereignty in the Philippines. The voices that survive in the documentary record explaining why people risked their lives to protect the Spanish empire overwhelmingly belong to the colonial elite, including Spaniards, Chinese mestizos, and the Indigenous principalia, and these tend to follow established scripts of loyal subjecthood. Analyzing an array of evidence makes it possible to fill these gaps and present a fuller picture of people's multiple and overlapping motivations to fight.

The loyalists, the invaders, and the insurgents all bargained with fighting men for their labor, although negotiations occurred in the context of extreme violence and coercion. As soon as war broke out in 1762, it was immediately established that the competing armed forces mobilized in Luzon would severely punish anyone who opposed them or otherwise got in their way. The British forces, Anda and his followers, and those who rose up in rebellion all threatened and committed violence, inflicting brutal bodily injuries and even killing people who refused to support them or submit to their authority. During the siege of Intramuros, loyalists captured the British Mr. Fryer, and "sent out [his] headless trunk . . . maimed in the most inhuman manner."[73] British and sepoy soldiers took revenge on the city's population after they breached the walls of Intramuros, committing atrocities that included hanging one man to die on the tall cross that stood in the patio of the church of San Francisco.[74] Such brutality influenced individual and community responses to the war and decisions to join the loyalists.

Manileños were the first people who were displaced by war. Thousands of people fled the city as it was overrun by enemy soldiers in October of 1762. Refugees, especially those who were single Indigenous and Chinese men, risked dangerous confrontations with untrusting parties as they traveled into the provinces beyond the capital. One ill-fated group of refugees' experiences are well documented. That month, the priest and gobernadorcillo in the Pampangan town of San Miguel de Mayumo arrested six men and a boy who had tried to pass through the pueblo on their way to Pangasinan. All had been living and working as domestic servants in Manila when the British invaded. Four of the men—thirty-four-year-old Benito Carlos Balthazar, thirty-two-year-old Joan Cervantes, thirty-five-year-old Joan Pagliguan, and forty-year-old Sebastian Pérez—were native to Pangasinan and had all been employed as coachmen in the capital. Another Pangasinan native in the group, Santiago de Galicia, had been working as a baker in Binondo. Joseph Francisco de la Cruz, originally from Bulacan, and the twelve-year-old Macao-born Joseph Rodríguez were servants in Manuel de Castro's household. Castro was the sublieutenant of the Parián gate and had been killed during the siege.[75] These workers had continued to follow their employers' orders in the early days of the invasion, including those to ferry their property and family members out of the city and away from harm. But when Manila fell to the enemy, they found themselves suddenly unemployed and homeless. The workers from Pangasinan decided to make the journey home, and with nowhere else to go, Castro's servants elected to join them.

This group of men made masterless by the war represent the multitude of subalterns who were neither devoted loyalists nor committed rebels or enemy collaborators. The refugees aroused suspicion when they reached San Miguel because the fall of Manila had triggered "an upsurge of heartlessness, iniquities, and banditry," making it dangerous to "go on the roads without an escort of well-armed men."[76] Strangers were not trusted in this climate.

The group traveled with two horses loaded up with valuable goods that appeared to be stolen: a couple of rifles, pistols, and bows and arrows, an assortment of clothing, and a few bundles of textiles. San Miguel's priest and gobernadorcillo considered this haul as evidence that the refugees were dangerous thieves, and probably murderers. They arrested the group and locked them up in the town's jail.

Over several days, local officials publicly humiliated and abused the refugee prisoners, parading them through the town on top of horses and carabao, and interrogating them under torture as townsfolk looked on. At one point, a local guard held a gun to Pagliguan's head and shot blanks to terrify him. They also whipped the refugees. In between lashes that left their backs raw and bleeding, the men pleaded their innocence; they were only guilty of fleeing the capital, as their masters had done. Balthazar explained that "he didn't want the English to grab him" and be forced to "enter their service."[77] The baker had got away quickly with only his clothes on his back, and "not a single coin or grain of rice" in his pocket. The others had managed to take along some of their masters' possessions, reasoning that this was better than leaving them for the enemy to snatch. Balthazar eventually made a false confession under torture. "When he couldn't take any more lashes," he admitted that he witnessed Pagliguan kill two Spaniards and an indio.[78] He was convinced that his captors would kill him if he refused to cooperate. The refugees remained in prison until Anda reviewed their case in December. Anda condemned Mayumo's officials for their abhorrent management of the criminal trial and set the men free. Irrespective of Anda's condemnation, the group's treatment at the hands of loyalists highlights how vulnerable the itinerant poor were to violence during the war. Single men venturing beyond their villages continued to be treated with suspicion. In 1763, the Spanish government-in-exile warned loyalist towns to be wary of "outsiders and travelers, because they could be spies."[79]

In the provinces that rose up in rebellion, Indigenous rebels who fell into loyalist hands faced severe punishment, too. For example, loyalists arrested the sixty-year-old Antonio de la Cruz and his thirty-one-year-old son, Miguel de la Cruz, in the Ilocos town of Santo Domingo. Antonio, who was also known as Butarga, was an apoderado. The father and son were carrying incriminating letters written by Diego Silang when they were captured, and they were thus accused not only of joining the revolt, but of recruiting others to support it. Laoag's gobernador and three local judges put the pair on trial. Antonio and Miguel pleaded their innocence and insisted that they had been forced into moving rebel mail. The tribunal found them guilty of treason and sentenced them to hang until dead. "To make an example and to terrorize" people who were still persuaded by merits of the revolt, local officials decided to leave the victims' lifeless bodies on the gallows for three hours before they decapitated and quartered them. They then sent Antonio's head to Panay in the Visayas and Miguel's head to Dingras in Ilocos Norte. Their limbs were distributed to other towns in the province.[80] The morbid spectacle of rotting bodies would have forced observers to confront and weigh up the risks of disloyalty to Spain.

The loyalists' violent treatment of the rebels from Santo Domingo was unexceptional. Anda observed that gobernadorcillos continued to hang "people summarily for any crime; with the agreement of the principales and the elders, they could condemn criminals to the death penalty and execute them."[81] Anda himself claimed to have adjudicated a total of 664 civil and military trials like this one during the war.[82] Stories circulated that loyalists hanged anyone that they captured carrying rupees, the currency that the British used to pay their soldiers and collaborators.[83] Priests like Padre Montero, the prior of the Augustinian convent at Lipa, threatened to cut out the tongues of Indigenous traitors.[84] The previous chapter showed that insurgents used similar threats to coax communities into supporting their revolt. The decision to favor one party over another could have been influenced by which group was perceived to offer the highest level of security at a particular time.

British officials also used violence in Manila to persuade its soldiers as well as occupied communities to comply with their commands. Fray Castro remarked that the "British hanged an extraordinary number of people" without any semblance of a trial.[85] Drake ordered British captains to "punish severely any one who shall dare to disobey your orders," and to execute deserters "captured in arms."[86] Royal Navy Captain William Breton hanged a boatswain that he found guilty of plotting a mutiny.[87] British officers punished local men they caught selling arak to their soldiers with "a very severe flogging" and forced them to "work in the naval yard with irons to prevent their escape."[88] They executed Manileños who were caught aiding the loyalists. British officials arrested Francisco de la Cruz, a man described as "a Malay," who was encouraging two sepoys to defect to Anda's army in August 1763. Drake and his advisors deemed it necessary to make an example of Cruz in light of the "frequent desertions, and the town and suburbs swarming with these seducers." They sentenced him to be marched across the city of Manila, "through the suburbs of Santa Cruz . . . causing his crime to be published at the corner of every street, until he reaches Quiapo, and that he there be hanged . . . to deter others from following his example."[89]

Material rewards for military service were an important incentive to fight when the threat of such punishments loomed large. Silver was decisive to the loyalist's success. It is difficult to imagine how Anda could have established and preserved his loyalist army without the millions of silver pesos that were at his disposal after he acquired the *Filipino* galleon's silver.[90] Anda paid loyalist soldiers well. Fray Castro cynically suggested that Manila's Spanish vecinos, those "brave subjects who take arms for silver instead of patriotism or religion," only went looking for the governor in exile after they heard that he had obtained the famed treasure ship's riches.[91] Pieces of eight certainly attracted defectors to the loyalist army. In May of 1763, Anda sent word to soldiers in the British forces stationed at "the little fort at Pasig" that he was preparing to attack with "five hundred good Spanish soldiers with the French company consisting of fifty men, six thousand Pampangoes [sic], and thirty Malabares, and six pieces of cannon."[92] He invited the troops to defect and "deliver up the garrison guns [and] ammunition" to the Spanish army for a fifteen-dollar reward. Later that month, Anda tempted defectors with the promise of paying them "no less than 100 Dollars per man," which was equivalent to more than twice the annual salary that the British ordinarily paid these soldiers.[93] For their part, British officials tolerated their soldiers' widespread pillaging, recognizing that prize-taking supplemented fighting mens' pay.[94] They agreed to soldiers' requests for pay rises, increased alcohol rations, and other demands, with the Manila Council noting that it was "highly necessary to allow [the troops] all possible indulgences in order to prevent any murmurings or application to return to the [Coromandel] coast."[95]

Anda understood that silver could encourage support for the loyalist cause across colonial society. He ordered his army to pay for the weapons or animals that they requisitioned from Indigenous communities, which his plentiful silver reserves made possible. Additionally, galleon silver paid for "ironworks, armories, the founding of cannon and shot, gunpowder production, and the construction of boats to guard the mouths of rivers;" resources that the loyalists deployed against the foreign invaders and Indigenous insurgents.[96] Silver even funded the Spanish colonial government's trade missions to purchase essential military supplies in port cities across maritime Asia. Jorge de San Clemente went to China with galleon silver to buy copper and iron that were essential to the production of weapons and ammunition.[97] East India Company officials in Madras also suspected that Spanish and

Dutch vessels were coming to Manila Bay from Batavia and selling "cannon, fire arms, ammunition, etc" to the "malecontents," as they called the loyalists. The occupying forces were incapable of halting this trade.[98]

The long history of war in the Philippines and the martial colonial culture that it fostered meant that the archipelago's multiethnic population understood that the Crown rewarded loyalty on the battlefield. Kings often rewarded unfree individuals who showed bravery on battlefields across the global Spanish empire with liberty. The governor of Cuba, for example, held out freedom to enslaved people who joined the Spanish military campaign against the British in Havana in 1762.[99] In Luzon, Anda held out liberty to soldiers who came across from British ranks, promising defectors the right to choose to remain in the Philippines and in the ranks for his army, for which they would be paid high wages, or the right to travel to "New Spain or any other place that you think proper."[100] Mexican forzados might have anticipated that the Crown would reward their dedicated service with shortened sentences and the right to return home to Mexico. Tribute-paying fighting men who became war heroes were traditionally rewarded with freedom from their obligations to pay the burdensome head tax and to perform polo labor. Fray Bautista Areros promised these prizes to fighters from north Ilocos that joined the military campaign against the Indigenous rebellion.[101]

Rewards could also flow to groups that collectively showed loyalty to the Crown. Spanish monarchs routinely granted collective privileges to Indigenous communities that sent soldiers to fight to defend its sovereignty. Raquel Güereca Durán's research on Indigenous militias in eighteenth-century Mexico highlighted that Indigenous communities expected that military service would safeguard them in future disputes that might arise with priests, colonial officials, and other adversaries over vital issues including land ownership, tribute, and labor obligations. Indigenous towns in New Spain that raised militias invested in the creation of official records that certified military service, ensuring that they could be used to protect their interests in future litigations.[102] Communities in the Philippines did the same thing. The documents that Anda prepared to certify Pampangan and other Indigenous contributions to the multifront war surely responded to community demands for this paper trail. The archive demonstrates Indigenous agency and reflects the principalia's appreciation of the future utility of military service.[103]

The widespread expectation of material rewards for military service is evidenced by the flood of petitions that vassals in the Philippines seeking privileges sent to Spain in the aftermath of the conflict. José Peréz del Busto, the Spanish engineer who proved himself to be one of Anda's most reliable generals during the war, was among these petitioners. Anda promoted Busto to alcalde mayor and captain of war in Tondo during the war, before making him lieutenant general in charge of the troops who laid siege to Intramuros, where the British were holed up in the final stages of the conflict. The Crown approved Busto's 1768 request for the title and salary of *coronel* and an *encomenda* in the military orders, which he likely made in person at the royal court in Madrid.[104] In February of 1767, Matheo de Los Angeles, the wartime captain of the Chinese mestizo militia, requested a license to travel to Spain so that he too could put his case for a reward for his wartime loyalty before the king. Bureaucrats denied Los Angeles's application to travel, forcing him to rely on lawyers to represent him in the royal court.[105] Los Angeles's faithful and effective military service not only against the British, but also in campaigns against the "infidel *cimarrones* and Igorots" in the gold-rich mountains that soared over Manila, persuaded the Council of the Indies to promote him to alcalde mayor of Camarines Province in August 1769.[106]

Even missionaries petitioned the Crown for rewards for their wartime service. The king approved the Franciscan friar Bernado de Corral's request to be promoted to chaplain of the newly established Tagalog militia, and approved the five-hundred peso annual salary that Corral suggested was appropriate remuneration for this work. The monarch also agreed to financially support Corral's sister, who was a nun in the La Concepción convent in Cuenca's Villa de Moya. Corral emphasized that his sister was so poor that she was surviving on a diet of "two eggs and sixteen ounces of bread a day," implying financial need and the physical frailty that complemented contemporary notions of female piety.[107]

Simón de Anda also invested heavily in ensuring that he was handsomely compensated for his leadership of the victorious military campaign. He traveled to Spain shortly after the war. In the metropole, he took advantage of opportunities to regale King Charles III with stories of his heroic battlefield exploits, in addition to preparing the formulaic, formal written reports documenting his "merits and services" to the Crown. Anda likely commissioned the production of a grand artwork that celebrated his military achievements.[108] The *Alegoría de la defensa de Filipinas por el Alavés Don Simón de Anda,* a huge painting that offers a visual retelling of the main events of the war against the British and Chinese and Indigenous insurgents, underscored

Anda's personal contribution to the effort to return the archipelago to Spain. The king honored Anda with a 36,000-peso prize, and promoted him to governor of the Philippines, a position that he held from 1770 until his death in 1776.[109] All of this lobbying for rewards underscores eighteenth-century vassals' understanding of the bargain at the heart of empire; they were duty bound to defend the monarch's interests, even sacrificing their lives for the monarch if it became necessary, and the monarch was obliged to compensate vassals for their fidelity.

Catholicism was also crucial to the formation and success of the loyalist army. The conviction that the loyalists' multifront war was mandated by the Almighty, and was being waged to preserve the Catholic faith and the Mother Church in the Philippines, compelled many Catholics to join its ranks. Imagining the Seven Years' War as a holy war also created continuity with Catholic military campaigns against Moro pirates. The Indigenous people were told that God himself commanded them to follow their priests into battle. Multiple elements of the loyalist campaign underscored its Catholic character. One of these was the conspicuous integration of the clergy into its ranks. Most of the priests in the Philippines at this time were European or American born and belonged to missionary orders, although the number of secular, island-born Indigenous priests increased in the eighteenth century. By the 1760s, native priests oversaw an estimated one-quarter of the Philippines' parishes and mission stations. The Tagalog priest, Bartolomé Saguinsín, for example, fought against the British in Manila, and the Pampangan priest Tomás Millán supported the counterrevolutionary offensive in Ilocos.[110] As language education was integral to missionary training, Spanish and Mexican priests could converse with their parishioners about God and war in Filipino languages.[111] Priests led fighters in prayer before and after battles, and they listened to the fighters' confessions and absolved their sins so that if they died, their souls would go to paradise.

A shared Catholicism played a part in amalgamating loyalist fighters from different parts of the Philippines, and other places in the world beyond. Faith convinced French fighters to flock to the loyalists.[112] Along the riverbanks of loyalist camps, priests baptized other Protestant European and non-Catholic South Asian defectors from the British army.[113] Catholic symbols created a sense of coherence among the polycentric loyalist militias. Some five hundred Pampangan and Cagayan fighting men marched into battle against Indigenous rebels at Bayamban in Pangasinan under a Dominican flag described as "the flag of religion and the *patria*."[114] At the bloody battle against insurgent fighters that took place at Calasiao in December of 1763, loyalists marched under a large flag that featured two-headed eagles in each of its four corners that represented the Hispanic monarchy, and a shield bearing the Dominican coat of arms in the center. The banner perfectly captured the army's goals of restoring monarchical and church authority over the peoples and lands swept up in revolt.[115]

Loyalist rhetoric also revealed the army's deeply religious character. The Pampangan principalia from Minalin pueblo wrote a long, sermon-like letter to Anda in response to the formation of the Alabarderos company. The letter described Pampangan soldiers as "Catholic troops defending the holy Catholic faith in the militant Apostolic Roman Church."[116] It celebrated the long history of Pampangan service to the Crown and the Church in a way that blurred the lines between tributary labor and voluntary military service. It recalled how, for centuries, Pampangan soldiers had toiled "cutting trees, building boats . . . constructing walls, forts, and castles for infantry, and [providing] troops to defend this city and presidios, and other many works in the service of both majesties."[117] Minalin's elites framed their contribution to this war in biblical terms, comparing Anda's appeal to enlist their first-born sons in the loyalist forces to God's request to Jacob to sacrifice his son, Isaac, in the Old Testament's ultimate test of faith. The profound sacred tenor of the loyalist campaign convinced Castro that the Spanish empire survived in the Philippines "because of the Catholic hearts that trusted in God." "Even without silver," he reasoned, "Anda still would have been successful, because God was guiding him in what he did, and consequently he was followed."[118] While it is difficult to see a path to victory for the loyalists if they had not had such huge quantities of silver at their disposal, success would also have been impossible without faith.

Feelings of personal connection with the king of Spain was another factor that impacted decisions to join the loyalist forces. Early modern Spanish monarchs had a presence in the Philippines despite never setting foot in the islands. Public festivities that were staged to celebrate royal births and marriages and to grieve royal deaths fostered a sense of closeness to the monarchy.[119] The king was also "present" in local celebrations of victories over pirate enemies past and present. Megan Thomas has argued that Diego Silang avoided insulting the Crown in his many addresses to Indigenous crowds to avoid offending their monarchical sensibilities.[120] Family connections also pulled men into the loyalist army and kept them there. The local organization of military units ensured that men who fought together were often blood relatives—brothers, fathers, sons, uncles, and cousins—men bound together by an organic network of personal loyalties and kinship.[121]

Antipiracy politics also contributed to support for the loyalists. British officials in Manila resented being associated with pirates. They complained about Spanish proclamations circulating in 1763 that "stigmatizes HBM's [His British Majesty's] forces with the names of pirates and robbers acting in open contempt of public faith, religion, and humanity."[122] Yet the invading British forces acted like Filipinos' familiar pirate enemies, which bolstered the popular campaign against them. British attacks on sacred buildings, which echoed Moro pirate attacks on coastal churches, would have convinced devout locals that they were pirates and enemies of God. The invading army turned three Manila churches into rubble during the 1762 siege.[123] Soldiers destroyed or stole numerous religious images venerated by local communities. One of these was the image of Our Lady of Guadalupe that was housed in the Augustinian convent along the Pasig River in San Pedro Makati. In a win to win over local support for British colonial rule, the British Manila Council ordered Captain Backhouse to return this "Malay virgin and black Jesus" to its sanctuary in March of 1763. Backhouse reported that the community staged an elaborate celebration to welcome home the revered icon. He described how "the Virgin Mary . . . was carried away in great state and procession, she was accompanied by a thousand people at least in canoes and boats finely decorated."[124] The captain believed that the restoration of the icon "had good effect, and numbers of the Malays, men and women, came to Pasig the same night to return thanks for the honor I had done." Yet it is also possible to read Backhouse's words against the grain, as suggestive of this Tagalog community's deep resentment and anger toward the British for the desecration of their revered religious icon.

Beyond sacking churches, the invading army continued to strike villages and farms, frequently stealing cattle and livestock from Indigenous pueblos.[125] The British pursued a scorched-earth policy in smaller towns and agricultural regions surrounding the capital, burning villages to the ground to eliminate places where enemy armies could hide or congregate.[126] Violence by the invading forces against Indigenous Filipinos was the norm in 1762–1764. As Backhouse poetically observed, "war in her mildest dress is too severe where the innocent fall in her way."[127]

The British government's conspicuous associations with Azim ud-Din and his son Mohammed Israel would have only strengthened the invaders' reputation for being enemies of the Catholic Church. British Moro diplomacy was on full display in the occupied capital. Drake presented gifts to "the king of Mindanao" to celebrate the British-Sulu treaty that the parties brokered. The gift-giving was likely a part of an elaborate public ceremony that the British were known to stage in the occupied city. Another grand celebration would take place to mark Azim ud-Din and Israel's departure from Manila to Jolo, where the prince had promised to help the British to establish a new trading outpost.[128] In the eyes of locals, these performances of friendship would have reaffirmed the religious dimensions of the war and the perceived connections between the redcoats and other pirates in maritime Southeast Asia.

Six months into the British occupation of Manila, it was clear that the invaders were losing the war. The occupying army struggled to obtain enough food to feed its soldiers, and hungry men deserted in droves. Anda's plan to blockade Manila and "crush the enemy by hunger" was working.[129] In February of 1763, Lieutenant Bonjour reported to Backhouse that he had no provisions on his ship in Manila Bay, and "that if he lets the men go on shore he will lose them, and if he keeps them on board they must starve."[130] Soldiers in the invading army faced a constant threat of ambush from loyalists who attacked fighting men whenever they ventured out of the walled city of Manila. Captain Backhouse reminded officers to "secure your men from straggling in the Woods and getting drunk" to protect them from "having their Throats Cut."[131]

The loyalists and the British also faced off in major battles. British forces attacked the loyalists at Malolos, a town with an Augustinian convent north of the capital, in January of 1763. Although the invading army overwhelmed the loyalists, the British suffered many casualties and were forced to withdraw to Manila.[132] In July, a major battle at Malinta, roughly thirteen kilometers north of Fort Santiago, was a turning point in the war. The British army struck the town and convent fortified by loyalists with a fifteen-hundred-strong battalion, which included an estimated one thousand Chinese soldiers. The ensuing engagement was deafening and deadly. Both sides shot their heavy muskets and cannon, filling the air with thick smoke that stung combatants' eyes. Shot and arrows whistled past the soldiers' heads. A French artilleryman who had defected to the loyalists landed a shot at the invading army's gunpowder barrels, causing a booming explosion that sent soldiers flying into the air. The British forces were forced to retreat. Loyalists kept up attacks on the enemy as they marched back to Manila. Castro observed that "our indios, hidden in the trees, killed many with bows and arrows."[133] The missionary noted that after this encounter, the invaders were too scared to leave Intramuros, and they were "more like prisoners in a presidio of the Catholic king than soldiers who had conquered a city."[134]

Defeating the Indigenous Revolt

The Spanish saw the defeat of the British as a certainty by the middle of 1763; however, the fate of the Indigenous insurgency was not so obvious. Drake and the Manila Council noted that even if the British withdrew and "the islands restored to the Crown of Spain, their monarch will find himself either obliged to abandon them to the Indians or conquer them at an immense expense of treasure and men."[135] Priests who were caught up in the uprisings that roared across Luzon described being utterly disorientated by these events. One priest, Fray Maldonado, wrote that "everything is a riot without feet, or a head . . . and no one can speak."[136] Another described the country in revolt as "all confusion, tears, and commotion."[137] Armed rebels and loyalists blocked roads and rivers, making travel through Luzon difficult and dangerous. The restricted movement of people and information across the countryside meant a lack of reliable news about what was happening. Amid this chaos, colonial officials and the clergy deployed various strategies to suppress the rebellion, including bargaining with Indigenous communities to disavow the insurgency, and using brute force to make them do so. Anda repeatedly promised to punish traitors with blood and fire, until the revolt was anemic and extinguished.

The clergy's central role in the counterrevolution substantiates the orthodox view that priests were central to the longevity of Spanish colonial rule in the Philippines.[138] Priests used various strategies to discourage people from backing the revolt, and to rouse support for the loyalist forces that were mobilizing against it. They condemned the rebellion from the pulpit. In the small Ilocos town of Dingras, which stands some twenty kilometers inland from the sea on the banks of the Padsan River, the Augustinian friar Manuel Álvarez preached that Silang and corporals were enemies of God and the king, and that their followers would burn in hell.[139] Priests made dramatic, emotional appeals to their congregations to end their rebellion. In Lingayen, Padre Melendez got down on his knees before his parishioners, and with tears running down his face, he begged them "to desist from this crazy business."[140] The clergy also continued to bargain with people for peace. Although Bernardo Ustaríz, the Bishop of Nueva Segovia, never ceased to defend tribute as a fair contribution that Indigenous vassals were obligated to make to the

greater costs that the monarchy incurred in maintaining Catholicism in
the Philippines, he granted a temporary one-year exemption from tribute
to the communities that were refusing to pay, in the hope that this would
convince them to abandon the revolt.[141]

Priests undermined the rebellion by spreading rumors that cast doubt on
Silang's Catholic identity. The gossip they spread included an apocryphal biography of Silang that highlighted his ties to the mountain-dwelling infidels
of the cordillera, people whom the Spaniards and lowland Indigenous communities regarded as vicious cannibals, and the descendants of the Chinese
pirate Limahong and his crew.[142] It told that these uplanders had taken Silang captive when he was just a boy. Silang allegedly lived with a tribe for
years, learning about their *anitos* (amulets), until an Augustine Recollect friar
eventually rescued him by buying his freedom for a piece of cloth.[143] This narrative implied that Silang's Catholic faith was corrupted by his time among
the mountain people.

Stories of Diego Silang and his followers' cannibalism and macabre violence against their enemies further damaged the devout Catholic persona that
the rebel leader strived to cultivate. Pedro de Vivar, the Spanish Augustinian friar who was in Ilocos for the duration of the revolt, recounted that after
Silang killed the mestizo loyalist Miguel Pinzón, he threw his dead body from
a second-story window onto the waiting pikes of his bloodthirsty soldiers,
who tore apart and ate the corpse in a frenzied feast. One of Silang's brothers-
in-law allegedly ate Pinzón's heart while raving through bloody mouthfuls
of muscle about how brave it was to eat hearts.[144] On another occasion, Silang was said to have made an enemy corpse the guest of honor at a drunken
party that he hosted to celebrate a victory against loyalists on the battlefield.
He placed a deceased loyalist soldier's severed head in a clay pot and danced
around it before handing the body over to uplander fighting men to divide
up among themselves.[145] These rumors may have contained elements of truth.
The ritual consumption of human body parts was practiced in the cordillera.[146] Vivar and other priests interpreted these anecdotes as evidence that
the Silanistas were fallen Christians, possessed by the devil. These tales would
have diminished native Catholics' enthusiasm for the revolt.[147] Other rumors
that Sangleyes were coming to Luzon from China to assist Indigenous insurgents would have added to the idea that the revolt was not a Catholic movement. Futhermore, they evoked memories of the past century's Chinese
pirates, and weaponized popular Sinophobia against the predominately Indigenous campaign.[148]

The Catholic Church was a formidable adversary. Priests went on strike in rebel districts, withdrawing their spiritual labor from communities in rebellion. These men of religion understood that their unique power stemmed from their ability and authority to perform Catholic sacraments, which included baptisms of newborn babies, and the anointing of the sick at the end of life, in addition to marriage, the eucharist, and penance. The importance of these religious ceremonies was rooted in their necessity for salvation. Many Catholics would have believed that if they or their kin died without receiving these sacraments, their souls would be damned to suffer in hell for all eternity.[149] The leaders of the missionary orders directed coordinated walkouts from churches in rebel pueblos. In February, Dominican missionaries in Pangasinan followed their provincial's orders to leave their parishes. The Dominican friar Melendez had to escape from his house by climbing out of his bedroom window in the middle of the night. He traveled with other priests to Asingan, a town that remained a loyalist stronghold. The priests sent proclamations throughout the province that promised that they would return to minister to their flocks as soon as the people agreed to their requirements.

The insurgents had put their demands on the table, and now it was the priests' turn to do the same. The clergy insisted that communities recognize the Spanish Crown's sovereignty in the Philippines by swearing oaths of loyalty to the king, acknowledging Anda as governor of the islands, and accepting a Spanish alcalde mayor in Pangasinan. In addition, they demanded that the revolt's leaders be expelled from the province, along with all single Chinese men whom they deemed "public enemies."[150] The Church in Ilocos followed suit. Bishop Ustaríz ordered the clergy in the province to close their churches and refuse all sacraments with the exception of the baptisms of newborns. While the rebellion raged, countless sick and injured people of faith died without a priest hearing their final confessions and absolving their sins, and their bodies were buried without Catholic funeral rites.[151] Catholic sacraments proved to be a powerful bargaining chip.

The Church-baked counterrevolutionary campaign must have been working, as Silang slammed the friars for undermining his movement for change. He singled out the Augustinians as his worst enemies, claiming that they "have pursued us as if we were wild boars, [and] neither has our submission, nor laying down our arms and crying for mercy availed us in the least for a further security."[152] Recognizing that the clergy's strike was weakening support for the revolt, Silang repeatedly exhorted friars to return to their pueblos, and urged them to hear his corporal's confessions and absolve their sins.

Falling back on the language of Catholic anti-piracy, he urged the missionaries to do God's work to defeat the English. Silang relied on coercion when persuasion failed. He sent armed guards to escort two clerics to Pangasinan when they refused to go voluntarily.[153] All of these efforts to secure the clergy's cooperation failed.

Silang was a shrewd negotiator. In the first few months of 1763, he maintained a line of communication with exiled Spanish governor of the Philippines Simón de Anda, and the British governor in Manila, Dawsonne Drake, exploiting the rivalry between the rival European empires to advance his own personal interests and those of the Indigenous communities that he claimed to speak for.[154] In a letter to Anda, Silang emphasized that he was still a loyal vassal of the Spanish Crown and was committed to defeating the British, and he clarified that his ultimate objective was to remove the corrupt Principalia from power. All parties recognized that replacing some Indigenous gobernadorcillos with others would not fundamentally change colonial society. Silang hoped that such reassurances would persuade Anda to call off the loyalist attacks on the rebels. They did not.

Drake was much more receptive to Silang. The British had, after all, expected to meet disgruntled Indigenous men like him in the Philippines, and they enthusiastically embraced this leader who "after throwing off the Spanish yoke has taken upon himself the Government of Ilocos."[155] The British Manila Council and Silang bargained the terms of an alliance through a series of letters, with the Spanish traitor Orendaín likely assisting as a translator. They formalized their accord in May of 1763. Silang pledged loyalty to Britain's King George III and was appointed to various posts in the new British government of the Philippines, including maestre de campo general and governor, alcalde mayor, and sargento mayor of Ilocos. Drake sent Silang gifts of silver pistols, a golden sword, and a staff—all symbols of political authority in the Philippines that acknowledged Silang's sovereignty in the province.[156] The British provided Silang with as much military support as they could muster given the constraints of their small and shrinking army. Drake dispatched fifty soldiers (including twenty Europeans and thirty sepoys) with weapons and ammunition to Ilocos to support his ally's war against the loyalists. The arrival of British forces in the province coincided with proclamations circulating in the local languages that advertised Silang's new titles and ordered missionaries to swear oaths of allegiance to the king of England, which they of course refused.[157] The Manila Council made attempts to broker a similar alliance with the leaders of the revolt in

Pangasinan. Although they were unsure of their identities, Drake dispatched letters offering the rebels "our friendship and protection," and invited them to combine their armies "to crush Mr. Anda and his faction."[158] It is not clear if British letters reached Palaris or other insurgents in Pangasinan. If they did, the insurgents apparently chose to ignore this correspondence; they did not desire liberation by the British.

Silang's decision to join forces with the British also seems to have soured popular support for his armed struggle. The Anglo-Ilocano alliance played into the friars' hands. Locals did not trust the invaders, and they were wary of parties that brokered an alliance with them. Bishop Ustaríz issued proclamations stating that Silang's real goal was to enslave Ilocanos and suppress Catholicism in the Philippines. He called on the people to fight the rebels "until glorious death in defense against the furious force of these tyrants and enemies."[159] The fact that Silang waited a long six months into the rebellion before he firmed up a deal with the British suggests that he was concerned about its potential to backfire and hurt his campaign. The truth is that Silang was growing desperate when he brokered this partnership. He was running short on supplies of silver and food that were necessary to sustain a revolutionary army. War and typhoons brought an acute hunger to Ilocos that emptied towns of people. Entire families fled to the mountains searching for something to eat.[160] The people's appetite for rebellion diminished as their hunger grew.

Silang promised a world in which taxes, forced labor, and the forced sale of goods would vanish, and people would be free. But then he delivered the opposite. To feed and arm his revolutionary army, Silang tried to reimpose tribute on Indigenous peoples, demanding that every *timawa* (peasant) pay a head tax to his government. In addition, he demanded that communities surrender to his army whatever material goods that they produced—cotton manufactured in the north of Ilocos and the fruits and vegetables grown in the south. Locals would have recognized this as a version of the Spanish colonial government's bandala system. Like the British, Silanistas confiscated cattle too, seizing buffalo from small towns and herding them to Vigan. There were rumors that Gabriela Silang herself butchered the animals.[161] By the end of May of 1763, the self-proclaimed leader of a rebellion that had been committed to tribute abolition and radical Catholic anti-piracy was in an open alliance with pirate enemies of the Church, and was trying to reimpose a version of the extractive, exploitative colonial system that his followers despised. Popular support for the revolt waned as famine and hypocrisy fed resentment.

For the duration of the rebellion, the loyalists sustained violent attacks on the rebels that gradually quashed the armed insurgency. Priests' pleas to their parishioners to end their revolt were accompanied by assaults mounted by heterogeneous loyalist forces. As Silang predicted, Anda sent a "Spanish and Indigenous army" to "finish us with blood and fire, men as well as our women and children."[162] The friars and the Spanish colonial government-in-exile wanted the leaders of the Indigenous revolt dead. Bishop Ustaríz and Pedro Becbec, an apoderadillo from Santa Ana, organized for Miguel Vicos to kill Silang.[163] We know little about Vicos, except that the colonial archive described him as "an indio." On the eve of the murder, Ustaríz heard the assassin's confession, blessed him, and gifted him a precious relic, as though the killing was a sacred mission. Vicos shot Silang with a blunderbuss, killing him instantly, between three and four o'clock in the afternoon on the twenty-eighth of May. A crowd gathered for an impromptu celebration of Silang's execution that night. They took turns stabbing his corpse, and they dressed up the body and placed a staff in his hand, mockingly referring to the deceased as alcalde mayor.[164] Anda paid Vicos one thousand pesos in recognition of his service to the empire, and promoted Becbec to justicia mayor of Ilocos.[165] The Crown later granted Vicos and Becbec and their sons permanent exemptions from tribute as a reward for their exemplary loyalty.[166] The politics of patronage and the tradition of the monarch rewarding loyal service greased the wheels of Silang's assassination.

The Spaniards had hoped that the revolt in Ilocos would die with Silang. After holding a celebratory te deum mass that offered thanks to God for the rebel's execution, Bishop Ustaríz issued declarations in Ilocano and Spanish to pueblos across the province that reported Silang's demise and offered a general pardon to all who put down their weapons.[167] To make peace a more attractive proposition, the declaration reiterated earlier reassurances that people did not have to pay tribute as long as the British occupied Manila, and promised that the Spanish government would return property that Silang and his followers had stolen to their rightful owners. However, instead of restoring order, Silang's murder fanned the flames of rebellion. The insurgents were like a hydra—that mythical many-headed beast—and the loyalists found that if they cut off its head, more would grow back in its place. Padre Arenos, a priest in Santa Catalina, wrote in July that the "head of every town is a Silang and all are in agreement to avenge Silang's death."[168] The armed insurgency continued with Gabriela Silang, Diego's widow, as the head of the radical movement. Fray Juan Baptista wrote that "the people who have taken over all love Silang's woman."[169] Some communities' resolve to continue the rebellion was encouraged by the fact that the men that Anda appointed to govern Ilocos—the veteran soldier Antonio Pimentel, whom he promoted to alcalde mayor, and Pedro Becbec, serving as justicia mayor—attempted to collect tribute, contradicting Anda's promises that the head tax collection would be paused.[170] Vivar believed that mistrust of the Spanish, rather than the desire for revenge, was another obstacle to peace. The peasantry refused to lay down their weapons because they did not trust promises of pardons and feared they would be punished severely for their uprising.[171]

In June and July, rebels and loyalists clashed in skirmishes and battles across the insurgent provinces. The rival forces continued to compete for local support, sending calls to towns to send men and horses to fight against their opponents. The people of San Esteban penned a letter to "los señores de Abagatan" that called on them to send thirty men with horses to come and fight the enemy. They threatened to "give them ashes"—to burn everything—if they refused.[172] Militias marched into pueblos, forcing their residents to fight, hide, or flee. Rebels and loyalist armies alike destroyed people's homes and their livelihoods as they moved across the countryside. Santa Catalina, Becbec's hometown in Ilocos, was one that rebels destroyed. The parish priest, Padre Arenos, wrote that "I do not know how to explain that day" when armed enemies marched through, "but for hours I was with an army of infinite drunkards." The rebels stripped the convent bare, "leaving not even the chickens."[173] There was a major battle between loyalists and rebels between Sinait and Cabugao, that left hundreds of people dead on both sides. The majority of loyalist fighters at this engagement were Indigenous, including a large contingent of men from Laoag, and "negros flecheros" (Black archers) from the cordillera.[174]

The insurgency in Ilocos suffered a serious blow at a major battle in Vigan at the end of July. An estimated twenty thousand people participated in the bloody confrontation, making this the largest military engagement of the entire Seven Years' War in the Philippines. The loyalists overwhelmed the rebels. They attributed their victory to divine intervention. The insurgents had been tricked by the illusion of the coppices of Vigan's churches appearing as thousands of loyalist soldiers, prompting many to flee. Missionaries accredited this miracle to the Virgin of Caridad, a sacred image of the mother of God that was venerated in the nearby town of Bantay, whose residents had shunned the uprising.[175] Juan Manuel de Arza y Urrita, the alcalde mayor of Pangasinan, led a company of loyalist troops that hunted down and arrested

Gabriela Silang and her militia. Arza and his men hanged Silang until dead, and used a kind of trapiche to kill more than ninety of her corporals and soldiers.[176] They gave "a good ration of whippings" to other arrested rebels before setting them free. After Vigan, the loyalist path to victory appeared more certain.

As David A. Bell remarked in his study of early modern warfare, "armies never pose a greater threat to prisoners and noncombatants than when they have won a major engagement, are shuddering with pent-up tensions and fear, and have their enemy at their mercy."[177] This was certainly the case in Ilocos in 1763. The triumphant loyalist army left a trail of destruction as they left Vigan. Agustín de la Encarnación, an Augustinian Recollect missionary, vividly described the army's brutal treatment of the innocent people caught up in the web of war. Fearful locals hid in their church or fled to the mountains when an estimated nine or ten thousand men belonging to the "so-called Catholic forces" arrived in his town of Bantay. Not satisfied with the loot that they raided from the community, which included all of their animals, the soldiers broke down the church doors and dragged people onto the patio. A principal from Dingras and one of the militia commanders subjected various town residents to a hurried trial, accusing the locals of crimes that the priest said "they never committed." The appointed judge for the day then forced the people to buy their freedom. The soldiers "raped the women without the fear of God" and murdered many of the men they found, even though they were unarmed, "slaughtering them as though they were animals." Encarnación estimated that more than one thousand people were killed, and the soldiers left survivors "not even the ploughs that are the indios' hands and feet."[178] This scene of brutalization and destruction was repeated in town after town across Ilocos, extinguishing the rebellion.

The revolt lasted longer in Pangasinan. In the second half of 1763, the loyalist army brought blood and fire to pueblos in the province that were known to be "notoriously rebellious" and unwavering in their support of the insurgency, including Calasiao, Baimamban, Binalatongan, and Magaldan. As violent clashes and battles continued in the province, Dominican missionaries worked to persuade people, town by town, to abandon the rebellion. Priests collected a reported four thousand pledges from Indigenous men to join the loyalists and fight against their rebel neighbors. In mid-September rebels had gathered at a conference with the friars in Binalatongan where they accepted Anda's offers of an amnesty. They agreed to lay down their weapons and end the insurgency on the assurance that they would be pardoned for their roles in the insurrection. The missionaries were forced to make concessions to achieve this peace, which included freeing certain rebel leaders, such as Thomas Casiqpi. In a report on the revolt that they prepared for the Crown, Spanish colonial officials in Manila noted that while such actions "seem irregular, they were necessary in that moment."[179] The balance of power still forced agents of empire to bargain with rebels.

Mistrust of colonial officials made peace in Pangasinan fragile. When the new Spanish alcalde mayor arrived in Paniqui to take over the government of the province, the insurgents refused to surrender their firearms as they had promised. Their hesitancy can be attributed to rumors that Arza had issued a proclamation ordering that all disloyal chiefs in Ilocos, Pangasinan, and Cagayan be arrested and transported to Vigan for punishment, and the people feared that this order would be carried out as soon as they gave up their arsenal.[180] In December, Pangasinense rebels kidnapped the the justicia mayor of San Jacinto, Francisco Vargas y Machuca, while he was supervising polo workers felling trees.[181] Evidently, coerced labor systems continued to nurture tension between locals and colonial officials. The assault on the justicia mayor prompted the loyalist forces to march into the province again. Armed bands burned various villages in the name of the king, including towns like Bayambang that they found abandoned.[182] The loyalist army, bolstered by a significant contingent of fighting men from Cagayan, crossed the river at Bayambang and attacked Binalatongan, where armed rebels had dug in and prepared for battle. The entire town of Binalatongan was destroyed when the two armies clashed. Loyalists ensured that fire totally consumed the town, leaving only the shells of the burned-out church, convent, and schoolhouse. Notably, the Spanish colonial government decided against rebuilding the town. To erase the memory of the revolt, they constructed a new town that they named San Carlos a few kilometers away from Binalatongan's ruins.[183] The last major battle between rebels and loyalists in Pangasinan took place in Calasiao in early 1764, forcing priests and principales to temporarily escape. The revolt petered out after this confrontation. Loyalists pursued rebel leaders, whom they captured and hanged, and whose body parts they distributed across the region. Palaris was finally captured and killed in late 1765.[184]

Even in the face of this devastation, there were voices that called for the rebels to be punished even more harshly. Bishop Millán, for example, was furious that insurgents had been allowed to escape from Vigan on foot and by boat, instead of being put to death, which he strongly felt was a just punishment for their crimes. Vivar was also frustrated that the traitors got off lightly. In his view, the entire city of Vigan was a rotten apple, and it should have been annihilated.[185] In contrast, the Augustinian missionary Encarnación was one of the voices that called for a general pardon of the insurgents. He made a moral argument for a gentler response, emphasizing that a pardon was the Christian thing to do. He also made a pragmatic case: peace was necessary to revive the colonial political economy, to restore the conditions that were necessary for Indigenous and mestizo communities to complete the harvest and to pay tribute.[186] Ultimately, Encarnación's view won out. The colonial government pardoned the majority of rebels, conveniently claiming they had been forced into rebellion. In ceremonies staged in towns across Luzon, survivors of the war swore loyalty oaths to the Crown, marking the end of the revolt. At the urging of the friars, the Spanish colonial government banned apoderadillos as preventative measure against future rebellions.[187]

The price paid for peace, and for empire, was mighty high. So much of the country was in ruins when the revolt was finally suppressed. The war had washed over Luzon like a tsunami of death. Tribute records show that Pangasinan's population plummeted in 1762–1764, falling by more than twenty-five thousand in these few years. This decline reflects a combination of families fleeing the war-torn province and the demise of so many men of fighting age.[188] There were many who saw this as a fragile peace. Vivar pointed out that "the many promises made [to Indigenous peoples] in the name of the king are still only words, and the women's husbands are still dead." "God wants the Spaniards to know that the islands were conserved not by their efforts, but by his special providence," he said.[189] The restored colonial order may have been precarious, but it would prove to be long-lived. The war demonstrated the tremendous cost of an uprising against colonial rule: destruction and death wrought by revolutionary and counterrevolutionary armies. A generation of rebel leaders were either killed or disheartened by the insurgency's defeat, crippling the potential of future armed struggles against the empire.

Conclusion

Spain's Asian empire was forged from below. The diverse, counterrevolutionary loyalist army that mobilized in 1762 and 1763 to defend Spanish sovereignty in the Philippines delivered a decisive victory over the British Royal Navy and East India Company forces that attacked Manila from the sea, and the home-grown insurgency that the invasion triggered. The Seven Years' War in the Philippines ushered in a long peace. This chapter demonstrated that the multifront war firmed up the Spanish colonial government's alliances with Indigenous and Chinese mestizo elites who were loyal to the Crown during these years of crisis, and reinforced important popular assumptions that the monarch and his delegates in the islands would reward faithful service to the Crown. It also reified that disloyalty would be harshly punished. The loyalist victory signaled the colonial government's potency and capacity to crush challenges to Spanish sovereignty. Another major Indigenous uprising would not emerge in the Philippines until 1807.[190]

War scarred the landscape, leaving coasts and valleys spotted with the ruins of burned-out churches and the remains of destroyed villages, and countless graves. Filipinos may have experienced the damaged countryside as the physical expression of the fragility of colonial rule, the unhealed wounds inflicted on the state by its enemies. Or they could have encountered the landscape as the embodiment of the Spanish empire's resilience. The ruins of the large Pangasinan town of Binalatongan—never to be rebuilt—remained standing as a haunting monument to the insurgency's defeat. The gallows that loyalists erected to hang captured insurgents in Malasiqui, another Pangasinan pueblo, were left standing for two decades.[191] Painted murals depicting the execution of Gabriela Silang decorated the roof of the episcopal palace in Vigan and the walls of a convent at Laoag.[192] These memorials evoked the power of the colonial government, the clergy, the principalia, and Chinese mestizo elites, who had proved their capacity to mobilize armies to quash serious threats to Spanish rule.

The war between the loyalists and the British dragged on into 1764, even though it was clear after the battle at Malinta that the invading army was conquered. In early 1763, the rulers of Britain, Spain, and France agreed to a peace treaty that ended the war, and returned Manila to Spain. News of peace made its way to the Philippines from Madras as early as the middle of that year, however, Anda refused to acknowledge it until he received official notification of the armistice from his king. This finally arrived aboard the *Santa Rosa* galleon that reached Manila from Acapulco in March of 1764.[193] Diplomats in Europe continued to debate whether Spain still owed the British a ransom for Manila. The Spanish never paid a peso more than what the British forces stole or otherwise ignobly procured during the occupation.[194]

Anda and his loyalist army triumphantly reentered Manila at nine in the morning on the sixteenth of March, days after the galleon weighed anchor in Manila Bay. The Spanish governor rode into the city on horseback. More than five thousand fighting men followed him, marching alongside carriages loaded with cannon and ammunition. Echoing the capital's historic celebrations of victories over pirates, the military parade proclaimed the restoration of Spanish sovereignty over the capital and the provinces beyond. The festivities also lauded the preservation of the colonial social hierarchy. Chinese mestizos and Indigenous veterans processed behind the Spanish governor, simultaneously performing the part of triumphant soldiers and vanquished others.[195] The procession ended in a thanksgiving mass in the cathedral, where government officials, the clergy, and multiethnic elites gave thanks to God for the victory he delivered them.[196] Relations between Anda and Drake were surprisingly amicable at the end of the war. Anda even accepted Drake's invitation to a soiree on the British flagship at the end of March before the defeated fleet departed. The Spanish governor was sincerely impressed by the "magnificent" celebration aboard the "richly adorned" boat, and the three artillery salutes that the British fleet made in Anda's honor. At the end of the night, Anda accepted Drake's gift of a decorated shotgun and a pair of exquisite pistols. Anda sent Drake a cow, several chickens, and fruits for his return voyage to India the following day.[197]

The final act in the great drama of the British invasion and occupation of Manila took place a little over a year later. Many of the European and South Asian soldiers who defected to the loyalists from British forces elected to remain in the Philippines and enlisted in the Spanish military after war.[198] These men may have had little real choice in the matter, as they risked being punished as traitors if they returned to British outposts in India or to other cities in the British empire. In May of 1765, the soldiers in the Spanish army's new English artillery unit that was guarding Fort Santiago mutinied over poor pay and labor conditions. Peace had diminished their bargaining power, and the days of one-hundred-peso handouts were far behind them. The troops locked themselves inside the fort, aimed its bronze cannons at the government palace, the cathedral tower, and the barracks, all of which were within range, and demanded a pay rise and other concessions. The mutineers fired a few cannon shots before the new Spanish Governor De la Torre sent in other soldiers to overrun and arrest them. Manila's war council conducted an investigation into the incident that identified the twenty-seven-year-old, Kent-born English artillery captain Mariano José Bustos Lent as the ringleader of the rebellion. They sentenced him to perpetual banishment from the colony and subjected his fellow mutineers to the same punishment "for being Protestants."[199] The quick suppression of the soldiers' rebellion was yet another salient display of the Spanish colonial government's restored authority. The expulsion of Manila's newest migrants also demonstrated that the changing dynamics of maritime violence in Philippine waters impacted who was permitted to live in the Spanish colony and who would be forced to leave it. The next chapter examines how the invasion of Manila fundamentally altered the politics of belonging in the archipelago, and triggered the forced repatriation of the island's Chinese migrants.

CHAPTER 5

Empire by Expulsion

The Forced Repatriation of Chinese Migrants
from the Philippines

Seven boats waited at the mouth of the Pasig River, readying to sail to South-western China in August of 1769. Between them, the two European-style boats and five sampans were carrying 575 Chinese men whom the colonial government was forcibly repatriating to their homeland. A new law required that every ship departing from Manila for China was to take as many exiled Sangleyes as it could safely carry. The Chinese *cabecila general de la nación* Ignacio Phoco, and the government notaries Juan de la Cruz and Salvador de Jesús, inspected the ships and their human cargo. Aboard Captain Juan Ong-Silo's crowded boat, the *Tec Sen*, the trio counted and questioned two hundred deportees. They recorded the passengers' names and places of birth, and they scrutinized their bodies, examining faces, torsos, and limbs for any defining physical features. Juan Lin Tatlo of Leonque (Longxi) had a wart above his belly button. There was a scar on Joseph Nagco of Huajay's chest, and Juan Kan-Lao from Tangua (Tong'an) had a mole inside his right ear. The government planned to use this data to verify the men's identities in case they ever attempted to return to Manila, which they law prohibited them from doing.[1] The inspectors also verified that the boats were not carrying any contraband: the expelled men's wives, daughters, or any children under twelve years of age whom the Crown had banned from leaving the Philippines, or any weapons lest the passengers were tempted to turn pirate.

King Charles III's 1766 order to expel all China-born males older than twelve from the Philippines resulted in several flotillas like this one departing Manila in the decade after the war. The British invasion and occupation

of the capital were a watershed in Sino-Spanish relations. They radically altered Spanish perceptions of the Chinese in the Philippines and triggered a
sweeping government program to purge Sangleyes from the archipelago. The
longstanding royal protection for baptized Chinese migrants was withdrawn,
and the number of Chinese migrants living in the Spanish-controlled territories of the archipelago plummeted from an estimated seven thousand men
in 1762 to less than one hundred a decade later.[2] This chapter analyzes Chinese expulsion in depth, examining its ideological foundations, how forced
displacement on this scale was organized, and how the expelled experienced
and responded to this crisis.

This chapter reconstructs the two-stage forced migration of thousands
of Chinese migrants in the post–Seven Years' War Philippines. The first stage
saw Chinese men, in some cases accompanied by their families, evicted from
their homes, dispossessed of their land and belongings, and forcibly transported to Manila's Alcaicería, the market building that was transformed into
an internment camp. After lengthy periods of imprisonment, Chinese migrants endured the second stage of forced displacement, boarding private
merchant vessels that promised to deliver them to China. Expulsion depended
on the assistance of numerous people in the islands. Spaniards, Indigenous
Filipinos, Chinese mestizos, and Chinese migrants who occupied a range
of positions in colonial society, from senior government officials to priests,
prison guards, and merchants, became the state's essential partners in this
process. This chapter also recovers the strategies that Chinese migrants and
their kin deployed to avoid expulsion, or to ameliorate the dire conditions
that they were subject to during this protracted process. Some migrants ran
away or committed suicide, whereas others worked within the colonial system, utilizing its well-established pathways for seeking justice and mercy from
the king and his representatives in the islands. The historian Alf Lüdtke observed that forced migration archives compiled by governments often silence
the "emotional charge on both sides: the rage and revenge (if not pleasure)
among those who did the expelling; the mixture of revenge, anger, despera-
tion, and hatred among those who were expelled, hatred of those who inflicted
(or seemed to inflict) misery and grief."[3] This chapter digs deep into the expulsion records created by many hands in the Philippines and in Spain to
salvage glimpses of the raw and complex human experience of forced migration in the islands.

Deepening our understanding of the ideas that made expulsion possible,
and even desirable for many Manileños, this chapter excavates the toxic tropes

and stories about the Chinese that circulated in Manila in the aftermath of the Seven Years' War. It reveals that in the immediate postwar years, many people living in the capital remembered the conflict in the Philippines as a civil war that had pitted the pirate-like Sangleyes—brutes who had raided homes and committed extreme acts of violence—against their Spanish, Indigenous, and Chinese mestizo enemies, pushing the British to the sidelines of history. The texture of postwar Sinophobia overturns the simplistic idea that the Chinese faced systemic discrimination in Manila because of their wealth and success in business.[4] This chapter also highlights the global dimensions of Chinese forced displacement. The expulsion of the Jews and Moriscos from Spain in the late fifteenth and early sixteenth centuries served as models for eighteenth-century Chinese expulsion. Using the term "expulsion" to describe this forced migration, as contemporaries did, preserves this important imagined connection between the Iberian Mediterranean world and the Iberian Pacific. It also mattered that Chinese expulsion was implemented in the context of a broad transoceanic campaign to reform and strengthen the Spanish empire in the wake of a global war that made Britain a more potent enemy. The Pacific was not governed in isolation from the rest of the global Hispanic Monarchy.

Expulsion transfigured the politics of belonging in Manila. Counterintuitively, it had a positive impact on Chinese mestizos in the islands, creating new opportunities for mestizo elites to distinguish themselves from Sangleyes and bolster their identities as faithful vassals of the monarchy on earth and God in heaven. Chinese expulsion ultimately had a limited lifespan. The final section of this chapter shows that by the late 1770s, powerful voices in the Philippines were calling on the Crown to readmit Sangley migrants to the islands. In a passionate petition to resume Chinese migration to the islands, the Franciscan friar Juan de Concepción declared that "the Sangleyes are the blood that keeps this Christian body alive, and without them we will continue to deteriorate."[5] By the end of the decade, the colonial government was actively recruiting Chinese men to settle in the colony. The fact that the Spanish commitment to a Philippines free of Chinese migrants only endured for a decade has contributed to historians dismissing and disengaging from expulsion.[6] However, instead of rendering expulsion insignificant, its abandonment accentuates the dynamic nature of Sino-Spanish relations, and the extent to which the Chinese Question in the Philippines was influenced by vacillating regional politics.[7]

Enemies of God, the King, and the Republic: Popular
Memories of War and the Origins of Expulsion

The postwar push to purge the Philippines of Chinese men originated in the Southeast Asian archipelago.[8] Having led the loyalist forces to victory, the oidor Simón de Anda urged King Charles III to rid the Philippines of Sangleyes in a June 1764 letter, only weeks after the last British soldiers left Luzon.[9] Anda had no intention of harming trade between Manila and China, but he insisted that a general expulsion of Chinese migrants was necessary in light of their collective betrayal of Spain and God, not only during the British invasion, but throughout the long history of Spanish colonial rule in the islands. He connected recent Chinese collaboration with the British to past Chinese rebellions against Spanish sovereignty dating back to the pirate Limahong's 1574 attack on Manila. Time and time again, Anda argued, the Sangleyes had proven themselves to be the loyal allies of the pirates. When Francisco Javier de la Torre arrived in Manila in 1764 to take up the post of governor of the Philippines, he reiterated Anda's calls for expulsion.[10] Piracy was interwoven with the othering of Chinese migrants, locating them outside of the Catholic Hispanic nation.

The clergy enthusiastically threw their support behind the expulsion campaign. In June 1764, Governor de la Torre asked the leaders of the religious orders in the islands to report on the Sangleyes' wartime actions.[11] All were quick to return scathing letters that passionately recommended the Chinese be banished from the Philippines. The provincial of Franciscans, Fray Roque de la Purificación, insisted that expulsion was necessary since the Sangleyes had tried to "erase the Spanish name from these islands."[12] The Jesuit superior Fray Bernando Pazuengos declared that the Sangleyes were "more bloodthirsty than the English, the Moros, and the Malabars and Sepoys in the British army."[13] Fray Pedro Ire, the Dominican provincial, suggested that the Sangleyes' rebellion against the Spanish during the British invasion, on top of their repeated revolts that preceded this most recent crisis, amounted to proof of the disappointing failure of the two-centuries-long experiment in Chinese evangelism.[14] Their unanimity is astonishing given the long history of tension and conflict between the mendicant orders in the Philippines. The religious voices that had spoken out against Chinese expulsion a decade earlier had fallen silent.

Surely Anda and the clergy understood that someone had to be held to account for the British invasion and occupation of Manila. Elite Manileños

would have been aware of the dangerous accusations of treason that were pil-
ing up against Havana's rich and powerful men who allegedly collaborated
with the British during the simultaneous occupation of the Cuban capital.
The apparent incompetence of Juan de Prado, who was governor of Havana
and captain general of Cuba when the British attacked, led him to be placed
under house arrest in Madrid in 1763, tried for treason in a very public trial,
and handed down a death sentence that was commuted to a decade in
prison. The Crown also embargoed the property of two other wealthy Havana residents and brought them to Spain to answer to treason charges.
Both were found guilty and executed as punishment for their crimes.[15]
Scapegoating the Chinese meant that the Crown was less likely to try to
blame Spaniards for the temporary loss of Manila.

Powerful voices from Manila persuaded the king to take action against
the Chinese. On the seventeenth of April in 1766, the king decreed that all of
the Catholic Sangleyes that had committed infidelity, apostasy (abandoning
or renouncing the Catholic faith), and other "ugly and abominable crimes"
during the British occupation were to be expelled from the islands, regardless of whether they were single or married to local women.[16] The order
targeted baptized Chinese migrants because there were already laws in place
that prohibited nonbaptized Chinese from residing in the islands.[17] This
royal expulsion order was a major shift away from historic precedent. Previous expulsion orders had applied only to Chinese "infidels." The royal
decree did allow for baptized Chinese men who had remained loyal to Spain
during the British invasion to remain in the Philippines, albeit under new
restrictions on their mobility and their economic activities. Borrowing provisions from an old 1620 law that was still on the books, the 1766 decree
permitted baptized Chinese men who were married to Indigenous women
to settle in segregated rural towns that the government designated for this
purpose. Cut off from urban centers, and without the right to bear arms,
these men would be encouraged to work in agriculture or in skilled and ar-
tisanal trades, but they were prohibited from renting lucrative government
monopolies or engaging in commerce.[18] Colonial officials in the Philippines
were left to determine how to put this clause into effect.

Although demands for Chinese expulsion came from Manila, bigger
transoceanic processes impacted this policy. The idea of banishing the Chinese was inspired by the Crown's late fifteenth- and early sixteenth-century
expulsions of Jews, Muslims, and Moriscos from Iberian Peninsula. These
precedents established expulsion as a tool for managing populations that the

Crown deemed threats to Spanish sovereignty and the nation's religious purity. The links between these expulsions across time and vast distances are evident in the letter of the law. The 1766 order expelling the Chinese from the Philippines copied provisions from these earlier expulsion orders, including the exemption of baptized children from banishment.[19] Expelling the Chinese also responded to the new, post–Seven Years' War dynamics of interimperial rivalry operating on a transregional and global scale. Although Manila and Havana were returned to Spain in the Treaty of Paris, the British empire emerged from the war far bigger and bolder than ever before. Having seized Frances's former colonies in the Indian subcontinent and North America, postwar Britain claimed to rule over a vast territory that spanned the Indo-Pacific and Atlantic worlds. Colonial officials across the Spanish empire feared that it was only a matter of time before the emboldened British attempted another conquest of Spain's Asian and American colonies. Rattled by the invasion and occupation of its most strategic port cities, the Spanish empire's top military strategists feared that Britain could feasibly attack them again and even conquer Mexico. The forced displacement of Chinese migrants in the Philippines must be understood as part of an extensive program of reforms that Bourbon monarchs pursued in this context to shore up the empire against anticipated future enemy attacks.[20] Notably, Chinese expulsion also coincided with the expulsion of the Jesuits from the Spanish monarch's global domains. The royal pragmatic expelling the Jesuits was decreed in April of 1767, and resulted in the forced resettlement of more than five thousand Jesuits worldwide, with most seeking refuge in Italy under the pope's protection. Conflict over land and Indigenous subjects in Rio de la Plata drove this radical policy.[21] The expulsion of the Chinese from the Philippines was embraced in a moment of flux and change in the global Spanish empire, along with overhauls of colonial militias, the expansion of fortifications, and economic policies that sought to put more money in the royal treasury to fund these expensive projects.[22]

Expulsion was not a uniquely Spanish tool of population control. The British expelled the Arcadians from its North American colonies following the Seven Years' War, giving this French-speaking Catholic people eighteen months to leave British colonies in North America in 1763. This policy could have whetted the Spanish king and the Council of the Indies' appetites for banishing "foreign" communities.[23] The Dutch East India Company regularly forcibly repatriated undocumented Chinese migrants from Batavia and transported others to the Cape of Good Hope, offering another model for the

Spanish to copy.[24] European empires were keenly aware of what their imperial rivals were doing and often mimicked each other's strategies.[25]

Shattered Convivencia

The British invasion of Manila shattered the *convivencia* or relatively peaceful coexistence that Chinese and Spaniards had forged in the Philippines through Catholic anti-piracy in the eighteenth century. Simón de Anda's government-in-exile escalated violence against the Chinese during the 1762–1764 war, including forced migration, years before the Crown decreed expulsion. Chapter 3 discussed the government-authorized executions of at least 180 Chinese men at Guagua who were allegedly guilty of plotting to slaughter Spaniards attending Christmas religious services. Anda imposed tough new restrictions on Chinese mobility in the wake of this Christmas conspiracy. Sangleyes residing in pueblos outside of Manila were required to report in person to their local *gobernador de naturales* three times a day: at morning, at midday, and at sunset. They were also prohibited from traveling between villages without a license issued by their hometown's gobernadorcillo that specified where they were going and why. Anda ordered local officials to whip Sangleyes who broke these new rules, and to kill any found in possession of a weapon.[26] During the war, alcaldes mayores confiscated the property of Sangleyes who were accused of aiding the British. In Apalit, a town in Bulacan, local officials seized the mestiza de Sangley Gabriela Josepha's house and all of its contents because her Chinese husband had allegedly joined the British forces.[27]

Between two thousand and three thousand Chinese men fled the Philippines during the war to escape accelerating persecution. These migrants may have returned to China or other port cities in maritime Asia with substantial Chinese populations. Fray Remigio Hernández, the provincial of the Augustinians in the Philippines, claimed that many Sangleyes left Manila with as much silver as they could carry when it became obvious that the Spanish were gaining the upper hand in the war.[28] Almost fifteen hundred Sangleyes left Manila with the British East India Company. This includes approximately two hundred Chinese men who boarded British ships bound for the west coast of India in early 1763, and another twelve hundred who accompanied Alexander Dalrymple to Balambangan on the northern tip of Borneo later that year, where the British were attempting to set up a new trading outpost.[29]

The end of the war did not bring peace for the Chinese who stayed in the Philippines. The restoration of Spanish sovereignty in Manila only intensified the colonial government's repression of Sangleyes. In early 1765, Manila's Audiencia shut down Chinese-owned shops, and ordered baptized Sangleyes to pay the tribute that they owed for the preceding years when the head tax collection was interrupted by the British occupation.[30] Governor Francisco de la Torre forced five hundred Sangleyes to labor without pay on the massive fortification projects that were underway in the capital to repair the city's war-damaged defenses.[31] This was arduous work that involved digging deep and wide holes for wells and trenches for new, thicker, and stronger city walls. Forced Chinese migrant workers labored alongside three thousand Indigenous Filipinos who were mostly tribute workers mobilized from nearby provinces through the polo system, and were paid half a real and a rice ration each day. Even in this tense time, Chinese community leaders attempted to negotiate a way out of this new forced labor mandate. Parián officials persuaded de la Torre to accept a payment of twenty thousand pesos to liberate the Chinese workers. The governor gloated about this deal, which in his view asserted Spanish power over the Sangleyes, and ensured that they paid for the wall.[32] Bargaining continued to characterize relationships between the Spanish and the Chinese in the context of escalating oppression and control.

The colonial government's efforts to forcibly resettle Chinese migrants and their families from their homes in villages across Luzon to Manila's Alcaicería de San Fernando and the Parián started before the Seven Years' War had ended. There was a push to segregate Chinese migrants in Manila when the British still ruled the capital. In December of 1763, the British governor of Manila Dawsonne Drake "signed a proclamation directing all the inhabitants of Santa Cruz," most of whom were Chinese and Chinese mestizos, to relocate to the Parián, where they could be placed under surveillance.[33] It was around that time that Simón de Anda ordered the Indigenous principalia and military leaders to kill any Chinese man discovered in Pampanga, which resulted in a Chinese exodus from the province. In January of 1765, Governor Raón ordered alcaldes mayores across the Philippines to send the wives and children of Sangleyes to Manila to join their husbands and fathers who had already been sent to the capital.[34] Fragmentary evidence shows that local Indigenous officials collaborated with the government to rid the provinces of Chinese migrants and their kin. Twenty-three women and fifty-six children were forced to make the two-hundred-kilometer journey from their Pangasinan village of Lingayen to Manila in April that year, including Rosa

Vitacay and her three children, Maria Guatnio, Manuel Dizón, and Nicolas Samson.[35] The Chinese mestizo man Andrés Vengzon, Lingayen's lieutenant of the gobernadorcillo of the Chinese mestizos, accompanied the group to ensure that they did not flee into the mountains.

The postwar internal forced migration of the Chinese extended beyond Luzon. Petitions for exemptions from expulsion coming from the Visayas show that the push to cleanse the archipelago of Chinese people reached far across the islands. In Cebu, seven Chinese men jointly petitioned the colonial government to grant them and their families permission to remain in the city's Pariancillo and the Chinese neighborhood of San Juan Baptista. Domingo Canleong, Juan José Chengleong, Juan José Cue, Jacinto Chanco, Antonio Conguan, Francisco Tianga, and Eugenio Sulóng made the case that they should be granted permission to remain in Cebu because they were loyal Catholic vassals of the Crown, as their ancestors had been. Their petition pointed out that Cebu had never witnessed a Sangley uprising before or after the 1614 founding of the city's Pariancillo. In recent times, loyal Sangleyes had supported the holy war against the islands' Muslim pirates by generously donating rice and boats to the Catholic armadas mobilized to fight against them.[36] When news of the British attack on Manila reached Cebu, this community formed a militia to defend the city in case the British or Moro pirates tried to attack them. During the late war, the militia captain Domingo Canleong also donated one thousand *cavanes* of rice to feed the troops at the Spanish presidios at Misamis and Caraga, and he gifted silver to Cebu's Bishop Lino de Espeleta to support the expedition against Indigenous rebels in Loon, a village on the nearby island of Bohol.[37] Bishop Espeleta, along with the local Jesuit and Recollect missionaries and local Spanish military officials, all wrote strong letters in support of the Sangleyes of Cebu that verified their cited services to the Crown.[38] As a result, Manila's Audiencia decreed in November 1765 that Cebu's Sangleyes were "good and loyal vassals" who were not involved in their compatriots' rebellion, and granted them an exemption from the forced relocation. This proved to be a temporary reprieve.[39]

The royal expulsion order arrived in the Philippines in 1767. Governor Raón dispatched copies of the royal order to alcaldes mayores and missionaries across the Philippines, along with renewed orders to round up any remaining Sangleyes and their families and send them to Manila. Government officials and the clergy cooperated. Domingo Canleong's group were among the migrants who were forced to travel to Manila at this time.[40] In Pampanga, the alcalde mayor rounded up enough Chinese Christians and their families in the province to fill four sampans that he dispatched to the capital.[41] Fray Joseph de San Buenaventura, the provincial of the Augustinian recollects, helped to deport forty-eight families from towns in Pampanga and Bulacan provinces.[42] Colonial officials in Cavite also sent baptized Sangleyes and their families to Manila.[43] Local authorities in Panasajan sent adult Chinese men to Manila, but allowed their wives and children to remain on the grounds that there was no one else to look after the few belongings that these people had.[44] Vigan also sent only Sangley men to Manila.[45]

The journey to Manila from the provinces could be a dangerous one. Moro pirates continued to pose a risk to anyone traveling on the open sea, and bands of highwaymen threatened overland travelers.[46] A letter from Bacan informed Governor Raón that Moros captured a boat that was transporting Chinese prisoners to Manila, and the Chinese prisoner-passengers escaped. It is possible that the official concocted this story to protect a group that successfully evaded forced resettlement in the Manila internment camp. Some resettled families succeeded in running away. Pangasinan's alcalde mayor reported that a group of women who were married to arrested Sangleyes had fled to the mountains.[47] But many made it to the capital.

The displaced Sangleyes were forced into the Alcaicería when they arrived in Manila. This market hall had been built on the northern bank of the Pasig River in the 1750s—well within the firing range of Fort Santiago's big guns—to house visiting non-Christian Chinese migrants and maritime workers. It was subsequently transformed into an internment camp in the expulsion era. Some Chinese migrants may have voluntarily left the Philippines if they managed to secure a passage on a boat out of the archipelago, but the government was not putting them on ships departing from the islands in large numbers in 1767 and 1768. In 1767, the government forcibly repatriated to China only 213 men, who were all prisoners collected from jails in Manila and nearby pueblos.[48] The 255 Chinese men dispatched to China the following year included 164 criminals and vagabonds and 91 "infidels" who were shipwrecked in Ilocos.[49] Chinese survivors of shipwrecks were regularly deported from the Philippines in the eighteenth century. The capital was also traditionally cleansed of those undesirable men who wound up in jail for being vagrants or were guilty of other crimes; however, before the war many of these men would have been dispatched to labor-hungry presidios instead of to China.[50] In the wake of the war, these strategic defensive outposts must have been deemed too vulnerable to be turned over to political prisoners.

The slow pace of Chinese expulsions frustrated some Spanish colonial officials. The French astronomer Le Gentil, who came to Manila to document the transit of Venus, suggested that the Spanish governor was taking bribes from the Chinese to delay the expulsion.[51] When Antonio Andrade arrived in Manila in 1769 to take up the position of *fiscal*, he was offended by the liberties that Chinese people were apparently enjoying in the Philippines. He complained in a letter to the king that "when I arrived in the islands, I noticed . . . the infidel Chinese—apostates and traitors—were just placed under the charge of their cabecilla in Parián, and the Chinese in the provinces remained there under frivolous pretexts."[52] The king and the Council of the Indies were unhappy to receive this news, and urged the governor to hasten the expulsion.[53]

Memories of War and Malignant Sinophobia

Efforts to expel the Chinese gained speed when José Antonio Raón y Gutiérrez took over the reigns as governor of the Philippines. Raón put the oidor Juan Antonio de Uruñuela Aransay in charge of expulsion in June 1769. Uruñuela hastily undertook a formal inquiry into the Sangleyes' wartime activities that would ostensibly determine who was guilty of betraying Spain and abandoning their Catholic faith. This investigation resembled the trial of Cuba's former governor that was conducted in Spain. These rituals of scapegoating placed all of the blame for Spain's embarrassing military defeat in the Caribbean on the shoulders of a select group of men, deflecting criticism from the Crown and other colonial subjects. A notable difference was that in the Cuban case, a small group of individuals were on trial, whereas in the Philippines, an entire nation of people were accused of being traitors.[54] Although the royal expulsion order stated that only Chinese migrants who were guilty of these crimes were to be expelled from the Philippines, Uruñuela made no effort to assess individual's actions. Although the investigation turned up evidence of Chinese migrants who had remained faithful to the Spanish during the war, Uruñuela concluded that the Sangleyes in the Philippines were collectively guilty of treachery and apostasy, and every single one of them must be banished from the islands.

Uruñuela's two-week-long investigation saw him interview seventy-two Manileños about Sangleyes' wartime activities. The surviving collection of testimonies that scribes transcribed offers rich insight into the stories about the Chinese and the Seven Years' War that circulated in Manila in the aftermath of the conflict. These narratives reveal the texture of Sinophobia that flourished in this era and shed light on why Chinese expulsion was desired, or at least not opposed in any meaningful way, by non-Chinese communities in the Philippines. Uruñuela questioned colonial officials including alcaldes mayores, scribes, and the administrator of the royal hospital, in addition to high-ranking soldiers and militiamen who had fought in Anda's army. Although these people were not representative of Manileño society, they were not all males and Spanish. Two witnesses were women. Uruñuela questioned one Indigenous Filipino, one Armenian, and one Malabar. The eleven Chinese mestizos that he interrogated embraced the opportunity to distinguish themselves from Chinese migrants.

Multiple witnesses repeated the claim that the Chinese were eager collaborators with the British during the war. Several recalled that the Sangleyes' first bold act of treason in 1762 was the elaborate public ceremony that they staged to formally swear allegiance to the newly installed British governor of Manila three or four days after the city fell. The Sangleyes allegedly paraded through Manila and into Intramuros. The most senior Parián officials rode on horseback accompanied by musicians playing instruments, and others carrying colored arches as well as gifts of fruit, bread, sugar, and chickens for Manila's conquerors. The crowd made its way to the British governor's palace, where Sangley elites declared their loyalty to the invaders.[55] British archives do not mention this event at all, which casts doubt on its occurrence. Descriptions of the whole production evoke the Hispanic tradition of governors' and archbishops' ceremonial entries into Manila and other colonial cities, which may have inspired witnesses' imaginations.[56] But witnesses provided plenty of substantiated examples of the Chinese aiding the invaders throughout the nineteen-month occupation. Sangley farmers and cooks had supplied the British army with food, and artisans manufactured their weapons, including lances and swords.[57]

It is striking that so many wartime memories captured by the government inquiry almost erase British officials and their multiethnic armies from this conflict, and reimagine 1762–1764 as a period of civil war in the islands waged between the heathen Sangleyes and the loyalist Catholic Hispano-Filipino armies. In the theater of popular memory, the British were cast as supporting actors to the Chinese protagonists and their campaign to seize control of the archipelago. Uruñuela collected testimonies that painted a picture of a highly organized Sangley army that mobilized against Hispano-Filipino

forces. Witnesses remembered Chinese infantry and calvary companies, each
with its own emblems, flags, and banners, training with British soldiers in
drills before marching into battle against the Catholics.[58] The Manileños suggested that all Sangleyes were somehow involved in this army; even those
who had been too cowardly to fight had donated money and other resources
to the Chinese war effort.[59] Some of Uruñuela's witnesses were convinced that
the Chinese were the true ringleaders of the uprisings in Pangasinan and
Pampanga, shifting the blame for these massive revolts from Indigenous
communities to migrants.[60] Joseph de Ayusso, a lawyer attached to Manila's Audiencia, was unique in acknowledging that coercion shaped the
Sangleyes' decisions to take up arms against the Spanish. Ayusso had seen
the British fire shots at Chinese soldiers at Malinta when they refused to join
the vanguard of troops that were rushing into battle against Anda's forces,
and was empathetic to their plight.[61] It may be common sense that people can
be compelled to do things they morally object to under the threat of violence, but few Manileños were willing to admit this in 1769.

Religion was a central theme in stories about the Chinese in the war. For
Manileños, abandoning Catholicism went hand in hand with treason. They
considered the Sangleyes' conspicuous physical transformations during the
war as proof of their apostasy. Witnesses explained that rosary beads were
the only thing that had distinguished Christian Sangleyes from their infidel
countrymen before the war. When the British invaded, the Sangleyes sup-
posedly tore these Catholic prayer beads from their necks, shouting "I'm done
with Santa Maria."[62] The merchant Don Pedro Galarraga noted that Sangleyes
also "cut their hair very short in the style of gentiles" soon after the British
seized control. In a society that understood faith as embodied, changes to
hair and dress could be read as expressions of religious beliefs or identities.[63]

During the war, Chinese apostasy had transformed Manila's urban space.
Manileños recalled being shocked when the Chinese established a large
temple in the Arroceros neighborhood. Curiosity drove some Spanish vecinos to take a closer look. Sebastián de Aramburú admitted to entering the
temple in his capacity as a familiar of the Inquisition. He saw that the Sangleyes had adorned the exterior of the building with banners and pieces of
silk. Inside they had erected an altar, where they had placed a pig's head on
a silver tray surrounded by fruit, sweets, incense, and "ten thousand candles." These were common offerings to ancestors and deities in Confucian
and Taoist rituals including in Southeastern China. Sangleyes knelt before
the altar holding colored candles in their hands.[64] The blacksmith's guild

hall in the Parián was also converted into a temple.[65] It is plausible that the Parián's Sangley guilds had a secret religious function before the war, comparable to Cuba's African *cabildos de nación*. A degree of religious plurality was characteristic of multiethnic Manila for the duration of Spanish colonial rule.[66] The government and the various arms of the organized Church had ensured that non-Catholic traditions were suppressed and forced into private spaces beyond state scrutiny. Spain's temporary loss of sovereignty created opportunities for non-Catholic religious practices to come out into the open.

In early 1763, a sampan from China delivered a statue of the Chinese god of vengeance to Manila, which local Sangleyes installed in the Arroceros temple with great ceremony. This deity was probably Guandi, the god of war, who became one of the most important gods in China in the eighteenth century. Villages across China built temples in Guandi's honor, and "his statue was found in every corner of the empire."[67] The statue frightened Manileños. Doña Ana Monterro had heard that this icon had crossed the sea to avenge the deaths of the Sangleyes who were slaughtered at Guagua, and to kill Simón de Anda.[68] Sangleyes had dressed in their best clothes to welcome the god to Manila, escorting the statue in a candlelit parade from the beach where it came ashore to the Alcaicería de San Fernando, and finally to the Arroceros temple. There they burned offerings of colored paper money before the statue and drank tea and ate sweets.[69] Whereas this Chinese celebration had proceeded unencumbered, Don Matthias de Porras recalled a contemporaneous Catholic procession of the image Nuestra Señora de Consolacíon through the city, where participants faced heckling and ridicule from Sangley onlookers.[70] For Porras, this incident was the epitome of a world turned upside down.

Sangleyes manifest as pirates in Manileños' memories of the war, pillaging prized possessions and murdering people. Uruñuela's witnesses remembered that it was Sangleyes (rather than British and Sepoy soldiers or opportunistic Indigenous people) who sacked Manila after the city fell in 1762. Don Francisco Xavier Salgado reported that he had to pay a hefty price to a Chinese merchant to buy the large ornamental silver and glass spider that had been stolen from his house during the sack.[71] Juan Salvador de la Soledad, a mestizo de Sangley from Binondo, said that during the war he had seen Sangleyes in the Parián selling items that had obviously been stolen from churches, including sacramental silver chalices and the small bells that priests used in the Catholic mass, as well as the habits worn by the Jesus of Nazareth confraternity.[72] Even stories about Sangley robberies emphasized their disrespect of the Catholic religion.

Witnesses attributed the war's most brutal acts of unrestrained violence to Sangleyes. They were captivated by rumors of the Chinese torturing and murdering Catholic priests, offering up many examples to Uruñuela. Santiago del Barrio, a Chinese mestizo, testified that the Sangleyes had cut off the noses and ears of several priests at Bulacan before murdering them.[73] Revealing the colonial rumor mill in operation, del Barrio clarified that he had not seen this crime with his own eyes, but he had heard about it from a friend. Several witnesses vaguely mentioned that somewhere in Batangas, the province south of Manila, a band of vicious Sangleyes had beaten friars to a pulp before handing them over to the British, and at least one had died from his injuries. Some witnesses added more details to accounts of this incident. Domingo Hurtado identified the priests as the Augustinian friars Manuel Cavallero and Pedro Cordojuela, and claimed that the Sangleyes had "painted their faces with excrement."[74] Other Manileños postulated that a band of Sangleyes had forced Padre Thomas Parada to drink horse urine from a sacramental silver chalice before tying him to a tree and whipping him, then killing him. The Sangleyes crucified one priest on a cross, others testified, mocking the God that Catholics worshipped.[75] These were the kinds of atrocities that pirates were known to commit.

Some witnesses testified that they had personally sustained injuries from Sangleyes during the war. Vicente Barzina, a Spaniard employed as a guard in the Arroceros neighborhood, claimed that he had been captured and seriously injured by a band of Sangleyes in 1762. The assault left him with lasting injuries, including a scar that ran so deep on his upper right arm that he appeared to be "missing a chunk [of flesh]," and thick scars on his skull and left wrist.[76] Other witnesses disclosed that their family members had fallen victim to the Sangleyes. The captain of the Chinese mestizo militia, Domingo Garcia, testified that Sangleyes had arrested his young cousin and proceeded to beat him, tie him up, and throw him into a river while he was still alive and screaming for mercy, leaving him to drown.[77] Such personal encounters fueled Sinophobia.

Several versions of Chinese conspiracies to exterminate Spaniards during the war persisted in 1769. These included the rumor that the Chinese had planned to attack and kill all the Spaniards when they attended mass on Christmas Eve in 1763, which had led Anda's government-in-exile to execute at least 180 Chinese men.[78] Several Manileños reported that the Chinese had offered the British governor of Manila a large sum of money for a license to kill all of the Spaniards. When Chinese mestizos relayed this conspiracy to Uruñuela, they insisted that the Sangleyes had intended to kill them, too. Rumors about this license to kill were surprisingly detailed. Manileños were specific about just how much blood money the Sangleyes had offered, citing sums that ranged from ten thousand to thirty thousand pesos. Some shared knowledge that the Swiss mercenary, merchant, and long-term Manila resident Cesár Falliet had drawn up and presented a contract to the British that outlined the terms of the planned killings. This could have struck people as plausible because Falliet became an important advisor to the British occupiers and helped them to acquire the contents of the Augustinian Library. The British took on the unlikely role of heroes in this story, as it was apparently their refusal to accept Sangley bribes that saved the Spaniards and mestizos from slaughter. It is interesting that no references to this plot survive from the war years; it gained currency only in the aftermath of the conflict.[79]

If this massacre was thwarted, the 1769 testimonies show that Manileños believed that the Sangleyes had succeeded in carrying out three distinct massacres of Spaniards, Philippine indios, and Chinese mestizos during the war. The first alleged mass killing involved the Chinese boatmen who had accepted money to ferry families of Spanish refugees across the Pasig River as they tried to flee the British during the siege of the city. The boatmen were accused of robbing their passengers, taking even the clothes from their backs, and then killing them.[80] The second massacre was the slaughter of Indigenous refugees, including women and children, inside the Quiapo church. This attack certainly occurred, and the parish priest Bartolome Saguinsin survived and reported this incident.[81] The third was the mass murder of Hispano-Filipino soldiers who had fallen into enemy hands at Bulacan. The British had allegedly handed over these prisoners of war to their eager Sangley executioners, who led them to a river bank and slit their throats one by one. Perhaps this story gained popularity because it had a hero. An unidentified captive militiaman from Anda's army was said to have made a lucky escape by wrestling his hands free from the ropes that tied them together behind his back. Grabbing the knife that was about to slash open his throat, he cut the cords that bound him, and dived into the river, swimming away to safety.[82]

Hateful art created in Manila in the immediate postwar era indicates that the idea of the Seven Years' War as a Chinese rebellion was widespread in this colonial society. One contemporary sketch of Simón de Anda depicts him towering over the severed heads of seven Chinese men as a church burns in the distance behind him, implying that the dead had been punished for their betrayal of the Catholic republic (Figure 6). There are no visual references to the British role in the war at all in this particular image. The decapitated heads of dead men, whose Chinese identity is marked by their queues, trail blood and gore.[83] Trophy heads were a common symbol of Christian triumph in military art.[84] This gruesome scene evokes images of Santiago the moor-slayer trampling over the heads of dead Muslims, an icon that was carved above the main entrance to the Intramuros fort.

Bartholomé Saguinsín, a proud Tagalog, a poet, and the parish priest of Quiapo, penned a collection of Latin epigrams celebrating Simón de Anda's victory over the British and the Sangleyes.[85] The poem emphasized the un-reformable evilness of the Sangleyes, citing their attack on his own church, as well as the Guagua conspiracy as proof. Saguinsín portrayed Sangleyes "as having a bio-moral inclination to violence, treachery, and rebellion that went beyond even that of the most fickle and wicked indios from distant provinces."[86] This is clear in the verse where Saguinsín addresses his ene-mies directly:

> O Sangleyes, what frenzy lashes your souls
> And mysteriously overwhelms your hearts?
> Such madness digs for you wide graves!
> For whoever sets snares for others, falls in himself.
> This is the work of violent passions and a godless people.[87]

The popular Sinophobia that swept over Manila made the colonial govern-ment's radical Chinese expulsion experiment feasible.

The Alcaicería de San Fernando: Manila's First Internment Camp

The Spanish colonial government doubled down on its campaign to banish baptized Chinese men from the Philippines as soon as Uruñuela's rushed in-quiry wrapped in the middle of 1769. Two hundred noisy soldiers descended on Manila's Chinese districts in the dusky hours before dawn on the eigh-teenth of July. In the Parián, Arroceros, Binondo, and Santa Cruz, soldiers startled sleeping families awake with shouting and angry palms pummeling the doors of house after house, demanding to be let in. They swooped into

Figure 6. This unpublished engraving depicts Simón de Anda y Salazar towering over a desk next to a man who might be his son. The severed heads of Chinese men trailing gore are visible along the bottom edge of the image. It echoes images of Santiago Matamoros and Mata-Indios, trampling over enemy corpses. Newberry Library, Ayer MS 1921, N.23.

darkened bedrooms and arrested every Sangley man they found, along with their wives and children. Armed guards patrolled the streets and passageways that led in and out of these neighborhoods to catch anyone who tried to escape. By the time the midday sun was high in the sky, the soldiers had imprisoned fifteen hundred more Sangley men in the Alcaicería de San Fernando. Whatever worldly possessions the prisoners had been forced to leave behind were abandoned to "the insatiable greed" of thieves.[88] Days after the mass arrests in Manila, Uruñuela dispatched instructions to alcaldes mayores in the provinces to round up any Sangleyes who remained in their respective districts and send them to the capital.[89] Between the nineteenth of July in 1769 and the end of 1772, a total of 2,294 male Chinese migrant prisoners were imprisoned in the Alcaicería. This forced resettlement impacted Chinese migrants living across the Philippines. The majority of interred migrants had been living in Manila before they were arrested, but others came from northern Luzon, the Visayas, and Mindanao.

Surviving local records documenting the forced migration of the Chinese from Pampanga to the Alcaicería in 1769 offer rare insight into how this process was organized and experienced on the ground.[90] Expelling the Chinese depended on the support of many different people, including the highest ranked provincial officials. Pedro Antonio de Aguirre, the alcalde mayor of Pampanga, resided in the provincial capital of Bacolor. On receiving Uruñuela's instructions to expel the Chinese in July, Aguirre used a circular letter to disseminate the expulsion order to gobernadorcillos de naturales and gobernadorcillos de mestizos in pueblos throughout the province. Scribes in Bacolor made copies of Uruñuela's instructions, and runners delivered them to chains of towns that were relatively close to each other. In each pueblo, gobernadorcillos read the copied orders and then added their names to the bottom of the document to certify that they understood and promised to comply with them. These local Indigenous and Chinese mestizo officials were responsible for arresting Sangleyes in their jurisdictions— men who were often their neighbors. They locked them up in the town jail until they could be escorted to Bacolor by an armed guard, from where bigger groups of forced migrants would be sent to Manila.

Pampanga's postwar Chinese population was small. Towns in the province were usually home to no more than five Catholic Chinese men and their families. Forty Sangleyes were forcibly migrated from Pampangan towns to Manila between August and October 1769. Most had lived in the province for many years and were either married or widowed and were fathers to children.

The shopkeeper Pedro Leyeng was typical in this sense. After being baptized in 1747, he settled in Bacolor with his wife, Juana Tuano.[91] The shopkeeper Esteban Herrian was wealthier than average. His house was furnished with chairs made of wood and leather, and his shop stored five hundred *cavanes* of rice.[92] Pampanga's Sangleyes were mostly poor, owning little more than their simple thatched houses, a couple of pieces of furniture, such as a small table and bench, and a few items of well-worn clothing. The sole possession of Juan Coquenco, the only Chinese migrant living in Lubao, was his skinny horse.[93]

There is no evidence that these migrants helped the British during the war. In fact, Pampanga's gobernadorcillos reported that the majority of the resident Sangleyes had remained in their respective pueblos for the duration of the British occupation. Nor was there any proof of apostasy. To the contrary, the expulsion archive documents Catholic devotion. Local officials compiled inventories of the displaced Sangleyes' property that point to piety. Among Esteban Herrian's things was a small, gold-painted tabernacle that held a gilded image of Our Lady.[94] Despite their lack of treachery and apostasy, only five Sangleyes were permitted to remain in the Pampanga on the grounds that they were too sick and elderly to travel. They included Pedro Leyeng, who was suffering from a sickness that filled his mouth with blood and gave him such severe stomach pain that he was completely unable to walk.[95] The colonial government permitted similar exemptions for old and sick Jesuits who were also being expelled from the islands at this time.[96]

The trauma of being torn from family and community is conveyed in the account of Joseph Luis Chiucong's suicide, which painfully disrupts the emotionless lists of the names of the expelled and the inventories of their belongings that local government representatives compiled. Chiucong was born in Leongque and had lived in the Philippines for twenty-four years by 1769. At first he had resided in Manila, and he was baptized in the Parián. He then resided in Laguna for seven years before settling in the Pampangan town of Mexico. Chiucong married his wife, Rosa, only weeks before he was arrested and locked up in Mexico's small jail. Late in the evening of the twenty-first of October, Pampangan soldiers guarding Chuicong and other imprisoned Sangleyes watched him roll tobacco into a cigar and reach over to light it on the oil lamp that illuminated his dark cell. Chiucong then threw the lamp to the floor where it shattered, plunging the cell into darkness. When guards rushed in to the cell with a candle, they saw Chiucong tearing at his throat with the sharp shards of broken lamp. By the time the guards wrestled

Chiucong's hands from his face, he had a five-centimeter-wide gash across his neck and his mouth was filling with blood. The guards called a priest to give the dying man his last rites, but Chiucong was unconscious when the priest arrived on the scene, and he took his final breath shortly after.[97]

We can only wonder what thoughts flashed through the minds of those who witnessed this desperate act. Did they feel responsible? Did the guards ask the priest to forgive their sins as well as those of the dying man? There are many possible ways to interpret the anonymous scribe's decision to write about Chiucong and document his violent death, and to disclose that he had been a neighbor and was newly married. Was this a kind of protest against the forced repatriation of the Sangleyes? Or did the scribe write down what happened to avoid being blamed for the death of a man in their care, hoping to avoid punishment?

Government scribes recorded only basic information about the forced Sangley migrants when they arrived in the Alcaicería. Analyzing the data they collected reveals that the average interred migrant was forty-seven years old, had resided in the Philippines for two decades, and had been baptized for sixteen years. At nineteen years of age, Miguel Tin Yocco and Francisco Go Usay were the youngest migrant prisoners in the market-turned-prison. Miguel had come to Manila from China only two years earlier and was baptized in the Parián church shortly after his arrival. Francisco had come to the Philippines when he was ten years old. At eighty-eight years of age, Jacinto Locco was the oldest prisoner, and one of two octogenarians detained in the camp. Locco migrated to the Philippines when he was sixty-six and had settled in Catbalogan, a coastal town on the Visayan island of Samar, where he was baptized and married. The majority of migrants imprisoned in the Alcaicería were unskilled workers with no declared occupation. Many worked in low-paid jobs, including as dockworkers and fishermen. Street hawkers who sold sweets, snacks, and tobacco were also well represented among the imprisoned, as were skilled tailors, cobblers, carpenters, and butchers.[98] Sangleyes faced a stay of months or even years in the Alcaicería de San Fernando as they waited for a passage to China. The seventy-five-year-old Thomas Sunco, a native of Leonque, was arrested on the eighteenth of July 1769 in the Santa Cruz home that he shared with his wife of fifteen years. He was held in the camp for more than a year before he was deported to China in August the following year.[99]

It is odd that some scholars have described the Alcaicería as a symbol of Sino-Spanish cooperation, because the colonial government constructed this octagonal, two-story market building in the 1750s to more effectively surveil and control itinerant Chinese men.[100] Before the British invasion, the Spanish colonial government in Manila had required nonbaptized Chinese visitors who were temporarily calling in to the city, including merchants and maritime workers, to sleep and conduct their business in this structure. These temporary residents were able to move about the city freely during the day, but they were required to return to the building during the night.[101] After the war, when baptized Chinese Catholics who had lived in the Philippines for many years were forced to join the sojourners in the market hall, it became very difficult for its residents to leave. A company of Pampangan infantrymen was posted at the gates to guard the prisoners and prevent escapes. With so many people crowded into the Alcaicería, the situation inside grew dire during the expulsion years.

The hierarchical structures that organized life within Manila's Chinese community remained intact during the expulsion era. Go-betweens continued to act as mediators between the Sangleyes and the colonial government. In the mid-1760s, trapped Sangley seamen complained to the Parián's gobernadorcillo about being extorted and abused by Don Andrés Barreto, the alcalde of the Alcaicería.[102] Barreto permitted the Chinese to leave the building only if they paid the exorbitant 100-peso fee for a license to do so.[103] He set up an illegal monopoly on essential items that he sold to the prison's residents at steeply inflated prices, including rice, pork, wine, and firewood. Barreto was ruthless. He punished the prisoners who broke his rules, brutally whipping a man who smuggled a quarter-hog into the Alcaicería to sell. On top of this, Baretto confiscated whatever goods he wanted from the migrants being held in the market hall. This situation created public outcry in Manila as Spanish merchants became anxious that this abuse would damage trade with China.[104] The Chinese gobernadorcillo lobbied the Spanish governor to address this miserable situation. Manila's Audiencia eventually intervened and disciplined Barreto for corruption. A judge deemed poverty to be the root cause of the alcalde's criminal activities. He noted that Barreto was "a poor man without fortune," and "experience has taught the universe that when the poor enter office, they build huge fortunes through extortion."[105] Surely the rise of Sinophobia emboldened Baretto's petty dictatorship.

Joseph Camco, the gobernadorcillo of Sangleyes, petitioned Uruñuela to improve camp conditions in late 1769. Camco convinced Uruñuela to allow twenty-five prisoners to leave the Alcaicería each day so they could work and earn money to support themselves. Uruñuela agreed, but he warned that the prisoners would be punished with two hundred lashes if they failed to return before the five o'clock curfew.[106] The Spanish official was angered by Camco's claims that the poorest Sangleyes were starving in this prison, characterizing these as "false rumors" spread by the "inherently untrustworthy" Sangleyes in an effort to malign his character and gain their freedom, yet he agreed to demands to provide rice rations to those prisoners who required it.[107] Even in such awful conditions, there continued to be some opportunities for negotiation.

The Spanish colonial government utilized the existing, private infrastructure of inter-Asian commerce to repatriate Sangleyes from the Alcaicería to China.[108] The 2,653 Sangleyes who were forcibly repatriated to China between August 1769 and August 1772 made the journey on merchant ships: privately owned vessels of various sizes that regularly sailed between Manila and China and other ports across maritime Asia. There was no attempt to return the expelled men to their towns or cities of origin.[109] Instead, the refugees were delivered to whatever ports in Southwestern China that captains deemed convenient, including Emuy, Canton, Macao, Chianchiu, and Huajay.[110] The majority of the expelled were forcibly repatriated to China in the two and a half years that followed the sweeping mass arrests in Manila in July 1769: 1,006 were deported that year, 809 followed in 1770, and 783 in 1771. Only fifty-five Sangleyes were deported in 1772, as by this time, no other "expellable" Sangleyes remained in the Philippines archipelago. In the same four-year period, the government expelled 119 Jesuits and lay brothers from the Philippines.[111] Only eighty-nine Sangleyes remained in the Philippines in 1772, and all were men who were too old or too sick to travel.[112]

Spanish merchant vecinos of Manila captained six of the thirty-four voyages that transported expelled Sangleyes to China in these years. The example of Francisco Casten shows how seamlessly merchants integrated human trafficking into their thriving long-distance trade routes. Typical of the mid-eighteenth-century ships' captains in maritime Asia, Casten combined an expert knowledge of sailing and navigation with market nous. In September 1769, he steered the large goleta *Nuestra Señora del Rosario* into Manila Bay after a voyage to Java and Malaya. He filled his ship with luxury goods in Batavia, the center of the Dutch empire in Asia that doubled as a global emporium. In addition to bundles of colorful printed cottons and other textiles from India, the ship's hold was packed with fine European foods for Manileño elites. Casten had invested in a huge amount of alcohol: thirty-six bottles of aguardiente, eighty bottles of beer, and more than a thousand bottles of wine. He also carried barrels of Spanish olive oil, olives, more than one hundred round cheeses, butter, and preserved salmon.[113] A few weeks after arriving in Manila, Casten set off for Macao with fifty-two exiled Chinese men crowded onto his boat.[114] He returned to Manila in February 1770 with 92,000 pesos' worth of cargo, including cinnamon and Chinese silks, and departed for China once more in October with another fifty expelled Sangleyes on board.

Chinese sea captains were also willing to integrate deporting exiled migrants from the Philippines into their established inter-Asian trading routes. They transported exiles to China in twenty-eight separate voyages. Captain Chu Dimquia brought the sampan called *Sin Jin* to Manila in June 1771 with twenty crew and a modest 1,635 pesos' worth of trade goods on board, including some five thousand ordinary porcelain plates.[115] The cargo's low value suggests that the *Sin Jin* was a small boat. In August the following year, Dimquia left Manila for Huahay on a different sampan—the *Taigua*—with eight expelled Sangleyes aboard. Chy Juaqua, the captain of the *Pechingeng*, arrived in Manila Bay in February 1772 from Emuy. His cargo, valued at 85,448 pesos, included silks and boxes of fine stockings—white for men and colored varieties for women—in addition to the spice *anís*.[116] Six months later, he made the return voyage to China with ten expelled Sangleyes aboard the same boat.[117] Other Chinese captains carried much larger numbers of deportees. Captain Bartolome Pitco transported 178 Sangleyes in two separate voyages in 1771 and 1772, more than any other individual merchant.[118]

Multiple factors influenced captains' decisions to cooperate in the expulsion of the Chinese from the Philippines. Some may have had little choice in transporting migrants. In 1769, the colonial government introduced a regulation that required all vessels destined for China to repatriate as many exiled men as they could carry in addition to the crew and passengers that they had brought to the Philippines. The government deployed two pilots to assess each boat's capacity for human cargo to enforce this rule.[119] However, all ships that sailed to China that year ultimately carried less than their government-assessed capacity of deportees, as captains successfully claimed that larger crews and trade goods left less space for exiled men.[120]

Toxic Sinophobia surely played a part in encouraging Spanish captains to participate in the expulsion. Thomas Perez Dorado, a vecino of Manila and captain of the goleta *Nuestra Señora del Rosario*, transported twelve expelled Sangleyes to Canton in early 1770.[121] Dorado revealed his hatred of the Sangleyes when he testified in Uruñuela's investigation, accusing the group of engineering the Indigenous uprisings that erupted in Pangasinan and Pampanga during the British invasion of Luzon.[122] Other Spanish captains probably shared his views, harboring resentment that their property had been stolen or destroyed in the war.

There were significant economic incentives for captains to assist in the expulsion. The archive holds clues that captains of ships were paid to ferry these forced passengers to China. For example, in late 1779, Parián officials informed the government that they had paid two and a half thousand pesos for two large sampans to return to Manila the following year to repatriate exiled Sangleyes to China.[123] For Chinese merchants, transporting forced migrants was a strategy for continuing to trade in Manila during the era of the expulsion. In 1770, the colonial government received Bartolome Pitco's request for permission to return to Manila from China the following year with a large sampan that could repatriate a sizable group of exiled men to their homeland. Uruñuela agreed with the caveat that if Pitco arrived with a small boat, the government would confiscate it. Uruñuela sternly warned that Sangleyes like Pitco should not use promises of repatriation as a ruse to trade, yet this is exactly what Pitco did.[124] Pitco correctly assumed that aiding the expulsion would have served his personal interests in the long term. He continued his profitable shipping enterprise into the 1770s, captaining two boats that brought trade goods into Manila in 1773 and 1775.[125]

For Miguel Ygnacio Mayoralgo Gou Quic, working with the government to facilitate expulsion proved a successful strategy for avoiding this fate himself. Mayoralgo acted as a middleman between the colonial government and Chinese merchants, bargaining with Chinese sea captains on the government's behalf to buy or rent space on sampans to deport the banished men to China.[126] Mayoralgo hired *apoderados* (lawyers) in Spain to petition the Crown for an exemption from the expulsion in 1770. Francisco Gómez and Antonio Rumualdo de Marín Martínez, both vecinos and residents of the royal court of Madrid, succeeded in convincing the monarch to defend Mayoralgo's right to remain in the Philippines.[127] Mayoralgo was a long-time resident of Binondo and had been an important go-between in the prewar capital for many years. In the mid-1750s, Mayoralgo rented the *ramo de boletas* from the government, which meant that he was responsible for collecting Chinese tribute in Manila and its hinterland as part of the tax-farming system that existed in the Philippines. He helped the government to enforce the expulsion of non-Christian Chinese from Manila during Arandia's government. In 1759 Manila's archbishop appointed Mayoralgo to the position of *fiscal zelador*.[128] This made Mayoralgo a kind of moral policeman, responsible for monitoring "public sins," reporting instances of heresy, idolatry, and witchcraft to the archbishop, and encouraging Sangleyes in his neighborhood to attend Catholic mass and participate in catechism. In 1761 Mayoralgo became the *cabecilla principal* of the Sangleyes. During the British occupation, he supported Anda's government-in-exile by making at least two voyages to China to purchase supplies for Anda's army, including bronze, guns, artillery, wheat, and paper.[129] Mayoralgo was not the only Chinese migrant to loyally serve the colonial government in wartime, but he was the only one whose loyalty delivered an exemption from expulsion.

The almost complete eradication of Chinese migrants from Manila transformed the city's urban space.[130] The Alcaicería's transformation into an internment camp was one of the most obvious changes. When Simón de Anda returned to the Philippines as governor in 1770, he ordered the San Gabriel Hospital in Binondo, which had long served sick and dying Sangleyes, to close its doors. By 1775, the Dominicans had renovated and reopened the hospital as a chapel for Indigenous Filipino parishioners, complete with a new door to the street and an elaborate frontispiece.[131] The Parián church dedicated to the Magi that had primarily served Sangleyes was also closed down. Manila's archbishop Basilio Sancho de Santa Justa y Ruffina led a spirited campaign to erase the physical traces of the Sangley presence in the city, too. In April 1771, he ordered Manileños to remove the figures of snakes and alligators that Chinese builders had crafted in the eaves of the roofs of houses they had constructed across the cosmopolis. The archbishop suggested that these symbols, which he denounced as false idols, could be replaced with crosses, being the "sign and banner of true Christianity."[132] The expulsion of the Jesuits from the Philippines set a precedent for this makeover of public space. In 1770, Governor Anda ordered the removal of the Jesuit coats of arms that were chiseled into the order's former colleges, houses, and other buildings. Anda ordered that these symbols of Jesuit authority be replaced with King Charles III's royal coat of arms.[133]

Reevaluating Sangley Settler Colonialism in the Philippines

Support for a Philippines free of Chinese migrants began to wane in Spain after the final ships repatriating exiled men departed Manila for China. Pedro Calderón, a former oidor in Manila's Audiencia who was serving as a minister of the Council of the Indies in Spain, recommended that the monarch repeal the Chinese expulsion law in 1772. Calderón presented several arguments in favor of welcoming Chinese migrants back to the islands, which he laid out in a long letter to the Crown.[134] The minister's case was grounded in an alternative interpretation of the history of the British invasion of Manila that challenged the myth of the bloodthirsty Sangley bent on destroying the Spanish that had underpinned expulsion. Calderón acknowledged that one thousand or so Chinese migrants had joined forces with the British in Manila, yet these men were "dockworkers, boatmen, and poor people" who were motivated more by the fifteen pesos a day that the British put in their pockets than by an innate hatred of the Spanish. He rejected wartime stories of Sangley brutality. The one group of Chinese men who were guilty of conspiring against the government were outliers who got the punishment that they deserved at Guagua. He dismissed stories of Chinese migrant boatmen murdering Spanish families fleeing the British in Manila as lies. He denied that the Chinese participated in the infamous sacking of the city when it fell.[135] Calderón also drew attention to Chinese loyalty to Spain during the war, pointing out that they had supplied Anda's army with food and other essentials throughout the conflict. He recast memories of wartime Chinese religiosity in a favorable light, denying that Catholic Sangleyes had tossed away their rosaries, and clarifying that Manileños had mistakenly confused a solemn Chinese Catholic celebration on the day of the Magi—the patron saints of the Parián church—for the public worship of heathen gods. The pirates in Calderón's history of the war were not the Chinese but the British who burned down churches, and the Indigenous peoples who raided and robbed the houses of Spaniards and revolted in Ilocos and Pangasinan.[136]

Appealing to the king's sense of justice, Calderón pointed to acute flaws in the expulsion process that rendered it illegitimate. Anda's and Uruñuela's reports to the Crown on Chinese treachery and apostasy were full of "exaggerations and generalizations," he claimed.[137] To say that all Sangleyes are bad was a "merciless and reckless" proposition.[138] Calderón condemned Uruñuela for failing to make any real effort to distinguish guilty Sangleyes from the innocent. He pointed to the government's response to the massive 1745 Indigenous uprisings in Bulacan as an example that Uruñuela should have been followed. Calderón himself had been involved in formulating the government's response to this earlier crisis. Back then, he had offered prizes for the heads of the two ringleaders only, "because one never punishes the multitude."[139] Calderón claimed that even those baptized Sangleyes who had aided the British and slipped into apostasy should never have been banished from the islands. This was an unprecedented and unjust punishment for Catholics, and forced labor would have been a more appropriate penalty for disloyalty.[140] He argued that it was wrong to compare Christian Sangleyes in the Philippines to the Moriscos of the Mediterranean world. The Sangleyes were more like the Crown's Indigenous vassals. Indeed, he reminded his audience that the laws of the Indies recognized "indios Sangleyes," and they were therefore deserving of royal protection. "Indios apostatize many times, and with their tenderness, the missionaries bring them back to the true path."[141] It was unethical for the king to force baptized Sangleyes to return to China, where they would struggle to live as Catholics. This was a kingdom that persecuted Catholics. Without priests to guide them, exiled Catholics would be tempted to return to live with their heathen wives, who would also encourage their drift from the Church.[142]

For Calderón, the loyal Catholic Chinese mestizo was proof of the profound flaws and shortsightedness of Chinese expulsion. The fact that Manila's archbishop had ordained "the sons of Sangleyes" was a testament to their strong faith, he argued.[143] He had seen firsthand in 1745 how baptized Chinese and Chinese mestizo merchants and sea captains had supported the state's campaign against the Indigenous communities who rose up in rebellion across Southern Luzon by organizing and funding eight Sangley militia companies to support the government's military campaign against them.[144] Calderón reasoned that if the sons and daughters of Sangleyes were such good vassals, then it was impossible that their parents were the bloodthirsty pirate-like villains portrayed by the likes of Anda and Uruñuela. Evidently, the debate about the Chinese in the Philippines created spaces for the colony's learned men to speak to the virtues of Chinese mestizos. It is difficult to measure but also to deny the positive impact that this had on the Chinese mestizo's integration into colonial society.

Economic considerations mattered to Calderón, even though they were not driving his case against expulsion. He made familiar arguments about the colony's dependence on hardworking and industrious Chinese. He put it in the most simple terms: "the town without Sangleyes is poor and unhappy," and towns with Sangleyes prosper.[145] He explained that Chinese migrants stimulated economic growth in the Philippines not only by planting sugar crops and building sugar mills, but also by setting a good example for Indigenous populations to follow. Furthermore, Sangleyes made more reliable business partners than the colony's impoverished Europeans. "A vecino of

Manila would rather trust his money to a mestizo de Sangley than a shirt-less Spaniard," he emphasized[146] In contrast to upstanding Chinese settlers, the "criollos of New Spain," are "so scatterbrained and useless that they can only serve as soldiers."[147]

By this time the Philippines were in the grip of an acute economic reces-sion that trailed the Seven Years' War and opened the vecinos' minds to the option of welcoming the Chinese back to the islands. Recession in the Phil-ippines occurred in the context of an economic downturn that reverberated across the Americas and Europe.[148] Yet elite Manileños attributed the eco-nomic crisis to the Chinese expulsion. Trade with China had declined, with the average number of ships visiting Manila each year falling to nine in 1764–1780, down from fifteen in 1721–1760.[149] The miserable state of the economy prompted Manileños to recognize the colony's apparent dependence on the Chinese, and calls to renew Chinese migration to the islands became louder.

The Franciscan friar Concepción's impassioned April 1777 plea to the king to welcome Sangleyes to the Philippines again framed this as the only solution to the colony's economic woes. "The Sangleyes are necessary for every thing that you want to do in the Philippines, and without them little, or nothing, can be achieved in these lands in which only they are equipped for every-thing," he reasoned.[150] Concepción envisioned the Sangleyes as ideal part-ners of the Spanish in a successful colonial project. "Everything depends on the Sangleyes. The Spaniards with their commerce by sea, are helped by the Chinese on land, as it has always been, and without them, we cannot live."[151] For Concepción, the temporal and spiritual were entangled concerns. Extreme poverty undermined conversion efforts, and economic prosperity was necessary to sustain and spread Christianity in the Philippines. To il-lustrate this point, Concepción claimed that many Indigenous people in the islands were too poor to participate in religious services. Too many men and women were without a single decent shirt or skirt to wear to mass. A Sangley-driven economic recovery was necessary to overcome this "shame of entering the church."[152]

The friar also made the case that the Crown's treatment of Chinese mi-grants had an impact on Catholicism in maritime Asia beyond the Philip-pines. He recommended that in addition to permitting Chinese migrants to return to the Philippines, the king should also allow them to become priests. Specifically, he suggested that young boys between ten and twelve years of age be brought from China to Manila to train to enter the clergy. Concep-ción hoped that these "pure Chinese priests" would eventually serve Catholic Chinese communities in the Philippines as well as in China, preaching to the Chinese "in their language and imprinting in them the love of Religion." Concepción thought that the proximity of China to the Philippines made it a sensible place to train priests; he imagined Manila as the "Rome of the Orient."[153] This global view of Philippines affairs shaped shifting opinions on mobility and migration in the Spanish Pacific.

The Crown abandoned expulsion in the late 1770s. Simón de Anda's death in 1776 paved the way for interim Philippines Governor Pedro Sarrio to seek and obtain the Crown's permission to recruit skilled workers from China to labor in the Philippines' new copper and indigo factories.[154] In 1777, the king approved a proposal for Domingo Canleong and his compatriots from Cebu, the group who had successfully petitioned against forced repatriation to China, to be sent to work in Francisco Xavier Salgado's new copper mine and indigo plant in Masbate, a town in Albay Province.[155] In 1778 Sarrio's successor, Governor Basco y Vargas, commissioned Bartolome Pitco to go to China to recruit four thousand Christian migrant workers. The governor was hopeful that Pitco could convince skilled workers to emigrate to Luzon, specifically "porcelain manufacturers, dyers, foundrymen, blacksmiths, miners, master artisans in lacquer production and those skilled in mulberry silk culture."[156] Ultimately Pitco succeeded in bringing only a few hundred men to the Philippines, and most were farmers and merchants. A 1778 census counted fewer than one thousand Chinese men in Manila, including 576 Catholics and 138 who were not baptized. It is possible that many were returnees.[157] The colonial government relaxed restrictions on the movement of Chinese within the colony. In 1783, it authorized Sangleyes to live "in any province of the Philippines," as long as they bought the requisite six-peso license each year.[158] Yet Chinese migrants were slow to return to the Philippines. A decade later, an estimated 1,500 Sangleyes were living in Manila, of whom 1,200 were catechumens, or people receiving instruction in Catholic doctrine and discipline in preparation for baptism.[159]

The era of Chinese expulsion was counterintuitively an era of Chinese mestizo ascendency. The new Chinese mestizo militia that was established in Manila in 1769 with Antonio Tuason as its lieutenant colonel was powerful proof of Chinese mestizos' elevated status in the postwar Catholic Republic.[160] Officially called the Royal Prince Regiment, the Chinese mestizo militia comprised seven companies with sixty-three men in each, including one company of grenadiers.[161] This move formalized the irregular units of Chinese mestizos that were mobilized to fight against the invading British forces during the Seven Years' War and was part of the larger campaign to reform militias across the global Spanish empire and incorporate these into the king's army, enhancing their ability to confront future threats.[162]

After the Seven Years' War, Chinese mestizos secured the right to graduate from Manila's universities with higher degrees. Faustino Bautista and Juan Thomas de Legaspi, both Chinese mestizo clerics, graduated from the University of Santo Thomás with the advanced degree of licentiate in arts in 1765.[163] Francisco Borja de los Santos and Gregorio de los Reyes were awarded licentiates in philosophy from the university in 1776.[164] In 1785, two young Chinese mestizo men whose Sangley fathers had been expelled from the Philippines successfully defended their right to graduate with licentiates from the same university.[165] This does not mean that Chinese mestizos no longer faced discrimination. In the same decade, mestizas de Sangley were refused admission to the Franciscan Santa Clara convent and the Beaterio de Santa Cathalina de Sena, an institution for laywomen devoted to prayer. A Dominican-backed campaign to establish a new beaterio in the city exclusively for the daughters of elite mestizos de Sangley also failed. The Crown refused to approve the beaterio, citing insufficient funds.[166]

Previously, historians looked to the colonial economy to explain the privileges that Chinese mestizos' gained in the postwar era, attributing them to increased Chinese mestizo wealth that came from their taking advantage of the economic opportunities created by the expulsion of the Sangleyes and effectively replacing the banished migrants.[167] But this analysis ignores the important ways in which the Seven Years' War and Chinese expulsion allowed Chinese mestizos to demonstrate their devout Catholic faith and devoted loyalty to Spain, and to distinguish themselves from Chinese migrants. The colonial government's decision to arm Chinese mestizos in a militia and granting its members all the benefits that militia service conferred, and to afford Chinese mestizos access to university education, became possible because the war and expulsion brought about a fundamental change in how colonial elites perceived mestizos de Sangley. Chinese mestizos marked themselves as distinct from Chinese migrants through their support for the Hispano-Filipino military campaign against the British, and then by lending assistance to the state's efforts to forcibly migrate Chinese migrants in the islands. This support ranged from testifying against Sangleyes in Uruñuela's investigation to helping the government transport the expelled men, first from the villages they resided in to the Alcaicería, and then onto the boats that carried them across the sea. The politics of expulsion fundamentally shaped Chinese mestizo ascendancy.

Conclusion

Historians have been reluctant to categorize Manila as a Spanish city. Dennis O. Flynn, Arturo Giráldez, and Raquel Reyes characterize early modern Manila as a uniquely global city due to its historic role as a hub of transoceanic trade that connected Asia to the Americas across the vast Pacific Ocean, a function that gave rise to a diverse human population.[168] Others have emphasized that Manila was a Chinese city. In the first half of the eighteenth century, Manileños who had been born in China or were descended from Chinese migrants far outnumbered those who were born in Spain or counted *peninsulares* among their ancestors. Rallying against studies of the Hispanization of the Philippines, John. D. Blanco recently called for "reorienting world history around the Sinicization of the Philippines and the Pacific . . . [and] Spain and Europe's insertion and assimilation into a Sinocentric world economy.[169] If we gaze at the early modern Pacific world in this period through the lens of trade and the circulation of commodities, the Spanish empire certainly figures as one part of a large system that it never dominated. Yet when we look at the Philippines through the lens of migration—the circulation of people in and through the islands in the archipelago over which the Spanish claimed jurisdiction—the Spanish empire appears less weak and abstract and more of a potent force that policed mobility and determined where people could live and travel, and under what terms.

In the aftermath of the Seven Years' War, the Spanish colonial government expelled more than two thousand Chinese migrants from the Philippines. In the decade after 1763, men ranging in age from their late teens to their late eighties were arrested across Luzon and the Visayas, torn from their families and homes, forcibly resettled in a Manila internment camp, and then compelled to board ships bound for distant shores. These refugees encountered empire as a very real force in their lives. This is not to say that they were powerless, or without agency. This chapter has recovered a range of strategies that Sangleyes experimented with to avoid expulsion and remain in the islands with their kin; however, these were rarely fruitful. Their collective efforts to improve the dire conditions they suffered during their forced displacement, which included improving access to food, must have helped to ensure that refugees survived this ordeal.

Chinese expulsion was certainly influenced by global dynamics, but men and women in the Philippine islands drove this cruel policy and ensured that it was implemented. Through interrogating the beliefs and prejudices that contributed to the colonial government's commitment to Chinese expulsion, and the mechanisms through which this radical policy was put into effect, this chapter has illuminated the complexity and dynamism of Sino-Spanish relationships in the Philippines, and the great extent to which these were defined by the waves of piracy that rippled across the region. Maritime violence and attacks from the sea profoundly influenced shifting attitudes toward Chinese migrants in the Philippines and the policies that they ultimately gave rise to. In the minds of many local residents, the British invasion and occupation of the Philippines transformed Sangleyes from allies in the war against Islamic piracy to adversaries in the war against the British: a different pirate enemy. This metamorphosis established the conditions for expulsion.

Significantly, this chapter has illustrated that expulsion could not have been achieved without popular support, or at least the willingness of numerous colonial subjects to follow orders to take action that implemented forced migration on this scale. The archive provides insight into the hateful stories about the Chinese and the war that circulated in the Philippines in the years after the conflict, the rumors that made forced repatriation tolerable, if not preferable, to many Manileños. Chinese mestizos, and particularly the elites within their ranks, aided Sangley expulsion in various ways, and ultimately benefited from the distinction it solidified between Sangleyes and mestizos de Sangley. The push for the reversal of Chinese expulsion in the mid-1770s similarly originated in the Philippines. If there was a "reconquest" of the archipelago in the aftermath of the Seven Years' War, it was one driven by men and women on the ground.

Epilogue

Piracy and Empire in the Age of Revolutions and Beyond

In April of 1776 the small Spanish ship *Nuestra Señora del Carmen* arrived at Mangalore (Mangaluru), the busy port city at the confluence of the Guru-pura and Netravati rivers in the southern Indian kingdom of Mysore. On board were Commander Ramón de Ysassi and the military engineer Miguel Antonio Gómez, two men that the Philippines governor Simón de Anda had handpicked to firm up a new alliance between Spain's King Charles III and Sultan Haidar Ali, Mysore's sovereign ruler. The two-and-a-half-month voy-age from Manila had taken the ship and its crew across seas and littoral zones transformed by globalization and imperial expansion. The *Nuestra Se-ñora del Carmen* called in to the Dutch-controlled ports of Malacca and Cochín (Kochi). Gómez spotted towers and forts flying British and "Moro" flags when they sailed past Calicut (Kozhikode). There was a heavy British naval presence along the Indian subcontinent's western coast, and ships flying British colors intercepted the Spanish vessel and inquired about whom it was carrying and where they were headed. The Manileños pre-tended to be Portuguese to avoid trouble. Haidar Ali sent an armada to greet the Spanish ship and guide it into the mouth of the river at Manga-lore. The Manileños invited the sultan's commander on board, welcoming him with music played by "trumpets, flutes, and violins," and a meal. Ysassi and Gómez served coffee, tea, and chocolate, "and the best sweets that we had brought," and the Mysore commander offered a rich "Arabian conserve made from dates, goat milk, egg yolks and cardamon."[1] Spain's push to ex-pand its Asian empire westward into the Indian Ocean world was off to a sweet beginning.

The meeting at Mangalore was the product of truly global processes and imaginaries. The Manila embassy was set in motion when Isaac Goldsmith arrived in Madrid in 1773. Goldsmith identified himself as a Prussian Jew who had spent many years in India and as a representative of Mysore's Sultan

Haidar Ali, who had sent him to Europe to broker an alliance with Spain.
The sultan and the king shared a mutual desire to limit the expansion of the
burgeoning British empire in Asia. Haidar Ali was at war with the British
and rival Indian kingdoms. British Royal Navy and East India Company
fleets had invaded Haidar Ali's territory, sunk his ships, bombarded his
forts, and blockaded the Malabar coastline. The sultan mounted a fierce
resistance. He was building up Mysore's navy and its coastal defense systems "to free the Indian Ocean one day from the European pirates."[2] He
wanted a powerful European ally who could help to shore up his kingdom
and shift the balance of power in the region in his favor. The Spanish were
all ears. Goldsmith gained access to the Crown's most senior and influential
advisors in Madrid, including Spain's chief minister the Marquez de
Grimaldi and Julian de Arriaga, who was secretary of state for the Indies.
These men made sure that Haidar Ali's proposal reached the king.[3]

The alliance that Haidar Ali proposed to the Spanish via his cosmopolitan emissary was a military one first and foremost. Goldsmith presented a
draft nine-point treaty that offered Spanish subjects the exclusive right to reside and do business in Mysore. The goods that the sultan most wanted to
buy from the Spaniards were military supplies. He needed iron and bronze
cannon, as well as cannonballs, rifles, gunpowder, and copper. The sultan also
wanted hats and feathers for his soldiers' uniforms. Additionally, he requested
that the Crown send "some people highly knowledgeable in military arts" to
share their expertise on the design and construction of fortifications and
ships.[4] In return, Haidar Ali promised to give Spanish traders access to spices
including black pepper, cinnamon, and cardamon, in addition to pearls and
printed cottons that generated big profits for European merchants. He offered
the Spaniards land to build a fort and a dock: a "factory" in the image of
Dutch and British trading company outposts. Familiar with the politics
of conversion diplomacy, the sultan also assured his new allies that Catholic missionaries would be welcome in his kingdom. He promised to provide
protection for Catholic friars, as well as land to build churches. Haidar Ali
invited Charles III to send delegates to his court in the inland city of Seringapatam to finalize the terms of "an offensive and defensive alliance for the
good and conservation of the two states mutually located in the Oriental
Indies, which will produce great advantages for both sides."[5] Although
the king's advisors did not entirely trust Goldsmith, they considered the
potential advantages of the proposed deal worth the risk of engaging with a

somewhat suspicious character. The king ordered three thousand rifles with bayonets and fifty thousand bullets destined for Mysore to be loaded on to the next ship at Cadíz bound for the Philippines. Goldsmith would accompany this cargo, traveling at the king's expense. The king and his advisors trusted Governor Anda to take charge of the alliance-making in Manila, upholding the level of local autonomy that characterized colonial rule in the Philippines.

The Spanish-Mysore pact resembled others that the Crown and its delegates in the Philippines had previously brokered with sovereign rulers in maritime Asia and with Indigenous elites within the archipelago. In this regard, the Crown's commitment to diplomacy in the 1770s shows continuity in how the Spanish empire in this part of the globe functioned over the long durée. Yet the Manila embassy to Haidar Ali's kingdom also indicated that the empire was moving in a new direction. This was the first time since the end of the Iberian union in 1640 that Spain seriously pursued a partnership with an Indian state, and one that would potentially lead to the establishment of new Spanish settlements in the subcontinent. Shifts in maritime violence in the Pacific set in motion new transcultural and transoceanic alliances and expanded the horizons of Spanish colonialism in the region.[6]

Pirates still "infested" the seas surrounding the Philippine islands in the late eighteenth century. Moro pirates continued to pose an existential threat to Spanish colonial rule. Fray Manuel de la Concepción declared that Moro pirates "owned these seas."[7] Simón de Anda reported that these Muslim raiders had acquired better weapons, including "cannon and rifles," making them a more potent enemy than they had been even in the recent past.[8] Captive-taking raids in watery Philippine borderlands continued to occur at an alarming rate. The Spanish also feared that Moro pirates were infiltrating Manila and its hinterland, with Anda claiming that they were calling into Manila Bay disguised as fishermen. Violent clashes between pirates and Hispano-Filipino forces were occurring off the Pampangan coast, too.[9] It seemed that Moro pirates were closing in on the capital.

And now Britain's militarized Pacific turn was in full swing. The British were using their expanded naval power to aggressively add land and people to its expanding empire. Although settler colonists in Britain's North American possessions declared independence in 1776, the Spanish were anxious about Britain's huge territorial acquisitions in India, their efforts to establish new outposts in the Sulu Zone that were within raiding distance of the

Philippines, and Captain Cook's voyages of discovery and conquest in the Pacific. Anda was not alone in thinking that the British would try to conquer Manila and the Philippines again, and soon. He reasoned that the British would not care about the Philippines "if these islands were as poor as the Malvinas." But "because they are not, and they are rich, and ideally located in the world for trade with all parts of Asia, Europe, and America," the archipelago continued to be coveted by Spain's imperial rivals.[10] It seemed inevitable to Anda and to other Spanish imperial strategists that British pirates and Moro pirates would unite and try to destroy Spanish sovereignty in the archipelago. This prediction propelled the Spanish into India.

Manila's mission to Mysore was ultimately not a successful one. The Spaniards had to wait for months in Seringapatam to obtain an audience with Haidar Ali, and during this time Ysassi died, and Goldsmith, who was being hounded by debtors, disappeared. Gómez eventually returned to Manila with the sultan's agreement to a treaty and with a young elephant gifted to the Spanish king to seal the deal. But no further steps were taken to advance this alliance. Haidar Ali did not pay for his large order of Spanish weapons and ammunition, and so Manila never delivered them.[11] Haidar Ali's son and successor, Fateh Ali Sahab Tipu, continued to wage war against the British until his death at the British siege and capture of Mysore's capital in 1799.[12] However, the strategies and aspirations that made Manila's mission to Mysore possible remain important despite its outcomes. The Manila embassy underscores that the king and his key advisors in Spain and powerful colonial officials in the islands recognized that alliances with sovereign Asian rulers were necessary to strengthen Spain's Asian empire in the face of entangled British and Moro piracy threats in the region in the final decades of the eighteenth century.

This book has demonstrated that real and imagined piracy threats fundamentally shaped the evolution of Spanish colonial rule in the Philippines up to this point. Maritime violence compelled agents of the Spanish empire to broker anti-piracy coalitions with Asian states as well as with the leaders of Indigenous and Chinese communities in the islands. Complicating the notion that Spaniards, Indigenous peoples, and Sangleyes were permanent adversaries with fixed opposing interests, this study has shown that piracy made alliance-making among these groups central to empire-building in the Philippines. Reading Spanish colonial rule in the islands through the lens of piracy suggests that loyalty to the Spanish empire was not an aberration in "an otherwise comprehensible past. We should be able to find meaning in it" without resorting to convenient explanations like naivety.[13]

Historians do not need to excavate many archival layers to find evidence of Indigenous and Chinese fidelity to Spain in the Philippines, yet the history of empire from below has been erased from public space. On the twenty-sixth of December in 1896, a firing squad executed the insurgent anti-colonialist José Rizal on the grassy Bagumbayan field that lies at the edge of the old walled city of Manila. Today this hallowed ground where Rizal's blood once soaked the earth is a park named for the Philippines' national hero. Visitors can trace Rizal's final footsteps from his prison cell in the old Spanish Fort Santiago inside Intramuros, which is now a shrine to Rizal, to the spot where he was shot dead. Rizal's mortal remains are interred in the park under the large obelisk monument that was erected in his honor. The uniformed soldiers of the Philippines Marine Corps permanently guard this grave. Other monuments in the park locate Rizal's resistance against the empire as the culmination of the archipelago's long history of struggle against Spanish colonial rule. A twelve-meter-tall statue of Lapu Lapu, the Mactan datu who killed Ferdinand Magellan in 1521, was unveiled at the north end of the park in 2004. In the gallery of heroes stand the bronze busts of men who led uprisings against the Spanish. They include the Tausug Datu Ache, who defeated the Hispano-Filipino armada headed by Governor Sebastian Hurtado de Corcuera in 1638; the Pampangan Francisco Maniago, who led an anti-colonial rebellion in the 1660s; Francisco Dagohoy, who headed the mid-eighteenth-century revolt in Bohol; and Diego Silang and Juan de la Cruz Palaris, who were prominent in the massive Indigenous revolts that broke out in Luzon during the British occupation of Manila.[14] The women leaders of revolts against empire, including Gracia Dagohoy and Gabriela Silang, are noticeably absent from the park. Filipinos who were loyal to empire are also missing from this memory space.

There are no historical markers in Fort Santiago or the adjacent park that inform visitors that the place where Rizal became a martyr for Philippine independence is also the site of historic battlefields where thousands of Filipino fighting men sacrificed their lives to preserve Spanish sovereignty in Manila. Indigenous people died alongside Spanish and Mexican soldiers at this place in the fighting against the Chinese pirate Limahong and his fleet, which attacked Manila in the late sixteenth century. Countless Indigenous men died in combat on the city walls and in Bagumbayan fighting against the Chinese migrants who rose up in rebellion on three separate occasions in the seventeenth century. Hundreds of Pampangans and other Indigenous soldiers and militiamen were slaughtered at Bagumbayan in the bloody battle for Manila in 1762, as they struggled to defend Intramuros against the surprise British attack on the city. Presently there are no visible traces of these loyalist fighting men's lives or deaths. Nor are there plaques indicating the location of the Catholic church in Bagumbayan that was destroyed in the British invasion, which was for many decades the final resting place for Pampangan soldiers who had been deployed across the Philippines archipelago and as far away as Taiwan and the Mariana Islands in the service of the Spanish empire.[15] There is no room for loyalists in teleologies of triumph either in Manila's commemorative landscape or in nationalist historiography.

This study has dug deep into empire's archives to recover the forgotten histories of Indigenous soldiers and militiamen, discover their identities and circumstances, and understand the complex reasons why they went to war to sustain Spanish colonial rule in the Philippines. It has analyzed the experiences and motivations of the people who joined the empire's armies and navies as part of a broader inquiry into the phenomenon of popular support for the Spanish rule in the archipelago, which is hardly discernible in the existing literature on the islands' early modern history. This revisionist account has illuminated how piracy influenced people's choices to throw their lot in with empire. Individuals and communities in Philippine borderlands as well as those located in and around Manila forged alliances with colonial governments to defend themselves from destructive and devastating pirate raids, and to secure the resources they required to carry out reprisal attacks against their enemies. Anti-piracy politics in the islands were deeply Catholic, and the widespread view that fighting pirates was ordained by God added to the fervor of campaigns to destroy sea-robbers. This study showed that times of real and rumored pirate invasions were moments when the Spanish empire in the Philippines appeared to be more fragile to islanders, and repeatedly sparked Indigenous and Chinese anti-colonial revolts. However, successive colonial governments were able to draw on long-standing militarized coalitions to raise armed forces that successfully suppressed these potent challenges to Spanish sovereignty in the islands.

Revealing piracy's impact on popular allegiances to Spain in the Philippines challenges condescending evaluations of loyalists as naive or foolish. This analysis has developed an alternative and more respectful evaluation of these ancestors, recognizing loyalists as people who had to make difficult decisions, often with the threat of violence hanging over their heads, and who exploited converging interests to chart a safer course through stormy seas and a changing world. This study has deepened our knowledge of the nature of Spanish colonial rule in the Pacific world, illuminating the sources of empire's surprising resilience leading up to the Seven Years' War and its immediate aftermath. Understanding how the Spanish empire in the Pacific was made from below is highly relevant to how we interpret the history of the larger, global Spanish empire, and the history of European imperial expansion. The array of pirates who converged in the Philippines archipelago—including Chinese, Southeast Asian, South Asian, and European marauders—shaped major historical processes of regional and global significance in the early modern world. Pirates influenced the contours of European empire-building efforts, and the development of economic, political, and spiritual and religious ties that connected polities across islands and oceans within and beyond the Pacific region.

This study ends in the 1770s, at the dawn of the Age of Revolutions that spanned the late eighteenth century to the late 1840s. This era witnessed polities across the Americas wage and win wars of independence against European empires. Spain lost all of its territorial possessions on the American continent by 1830, leaving it with a nineteenth-century empire of islands that encompassed Cuba, Puerto Rico, and the Philippines. The uneven Age of Revolutions in the Spanish world reflected a larger global trend. The dissolution of empires in the Atlantic, in Clare Anderson's words, almost perfectly coincided "with the rapidly unfurling tentacles of European imperialism into the Indian Ocean region, to South-east Asia, and to Australia and the south Pacific in the late eighteenth and early nineteenth centuries."[16] The Philippines was increasingly surrounded by lands claimed by the bloating British, French, and Dutch empires in this epoch.

This book's core findings prompt us to consider how piracy influenced the survival of Spanish colonial rule in the Pacific in this turbulent era in world history. Future studies might examine how the experiences and perceptions of maritime violence and raiding in the islands shaped locals' responses to Napoleon's invasion of the Iberian Peninsula and the crisis of sovereignty that it triggered, and ultimately to the Latin American wars for independence. New research into piracy and popular perceptions of empire could expand scholarship that has already examined how economic reforms, including the creation of profitable government monopolies on tobacco and other commodities in the Philippines in the eighteenth century, contributed to empire's survival of the collapse of the galleon trade that accompanied

Mexico's hard-won independence from Spain.[17] Taking a more global perspective, historians including C. A. Bayly and Sujit Sivasundaram have argued that anti-colonial rebellions and revolutions in the Atlantic world led to
the development of "stronger, more intrusive" states that used their expanded
capacities for violence to extend and consolidate empire in the Pacific and
Indian Ocean worlds.[18] While we cannot dismiss the role of the repressive
apparatus of the state in sustaining Spain's nineteenth-century Asian empire, this study has shown that we also cannot ignore or underestimate the
significance of popular sources of support for colonial rule.

   Illuminating piracy's impact on the colonial politics of belonging in the
Philippines is another significant intervention this study has made. Shifts in
the character of maritime violence in Philippines waters impacted who
could be integrated into the Catholic nation as loyal vassals, and who was
othered and subject to systemic discrimination and violence. This book
illustrated that patterns and perceptions of large-scale Chinese piracy led to
three genocidal massacres of the Chinese in Manila and its hinterland in the
seventeenth century. In the early eighteenth-century the conceptualization of raiding in the islands as a crime perpetrated by Muslims encouraged
and legitimized Hispano-Filipino naval and land campaigns to destroy
Moro villages and fleets and enslave Moro captives. The escalation of Moro
piracy in this period coincided with the collapse of huge Chinese pirate
fleets, which combined to open up opportunities for Chinese migrants and
their mestizo descendants to become more integrated into the Catholic body
politic in Manila. The British attack on Manila in 1762, which many locals
saw as a pirate invasion, rapidly undermined this convivencia. Sangleyes
were subject to mass killings during the Seven Years' War in the Philippines,
and faced mass deportations in the years after this conflict when the Spanish attempted to rebuild an Asian empire free of Chinese migrants.

   Like the history of Indigenous loyalty to Spain, the history of anti-Chinese
violence is buried in public history in the Philippines. The Chinese museum
in Intramuros, for example, emphasizes cooperation and friendship between
Natives and Chinese newcomers and their descendants in Manila.[19] Confronting and thinking critically about the history of anti-Chinese politics in
the Philippines revealed in this book and the interesting ways that it intersected with anti-piracy ideologies and actions offers a deeper understanding
of the complex politics of othering and vassalage in the colonial Philippines.
This study might inspire future investigations of the interaction of maritime violence and the dynamics of exclusion in the Philippines after the 1770s,

during the final century of Spanish colonial rule in the islands and subsequent decades in the period of U.S. colonial rule and the national period. The legacies of empire include the persistent discrimination against Muslims and people of Chinese descent in the archipelago.

The archive of the Spanish empire in the Philippines, conceptualized as the "imagined totality of information accumulated by state apparatuses" about the islands, is vast.[20] This repository contains silences and gaps that were present at the moment of its creation, and over time it has been subject to irreparable destruction, with copious paper records created by colonial rule being damaged and ruined in successive wars and natural disasters. Yet much of the archive is intact and waiting to be read and pondered and written about. Historians can also engage with information about the past embedded in the archeological record, in visual and material culture, and in oral histories. Learning more about Spanish colonial rule in the Philippines not only will deepen our understanding of the histories of the many peoples who have lived and died in the islands, but will also deepen our knowledge of imperial expansion and the emergence of capitalism in maritime Asia and the wider early modern world.

NOTES

Introduction

1. Morga, *The Philippine Islands*, 16–20; San Augustin, *Conquistas de las Islas Philipinas*, 146–247; "Relation of the Conquest of the Island of Luzon," in *The Philippine Islands, 1493–1898*, 3:165; Sala-Boza, "The Genealogy of Hari'Tupas," 273–274, 288–289; Angeles, "The Battle of Mactan," 15; Beauchesne, "Trans-Pacific Connections," 13–15.

2. Gerilya, *Masigasig na Maynila*, 2020. Mural. Lagusnilad Underpass, Manila.

3. Rizal is best known for his two Spanish novels, affectionately known as the Noli and the Fili. Rizal, *Noli me tangere*; *El filibusterismo*. On the formation of Rizal as national hero, see Morley, *Cities and Nationhood*, 79–80, 94, 137.

4. Mulich, "Maritime Marronage," 133–148.

5. Constantino, *A History of the Philippines*, 6, 45. Starting in the late 1970s, historians focused on developing studies of a particular community or ethnic group's resistance to Spanish colonial rule over time. Reyaldo Clemeña Ileto's *Payson and Revolution* examined nineteenth-century Tagalog peasant revolts and their ties to a subversive Hispano-Filipino tradition of Easter week Pasyon (Passion) plays and remains a classic social history of anti-colonial rebellions in the Philippines from below. Rafael's *Contracting Colonialism* argued that sixteenth-century translations of Catholic texts into Tagalog uncovered earlier forms of resistance to Spanish rule and "the failure of authority to legitimize its claim to power in a stultifying colonial regime." Much of the literature on the Chinese in the Philippines prior to the nineteenth century emphasized antagonism and conflict between the people of the diaspora and the colonial government, which stands in contrast to the literature on the Chinese compradors or agents of empire in other parts of maritime Asia. Scott's history of the Igorots, the people who inhabit the mountainous Gran Cordillera region in central Luzon, highlighted their successful rebuff of multiple Hispano-Filipino military campaigns that repeatedly failed to conquer them. Majul wrote extensively about Islamic polities' strategies for preserving their independence from the Spanish empire. Ileto, *Pasyon and Revolution*; Rafael, *Contracting Colonialism*, 3; Wickberg, *The Chinese in Philippine Life*, 1–23; García-Abásalo, "Los chinos," 223–242; Chang, "Four Centuries"; Scott, *The Discovery of the Igorots*. See, for example, Majul, *Muslims in the Philippines*.

6. Studies pointing to priests as the key to the empire's expansion and survival include Phelan, *The Hispanization of the Philippines*; Andrés, *Entre frailes*. Economics-centered theories of imperial longevity include Legarda, *After the Galleons*; Fradera, *Filipinas, la colonia más peculiar*.

7. This study's broad conceptualization of pirate and piracy is consistent with the early modern understanding of these concepts in the Iberian world and reflects recent scholarship

that recognizes the fluid and expansive character of the pirate category. It challenges a body of literature that emphasizes that only acts of violence done on the sea by people acting independently of any politically organized society can be deemed piracy. See Lane, *Pillaging the Empire*, 2; Prange, "A Trade of No Dishonor," 1269–1272; Prange and Antony, "Piracy in Asian Waters," 6; Eklöf Amirel, *Pirates of Empire*, 7–15.

8. White, *The Middle Ground*, 50–93; Deloira, "What is the Middle Ground," 15–22; Yannakakis, *The Art of Being In-Between*. Cuadriello, *Las glorias*.

9. Echeverri, *Indian and Slave Royalists*, 14; Yannakakis, *The Art of Being In-Between*.

10. Hanna, *Pirate Nests*; Rediker, *Between the Devil and the Deep Blue Sea*. Rediker and Linebaugh, *The Many-Headed Hydra*.

11. Stoler, "Rethinking Colonial Categories," 137.

12. Lee's recent study is unique for analyzing entangled Indigenous and Chinese history through the prism of Catholic devotion. Lee, *Saints of Resistance*, 39–72.

13. Pratt, *Planetary Longings*, 84.

14. Owensby, *Empire of Law*, 24–25; van Deusen, "Seeing Indios," 205–230; Seijas, *Asian Slaves*, 5, 144–162, 212–246.

15. See for example, McManus and Leibsohn, "Eloquence and Ethnohistory," 526; AGI Filipinas 341, L8, f.196r–196v.

16. Dodds Pennock, *On Savage Shores*, xii–xvi.

17. Ting et al., "Modernity vs. Culture," 77–79; Paredes, "Fringe Histories"; CuUnjieng Aboitiz, *Asian Place, Filipino Nation*, 40–41, 64–65.

18. The most comprehensive study of maritime raiding and its impact on political economy, political organization, and culture in the Philippines in the centuries before Spanish rule and in the early Spanish period is Junker, *Raiding*.

19. I borrow the concept of maritime Asia from Tonio Andrade and Xing Hang. Andrade and Hang, "Introduction," 1–27.

20. Junker, *Raiding*, 219.

21. Andaya, *Early Modern Southeast Asia*, 93–95; Prange, *Monsoon Islam*, 25–91.

22. Padrón, *The Indies of the Setting Sun*, 240–245.

23. Mojares, "Lapulapu," 59–68.

24. Mundy, *The Death of Aztec Tenochtitlan*, 15–51, 76–77.

25. See Matthew and Oudijk, *Indian Conquistadors*, 5–27; Covey, *Inca Apocalypse*, 194–273; Valenzuela-Márquez, "Los indios cuzcos"; Restall, *Seven Myths*, 44–63.

26. For a concise overview of sixteenth-century Spanish voyages of discovery and conquest in the Pacific, see Reséndez, *Conquering the Pacific*, 17–41; Álvarez, "Caminos sobre la mar," 539–614. For evidence of the economic links between imperial expansion in the Pacific and northern New Spain, see Flint and Flint, "Guido de Lavezariis," 1–19.

27. See Schurz, *The Manila Galleon*; Flynn and Giráldez, "Cycles of Silver," 1–16; Yuste López, *Emporios transpacíficos*; Zapatero, "Intercambios culturales," 213–234; Giráldez, *The Age of Trade*; Priyadarshini, *Chinese Porcelain*.

28. Velarde, *Historia de la provincia de Philipinas*, 2:6.

29. Marquez, Plano del actual estado de la Plaza de Manila (1767), AGI MP-Filipinas, 51 BIS; Mancini, *Art and War in the Pacific World*, 100; Phelan, *The Hispanization*, 31–32.

30. Lee, *Saints of Resistance*, 6.

31. Scott has theorized extra-state and anti-state zones across upland Asia as a meta-region called "Zomia." James C. Scott, *The Art of Not Being Governed*. William Henry Scott

documented failed Spanish efforts to conquer the Cordillera in *The Discovery of the Igorots*. See also Newson, *Conquest and Pestilence*, 145, 213–229.

32. Velarde and de la Cruz Bagay, "Carta hydrographica."

33. Important studies include Vinson, *Bearing Arms*; Sartorius, *Ever Faithful*; Güereca Durán, *Milicias indígenas en Nueva España*. Echeverri, *Indian and Slave Royalists*. Schneider, *The Occupation of Havana*.

34. Echeverri makes this observation about Colombian historiography, yet it applies to the Philippines case. Echeverri, *Indian and Slave Royalists*, 2–3.

35. Sartorius, *Ever Faithful*, 9.

36. Amphibious thinking is inspired by Renisa Mawani and May Joseph's respective work. See Mawani, "Law, Settler Colonialism," 107–131; Sen and Joseph, "Terra Aqua," 1–6.

37. See Lesser, Hu-DeHart, and López-Calvo, "Why Asia and Latin America?," 1–16; Hau, "Transregional Southeast Asia," 4–16.

38. On method see Folger, *Writing as Poaching*, 13–66; Kars, *Blood on the River*, 22–23.

39. *The Philippine Islands, 1493–1898*, 55 vols.

40. The Indiana Republican senator Albert Beveridge is quoted speaking on the floor of the U.S. Senate in 1900, which appears in Kramer, *The Blood of Government*, 1. On the limitations of the Blair and Robertson volume, see Cano García, "Spanish Colonial Past"; Cano García, "La construcción del pasado español," 209–239.

41. On the destruction of archives see More, "The Colonial Latin American Archive," 300–302; Owens, *Nuns Navigating the Spanish Empire*, 137–140.

42. Scott, *Domination and the Arts of Resistance*.

43. Taylor, *Magistrates of the Sacred*, 4; Yannakakis, *The Art of Being In-Between*, 3.

44. See, for example, Yannakakis, *The Art of Being In-Between*; Grafe and Irigoin, "Bargaining for Absolutism"; Marichal, "Rethinking Negotiation," Vicuña Guengerich, "A Royalist Cacica."

45. See Kramer, *The Blood of Government*, 67–73, 123–124; Charbonneau, *Civilizational Imperatives*. For the post-Independence era, see Majul, "The Moro Struggle in the Philippines," 903–920; Nawab and Osman, "Understanding Islamophobia," 289–290.

46. Nightingale, "Before Race Mattered," 48–71; Lee, *The Making of Asian America*, 15–33; Ngai, *The Chinese Question*, 312–314.

Chapter 1

1. Anon., *Relación compendiosa*.

2. Scott, "Filipino Class Structure," 153; *Cracks*, 90.

3. Important works on the galleon include Schurz, *The Manila Galleon*; Yuste López, *Emporios transpacíficos*; Giráldez, *The Age of Trade*; Priyadarshini, *Chinese Porcelain in Colonial Mexico*; Reyes, "Flaunting It," 683–713.

4. Barrio Muñoz's in-depth study of the eighteenth-century Moro wars is centered on the Spanish governor of the Philippines. Valdés Tamón Barrio Muñoz, *Vientos de reforma*. Priest-centered studies of the Moro wars have a long lineage and can be traced back to the eighteenth century; see, for example, Torrubia, *Dissertación histórico-política*; "Compendio de los sucesos . . . se consiguieron contra los Mahometanos Enemigos" (1755). Newberry Library, Ayer MS 1328. More recent work includes Bernad, "Father Ducos," 690–728, and Schreurs, "The Royal Fort," 107–122. A study that celebrates Moro pirates as anti-colonial heroes is Majul, *Muslims in the Philippines*. Influential work on nineteenth-century piracy in Philippine waters

includes Warren, *Iranun and Balangingi* and *The Sulu Zone*. Hispano-Filipino military collaboration falls outside the scope of important historical anthropology studies by Junker and Angeles, in part due to the earlier time period they cover. Junker, *Raiding*; Angeles, "The Battle of Mactan," 3–52.

5. Martín de Rada (1573) cited in Álvarez, *El costo*, 100–101.

6. Heng, *The Invention of Race*, 113–122.

7. See Elliott, *Empires*, 18–20; Cook, *Forbidden Passages*, 34–36.

8. Fuchs, *Mimesis and Empire*, 74–76; Hernández Lefranc, "El trayecto," 51–92. The Spanish also conceptualized Asia and the Americas as being the dominions of Satan, or the devil. See Cañizares-Esguerra, "The Devil in the New World," 22–40; Flannery, "Can the Devil Cross the Deep Blue Sea?," 42–25.

9. Iglesias, "Moros en la costa," 8.

10. Prange, *Monsoon Islam*, 234–238; Andaya and Ishii, "Religious Developments," 508–571; Scott, *Barangay*, 77–93, 183–188; Brewer, *Shamanism*.

11. On the spread of Islam in Southeast Asia and the Philippines, see Prange, *Monsoon Islam*, 25–91, and Donoso, "The Philippines and Al-Andalus," 253–260.

12. In the twentieth century, Muslim-majority ethnolinguistic groups self-identified as Moro or Bangsamoro people. Majul, "The Moro Struggle," 897–922.

13. Tanner, *Societas Jesu*. For representations on Turks in early modern Europe, see van Duijnen, "Sacrificed," 179–200.

14. Heng, *The Invention of Race*, 111.

15. Letter from Melchior Davalos to Felipe II, in *The Philippine Islands, 1493–1898*, 6:61.

16. The rich literature exploring this historical politics of Muslim hate and its consequences tends to marginalize the Philippines, even though the islands counted the largest Muslim population in the Indies. See Ehlers, "The Spanish Encounter with Islam," 153–173; Vanoli, "Between Absence and Presence."

17. See Fuchs, "Virtual Spaniards," 15–16; Skemer, "An Arabic Book," 112; Tueller, "The Moriscos Who Stayed," 197–215; Soyer, "The Public Baptism," 506–523; Cook, *Forbidden Passages*, 140–152.

18. Crewe, "Transpacific Mestizo," 463–485.

19. Martinez, *Genealogical Fictions*; Böttcher, Hausberger, and Hering Torres, "Introducción," 9–28; Twinam, *Purchasing Wwhiteness*, 45, 86.

20. See Newberry Library, Ayer, MS 2179; Salas y Rodriguez, *Colección de documentos*, 319–329; Mawson, "Slavery, Conflict, and Empire," 256–283; Ireton, "Africans' Freedom," 1277–1319. Enslaving Muslims was also legal in other Catholic kingdoms in Europe, including France. See Martin and Weiss, *The Sun King*.

21. The large southern islands of Mindanao are excluded from this population count due to the lack of sources. Newson, *Conquest and Pestilence*, 4.

22. Muñoz and Alcina, *History of the Bisayan Islands*, 159; Scott, *Barangay*, 17–30, 54–76, 147–161, 217–243; Junker, *Raiding*, 339–347; Souza and Turley, *The Boxer Codex*, 64, 99–100; Angeles, "The Battle of Mactan," 3–52; Coballes and de la Cruz, "An Ethnography," 78–140; Kroupa, "Reading Beneath the Skin," 1252–1287.

23. Angeles, "The Battle of Mactan," 3–52; Junker, *Raiding*, 339–347.

24. For upland-lowland interconnections, see Paredes, "Rivers of Memory," 324–429; Brook, *The Troubled Empire*, 44–45; Junker, *Raiding*, 219.

25. Bobadilla, *Relación*, 11. See also AGI, Filipinas 6, R.9, N.173; Souza and Turley, *The Boxer Codex*, 65, 99–100.

26. Torrubia, *Dissertación histórico-política*.

27. Warren, *The Sulu Zone*, 169.

28. Ibid., xxii.

29. Rediker and Linebaugh, *The Many-Headed Hydra*; Lázaro, *The Misfortunes of Alonso Ramírez*, 10.

30. A group of Christian Filipinos from Batad in Iloilo who had been rescued from Moro captivity in 1753 informed Fray Roque de la Virgen del Carmen that they had encountered "white people shooting the artillery." The friar suspected that one of the men they had seen was Pedro Marcel, a soldier who was rumored to have escaped from the Zamboanga presidio and fled to the Kingdom of Mindanao. Stories circulated that Marcel lived there among the Moros for many years with his two wives and many sons and daughters. Anon., *Relación compendiosa*, f.11; AGI, Filipinas, 295, N.28 BIS, f.136–138; Torrubia, *Dissertación histórico-política*; Scammell, "European Exiles," 641–661. For the Chinese presence in pirate fleets, see Anon., *Relación compendiosa*; Barrio Muñoz, *Vientos de reforma*, 94, 143. The Dutch East India Company Captain Paulus De Brievings observed in the mid-seventeenth century that it was common for Chinese men "allured by the women" to convert to Islam, marry, and settle in the Sulu sultanate. Laarhoven, "The Chinese at Maguindanao," 40. Thomas Forrest, a Scottish navigator and British East India Company agent who traveled through the Sulu Zone in the second half of the eighteenth century, noted that there were "many Chinese settled" among the "Sooloos" Forrest, *A Voyage to New Guinea*, 87.

31. AGI, Filipinas, 706. This estimate is largely consistent with other contemporary assessments of the number of Filipinos taken captive by pirates. The anonymous author of *Manila Malgoberada*, a pamphlet that condemned the poor government of the Philippines, claimed that Moro pirates were robbing between three hundred and five hundred Christian captives each year. Newberry Library, Ayer MS 2161.

32. On social stratification and slavery in the pre-Hispanic and colonial Philippines, see Souza and Turley, *The Boxer Codex*, 99–100; Scott, *Barangay*, 4–5, 136–137, 222–229; Scott, *Slavery in the Spanish Philippines*; Scott, "Filipino Class Structure in the Sixteenth Century," 12–175.

33. Junker, *Raiding*, 25; Warren, *Iranun and Balangingi*, 218.

34. AGI, Filipinas, 192, N.108. Bugis merchants from southern Sulawesi visited Jolo to buy slaves that they transported to the Dutch East Indies. Other Spanish primary sources reveal that slave-raiders directly sold Filipino captives to merchants in Borneo, from where they were trafficked to Batavia. Warren, *Iranun and Balangingi*, 33.

35. Barrio Muñoz, *Vientos de reforma*, 56; Weber, *Bárbaros*.

36. Majul, *Muslims in the Philippines*. This claim is a source of contention among historians of the Philippines. Donoso suggests that Majul invented the martial Filipino subject in the service of a romantic, postcolonial nationalism. Donoso, "The Philippines and al-Andalus," 263–265. However, discussions of Muslims' obligations to wage war against European imperial forces are well documented in other parts of the Indo-Pacific world at this time. Prange shows that these ideas circulated in treatises and songs on the Portuguese-occupied Malabar coast, which discourages us from dismissing Majul's claims. Prange, *Monsoon Islam*, 148–153; Walravens, "Multiple Audiences," 226–236.

37. Warren makes this argument, and it has been criticized for its economic determinism. Warren, *The Sulu Zone*; *Iranun and Balangingi*. Sutherland, "The Sulu Zone Revisited."

38. Warren theorizes that the 1765 eruption of the Mount Macaturin volcano in Mindanao destroyed the local Iranun's villages and farms and forced thousands of refugee families to migrate to the Sulu Islands and beyond in search of subsistence. The Iranun diaspora subsequently rose to prominence as saltwater slave-raiders in the 1770s and 1780s. It is possible that earlier natural disasters had comparable effects. Warren, "Volcanoes, Refugees, and Raiders," 79–100.

39. Bernad, "Father Ducos," 697.

40. AGI, Filipinas, 706.

41. Barrio Muñoz, Vientos de reforma, 92.

42. Coello de la Rosa, Jesuits at the Margins, 337.

43. Ibid., 280.

44. This map uses data from several eighteenth-century sources including AGI, Mapas, Libros, y Manuscritos, 81, 12r; Biblioteca Nacional de España, MSS/19217 (H.11v–12r); AGI, Filipinas, 387, N.1.

45. Biblioteca Nacional de España, MSS/19217 (H.11v–12r), 75.

46. Ibid.

47. McEnroe, "A Sleeping Army," 128.

48. Neri et al., "The Archeology of Initao," 182–185; Canialo, "Isles of Garrisons."

49. Biblioteca Nacional de España, MSS/19217 (H.11v–12r), 62.

50. Javellana, Fortress of Empire; Lara, City, Temple, Stage; Luengo Gutiérrez, "La fortificación," 727–758; "Military Engineering," 4–27; "Fortificaciones," 197–213.

51. Coello de la Rosa, Jesuits at the Margins, 280.

52. Murillo Velarde and Bagay, "Carta hydrographica."

53. Andrés, "El 'Padre Capitán,'" 7–54. Entre frailes.

54. Entre frailes, 28.

55. For tribute, see Álvarez, El costo, 41–42, 216–217, 223–235; Fradera, Filipinas, la colonia más peculiar, 35–70. The Philippines was the only place in Spain's empire where the polo existed, but this institution was similar to the mita that forcibly recruited men to labor in the mines of Potosí. Bakewell, Miners of the Red Mountain; Barragán, "Working Silver," 193–222.

56. See Brewer, Shamanism; López Lázaro, The Misfortunes of Alonso Ramírez.

57. See Lee, Saints of Resistance.

58. McEnroe, "A Sleeping Army," 111.

59. The British East India Company pursued diplomacy with sultanates in the Sulu Zone from the late seventeenth century onward. Quiason, English "Country Trade," 112–125. See also León Portilla, "La Embajada," 215–242; Paredes, A Mountain of Difference.

60. Majul, "The Moro Struggle," 897.

61. Barrio Muñoz, Vientos de reforma, 157.

62. Francisco de San Antonio, Chronicas de la apostolica, 138–139; Mojarro Romero, "Notas en torno," 103–105.

63. Biedermann explores the politics of conversion diplomacy in early modern Sri Lanka. Biedermann, (Dis)connected Empires, 94–121.

64. Tiongson, Komedya, 11.

65. Díaz-Trechuelo, "Eighteenth Century Philippine Economy."

66. AGI, Filipinas, 192, N.108. For Spanish diplomacy with Siam in this period, see Llanes, "Dropping Artillery."

67. Newberry Library, Ayer, MS 2113.

68. Spanish sources referenced the China embassy. See Barrio Muñoz, *Vientos de reforma*, 128.

69. AGI, Filipinas, 227; Barrio Muñoz, *Vientos de reforma*, 133–227.

70. *Vientos de reforma*, 134–135.

71. Lilly Library, MS 21518, Mindanao.

72. Arechederra, *Continuacion de los progresos*; Saleeby, *The History of Sulu*, 180–181.

73. de la Costa et al., "Muhammad Alimuddin I," 49.

74. Twentieth-century historians have identified the tirones as the Orang Tedong of Eastern Borneo. The Malay word "tudung" means "to cover" and is commonly translated as a veil or headscarf and has been used to mark the group as Muslim; Mallari, "The Eighteenth Century Tirones," 297. Mid-eighteenth-century Spanish colonial officials were confused about the identity of the tirones and where they were from. Governor Arechederra wrote that these people inhabited a group of "innumerable" islands that lay between seven and four degrees on the map. The Jesuit historian de la Costa clarified that the 1747 campaign was carried out against the Orang Tedong; de Arechederra, *Puntual relación*; de la Costa et al., "Muhammad Alimuddin I," 45.

75. Jesuits claimed that Azim ud-Din contributed as many as 8,000 fighting men to the war, whereas Arechederra put this number at 750. See "Muhammad Alimuddin I," 45; Arechederra, *Puntual relación*.

76. Arechederra, *Puntual relación*.

77. Anon., *Relación de la entrada del sultan*.

78. Ramos, *Identity, Ritual, and Power*, 44–65; Cañeque, *The King's Living Image*, 26–35.

79. Anon., *Relación de la entrada del sultan*.

80. Fulchiero Spilimbergo or Espilimbergo, and Patricio de Barrio. The latter was vice provincial of the Jesuits in the Philippines. AGI, Filipinas, 458, N.20.

81. AGI, 292, N.13. Arechederra repeats this view; AGI, Filipinas, 458, N.20.

82. Hershenzon highlights equivalent suspicions in the Mediterranean. Hershenzon, *The Captive Sea*, 36.

83. AGI, Filipinas 292, N.33.

84. Ibid. The language in which Azim ud-Din and friars communicated is unclear. The report on the sultan's conversion states that Padre Patricio del Barrio, the vice provincial of the Jesuits in the Philippines and one of the sultan's religious instructors, could communicate in Azim ud-Din's native tongue, and that the sultan could communicate in Spanish. Yet there is evidence that translators also facilitated communication. Alferez Diego Santiago Ravelo was employed as an interpreter of the Joloana language, based in the sultan's Binondo home in 1749–1750. AGI, Filipinas, 458, N.20.

85. AGI, Filipinas, 292, N.33.

86. Ibid.

87. Ibid.

88. Another factor that likely influenced Martínez's opposition to Moro diplomacy was his grudge against Arechederra for denying him the opportunity to serve as interim governor of the Philippines. Spanish royal decrees directed that when the Philippines governor died in office, the archbishop of Manila should serve as governor until a replacement official, appointed by the Crown, arrived in the islands. Martínez had been appointed as Manila's archbishop and was in the middle of his long journey from Spain to the Philippines when Governor Gaspar de la Torre died in 1745. Arechederra was the bishop of Nueva Segovia, which made him next

in line for the interim governorship after Martínez. Arechederra refused to stand down when Martínez finally reached the colony. AGI, Filipinas, 458, N.20.

89. Original emphasis. AGI, Filipinas, 292, N.33.

90. AGI, Filipinas, 458, N.20.

91. Ibid.

92. Ibid., f.68–f.118. For the Sulu Middle Passage, see Warren, "The Iranun and Balangingi," 52–71.

93. AGI, Filipinas, 458, N.20.

94. Ibid.

95. Anon., *Relación de la entrada del sultan*. AGI, Filipinas, 458, N.20, f.117; Crailsheim, "The Baptism of Sultan Azim ud-Din."

96. Jawi script is Malay writing in Arabic characters. Jiménez, "El Islam en Filipinas," 21.

97. AGI, Filipinas, 706.

98. In Saleeby, *The History of Sulu*.

99. Ovando described the *kris* as "the weapon most used by these Moros." Newberry Library, Ayer MS 2113.

100. Ibid.

101. In December 1753, the sultan's daughter Fatima traveled to Jolo to negotiate her father's freedom in exchange for the liberation of Christian captives. The embassy included two Malaya interpreters: the Pampangan Diego Santiago Rauelo, and Mauricio Machado. Both men lived in Manila's Extramuros. Fatima returned to Manila with an ambassador, but no Christian captives. In March 1754 Ovando and Azim ud-Din made a new peace treaty, but it was largely ignored: the imprisoned Sultan had no power to enforce it. Foreman, *The Philippine Islands*, 138; AGI, Filipinas, 709.

102. Ovando, "Manifiesto, en que succintamente se exponen los motivos."

103. Ibid.

104. AGI, Filipinas, 385, N.25.

105. Ibid., f1v–1r.

106. AGI, Filipinas, 385, N.25.

107. This analysis of the 1754 expedition draws heavily on Commander Cesar Falliet's unpublished account of the expedition and an unpublished Jesuit account of the campaign. AGI, Filipinas, 920, N.23. Anon., *Relación compendiosa*. Concepción drew heavily on and reproduced large sections of the latter. Concepción, *Historia general de Philipinas*, 1, Chap. 12, 17.

108. Arechederra, *Puntual relación*, f.3–4. Kroupa, "Reading Beneath the Skin," 12.

109. Anon., *Relación compendiosa*.

110. On Father Ducos, see Bernad, "Father Ducos," 690–728; Schreurs, "The Royal Fort," 107–122. On the clergy in the war, see Torrubia, *Dissertación histórico-política*, 79; Blanco Andrés, "El 'Padre Capitán.'"

111. Newberry Library, Ayer MS 2113.

112. AGI, Filipinas, 295, N.28 BIS.

113. AGI, Filipinas, 385, N.25.

114. AGI, Filipinas, 385, N.25; Torrubia, *Dissertación histórico-política*, 5. See also Luengo Gutiérrez, "Fortificaciones Musulmanes en Joló"; ibid., 197–213.

115. Kreike, *Scorched Earth*, 2–3.

116. Concepción, *Historia general de Philipinas*, 1:378.

117. Angeles, "The Battle of Mactan," 23–25.

118. Concepción, *Historia general de Philipinas*, 13:16.

119. Anon., *Relación compendiosa*.

120. AGI, Filipinas, 706, f.91. Anon., *Relación compendiosa*.

121. On the concept of "Indian conquistadors," see Cuadriello, *Las glorias*.

122. Larkin, *The Pampangans*, 22–23; Phelan, *The Hispanization of the Philippines*, 146.

123. Mawson, "Philippine Indios," 388; Sales, "La escasez de soldados," 777–778; Fernández Palacios, "El papel activo"; Mawson, "Philippine Indios."

124. Pampangan soldiers brought their families to the Marianas as settler colonists. AGI, Filipinas, 349, N.6; Hezel and Driver, "From Conquest to Colonisation," 141; Borao Mateo, "Contextualizing the Pampangos."

125. Governor Valdés Tamón's 1739 report on military defenses reveals Pampangan soldiers were fully integrated into the Pacific presidio network and accounted for more than half of the deployed soldiers in some presidios. Biblioteca Nacional de España, MSS/19217 (H.11v–12r).

126. Cushner, "Meysapan," 25–53. Palanco Aguado, "The Tagalog Revolts," 45–77.

127. White, *The Middle Ground*, 33.

128. Prieto Lucena, *Filipinas durante*, 57–82; Constantino, "Identity and consciousness," 16.

129. Mawson, "Philippine Indios," 403.

130. Ibid., 385.

131. Biblioteca Nacional de España, MSS/19217 (H.11v–12r), 16–17.

132. AGI, 295, N.28 BIS.

133. Cushner, *Spain in the Philippines*, 45; Mehl, *Forced Migration*, 159–171.

134. Newberry Library, Ayer, MS 1325.

135. Donoso, "The Hispanic Moros," 93–94. On the komedya, see Tiongson, *Komedya*; Fernandez, "Princesa Miramar," 413–442.

136. There is a rich historiography exploring how patriotic theater with military themes encouraged white European men to enlist in the British royal navy in this era. See Wilson, *The Sense of the People*; Ennis, *Enter the Press-Gang*; Kinkel, *Disciplining the Empire*.

137. AGI, 198, N.32.

138. AGI, Escribania, 436A. On the chapel, see San Antonio, *Chronicas de la apostolica Provincia*, 193–194; Irving, *Colonial Counterpoint*, 182.

139. On average, Pampangan soldiers earned less than half of a Spanish soldier's salary. Biblioteca Nacional de España, MSS/19217 (H.11v–12rR), 25.

140. Anon., *Relación compendiosa*.

141. These include Lobo (Batangas), Loboc (Bohol), Luay (Mindanao), Yligan (Mindanao), Ynabligan, Baclayon, and Tagbilalan (Bohol), Malabohoc (Cebu), and Intao (Panay). Ibid. AGI, Filipinas, 920, N.23. Concepción's discussion of the raids copies information from the 1754 source. Concepción, *Historia general de Philipinas*, 1, Chap. 12, 17.

142. Junker, *Raiding*, 345.

143. Taylor, *Magistrates of the Sacred*, 221–223.

144. Anon., *Relación compendiosa*.

145. AGI, Filipinas, 706, f.91.

146. AGI, Filipinas, 162, N.8.

147. Sailors' salaries were fixed at two reales a month, in addition to rations of rice, salt, and tobacco. AGI, 295, N.28 BIS.

148. AGI, Filipinas, 140, N.12.

149. Ibid.

150. AGI, Filipinas, 162, N.8. Anon., *Relación compendiosa*.

151. AGI, Filipinas, 162, N.8. On the self-fashioning of loyal subjecthood, see Folger, *Writing as Poaching*, 13–66.

152. Paredes, *A Mountain of Difference*, 128–129.

153. Bianca Premo, *Children of the Father King*, 10–11.

154. Anon., *Relación compendiosa*.

155. Rescuing captives in the Philippines looked different to *recaste* in northern New Spain in this era, which involved missionaries buying or stealing unbaptized Indigenous children in trading fairs before baptizing and then selling them at a profit in a "thinly disguised labor market." Brooks, *Captives & Cousins*, 23, 49, 366.

156. AGI, Filipinas, 706.

157. AGN, Indiferente Virreinal, 6230–034.

158. Ibid.

159. Warren, "The Iranun and Balangingi Slaving Voyage," 56.

160. In Chakraborty and van Rossum, "Slave Trade and Slavery," 1. See also Eklöf Amirell, *Pirates of Empire*, 13.

161. AGI, Filipinas, 706.

162. Hämäläinen, *The Comanche Empire*, 30–51.

163. AGI, Filipinas, 706, 107r. On the Guaraní and Jesuit warfare, see Ganson, *The Guaraní Under Spanish Rule*; Jackson, *Regional Conflict*, 33–66.

164. Redden, "Priestly Violence," 81.

165. Lozano, *Historia de la Compañia de Jesus*.

166. Paredes, *A Mountain of Difference*, 21, 57.

167. AGI, Filipinas, 706, f.113.

168. NAP, Protoloco - Manila, 1755.

169. Ibid.

170. Anon., *Relación compendiosa*.

171. Ibid.

172. Junker, *Raiding*, 19; AGI, Filipinas, 162, N.8.

173. Londoño, *Discurso sobre la forma*.

174. Junker, *Raiding*, 237–238.

175. AGI, Filipinas, 162, N.8.

176. AGI, Filipinas, 706, f.113. AGI, Filipinas, 706.

177. Junker, *Raiding*, 138; Angeles, "The Battle of Mactan," 10–11,16; Paredes, *A Mountain of Difference*, 28–30.

178. AGI, Filipinas, 140, N.12.

179. Angeles, "The Battle of Mactan," 27.

180. Muñoz and Alcina, *History of the Bisayan Islands*, 3, 162.

181. Phillips, *Six Galleons for the King*, 158.

182. Anon., *Relación compendiosa*. For other miracles see AGN, Indiferente Virreinal, 6230–034; Torrubia, *Dissertación histórico-política*, 79; Lee, *Saints of Resistance*, 73–99.

183. Ileto, *Pasyon and Revolution*, 1–2, 22–28.

184. See Pérez-Mallaína Bueno, *Spain's Men of the Sea*, 237, 158–159.

185. Lilly Library, MS 21538, Lot 528.

186. Newberry Library, Ayer MS 2165.

187. See AGI, Filipinas, 453, N.2, f.35r–84r; Fray Juan de la Concepción, *Historia general de Philipinas*, 14:80–107.

188. *Historia general de Philipinas*, 14:91; AGI, Filipinas, 453, N.2, Exp.2, 5.

189. AGI, Filipinas, 453, N.2.

190. Ibid., Doc. 5, F.35.

191. Warren, *Iranun and Balangingi*, 11.

192. Cooper, *Colonialism in Question*, 157.

Chapter 2

1. Teochew refers to the people of the historical Chaoshan region in south China. In primary sources Limahong also appears as Limahon. This account is based on Sande, "Relation of the Philippine Islands," in *The Philippine Islands, 1493–1898*, 1:37–43. Concepción, *Historia general de Philipinas*, 1:422–434; Roman y Zamora, *Repúblicas de Indias*, 255–267; Callanta, *The Limahong Invasion*; Guingona, "A Ghost and His Apparition"; Kenji, "At the Crossroads"; Schultz, "Limahong's pirates," 315–342.

2. Juan Gil's foundational study offers an encyclopedic overview of Chinese migrants in Manila in the sixteenth and seventeenth centuries, drawing on Spanish archives. Gil, *Los Chinos en Manila*. Studies recovering negotiation between Chinese migrants and the colonial government in Manila include Buschmann, Slack, and Tueller, *Navigating the Spanish Lake*, 63–96; de Llobet, "Chinese mestizo and natives' disputes"; Gebhardt, "Microhistory and Microcosm"; Ruiz-Stovel, "Chinese Shipping and Merchant Networks"; Chen, "The Hokkiens"; Slack, "New Perspectives." Wickberg described the Sangleyes as "a despised cultural minority." Wickberg, *The Chinese in Philippine Life*, 9.

3. On the Chinese diaspora in the Pacific world, see Seijas, *Asian Slaves*; Hu-DeHart and López, "Asian Diasporas," 9–21; Hu-DeHart, "Indispensable Enemy," 65–102; Camacho, *Chinese Mexicans*; Chang, *Chino*; Ngai, *The Chinese Question*. For studies of how other non-Spanish migrants in Manila constructed loyal Catholic identities in opposition to Moro piracy, see Flannery and Ruiz-Stovel, "The Loyal Foreign Merchant Captain," 189–215; Flannery, "The Trans-Imperial Biography," 479–497.

4. Slack, "New Perspectives," 119.

5. Junker, "Trade Competition," 248; Go, "Ma'l in Chinese Records," 119–138; Go and Sy, *The Philippines in Ancient Chinese Maps*; Nicolas, "Gongs, Bells, and Cymbals," 62–93.

6. Tremml, "The Global and the Local," 559.

7. Cevera, *Cartas del Parián*, 85.

8. Mehl, *Forced Migration*, 234; Kueh, "The Manila Chinese," 38; Tremml, "The Global and the Local," 557.

9. Mawson, "Unruly Plebeians," 97; Mehl, *Forced Migration*, 267.

10. Newson, *Conquest and Pestilence*, 256–257.

11. Ibid.

12. Studies of these other migrant communities in Manila include Rafael, "From Mardicas to Filipinos," 343–362; Bhattacharya, "Making Money at the Blessed Place of Manila," 1–20; Baena Zapatero and Lamikiz, "Presencia de una diáspora global," 693–722; Tremml-Werner, "Marginal Players," 599–626; Crewe, "Occult Cosmopolitanism," 55–74.

13. Tremml, "The Global and the Local," 557.

14. For an overview of Chinese migration in this era, see Miles, *Chinese Diasporas*, 1–88; Blussé, *Visible cities*.

15. Siu, *Memories of a Future Home*, 11.

16. Miles, *Chinese Diasporas*, 45–47.

17. The term Hokkien "denotes a cluster of mutually comprehensible subdialects spoken in the Hokkien Province in southern China." Jones, "The Chiangchew Hokkiens," 42.

18. Ruiz-Stovel, "Chinese Shipping," 135–139. Chia discusses the challenges of extracting this data from extant Chinese sources. Chia, "The Butcher, the Baker," 513, 520–521. On nineteenth century migration patterns, see Chu, *Chinese and Chinese Mestizos*, 24–25.

19. Chu, *Chinese and Chinese Mestizos*, 25–34; Miles, *Chinese Diasporas*, 32–36.

20. Wang, *Writing Pirates*, 32–42.

21. Murakami, "Trade and Crisis," 220–222.

22. For "Sangley," see Ruíz Gutiérrez, "El Parián de Manila," 1616; Chu, *Chinese and Chinese Mestizos*, 69; Lee, "The Chinese Problem," 17; Kueh, "The Manila Chinese," 1; Ruiz-Stovel, "Chinese Shipping and Merchant Networks," 128–130; Tremml, "The Global and the Local," 555–588. The term "Sangley" was rarely used in New Spain. On the other side of the Pacific, Chinese migrants were lumped together with Indigenous Filipinos and other Asians as *chinos*. See Luis, "The Armed Chino"; Seijas, *Asian Slaves*, 1, 5–6.

23. For example, thirteen laws regulating Sangleyes were enacted between 1594 and 1627. *Recopilacíon de las leyes de indias*, libro VI, titulo 18.

24. Martínez, "Manila's Sangleys," 73–77.

25. Sangleyes and Chinese mestizos formed a single gremio in 1687. Wickberg, "The Chinese Mestizo," 70. Wickberg, *The Chinese in Philippine Life*, 190; Llobet, "Chinese mestizo and natives' disputes," 214–235; Chu, *Chinese and Chinese Mestizos*, 58–59.

26. Morga, *Sucesos*, 149. Gil also divided Sangleyes into two groups: wealthy merchants and an "exploited and unhappy" proletariat. Gil, *Los Chinos en Manila*, 458.

27. Gil, *Los Chinos en Manila*, 134–141, 335–392; Cevera, *Cartas del Parián*, 92; Luengo Gutiérrez, "European Architecture in Southeast Asia," 254–270.

28. Morga, *Sucesos*, 296.

29. Andrade conceptualized the Chinese as co-colonists of the Dutch East India Company in seventeenth-century Formosa (Taiwan). Busquets introduced this concept in the Philippines context. Andrade, *How Taiwan Became Chinese*, 116; Busquets, "Three Manila-Fujian Diplomatic Encounters," 449–453. The designation of Chinese and other Asian peoples as colonists or settler colonists is controversial. For an overview of the interdisciplinary debate over these concepts, see Iyko Day et al., "Settler Colonial Studies," 1–45.

30. Gil, *Los Chinos en Manila*, 125–136, 168–172. See Cobo's letter in Cevera, *Cartas del Parián*, 89.

31. Crewe, "Pacific Purgatory," 359; Martínez, "Manila's Sangleys," 75–76, 78. On baptisms of converts in other parts of the global Spanish empire, see Soyer, "The Public Baptism," 331–353; Prieto, "The Perils of Accommodation," 395–414.

32. Martínez, "Manila's Sangleys," 78. For a broader discussion of hair politics in seventeenth-century China, see Hang, "A Question of Hairdos," 246–280.

33. Tan, "The Chinese Mestizos," 144–146. On *padrinazgo* (godparenthood) see Kueh, "Adaptive Strategies," 364–371. There is a rich literature on padrinazgo in Black communities in the Spanish empire. See, for example, Stark, "Ties that Bind," 84–110; Salazar Carreño, "El compadrazgo," 467–494.

34. Cevera, *Cartas del Parián*, 90.

35. Martínez, "Manila's Sangleys," 79–80.

36. Minamiki, *The Chinese Rites Controversy*; Wang, "The Ancient Rites of China," 90–112.

37. Flannery, "Prohibited Games," 81–92; Brockey, "The First China Hands," 69–84; Newberry Library, Ayer MS 1458.

38. Clossey, *Salvation and Globalization*, 68–89; Brockey, *Journey to the East*; Brockey, "The First China Hands," 69–84; Brockey, "Conquests of Memory," 1–15; Hsia, "Introduction," 1–14; Hsia, "Imperial China and the Christian Mission," 344–364.

39. Ngai, *The Chinese Question*.

40. AGI, Filipinas, 28, N.131, f.1015; Gil, *Los Chinos en Manila*, 453.

41. Gil, *Los Chinos en Manila*, 283–286.

42. Tremml, "When Political Economies Meet," 110.

43. Rules regulating the Parián changed over time. The requirement for baptized Chinese to live in the Parián, for example, was subject to debate and was revised on multiple occasions. Other non-Catholic foreigners were also ordered to live in the Parián at various times. Gil, *Los Chinos en Manila*, 142–171.

44. AGI, Mapas y Planos, Filipinas, 10. Leibsohn, "Dentro y fuera de los muros"; Nightingale, "Before Race Mattered."

45. NAP, Spanish Manila 13816 (1721–1894), Exp. 1.

46. Gil, *Los Chinos en Manila*, 714. Gil has compiled a list of licenses conceded to Chinese to "keep shops and make journeys"; ibid.

47. Ibid., 714–748.

48. AGI, Filipinas, 712, N.1, f.102r.

49. Ruiz-Stovel, "Chinese Shipping," 164.

50. Tremml, "When Political Economies Meet," 263.

51. AGI, Filipinas, 202, N.1, f1406r–1407v.

52. NAP Consultas, 1771–1772, SDS-38, f.393r. Ruiz-Stovel, "Chinese Shipping," 461.

53. Schwaller, "For Honor and Defense," 239–266; Luis, "The Armed Chino."

54. Gil, *Los Chinos en Manila*, 125–136, 168–172.

55. My use of genocide as a concept is informed by studies of genocide in colonial contexts. See Ryan, "Digital map," 137; Lemarchand, "Introduction," 1–18.

56. Gil, *Los Chinos en Manila*, 496.

57. Ibid., 453, 457–458.

58. Tremml, *Spain, China and Japan in Manila*, 310.

59. Ibid. Hang, *Conflict and Commerce*, 117–143. Some historians have argued that the seventeenth century's environmental catastrophes generated political disruption and war on a global scale. Parker, "Crisis and Catastrophe," 1053–1079.

60. Gil, *Los Chinos en Manila*, 453.

61. Morga, *Sucesos*, Chapter 5.

62. Salazar y Salcedo, "Three Chinese Mandarins at Manila" in *The Philippine Islands, 1493–1898*, 12:83–94; Bartolomé Leonardo de Argensola, *Conquista de las Islas Malucas*, 315.

63. Colin and Chirino, *Labor evangelica*, 418–441; Argensola, *Conquista de las islas Malucas*, 210–212. Salazar y Salcedo, "Three Chinese Mandarins at Manila" in *The Philippine Islands, 1493–1898*. 12:83–97. See also Kueh, "The Manila Chinese," 40–42; Tremml, "The Global and the Local," 570; Borao, "The Massacre of 1603," 22–40.

64. Tremml notes, "there is no concrete evidence to support such huge numbers" and suggests that the death toll was inflated by the Spanish to convey their military superiority over the Chinese and by the Chinese to embellish their role as victims. Tremml, "The Global and

the Local," 570. What is clear is that the massacre was intended to destroy Manila's large Chinese population and almost succeeded. King Philip V claimed that there were no Chinese in Manila in 1603–1607 in the aftermath of the massacre. AGI, Filipinas, 202, N.1, 1406r–1407v.

65. Argensola, *Conquista de las Islas Malucas*, 335; Borao, "The Massacre of 1603," 31–32.

66. Borao analyzes Chinese sources revealing the Ming court's responses to the massacre. "The Massacre of 1603," 28–40.

67. Tremml, "The Global and the Local," 321.

68. Antony, *Like Froth Floating on the Sea*, 24–26, 74.

69. Li Guangpo, ibid., 139.

70. Hang, *Conflict and Commerce*, 99; Antony, *Like Froth Floating on the Sea*, 19–53; Antony, "Piracy on the South China Coast," 32–38.

71. Hang, *Conflict and Commerce*, 50–58.

72. Antony, *Like Froth Floating on the Sea*, 32–33. Note that Zheng Chenggong is also transliterated as Cogsen in Spanish publications.

73. Andrade, *How Taiwan Became Chinese*, 80–100.

74. These letters from Manila are not extant. One surviving account of the Chinese genocide emphasizes the Iquan connection. "Relation of the Insurrection of the Chinese," in *The Philippine Islands, 1493–1898*, 29:208–258. In contrast, Corcuera's account did not acknowledge Chinese pirates. Hurtado de Corquera, *Relacion del levantamiento*. See also Gil, *Los Chinos en Manila*, 492–509.

75. *Los Chinos en Manila*, 491–509.

76. Hurtado de Corquera, *Relacion del levantamiento*, 5r; Gil, *Los Chinos en Manila*, 494–495.

77. Hurtado de Corquera, *Relacion del levantamiento*, 14r. There is archival evidence of a genocide on this scale. Gil showed that in 1641, the governor claimed that of the forty thousand Chinese who had lived in Manila in 1639, no more than seven thousand remained. The Spanish official who led the residencia or formal assessment of the governor's term in office calculated that twenty-four thousand Sangleyes had died that year. Other historians agree with these figures. Gil, *Los Chinos en Manila*, 506–507; Tremml, *Spain, China and Japan*, 310.

78. Lilly Library, Philippine Manuscripts II, Legajo 1: MS 21529, 5–32; Lee, "The Chinese Problem," 5–32; Lee, *Saints of Resistance*, 39–72.

79. Andrade, "A Chinese Farmer," 575; Andrade, *How Taiwan Became Chinese*, 228–250.

80. Gil, *Los Chinos en Manila*, 514–515.

81. "Events in Manila, 1662–63" in *The Philippine Islands, 1493–1898*, 36:220–222.

82. Leibsohn, "Dentro y fuera de los muros," 242; "Events in Manila, 1662–63," in *The Philippine Islands, 1493–1898*, 36:243; AGI, Filipinas, N.9, R.2, N.34; Gil, *Los Chinos en Manila*, 522.

83. Gil, *Los Chinos en Manila*, 516.

84. "Events in Manila, 1662–63," in *The Philippine Islands, 1493–1898*, 36:222.

85. Hang, *Conflict and Commerce in Maritime East Asia*, 142–143. Gil highlights major inconsistencies in original Spanish accounts of the rebellion. Dominicans argued that the Chinese were planning a revolt that triggered and justified Spanish violence. In contrast, Jesuits claimed that the Chinese were innocent and were only trying to escape precedented, state-sponsored massacres. Gil, *Los Chinos en Manila*, 518.

86. Cheng, *War, Trade and Piracy*, 225–226.

87. On Mexican colonial government responses to rebellions, see Cope, *The Limits of Racial Domination*, 104, 153–155; Taylor, *Drinking, Homicide & Rebellion*, 113–151. For the 1612

Afro-Mexican conspiracy, see Martínez, "The Black Blood of New Spain," 479–481; Valerio, *Sovereign Joy*, 80–125.

88. Tardieu, *Cimarrones de Panamá*, 57; Gallup-Díaz, "A Legacy of Strife," 391–412.

89. Wang, *White Lotus Rebels*, 85–86; Antony, *Like Froth Floating on the Sea*, 112–116.

90. AGI, Filipinas, 28; Gil, *Los chinos en Manila*, 545–547.

91. Chia, "The Butcher, the Baker, and the Carpenter," 509–544; Gebhardt, "Microhistory and Microcosm," 167–192.

92. AGI, Filipinas, 202, N.1, f.166r–167v.

93. Ibid., f.168r–172r; Chia, "The Butcher, the Baker, and the Carpenter," 517–518.

94. AGI, Filipinas, 202, N.1, f.346r–348v, 351r.

95. The letter from the "infidel Sangleyes who reside in these islands," c.1690, ibid., f.410–412r.

96. Ibid., f.412r.

97. Ibid.

98. Ibid., f.410–412r.

99. Ibid., f.423r–424v. Special audits of Manila's bakeries where non-Christian Sangeleyes were rumored to be hiding from authorities were completed as part of the census. Note that Chinese agricultural workers outside of urban Manila are not identified in these censuses as they would have been registered in tribute records. Complementing the census, government officials also inspected Chinese passengers and crew aboard ships arriving in Manila. They recorded newcomers' defining physical features, including facial hair, moles, and scars, in addition to other personal information, data gathered in what could only have been intrusive, intimate inspections of the body. The intention was to use this biophysical information to ensure that non-Christian Chinese men who arrived in the Philippines later left the colony as the law required. Ibid., f.144v–f.165r, f.346r–348r, f.383r–391r.ibid., f.272–344v.

100. For examples of Manileños' complaints to the Crown regarding Sangleyes, see ibid., f.507v–509r, f.464r–471v.

101. Ibid., f.948r–955v.

102. Ibid., f.917v–939r.

103. Ibid., f.956v–964v.

104. "La total expulsión y extermino de los sangeleyes infieles que habiten esta islas," ibid., f.1406.

105. AGI, Filipinas, 712, N.1.

106. The records of the investigation are preserved in AGI, Filipinas, 712, N.1. See also Aguado, "The Tagalog Revolts," 56.

107. The rebellion lasted from February to October 1745. In addition to land ownership and land use rights, the revolting Indigenous communities demanded a slew of reforms to the colonial political economy. They sought a reduction in tribute, an overhaul of the *polo*—the tributary labor system that they claimed had workers suffering from inadequate rations and violent beatings from overseers—and modifications to the *bandala* system that required indigenous communities to buy goods from the state at set prices. Parish priests were instrumental in eventually persuading the rebels to put down their weapons. Aguado, "The Tagalog Revolts," 50–61.

108. AGI, Filipinas, 712, N.1. Alternative spellings of Yongco's name in Spanish documents include Juan Tangyongco and Juan Yngc.

109. Ibid., f.186v.

110. Ibid., f.181v.

111. Ibid., f.89r.

112. Ibid., f.267r.

113. Ibid., f.147v.

114. AGI, Filipinas, 292, N.60, f.1–22.

115. Ibid.

116. AGI, Filipinas, 60, N.21.

117. Ibid.

118. AGN, Filipinas, 5, Exp. 4, 215–219.

119. Concepción, *Historia general de Philipinas*, 1:431.

120. Lee, "The Chinese Problem," 11. In contrast, Armenian migrants' conversions to Catholicism in Manila in this period are well documented. Armenians were Christians, but Spanish Catholics regarded the Armenian Gregorian Church as heretical and schismatic, which obliged this community to seek baptisms in Manila. Aslanian, *From the Indian Ocean*, 60–63; Baena Zapatero and Lamikiz, "Presencia de una diáspora global," 693–722.

121. Nutini, "Syncretism and Acculturation," 301–321. Ramos, "Conversion of Indigenous People."

122. In 1694 and 1756, the government granted a stipend of two pesos per month and a rice ration to each member of a group of shipwrecked Japanese men following their baptisms. The men were in the care of Franciscan missionaries in Dilao. AGI, Filipinas, 165, N.62; AGI, Filipinas.

123. AGI, Filipinas, 712, N.1, f.90r–90v.

124. Ibid., f.86v.

125. Ibid., f.118v.

126. Lilly Library, Philippine Manuscripts II, Legajo 1, MS 21529; Hui, "Between Heaven and the Deep Sea"; Lee, *Saints of Resistance*, 39–72.

127. Newberry Library, Ayer MS 1325.

128. Lee, "The Chinese Problem."

129. Mazu is written as Ma-Cho in the Philippines today. On the early modern cult of Mazu in maritime Asia and the Philippines, see Ruitenbeek, "Mazu, the Patroness of Sailors," 281–289; Hui, "Between Heaven and the Deep Sea," 78; Lee, "The Chinese Problem," 5–32; *Saints of Resistance*, 39–72.

130. Scott, *Domination and the Arts of Resistance*, 25.

131. Warren, *The Sulu Zone*; Paredes, *A Mountain of Difference*; Lopez, "An Exploration," 105–120.

132. Hernández Lefranc, "El trayecto de Santiago," 51–92; Iglesias, "Moros en la costa."

133. Anon., "Sagrados trivmphos.".

134. Santísima Trinidad, *Carta pastoral*.

135. Ibid.

136. Anon., *Relación de la entrada del sultan*; Voigt, *Spectacular Wealth*, 14.

137. Anon., *Relación de la entrada del sultan*. Also see Crailsheim, "The Baptism of Sultan Azim ud-Din," 116.

138. On *gremios* in the Philippines, see Wickberg, *The Chinese in Philippine Life*, 95; Kueh, "The Manila Chinese," 56–57, 111–115.

139. Anon., *Relación de la entrada del sultan*.

140. Dean, *Inka Bodies*, 61.

141. Ibid.

142. Voigt, *Spectacular Wealth*, 121–149, 154.

143. Scott, *Domination and the Arts of Resistance*, xii; Ileto, *Pasyon and Revolution*, 16.

144. Crailsheim, "The Baptism of Sultan Azim ud-Din," 93–120; Trota Jose, "Imaging Our Lady."

145. Lane, *Pillaging the Empire*, 13–17; Mínguez, "Iconografía de Lepanto," 251–280.

146. Mawson, "Slavery, Conflict, and Empire," 256–258.

147. NAP, Cedulario, 31.

148. Ibid.

149. López Lázaro, *The Misfortunes of Alonso Ramírez*, 13.

150. NAP, Spanish Manila (1751–1846), 13820.

151. AGI, 295, N.28 BIS.

152. Marichal, *Bankruptcy of Empire*, 92.

153. NAP, Spanish Manila (1751–1846), 13820.

154. Ibid.

155. AGI, 295, N.28 BIS.

156. Ibid.

157. Hapsburg monarchs began soliciting contributions to military campaigns from the popular classes in the late sixteenth century. Royal requests for donations became more frequent after 1780 in order to fund escalating imperial wars. See Marichal, *Bankruptcy of Empire*, 97, 92.

158. Ibid., 86–94.

159. García-Abásalo, "Los chinos y el modelo colonial español en Filipinas," 225.

160. López Lázaro, *The Misfortunes of Alonso Ramírez*, 39.

161. AGI, 295, N.28 BIS, 136–138.

162. Wokou were Japanese, Chinese, and Korean. For an overview of the "Wo crisis," see So, *Japanese Piracy in Ming China*, 175. On Wo violence see Antony, *Like Froth Floating on the Sea*, 112–116; Antony, "Bloodthirsty Pirates," 482–483.

163. Tanaka Takeo, Kawakami Kei, ed. *Wo kou tu juan (Wakō zukan)* 倭寇圖卷. Tōkyō: Kondō Shuppansha, 1974.

164. Chaves, *The Columbia Book of Later Chinese Poetry*, 324.

165. Wang, *White Lotus Rebels*, 97–98.

166. Hui, "Between Heaven and the Deep Sea," 69–86.

167. Ruitenbeek, "Mazu, the Patroness of Sailors," 288–289, 315–318.

168. Marichal, *Bankruptcy of Empire*, 98; ibid.

Chapter 3

1. Quote from Cushner, *Documents*, 59–60. For rumors of war in Manila see *Documentos indispensables para la verdadera historia de Filipinas*, 58–59; Cushner, *Documents*, 59–60, 82–88.

2. For a discussion of total war, see Kreike, *Scorched Earth*, 16.

3. In Cushner, *Documents*, 73.

4. Vivar, "Relación de los alzamientos," 299–300.

5. Mancini has documented the extent of the theft of Manila's archives. Mancini, *Art and War in the Pacific World*, 75–77. Libraries and other civil and ecclesiastical archives were also lost in fires and damaged when the occupying army converted these buildings into stables and barracks. AGI, Filipinas, 605, N.3, 11v.

6. See Draper, *Colonel Draper's Answer*; Entick, *The General History of the Late War*, 441–433; Montero y Vidal, *Historia general de Filipinas*, 8–76; Tracy, *Manila Ransomed*; Fish, *When Britain Ruled the Philippines*; Vila Miranda, "Toma de Manila."

7. The Seven Years' War has inspired a vast historiography. The best general histories of the global war include Anderson, *Crucible of War*; Marshall, *The Making and Unmaking of Empires*. Several factors contributed to the marginalization of the Philippines in this literature. First, Spain entered the war late, in 1761, leading historians to conceptualize the conflict as a war between Britain and France, "the two most advanced monarchies of Europe," as Baugh noted. Baugh, *The Global Seven Years War*, 1. Second, historians have tended to prioritize Europe and North American theaters of war, paying less attention to Asia and the Pacific and "oceanic and insular conflict," as Mancini notes. Mancini, *Art and War in the Pacific World*, 70. Third, historiography has also largely neglected the actions and experiences of Black and Indigenous peoples who fought in global war, or whose lives were otherwise transformed by it.

8. Important new studies examining the Black and Indigenous revolts and wars that broke out in response to this interimperial conflict include McDonnell, *Masters of Empire*; Schneider, *The Occupation of Havana*; Kars, *Blood on the River*; Brown, *Tacky's Revolt*.

9. Marshall, *The Making and Unmaking of Empires*, 61.

10. The British used the term *Coffreys* to refer to the Africans recruited to the Manila campaign. Thomas discusses this category in her analysis of the British forces sent to Manila. Thomas, "Securing Trade," 130–134. For analysis of invading forces, see Leandro de Viana, "Diaro del sitio," 343; Cushner, *Documents*, 55–57; Marshall, *The Making and Unmaking of Empires*, 61–64. On the Indian Ocean slave trade see Machado, "A Forgotten Corner," 17–32.

11. Thomas, "Securing Trade," 130.

12. On meanings of piracy in the Spanish empire, see Lane, *Pillaging the Empire*, 4; Montanez Sanabria, "Challenging the Pacific Spanish Empire," 13–17. On the evolving and contested meanings of piracy in the British Atlantic world, see Coakley, "The Piracies of Some Little Privateers," 6–26. On the varied perceptions of maritime violence in the wider eighteenth-century world, see Risso, "Cross-Cultural Perceptions," 293–319.

13. Chet provides an overview of this literature and argues that historians have overstated the distinction between pirates and privateers in the eighteenth-century British Atlantic world. Chet, *The Ocean Is a Wilderness*, 5–6.

14. East India Company, *Manilha Consultations*, 1:1; BL, IOR, H/76, 1–134, 1–3.

15. For sieges in maritime Asia, see Schreurs, "The Royal Fort," 107–122. For the central role of sieges in early modern warfare, see Martens, "Siege Warfare," 1987–1994. For sieges in the Seven Year's War, see Schneider, *The Occupation of Havana*, 119–154.

16. Viana, "Diaro Del Sitio," 340–341. For the British military strategy in Manila, see Gutiérrez, "Military Engineering," 13–14. On siege tactics in the Philippines and Maritime Asia, see Barrio Muñoz, *Vientos de reforma*.

17. Stevenson's account of the siege, full of rich detail, is preserved in the British Library and was published in Cushner's valuable collection. BL, IOR, H/76, 1–134, 58–66; Cushner, *Documents*, 82–88. Original British reports or "diaries" on the invasion that were recorded as it unfolded include *Manilha Consultations*, vol. 1.

18. This is explicit in George Anson, *A Voyage Round the World*, 132, 386; BL, Add MS 19298, 3v. Historians have noted the connections between the black legend and British plans

to seize territory in the Spanish empire. Mapp, *The Elusive West*, 14–15. Montanez Sanabria, "Challenging the Pacific Spanish Empire."

19. Cushner, *Documents*, 82–88.

20. Ibid.

21. *Manilha Consultations*, 1:29; BL, IOR, H/77, 195.

22. *Manilha Consultations*, 1:29; Viana, "Diaro del sitio," 343–344.

23. Viana, "Diaro del sitio," 349, 352–353; Cushner, *Documents*, 81.

24. AFIO, 21/28; Viana, "Diaro del sitio," 359.

25. Viana, "Diaro del sitio," 364. Cushner, *Documents*, 81–82.

26. AGI, Filipinas, 922, N.5; B&R 49, 127–128

27. The exact count is 3,278. Newberry Library, Ayer, MS 1454, f.15r.

28. *Documentos indispensables para la verdadera historia de Filipinas*, 1:71; Viana, "Diaro del sitio," 359.

29. Entick, *The General History of the Late War*, v, 417.

30. Viana, "Diaro del sitio," 461–467.

31. *Manilha Consultations*, 1:29.

32. AGI, Estado, 44, N.6.

33. Viana, "Diaro del sitio," 365; Cushner, *Documents*, 70–82.

34. For the surrender, see Viana, "Diaro del sitio," 364. The capitulation agreement is printed in East India Company, *Manilha Consultations*, 1:16–17; Cushner, *Documents*, 120–124; Draper, *A Plain Narrative*.

35. Newberry Library, Ayer, MS 1292, f.14r–16r.

36. Cushner, *Documents*, 70–82.

37. Martens, "Siege Warfare," 1987–1994.

38. Newberry Library, Ayer, MS 1292, f.13r.

39. Cushner, *Documents*, 84–88; *Documentos indispensables para la verdadera historia de Filipinas*, 1:92.

40. Viana, "Diaro del sitio," 372.

41. Draper, *A Plain Narrative*, 21, 24; Huntington Library, Papers of Sir George Pocock, PO 1024.

42. Draper, *A Plain Narrative*, 22–24.

43. On the veneration of La Naval, see Lee, *Saints of Resistance*, 73–99. On the image's treatment during the war, see Trota Jose, "Imaging Our Lady"; Romero Mesaque, "Los comienzos de la cofradía"; Zurita, Adriano, and de Ire, *Oracion panegyrico-moral*. On the pillaging of churches see also AGI, Estado, 44, N.6; Cushner, *Documents*, 125–128. The inventory of Dawsonne Drake's property compiled on his death in 1787 features many items that he likely stole in Manila from churches and convents and private homes, including "a gold cross" and "seven Manila religious pictures" and "a very old fashioned piece of Manila furniture." Huntington Library, Papers of Sir George Pocock, PO 1104, 1781. Mancini identifies other ill-gotten wealth from Manila and makes a compelling argument that historians have underestimated the role of pillaging in the transfer of wealth to Great Britain. Mancini, *Art and War in the Pacific World*, 33.

44. Descripción de la ciudad de Manila (1763?), Newberry Library, Ayer, MS 1921, Folder 5; Cushner, *Documents*, 125.

45. East India Company, *Manilha Consultations*, 9 and 9A:18–20.

46. "Rojo's Journal," in *The Philippine Islands, 1493–1898*, 49:127–128.

47. The surviving copy of the letter is an English translation of the original. East India Company, *Manilha Consultations*, 6:153. On Falliet, see Flannery, "The Trans-imperial Biography," 479–497. On Dutch sources, see Borschberg, "Chinese Merchants."

48. Newberry Library, Ayer, MS 1292, f.5r.

49. Anda and Rojo contested each other's claim to the governorship. Ibid.

50. BL, IOR, H/77, 201–202.

51. Newberry Library, Ayer, MS 1292.

52. Ibid., f.5r.

53. Ibid., f.14r–16r.

54. Mancini develops the concept of a militarized Pacific turn. Mancini, *Art and War*, 34. For further analysis of Britain's aggressive push into the Pacific, see Mapp, *The Elusive West*, 262–272, 321–346; Pinzón Ríos, "En pos de nuevos botines," 45–76. Mancini, "Siege Mentalities." The more widely accepted view of the short-term motivations driving the British invasion is explicit in Fish, *When Britain Ruled the Philippines*; Vaughn, "The Ideological Origins," 21.

55. For Anson's attack on the galleon and its impact on the British plan to invade Manila and other Spanish colonies, see "Wednesday 4," *Gentleman's Magazine* 14:392; Mancini, *Art and War*, 42–50; Mapp, *The Elusive West*, 418; Paquette, "The Image of Imperial Spain," 194; Schneider, *The Occupation of Havana*, 23.

56. King George III's "secret instructions" for the Manila invasion directed his subjects to secure Mindanao as a British outpost. Cushner, *Documents*, 12–22. See also BL, Add MS 19298.

57. East India Company, *Manilha Consultations*, 1:6.

58. John Lewin Smith, Claud Russell, Henry Brooke, and Samuel Johnson joined Drake on the Manila Council.

59. Newberry Library, Ayer, MS 1292, f.17

60. For an additional examples of these announcements, see one dated September 24, 1762, ibid., 81, and another dated January 15, 1763 in BL, IOR, H/77, 153.

61. BL, Add MS 19298, 14v.

62. On maritime workers and information distribution in the eighteenth-century Indo-Pacific and Atlantic worlds, see Rediker and Linebaugh, *The Many-Headed Hydra*, 181–226; Bassi, *An Aqueous Territory*, 19–31, 70–82; Scott, *The Common Wind*; Flannery and Ruiz-Stovel, "The Loyal Foreign Merchant Captain."

63. BL, IOR, G/4/ 369–390.

64. East India Company, *Manilha Consultations*, 6:71–72; BL, IOR, G/4/ f.369–371.

65. East India Company, *Manilha Consultations*, 6:71–72; BL, IOR/G/4; BL, IOR, G/4/ f.369–371; Quiason, *English "Country Trade*," 121–131; Warren, "Balambangan," 73–93.

66. East India Company, *Manilha Consultations*, 6:61; AGI, Filipinas, 605, N.3 (parte 9), 9v, 23r.

67. Viana, "Diaro del sitio," 428; Cushner, *Documents*, 88–120.

68. East India Company, *Manilha Consultations*, 5:127–128; Huntington Library, Papers of George Pocock, PO 998; AGI Filipinas 292, N.33; United States Philippine Commission, *Report of the Philippine Commission, Part 1*, 814. For additional context on Irish and other non-Iberian Europeans in Manila, see Tremml-Werner, "Marginal Players," 599–626.

69. East India Company, *Manilha Consultations*, 6:128, 48.

70. Guatlo was also known as Nicolas Subang. NAP, Cedulario, 1766–1771. AGI, Filipinas, 716, 261v.

71. AGI, Filipinas, 386, N.35; AGI Filipinas, L.17, F.213v–221r. For beaterios in the Philippines, including their role as prisons, see Manchado López, "Religiosidad femenina," 171–202. On Arandía's government, see "Las relaciones entre la autoridad civil," 37–52. Zapata, who had also been part of Arandía's inner circle, was also thrown in jail at this time. AGI, Filipinas, 386, N.35.

72. East India Company, *Manilha Consultations*, 6:227–228.

73. AGN Inquisición, 1138, Exp. 22; AGN Inquisición, 973, Exp. 13.

74. East India Company, *Manilha Consultations*, 6:223–229, 237. Orendaín also petitioned the Manila Council to return his money that was aboard the captured Trinidad galleon, clearly expecting or hoping that his services to the British would protect his financial interests.

75. Ibid., 5:79.

76. Notably, Viana claimed that Azim ud-Din and his son Israel fought bravely with the Spanish at Pasig and were captured here by the British and brought into Manila as prisoners of war. This claim is not verified by other sources. Viana, "Diaro del sitio," 435. On these battles, see Viana, "Diario," 412–415, 428, 462, 381–382. For further discussion of Chinese assistance to the British in the war, see Flannery, "Battlefield Diplomacy," 467–488.

77. Flannery, "Battlefield Diplomacy," 470–472; *Documentos indispensables para la verdadera historia de Filipinas*, 1:67–68, 470–472.

78. East India Company, *Manilha Consultations*, 5:81; 6:96.

79. Viana, "Diaro del sitio," 470–472; Castro y Amuedo, "Relación sucinta," 67–68.

80. The Augustinian priest and historian Zúñiga asserted that "from the moment [the British] took possession of Manila, these Chinese gave them every aid and accompanied them in all their expeditions." Fish and other recent scholarship uncritically reproduced this claim. Martinez de Zuñiga, *An Historical View*, 655–668; Fish, *When Britain Ruled the Philippines* 160; Corpuz, *The Roots of the Filipino Nation*, 307–308.

81. Huntington Library, Papers of Sir George Pocock, PO 1024.

82. Newberry Library, Ayer, MS 1292, f.20.

83. Ibid., f.19–22.

84. Ibid., f.20–22.

85. Ibid., f.19.

86. Escoto mentions a Guagua plot to kill Anda but does not acknowledge the massacre. Escoto, "Expulsion of the Chinese," 48–76. The silencing of this violent past is also influenced by the modern Tsinoy community's preference to direct attention away from historical violence. Mayshle shows that the official museum of Chinese Filipinos downplays conflict and highlights cooperation between the people of the Chinese diaspora and other Filipinos. Mayshle, "Walled 'Memoria,'" 44–79.

87. Newberry Library, Ayer, MS 1292, f.20r–22v.

88. Ibid., f.24–27.

89. Ibid., f.20–23.

90. Fernandez, "Towards an Early History," 176, 182–183.

91. Collantes, *Historia de la provincia del Santisimo Rosario de Filipinas*, 641; *Documentos indispensables para la verdadera historia de Filipinas*, 1:73–75.

92. *Documentos indispensables para la verdadera historia de Filipinas*, 1:75.

93. Ibid.

94. Ferrando and Fonseca, *Historia de los PP. Dominicos*, 5:658–660.

95. Binalatongan was also known as San Carlos. AGI, Filipinas, 609, N.34. Collantes, *Historia de la provincia del Santisimo Rosario de Filipinas*, 637–642; Ferrando and Fonseca, *Historia de los PP. Dominicos*, 5:658–659; Mendoza Cortes, *Pangasinan, 1572–1800*, 172–178.

96. AGI, Filipinas, 609, N.34.

97. Viana, "Diaro del sitio," 397.

98. Collantes, *Historia de la provincia del Santisimo Rosario de Filipinas*, 642.

99. Vivar, "Relación de los alzamientos," 283–288.

100. Binmaley is also known as Dagupan.

101. AGI, Filipinas, 609, N.34; Collantes, *Historia de la provincia del Santisimo Rosario de Filipinas*, 641–642; Mendoza Cortes, *Pangasinan, 1572–1800*, 185–193.

102. For the protest, see Vivar, "Relación de los alzamientos"; Palanco and Arcilla, "Diego Silang's Revolt," 112–137. For Vigan in this era, see AGI, Filipinas, 293, N.79.

103. Vivar, "Relación de los alzamientos"; *Documentos indispensables para la verdadera historia de Filipinas*, 1:82–87; Palanco and Arcilla, "Diego Silang's Revolt," 112–137.

104. Phelan, *The People and the King*, 73–77, 238–244; Herzog, "¡Viva el rey, muera el mal gobierno!" 77–96; Exbalin, "Riot in Mexico City," 215–231.

105. AGI, Filipinas, 605, N.3, 13r–20v; Vivar, "Relación de los alzamientos," 292–294, 289, 300.

106. Gabriela is described as a *criada* in the archive. Historians suspect that criados or child servants in the Spanish empire were sometimes the illegitimate children of their masters. Premo, "Familiar," 305–306.

107. AGI, Filipinas, 605, N.3, f21r–22r.

108. Vivar, "Relación de los alzamientos," 286–287.

109. I borrow this concept from Yannakakis. Yannakakis, *The Art of Being In-Between*, 1–16.

110. Ibid., 3.

111. In 1962, the government of the Philippines issued a stamp commemorating the Silang revolt. Government of the Philippines, *Bicentennial Diego Silang Revolt Commemorative First Day Cover*. Gabriela Silang also features in murals celebrating Philippines history. Gonzalves, "When the Walls Speak a Nation." The heroes in millennial-era graphic novels and comic books pay homage to the Silangs. Flores, "Up in the Sky.," 73–86. Today, universities continue to perform plays dramatizing the life of Gabriela. Francisco, "Flipping the Script."

112. AGI, Filipinas, 609, N.34.

113. Thomas's important analysis of Diego Silang's rhetoric does not mention the Palaris revolt. Thomas, "Proclaiming Sovereignty," 79–104. Other studies acknowledge the simultaneity of the two rebellions, but approach them as independent from each other, including Arcilla, "The Pangasinan Uprising," 35–52; Routledge, *Diego Silang*.

114. AGI, Filipinas, 609, N.34.

115. Ibid., f.217r.

116. Vivar, "Relación de los alzamientos," 389.

117. See Newson, *Conquest and Pestilence*, 208–211. The Spanish referred to the multiple ethnolinguistic groups in the region as Cagayanes. Coballes and De La Cruz, "An Ethnography of Ibanag Warfare," 86–88.

118. Ferrando and Fonseca, *Historia de los PP. Dominicos*, 5:685. Newson, *Conquest and Pestilence*, 208. These towns are clearly shown in the digitized map. AGI, MP-Filipinas, 22BIS.

119. Constantino, *A History of the Philppines*, 103. Routledge, *Diego Silang*.

120. *Documentos indispensables para la verdadera historia de Filipinas*, 1:85–86. Ferrando and Fonseca, *Historia de los PP. Dominicos*, 5:685. On Spanish views of upland communities, see Ruíz Gutiérrez, "De indomables a almas temerosas," 227–261; Castro y Amuedo, "Relación sucinta," 84–88.

121. Anda repeatedly used these words when he advocated for war against the insurgents and the British. AGI, Filipinas, 605, N.3, 280r–282r.

122. In Mendoza Cortes, *Pangasinan, 1572–1800*, 198–199.

123. Vivar, "Relación de los alzamientos," 328; see also 348. AGI, Filipinas, 609, N.34. On the use of coral in fortifications see Luengo Gutiérrez, "Fortificaciones Musulmanes en Joló," 197–213.

124. Vivar, "Relación de los alzamientos," 329, 339.

125. AGI, Filipinas, 605, N.3, 14r–20v.

126. Vivar, "Relación de los alzamientos," 368. For Silang's writings see AGI, Filipinas, 605, N.3; Newberry Library, Ayer, MS 1292, 79, 83. Vivar's account includes copies of Silang's letters in addition to paraphrased speeches. Vivar, "Relación de los alzamientos," 351; East India Company, *Manilha Consultations*, 5:102–103.

127. Vivar, "Relación de los alzamientos," 368.

128. Ibid., 318, 368.

129. Bell, *The First Total War*, 269.

130. *Documentos indispensables para la verdadera historia de Filipinas*, 1:77.

131. Vivar, "Relación de los alzamientos," 322.

132. AGI, Filipinas, 605, N.3, 54v. Vivar, "Relación de los alzamientos," 287. For an overview of the cajas de comunidad (community chests) system, see Chiquín, "Administración y gasto," 216–219.

133. The bandala in the Philippines was equivalent to the repatrimiento in the Americas. Hidalgo Nuchera, "La encomienda en Filipinas," 476–480; Fradera, *Filipinas, la colonia más peculiar*, 46–47.

134. Vivar, "Relación de los alzamientos," 351.

135. Ibid., 287.

136. Serulnikov, *Revolution in the Andes*, 31–35, 68, 118–120; Walker, *The Tupac Amaru Rebellion*, 1–17, 52–53.

137. AGI, Filipinas, 609, N.34, see the first fifty folios, which are not numerated.

138. On tribute and the construction of calidad, see Fisher and O'Hara, "Introduction," 1–38; Gharala, *Taxing Blackness*, 2–8, 24–40; Pollack, "Hacia una historia social," 71, 81–89.

139. Timawa or timaua meant free person in Tagalog. Vivar, "Relación de los alzamientos," 300. On caste war see Serulnikov, *Revolution in the Andes*. Gabbert's important revisionist study of caste war in the Yucatan in the nineteenth century reveals the limitations of this interpretive framework, highlighting the complex politics that drew people into the war beyond the Native–not-Native binary. Gabbert, *Violence and the Caste War of Yucatán*.

140. Vivar, "Relación de los alzamientos," 307–308. Such expressions influenced the great Philippines historian and folklorist Isabelo Reyes to interpret the uprising as the "*kailianes* (the lower classes) rising up against the babakwáng (principales) and the priests." Reyes y Florentino, *Historia de Ilocos*, 178.

141. Mendoza Cortes, *Pangasinan, 1572–1800*, 199; Ferrando and Fonseca, *Historia de los PP. Dominicos en las islas Filipinas*, 5:682.

142. Vivar, "Relación de los alzamientos," 319.

143. Ibid., 322, 332.

144. Ibid., 366.

145. Routledge, *Diego Silang and the Origins of Philippine Nationalism*; Palanco and Arcilla, "Diego Silang's Revolt"; Thomas, "Proclaiming Sovereignty."

146. Vivar, "Relación de los alzamientos," 326–327.

147. Ibid., 351–352.

148. Ibid., 428.

149. Ibid., 336, 339.

150. Ibid.

151. AGI, Filipinas, 605, N.3, 108r–v, 99r–103r.

152. Ileto showed anting-anting in nineteenth century revolts. Ileto, *Pasyon and Revolution*. See also Borchgrevink, "Ideas of Power," 41–69. For Catholic sacred objects and war in eighteenth-century Europe, see Jonas, *France and the Cult of the Sacred Heart*, 97–117.

153. Vivar, "Relación de los alzamientos," 335.

154. Ibid., 336.

155. Borchgrevink, "Ideas of Power," 44–46; Ileto, *Pasyon and Revolution*, 23.

156. Güereca Durán, "Un profeta otomí en tiempos de crisis."

157. Zires, "Los mitos de la virgen," 291–306; Brading, *Mexican Phoenix*, 288–360.

158. Vivar, "Relación de los alzamientos," 351.

159. AGI, Filipinas, 605, N.3, f.21r–22r.

160. Ibid., 21r. This was not an isolated case. More friars were rounded up and imprisoned in the convent in Bantay in early 1763. Vivar, "Relación de los alzamientos," 353–354.

161. AGI, Filipinas, 605, N.3, f.21r–22r.

162. AGI, Filipinas, 609, N.34; *Documentos indispensables para la verdadera historia de Filipinas*, 1:62.

163. Viana, "Diaro del sitio," 429, 434–435.

164. Newberry Library, Ayer, MS 1292, f.47, 59–65; BL, IOR, H/76, 1–134, 91; Viana, "Diaro del sitio," 429, 447.

165. East India Company, *Manilha Consultations*, 5:20.

166. Viana, "Diaro del sitio," 456. See also the edict against Anda issued by Drake. Newberry Library, Ayer, MS 1921, Folder 27, Folder 7.

167. Huntington Library, Papers of Sir George Pocock, PO 1024.

168. AGI, Filipinas, 605, N.3, f.20r.

Chapter 4

1. See Newberry Library, Ayer, MS 1921, Folder 6. AGI, Filipinas, 716, 193v; Castro y Amuedo, "Relación sucinta," 72. The stated value of the *Filipino*'s silver treasure varies in the archive, ranging from 1.5 to 2 million pesos. Newberry Library, Ayer, MS 1921, Folder 27; Cruikshank, "Silver in the Provinces," 150.

2. East India Company, *Manilha Consultations*, 5:93–94; Cushner, *Documents*, 174–180.

3. AGI, Filipinas, 605, N.3, f.175v–177r.

4. Newberry Library, Ayer, MS 1921, Folder 27.

5. BL, IOR, H/77, 195.

6. Castro y Amuedo, "Relación sucinta," 67–68.

7. East India Company, *Manilha Consultations*, 5:127.

8. AGI, Filipinas, 605, N.3, 171r–178r. Newberry Library, Ayer, MS 1921, Folder 27.

9. The Spanish and Anglo "great men" interpretations of this history are exemplified by Tracy, *Manila Ransomed*; Fish, *When Britain Ruled the Philippines*; Dreaper, *Pitt's Gallant Conqueror*; Tracy, "The British Expedition," 461–486; Barco Ortega, "El gobierno de Manuel Antonio Rojo," 167–219. Luengo also glosses over the massive loyalist army and the insurgency. Luengo Gutiérrez, *Manila, Plaza Fuerte*.

10. This historiography is exemplified by David Routledge's short monograph on the Silang revolt. Routledge, *Diego Silang*. See also Constantino, *The Philippines: A Past Revisited*, 82–109; Arcilla, "The Pangasinan Uprising," 35–52; Palanco and Arcilla, "Diego Silang's Revolt," 522–537. Megan Thomas's important analysis of Silang's rhetoric avoids romanticizing the movement, but does not consider the loyalist campaign that suppressed it. Thomas, "Proclaiming Sovereignty," 125–147.

11. This concept is articulated in McEnroe, "A Sleeping Army," 128.

12. AGI, Filipinas, 605, N.3, 280r–282r.

13. Here the term "army" refers to a loosely organized body of armed people that formed with government approval to meet a particular need. "Army" should not be confused with "standing army," which refers to a permanent force of full-time soldiers. Spanish colonial officials and missionaries, as well as the insurgent Diego Silang, used the term "ejército" (army) to describe the loyalist forces. Vivar referred to the "Catholic army of the españoles and naturales." Vivar, "Relación de los alzamientos," 344. Castro also used the term "ejército." Castro y Amuedo, "Relación sucinta," 66.

14. See Lockhart, *The Men of Cajamarca*, 17–43, 121–156; Van Young, *The Other Rebellion*, 39–66. Vinson, *Bearing Arms*; Güereca Durán, *Milicias indígenas en Nueva España*; Walker, *The Tupac Amaru Rebellion*; Echeverri, *Indian and Slave Royalists*.

15. AGI, Filipinas, 387, N.1.

16. AGI, Filipinas, 605; BL, IOR, H/77, 145.

17. Castro y Amuedo, "Relación sucinta," 67–68. See Ganson, *The Guaraní Under Spanish Rule in the Río de la Plata*, especially Chapter 4.

18. East India Company, *Manilha Consultations*, 5:30.

19. Castro y Amuedo, "Relación sucinta," 61.

20. *Documentos indispensables para la verdadera historia de Filipinas*, 1:31–33.

21. Cruikshank, "The British Occupation of Manila."

22. East India Company, *Manilha Consultations*, 5:135–136.

23. Castro y Amuedo, "Relación sucinta," 71.

24. AGI, Filipinas, 605, 9v–10r.

25. Ibid., 13r–14v.

26. Biblioteca Nacional de España, MSS/19217 (H.11v–12r).

27. AGI, Filipinas, 923, N.59; Mehl, *Forced Migration*, 245; AGI, Filipinas, 923, N.59.

28. Mehl showed that Mexican "volunteers" often enlisted as soldiers under duress, including after being accused of vagrancy and facing penal servitude. Volunteering avoided the shame of impressment and allowed one to earn wages. Mehl, *Forced Migration*, 157. The precise number of Mexican soldiers in Manila is difficult to count accurately. Cáceres Menéndez and Patch counted 220 forzados sent to the Philippines between 1722 and 1728, of whom 83 percent were convicted criminals. Mehl counted a total of 3,999 soldiers transported from Mexico to Manila between 1765 and 1811, which equals an average of 87 recruits a year. However, annual arrivals fluctuated widely from no recruits between 1768 and 1771 to 451 in 1772. There must have been similar fluctuations in forzado arrivals to Manila in earlier

decades. Cáceres Menéndez and Patch, "«Gente de mal vivir»," 367. Mehl, *Forced Migration,* 277–278.

29. Cáceres Menéndez and Patch, "«Gente de mal vivir»"; Mawson, "Unruly Plebeians and the Forzado System," 701; Mehl, *Forced Migration,* 80–118, 156–158.

30. Mawson writes that "return migration, violence, disobedience and mutiny were persistent problems associated with every phase of the *forzado* system" in the seventeenth century. Mawson, "Unruly Plebeians," 718. Mehl comes to the same conclusion in her study of the forzado system that spans the post–Seven Years' War era to the early nineteenth century, when the Mexican war for independence ended the galleon trade. Mehl argued that "the presence of these men in the Philippines was unquestionably detrimental for the aspirations of the Spanish empire. Mehl, *Forced Migration,* 259.

31. Castro y Amuedo, "Relación sucinta," 59. An anonymous Jesuit report claimed there were one hundred Mexicans on the walls. Although there is a discrepancy in numbers, both sources show that Mexican soldiers actively defended Manila in the siege. Cushner, *Documents,* 88–120.

32. East India Company, *Manilha Consultations,* 5:61, 69.

33. AGI, Filipinas, 355, L.17, f.310r–317v.

34. AGI, Filipinas, 605.

35. Viana, "Diaro del sitio," 461–464.

36. Newberry Library, Ayer, MS 1454, f.16r.

37. AGI, Filipinas, 605, N.4.

38. Ibid.

39. Ibid., 12r–15r.

40. Ibid., f.31v–36v.

41. Brockey, *Journey to the East,* 227–228.

42. AGI, Filipinas, 683; Gomez Platero, *Catálogo biográfico de los religiosos franciscanos.*

43. AGI, Filipinas, 683.

44. Ibid.

45. AGI, Filipinas, 605, N.3, 196r.

46. Buschmann, Slack, and Tueller, *Navigating the Spanish Lake,* 94.

47. On the Tinajeros fort see AGI, MP-Filipinas,165. The importance of Chinese mestizos in battles in and around Vigan in late 1762 and early 1763 are highlighted in Vivar, "Relación de los alzamientos," 307–310.

48. AGI, Filipinas, 495, N.341.

49. AGI, Filipinas, 683. The white deer has received more attention from historians than Matheo de los Angeles has; Schurz, *The Manila Galleon,* 33. Gómez-Centurión Jiménez, "Curiosidades vivas," 186.

50. NAP, Spanish Manila (1751–1846), 13820.

51. Newberry Library, Ayer, MS 1292, 27.

52. Ibid., 25.

53. East India Company, *Manilha Consultations,* 5:131–132.

54. Ibid., 152.

55. Ibid.

56. Ibid., 232.

57. AGI, Filipinas, 605.

58. AGI, Filipinas, 923, N.11.

59. Ibid.

60. Castro y Amuedo, "Relación sucinta," 69.

61. Martínez de Zuñiga, *Estadismo de las Islas Filipinas*, 64.

62. East India Company, *Manilha Consultations*, 5:67–68.

63. Castro y Amuedo, "Relación sucinta," 69.

64. "Blacks, *sipayes*, and *malabares*" were numerous in the colony's standing army in 1766. In the late 1770s, the Spanish colonial government formally established the *Compañia de Malabares* (Malabar Company), in which approximately one hundred South Asian soldiers were enlisted. AGI, Filipinas, 923, N.24.

65. IOR E/4/300 (1760–1764), 213.

66. IOR E/4/300 (1760–1764), 250.

67. Viana, "Diaro del sitio," 364.

68. McManus and Leibsohn, "Eloquence and Ethnohistory."

69. Bastidas is a protagonist in Walker's analysis of the Andean revolt. Walker, *The Tupac Amaru Rebellion*.

70. Marjoleine Kars discusses the silences around women that persist in archives of eighteenth-century slave revolts. See Kars, "Dodging Rebellion," 57–60.

71. AGI, Filipinas, 609, N.34; Cushner, *Documents*, 88–120.

72. Van Young, *The Other Rebellion*, 23.

73. East India Company, *Manilha Consultations*, 1:29.

74. Viana, "Diaro del sitio," 372.

75. NAP, Erección de pueblos, Pampanga Leg 95, N.39, 414r–417r.

76. Cruikshank, "The British Occupation of Manila."

77. NAP, Erección de pueblos, Pampanga Leg 95, N.39, 414r–417r.

78. Ibid.

79. AGI, Filipinas, 605, N.3, 124r.

80. Ibid., f.104r–121r.

81. AGI, Filipinas, 605.

82. Newberry Library, Ayer, MS 1921, Folder 27.

83. East India Company, *Manilha Consultations*, 5:131–132.

84. Ibid., 135–136.

85. Castro y Amuedo, "Relación sucinta," 25. Other examples of hangings include *Manilha Consultations*, 5:79; ibid., 6:175.

86. East India Company, *Manilha Consultations*, 5:11.

87. Ibid., 6:157.

88. Ibid., 127.

89. Cruz allegedly promised to pay the men one hundred dollars each if they followed him to Anda's headquarters in Bacolor. Ibid., 175.

90. Anda took control of 110,000 pesos that were in the royal treasury, and at least 1,500,000 pesos that arrived aboard the Filipino galleon. By Anda's own accounts, he spent over 670,255 pesos on the war. AGI, Filipinas, 605, N.4, f.16r. Newberry Library, Ayer, MS 1921, Folder 27.

91. Castro y Amuedo, "Relación sucinta," 72.

92. East India Company, *Manilha Consultations*, 5:129–130.

93. *Manilha Consultations*, 5:129; ibid., 6:155. Annual wages for a soldier in the British army were approximately equivalent to forty-eight silver pesos a year. Way, "Rebellion of the Regulars," 761–792.

94. Pillaging was tolerated everywhere the British were deployed in the Seven Years' War. See Fred Anderson, *A People's Army*, 152.

95. East India Company, *Manilha Consultations*, 6:2; 5:170–171, 74, 164–165.

96. Newberry Library, Ayer MS1921, Folder 27.

97. AGI, Filipinas, 388, N.57.

98. East India Company, *Manilha Consultations*, 5:5.

99. Schneider, *The Occupation of Havana*; see Chapter 3.

100. East India Company, *Manilha Consultations*, 6:79; Fr. José Victoria and Fr. Manuel Rebollo, "Documento inédito," 31.

101. AGI, Filipinas, 605, N.3, f.240r.

102. For example, the people of San Andrés Chalchihuites in northern New Spain used such documents when they sought protection from forced or tribute labor in the mines. Güereca Durán, *Milicias indígenas*, 168–189.

103. AGI, Filipinas, 605.

104. AGI, Filipinas, 924. AGI, Contratación, 5512, N.1, R.5.

105. Few Indigenous people across the global Spanish empire succeeded in obtaining formal licenses to travel to Spain. De la Puente Luna, *Andean Cosmopolitans*, 8–9.

106. AGI, Filipinas, 683.

107. AGI, Filipinas, 683. Owens, *Nuns Navigating the Spanish Empire*, 35–36.

108. See Newberry Library, Ayer, MS 1921, Folder 27. Notably, Los Angeles financed the printing of Saguinsín's epigramatica in 1766. McManus and Leibsohn, "Eloquence and Ethnohistory," 526–527.

109. Newberry Library, MS1921, Folder 20.

110. De la Costa, "The development of the native clergy," 247. On the Indigenous clergy, see Santiago, *The Hidden Light*. On Saguinsín see McManus and Leibsohn, "Eloquence and Ethnohistory," 522–574. Routledge identified Milán as Pampangan. Routledge, *Diego Silang*, 13.

111. Santiago, *The Hidden Light*.

112. East India Company, *Manilha Consultations*, 3:37.

113. AGI, Filipinas, 605.

114. Ferrando and Fonseca, *Historia de los PP. Dominicos en las islas Filipinas*, 5:706.

115. AGI, Filipinas, 609, N.34. For the global proliferation of the imperial eagle symbol, see Inmaculada Rodríguez Moya, "El renacimiento del águila hispánica," 210–234.

116. AGI, Filipinas, 605.

117. Ibid.

118. Castro y Amuedo, "Relación sucinta," 71–72.

119. See, for example, this account of Manila's celebrations of King Charles IV's 1765 marriage. AGI, Filipinas, 683. For discussions of how festivals cultivated a sense of closeness to the monarchy across vast distances, see Cañeque, *The King's Living Image*, 119–141. Osorio, "Of National Boundaries," 100–130; Schneider, *The Occupation of Havana*, 146–148.

120. Thomas, "Proclaiming Sovereignty," 98–102.

121. Anderson makes this observation in relation to New England armies of the same era. Anderson, *A People's Army*, 45.

122. BL, IOR, H/77, 195.

123. Mancini, *Art and War*, 94–95.

124. East India Company, *Manilha Consultations*, 6:3. Manila's Guadalupe was probably a copy of the image of Our Lady of Guadalupe in Extremadura, Spain. I am grateful to Sir Regalado (Ricky) Trota José, who helped me to identify this image.

125. Ibid., 5:134.

126. Ibid., 162–163.

127. Ibid., 134.

128. Ibid., 6:73, 174–175.

129. IOR/H/77 N.17, f.145; Newberry Library, Ayer, MS 1292, f.1–13; AGI, Filipinas, 605, N.3, 185r.

130. East India Company, *Manilha Consultations*, 5:41.

131. Ibid., 56–57.

132. Castro y Amuedo, "Relación sucinta," 67; Viana, "Diaro del sitio," 470–472.

133. On the battle at Malinta, see Castro y Amuedo, "Relación sucinta," 69–71.

134. Ibid., 70.

135. BL, IOR, H/77, 195.

136. Maldonado used the term "boruca," meaning a racket, a commotion, a disturbance, or an uproar. People in the Bicol region of Luzon still use the term *nagbuburuca* today to describe people who are extremely angry and violent. AGI, Filipinas, 605, N.3, f.39v.

137. *Documentos indispensables para la verdadera historia de Filipinas*, 1:82–87.

138. Blanco Andrés makes this argument, focusing on the later eighteenth and nineteenth centuries. Blanco Andrés, *Entre frailes*; Blanco Andrés, "El 'Padre Capitán,'" 7–54.

139. Vivar, "Relación de los alzamientos," 364.

140. AGI, Filipinas, 609, N.34, 18r–v.

141. Vivar, "Relación de los alzamientos," 314.

142. Ibid., 458; Aguilar-Cariño, "The Igorot as Other."

143. Vivar, "Relación de los alzamientos," 298.

144. Ibid., 312.

145. Ibid., 332.

146. Junker discusses evidence of the ritual destruction of enemy corpses in the late pre-Hispanic Philippines. Junker, *Raiding*, 361–364. On ritual cannibalism in the cordillera, see Stanyukovich, "Peacemaking Ideology," 399–409.

147. Vivar, "Relación de los alzamientos," 332.

148. AGI, Filipinas, 605, N.3, f.228v.

149. Taylor, *Magistrates of the Sacred*; Jonas, *France and the Cult of the Sacred Heart*, 76.

150. AGI, Filipinas, 609, N.34, f.61r–66v.

151. Vivar, "Relación de los alzamientos," 389.

152. East India Company, *Manilha Consultations*, 5:133; Routledge, *Diego Silang*, 128–129.

153. Vivar, "Relación de los alzamientos," 374–377; AGI, Filipinas, 605, N.3, f.55r.

154. East India Company, *Manilha Consultations*, 5:102; Vivar, "Relación de los alzamientos," 301; Routledge, *Diego Silang*, 21.

155. East India Company, *Manilha Consultations*, 5:97–102.

156. AGI, Filipinas, 605, N.3 (parte 9), f.25r–26r, 47r.

157. East India Company, *Manilha Consultations*, 5:97–102.

158. Ibid., 76, 133.

159. Vivar, "Relación de los alzamientos," 314, 386.

160. AGI, Filipinas, 605, N.3, f.62v; Vivar, "Relación de los alzamientos," 386–387.

161. "Relación de los alzamientos," 354–355.

162. AGI, Filipinas, 605, N.3, 280r–282r.

163. Becbec is also written as Bicbic in original sources. Vivar identified Becbec as an apoderadillo. Vivar, "Relación de los alzamientos," 301; AGI, Filipinas, 335, L.17, F.319r–320v. Previous studies identified Miguel Bicus or Vicus or Vicos as a Spanish mestizo, yet the colonial archive described him as an "indio." Ibid. AGI, Filipinas, 605, N.3, f.75r–82r. Alip, *Political and Cultural History of the Philippines*, 22–25.

164. AGI, Filipinas, 605, N.3, f.75r–82r, 195r; Vivar, "Relación de los alzamientos," 395–400.

165. AGI, Filipinas, 605, N.3, f.195r.

166. Newberry Library, Ayer, MS 1921, Folder 27; AGI Filipinas 605, f.302r; Vivar, "Relación de los alzamientos," 395–400.

167. AGI, Filipinas, 605, N.3, 70r–89r.

168. Ibid., f.187v.

169. Ibid., 240r.

170. Ibid., 195r.

171. Vivar, "Relación de los alzamientos," 400.

172. AGI, Filipinas, 605, N.3, f.195r–196r.

173. Ibid., f.187v.

174. Ibid., f.233v. For an overview of key battles, see Ferrando, *Historia de los pp. Dominicos*, 660–739.

175. AGI, Filipinas, 605, N.3, f.185r–188r, 254r–258r; Reyes y Florentino, *Historia de Ilocos*, 2:189–190.

176. Vivar, "Relación de los alzamientos," 462–463; Castro y Amuedo, "Relación sucinta," 86–87.

177. Bell, *The First Total War*, 174.

178. AGI, Filipinas, 605, N.3, 269r–274v.

179. AGI, Filipinas, 609, N.34.

180. Ibid.

181. Cited in Mendoza Cortes, *Pangasinan, 1572–1800*, 206.

182. Ferrando, *Historia de los pp. Dominicos*, 4:722, 731.

183. Ibid., 721, 733–734; Mendoza Cortes, *Pangasinan, 1572–1800*, 209–210; Arcilla, "The Pangasinan Uprising," 39–44.

184. Ferrando, *Historia de los pp. Dominicos*, 4:721,716, 737–738. Palaris's confession in Pangasinense and Spanish are held in the Dominican archives, which point to the missionary order's role in his persecution and eventual execution. ASPR, Pangasinan Tomo 2 (1760–1782).

185. AGI, Filipinas, 605, N.3, 259v–274v. Vivar, "Relación de los alzamientos," 442–446.

186. AGI, Filipinas, 605, N.3, 269r–274v.

187. For loyalty oaths, see AGI, Filipinas, 605, N.3, 124r, 171r–178v. On the banning of apoderadillos, see Vivar, "Relación de los alzamientos," 464–466.

188. Ferrando, *Historia de los pp. Dominicos*, 4:739; Mendoza Cortes, *Pangasinan, 1572–1800*, 212–213.

189. Vivar, "Relación de los alzamientos," 472.

190. Roberto Blanco Andrés, "La revuelta de Ilocos de 1807," 43–72.

191. "Relación del viaje de D. José Basco y Vargas gobernador y capitán general de las Filipinas, a las provincias de Pangasinan e Ilocos." AMN, MS 136, Doc. 10 (1785), ff. 310–343.

192. These murals have not survived. They are described in Castro y Amuedo, "Relación sucinta," 86–87. Aponte mentions similar scenes of the death of Tupac Amaru painted in public spaces in the viceroyalty of Peru in the aftermath of his defeated revolt. Cohen Suarez, *Heaven, Hell, and Everything In Between*, 145–182.

193. Newberry Library, Ayer, MS 1921, Folder 27. On the Treaty of Paris see Calloway, *The Scratch of a Pen*, 3–18, 134.

194. See AGI, Estado, 44, N.35. As of March 2, 1763, the British Manila Council reported that it had seized an estimated 516,260 pesos or goods equivalent to this value. East India Company, *Manilha Consultations*, 3:36–37.

195. Dean, *Inka Bodies*, 32, 42–49.

196. Newberry Library, Ayer, MS 1921, Folder 27. The events leading to the Spanish repossession of Manila are documented in *Manilha Consultations*, 9, 9A.

197. Newberry Library, Ayer, MS 1921, Folder 27.

198. AGI, Filipinas, 924.

199. AGI, Filipinas, 335, N.17.

Chapter 5

1. AGI, Filipinas, 716, 1202r–1204r.

2. Ibid., 1302r.

3. Lüdtke, "Explaining Forced Migration," 18.

4. Reid, "Entrepreneurial Minorities," 33–72.

5. AGI, Filipinas, 714, N.1, 509r.

6. Historians have tended to dismiss Chinese expulsion as an insignificant event, with some even denying that it occurred. Kueh, for example, concluded that "authorities in the provinces either did not cooperate or were not able to round up the Chinese despite orders from the governor to do so immediately following the British Occupation." For Kueh, the fact that trade between Manila and China and the size of Manila's Chinese population both recovered by the end of the eighteenth century rendered expulsion a nonevent and unworthy of further study. Kueh, "The Manila Chinese," 165, 172–173. Salvador de Escoto's two articles on the expulsion are the only serious studies of the forced migration of Sangleyes in the postwar years, and they are tainted by the author's anti-Chinese politics. Escoto uncritically accepted the colonial government's assumption that all the Chinese in the Philippines betrayed Spain and aided the British during the war. Escoto, "Expulsion of the Chinese," 48–76; "A Supplement to the Expulsion," 209–234.

7. Juan Gil suggests that Spanish-Chinese relations were generally poor and characterized by violence. Gil, *Los Chinos en Manila*, 453.

8. This is consistent with studies that have revealed the American origins of many Bourbon reforms implemented across the Spanish empire. Paquette, *Enlightenment, Governance, and Reform*, 131.

9. AGI, Filipinas, 713, 953r–965v. An English summary appears in *Synopsis of Communications by Anda to Carlos III*, in *The Philippine Islands, 1493–1898*, 49:308.

10. AGI, Filipinas, 716, 290v.

11. Ibid., 253r.

12. Ibid., 265r.

13. Ibid., 268r.

14. Ibid., 272r, 283v.

15. Schneider, *The Occupation of Havana*, 251–266.

16. Various copies of the expulsion order survive in the colonial archive, including AGI, Filipinas, 621, N.9; AGI, Filipinas, 714, 279r–281v.

17. The 1744 expulsion of nonbaptized Sangleyes remained in effect. AGI, Filipinas, 202, N.1, f.1406.

18. Law 8, Title 18, Book 6. *Recopilación de las leyes de los reynos de las indias*, 272.

19. The 1501 order expelling Muslims from Granada exempted males under fourteen and females under twelve years of age. Harvey, *Muslims in Spain*, 56–58. On the exemptions of children from the 1609 expulsion orders, see Tueller, "The Moriscos Who Stayed Behind," 197–2015.

20. Schneider, *The Occupation of Havana*, 254. On the expansion of fortifications and campaigns to improve military defense, see Pinzón Ríos, *Acciones y reacciones*; Luengo Gutiérrez, *Manila, Plaza Fuerte*; Luengo Gutiérrez, "La fortificación."

21. Lynch, "The Expulsion of the Jesuits," 220–230; Cushner, "A Note on HM 4101," 83–88.

22. Schneider, *The Occupation of Havana*, 254. Pedro Luengo analyzed the expansion of Spanish fortifications in maritime Asia and the Caribbean after the Seven Years' War. Luengo Gutiérrez, *Manila, Plaza Fuerte*; Luengo Gutiérrez, "La fortificación." For broader studies of the Bourbon reforms, see Paquette, *Enlightenment, Governance, and Reform*; Kuethe and Andrien, *The Spanish Atlantic World*.

23. For the expulsion of the Arcadians, see Calloway, *The Scratch of a Pen*, 152–162.

24. Ward, *Networks of Empire*, 99.

25. Paquette, *Enlightenment, Governance, and Reform*.

26. Newberry Library, Ayer, MS 1292, N.26.

27. NAP, Cedulario, 1760–1768; NAP, Cedulario, 1766–1771.

28. AGI, Filipinas, 716, 261v. Anda estimated between two thousand and three thousand Chinese men had left the colony by the war's end. Escoto, "Expulsion of the Chinese," 4.

29. See letter dated March 26, 1764 (Fort Saint George), in IOR E/4/300 (1760–1764), and letter dated October 24, 1764, in IOR E/4/301.

30. AGI, Filipinas, 716, 1184v–1185r, 301r.

31. AGI, Filipinas, 388, N.77.

32. Ibid.

33. East India Company, *Manilha Consultations*, 5:232.

34. NAP, Consultas, 1731–1739, 194r.

35. Ibid.

36. AGI, Filipinas, 714, 373v.

37. Ibid., 355v–356r, 367r.

38. Ibid., 343r–385r.

39. Ibid., 385r–387v.

40. Ibid.

41. Frustratingly, no information about this group has survived, not even a head count. AGI, Filipinas, 715, 395r.

42. AGI, Filipinas, 714, 388r.

43. AGI, Filipinas, 715, 371–377.

44. Ibid., 404r.

45. Ibid., 412v.

46. Ibid.

47. Ibid., 404r–v.

48. Escoto, "Expulsion of the Chinese," 54.

49. Ibid., 58.

50. AGI, Filipinas, 157, N.3, 5r–5v; AGI, Filipinas, 292, N.60.

51. Le Gentil, *A Voyage to the Indian Seas*, 79.

52. Escoto, "Expulsion of the Chinese," 59. AGI 715

53. AGI, Filipinas, 621, N.9.

54. Schneider, *The Occupation of Havana*, 257.

55. AGI, Filipinas, 716, f.179v–80v, 128, 200v.

56. Ibid. For ceremonial entries and oath ceremonies see Hidalgo Nuchera, "La entrada de los gobernadores en Manila," 615–644; Ramos, *Identity, Ritual, and Power*, 44–45, 27. Cañeque, *The King's Living Image*, 123–125.

57. AGI, Filipinas, 716, f.134r.

58. Ibid., 33r, 187r.

59. Ibid., 33r, 179r.

60. Ibid., 221r.

61. Ibid., f.131v.

62. Ibid., 14v.

63. Crewe, "Pacific Purgatory," 360–361.

64. AGI, Filipinas, 716, 36r–v, 15v, 21r, 188r, 100r–105v; Liu, *Confucian Rituals*, 107; Dean, *Taoist Ritual*, 99–129.

65. AGI, Filipinas, 716, 37r.

66. Crewe, "Occult Cosmopolitanism," 55–74.

67. Liu, *Confucian Rituals*, 242–246; Dean, *Taoist Ritual*, 147, 214–216.

68. AGI, Filipinas, 716, 68v, 100r–105v.

69. Ibid.

70. Ibid., 21r.

71. Ibid., 238v.

72. Ibid., f.186v, 35r.

73. Ibid., 221v.

74. Ibid., 57r.

75. Ibid., 37r, 106v, 81r. In July 1764, Fray Remigio Hernandez, provincial of Augustinians in the Philippines, also recounted this story. Ibid., 261v.

76. Ibid., 139v.

77. Ibid., 182r.

78. Ibid., 26f, 48r, 77r, 82r–v, 100r.

79. Ibid., 42v, 182v, 231r, 42v.

80. Ibid., 304r.

81. Ibid., 23r, 58r, 116r, 413v.

82. Ibid., f.85r.

83. Newberry Library, Ayer MS 1921, N.23.

84. van Duijnen, "Sacrificed to the madness," 179–200.

85. The original published Latin poem is analyzed in depth in McManus and Leibsohn, "Eloquence and Ethnohistory," 522–574. An eighteenth-century Spanish translation is held in the Newberry Library, Ayer MS 1921, N.15.

86. McManus and Leibsohn, "Eloquence and Ethnohistory," 537.

87. Ibid., 538.

88. AGI, Filipinas, 621, N.12.

89. NAP, Erección de Pueblos, Pampanga, 1755–1833, f.110r, 147r.

90. Ibid.

91. Ibid., 113.

92. Ibid., f.152r–155r.

93. Ibid., f.132r.

94. Ibid., 152r–155r.

95. Ibid., f.113r.

96. Lynch, "The Expulsion of the Jesuits," 220–230; AFIO, 50/3.

97. NAP, Erecion de Pueblos, Pampanga, 1755–1833, f.89r–v, 113r.

98. This dataset collated and analyzed a sample using information for the first in every ten men appearing in the *padrón* (roll) of persons interred in the Alcaicería from July 19, 1769, to the end of 1772. In total this sample encompasses 230 of the 2,294 men who appear in this document. AGI, Filipinas, 716.

99. Ibid., 1255r–v.

100. Priyadarshini, *Chinese Porcelain in Colonial Mexico*, 63–96. Luengo emphasized the hybrid Sino-Spanish form of the building designed by the Chinese architect Antonio Mozo and the Spaniards Lucas de Jesús Maria. Gutiérrez, "European Architecture in Southeast Asia," 262–263. AGI, Mapas y Planes - Filipinas, 38.

101. AGI, Escribania, 330C, Cuaderno 7, f.294.

102. AGI, Filipinas, 724.

103. Ibid., f.81r–82r.

104. Ibid., f.242r.

105. Ibid.

106. AGI, Filipinas, 716, 1228r.

107. Ibid., 1225r–1226v.

108. Ibid., 1202r–1301v.

109. Colonial math does not always add up: 2,294 men are listed in the government log of baptized Sangleyes who were interred in the Alcaicería between mid-1769 and early 1772. After we add to this figure the 141 Sangley "infidels" who were expelled from the Philippines after being shipwrecked or arrested as vagrants, we still have 118 Sangley Christians who were deported without being registered in the Alcaicería camp records. AGI, Filipinas, 716, 1202r–1301v, 1043r–1181r.

110. Ibid., 1202r–1301v.

111. Burrus, "A Diary of Exiled Philippine Jesuits," 270–273; Baena Zapatero, "Regalos de Filipinas a Cádiz," 491–495.

112. AGI, Filipinas, 716, f.1302r.

113. AGI, Filipinas, 942, f.28r–62r.

114. AGI, Filipinas, 716, 1220r.

115. AGI, Filipinas, 942, 39r.

116. Ibid. Amoy is the Anglicized rendition of the Zangzhou pronunciation. Ruiz-Stovel, "Chinese Shipping and Merchant Networks," 3.

117. AGI, Filipinas, 716, 1295r.

118. Ibid., 1285r, 1297v.
119. AGI, Filipinas, 621, N.12, 15r–v; AGI, Filipinas, 621, N.9.
120. AGI, Filipinas, 716, 1221v.
121. Ibid., 1232r.
122. Ibid., f.153v.
123. Ibid., 1191r.
124. Ibid., 1253r.
125. AGI, Filipinas, 943, N.15; AGI, Filipinas, 943, N.16. See also Ruiz-Stovel, "Chinese Shipping and Merchant Networks," 157–159, 378–379.
126. AGI, Filipinas, 714, 307r, 328r, 335r.
127. AGI, Filipinas, 344, L.13, 49r–51r.
128. AGI, Filipinas, 714, 318v–319r.
129. Ibid., 307r, 328r, 335r.
130. The impact of the expulsion on the physical cityscape has been overlooked in the literature on postwar urban history that has focused on the expansion of Fort Santiago and other defensive military architecture in the city. Luengo Gutiérrez, *Manila, Plaza Fuerte*.
131. This fate of the San Gabriel hospital was controversial: the Council of the Indies accused the Dominicans of establishing a new church without the necessary permission from the Crown. AGI, Filipinas, 716.
132. AAM, Box 1, B.4, 2.
133. NAP, Spanish Manila, 13822.
134. AGI, Filipinas, 714, N.1, f200r–211v.
135. AGI, Filipinas, 714, 201, 282v–284r; AGI, Filipinas, 714, N.1, 202r.
136. AGI, Filipinas, 714, 201, 282v–284r; AGI, Filipinas, 714, N.1, 202r.
137. AGI, Filipinas, 714, 288v.
138. AGI, Filipinas, 714, N.1, 206v.
139. Ibid., 287r.
140. Calderón referred to a royal cedula from 1609 that enslaved 500 Sangleyes and forced them to labor aboard royal galleys and the arsenal of Cavite as punishment for participating in the 1606 revolt. AGI, Filipinas, 714.
141. Calderón cites law "tit. 18, lib. 6," AGI, Filipinas, 714, 211.
142. Ibid., 282–289.
143. Ibid., 287r.
144. AGI, Filipinas, 714, N.1, 506v, 209v.
145. Ibid., 506v.
146. Ibid., 210r.
147. Ibid., 201r.
148. Frank, "The World Economic System"; Klooster, *Revolutions in the Atlantic World*, 11, 27, 55–56.
149. Kueh attributes this trend to Manila's "hostile trading environment." Kueh, "The Manila Chinese," 169.
150. AGI, Filipinas, 714, N.1, 509v
151. Ibid., 503v.
152. Ibid., 501r, 505r
153. Ibid., 509r.

154. Sarrio hoped to recruit twelve master smelters or ironworkers and one carbonero, knowledgeable in coal production, in addition to fifteen unskilled laborers. AGI, Filipinas, 337, L.19, 205r–207r.

155. Simón de Anda presented this proposal to the Crown as an alternative to allowing Canleong and his group to return to Cebu's pariancillo. AGI, Filipinas, 714, f.294r–299v, 416r–v.

156. Kueh, "The Manila Chinese," 172.

157. Escoto, "Expulsion of the Chinese," 66.

158. Museo Naval, AMN 0553, MS 1664/030.

159. Kueh, "The Manila Chinese," 172–173.

160. AGI, Filipinas, 924. For an overview of the establishment of the Chinese mestizo militia, see Buschmann, Slack, and Tueller, *Navigating the Spanish Lake*, 63–97.

161. AGI, Filipinas, 924.

162. Vinson, *Bearing Arms*, 41–45.

163. Santiago, "The First Filipino Doctors," 259.

164. This was not a conflict-free process: some members of the university claustro opposed the conferral of decrees on mestizos de Sangley because they did not have the requisite *limpieza de sangre* (purity of blood), yet they were overruled. Villarroel, *A History of the University of Santo Tomas*, 222–223.

165. Ibid.

166. Manchado López, "El proyecto de convento," 171–202.

167. Kueh developed this argument in his recent dissertation, presenting evidence that mestizos de Sangley became tax collectors and invested in cash crops in the aftermath of the Seven Years' War, enhancing the wealth and power of the mestizo elite. Kueh, "The Manila Chinese," 186–187.

168. Flynn and Giráldez, "Cycles of Silver," 1–16; Giráldez, *The Age of Trade*, 1–6, 29–38; Reyes, "Flaunting It," 683–713.

169. Blanco, "Presumptions of Empire," 204.

Epilogue

1. There is much variation in how Haidar Ali's name is transcribed in colonial archives and in historiography. I use the spelling most widely used by Indian historians. This account of the Spanish-Mysore alliance draws on AGI, Estado, 45, C.6, 1r–9v; AHN, 3403, Exp.2; Escoto, "A Spaniard's Diary," 121–135; Escoto, "Haidar Alí."

2. In MacDougall, "British Seapower," 305. Haidar Ali bargained with other European powers. See Rai K., "Portuguese Hegemony," 619–620.

3. AHN, Estado, 3403, Exp.2.

4. Ibid.

5. Ibid.

6. The late eighteenth century also witnessed increased trade between Manila and India. See Ugartemendia, "Beyond the Galleons," 115–136.

7. AGI, Filipinas, 714, N.1, 499r–511v.

8. NAP, Cedulario. Consultas, 1771–1772, N.82.

9. AGI, Filipinas, 925, N.245.

10. NAP, Cedulario. Consultas, 1771–1772, N.228.

11. AGI, Estado, 45, C.6, 37v, 75r–90v; AHN, Estado, 3403, Exp.2; Gómez-Centurión, "Treasures Fit for a King"; Llanes, "Dropping Artillery."

12. MacDougall, *Naval Resistance*, 167–191; Conrad, "Enlightenment."

13. Ileto, *Payson and Revolution*, 2.

14. Morley, *Cities and Nationhood*, 76, 157.

15. AGI, Escribania, 436A.

16. Anderson et al., "Mutiny and Maritime Radicalism," 14.

17. Fradera, *Filipinas, la colonia más peculiar.* See also Legarda, *After the Galleons.*

18. Bayly, *The Birth of the Modern World*, 88–89; Sivasundaram, *Waves Across the South.* Historians have emphasized the role of violence in sustaining empire and slavery in Cuba in the first half of the nineteenth century. Reid-Vazquez, *The Year of the Lash*; Childs, *The 1812 Aponte Rebellion.*

19. Mayshle, "Walled 'Memoria,'" 49–79.

20. Folger, *Writing as Poaching*, 10–11.

BIBLIOGRAPHY

Archives

Archdiocesan Archives of Manila (AAM)
Archivo General de Indias, Seville (AGI)
Archive of the University of Santo Tomás, Quezon City (UST)
Archivo Franciscano Ibero-Oriental, Madrid (AFIO)
Archivo General de la Nación, Mexico City (AGN)
Archivo Histórico Nacional, Madrid (AHN)
Biblioteca Nacional de España (BNE), Madrid
British Library, London (BL)
British Library India Office Records, London (IOR)
Huntington Library, Pasadena, California
Lilly Library, Bloomington, Indiana
Museo Naval, Madrid (AMN)
Newberry Library, Chicago
National Archives of the Philippines (NAP)

Early Printed Books and Pamphlets

Anon. *Relación compendiosa de lo que con grande gloria de dios, lustre y honor de las cathólicas reales armas, ejecutó estas cristiandades de bisayas contra los enemigos moros mahometanos la real armada destacada al presidio de Yligan y sus costas en este año de 1754.* Manila: La Imprenta de la Compania de Jesus de Manila, 1754.

———. *Relación de la entrada del Sultán Rey de Joló Mahamad Alimuddin en esta ciudad de Manila: y del honor, y regocijos, con que le recibió en 20. de henero de 1749 el illmo, y rmo señor doctor y m[inst]ro D. Fr. Joan de Archederra del Orden de Predicadores del concejo de su mg. obispo electo de Nueva Segovia, gobernador y capitan g[ene]ral de estas islas, y presidente de su real chancilleria.* Manila: Imprenta de Santo Tomás, 1749.

———. *Sagrados trivmphos, célebres expressiones y festivos aplavsos con que la Santa Provincia del Santíssimo Rosario del Sagrado Orden de Predicadores; la de San Gregorio el Magno de Menores Descalzos, y su Venerable Orden Tercera de Penitencia celebraron . . . la dedicación solemne de el nuevo templo de mro. S.P.S. Francisco.* Sampaloc: Convento de Nuestra Señora de Loreto, 1743.

Anson, George. *A Voyage Round the World, in the Years MDCCXL, I, II, III, IV.* London: Printed for the author by John and Paul Knapton, 1748.

Antonio, Juan Francisco de San. *Chronicas de la apostolica Provincia de S. Gregorio de Religiosos Descalzos de N.S.P.S. Francisco en las islas Philipinas, China, Japon, &c.* Sampaloc:

Impressa en la imprenta del vso de la propria provincia, síta en el Convento de N[uest]ra. Señora de Loreto del pueblo de Sampaloc: Por Fr. Juan del Sotillo, 1738.

Argensola, Bartolomé Leonardo de. *Conquista de las islas Malucas.* por Alonso Martin, 1609.

Arechederra, Juan de. *Continuacion de los progresos, y resultas de las expediciones contra moros . . . en este año de 1748. Con noticia de los principios de las nuevas missiones de los reynos de Iolò y Mindanao, etc.* Manila, 1749.

———. *Puntual relación de lo acaecido en las expediciónes contra moros tirones, malanaos, y camucones destacadas en los de 746, y 47.* [Manila?] 1748.

Bobadilla, Diego de. *Relación de las gloriosas victorias que en mar, y tierra an tenido las armas de nuestro invictíssimo rey, y monarca Felipe IV, el grande, en las islas Filipinas, contra los moros de la gran isla de Mindanao, y su rey Cachil Corralat, debajo de la conducta de Don Sebastián Hurtado de Corcuera, caballero de la Orden de Alcántara, y del consejo de guerra de su majestad, gobernador y capitán general de aquellas islas.* Mexico: en la Imprenta de Pedro de Quiñones, 1638.

Colín, Francisco, and Pedro Chirino. *Labor evangélica, ministerios apostólicos de los obreros de la Compañía de Iesvs, fundación y progressos de su Provincia, en las Islas Filipinas.* 3 vols. Barcelona: Imprenta y litografía de Henrich y compañía, 1900.

Collantes, Domingo. *Historia de la Provincia del Santísimo Rosario de Filipinas, China, y Tunquin Orden de Predicadores: quarta parte desde el año de 1700 hasta el de 1765.* Manila: en la Imprenta de la Universidad del Santo Tomás por Iuan Franc. de los Santos, 1782.

Concepción, Juan de la. *Historia general de Philipinas: conquistas espirituales y temporales de estos españoles dominios, establecimientos progresos, y decadencias.* 14 vols. Manila: En la Impr. del Seminar, Conciliar, y Real de S. Carlos, por Agustín de la Rosa y Balagtas, 1788–1792.

Draper, William. *Colonel Draper's Answer, to the Spanish Arguments, Claiming the Galeon, and Refusing Payment of the Ransom Bills, for Preserving Manila from Pillage and Destruction: In a Letter Addressed to the Earl of Halifax.* London: J. Dodsley, 1764.

———. *A Plain Narrative of the Reduction of Manila and the Phillippine Islands.* London [1764?].

Entick, John. *The General History of the Late War: Containing It's Rise, Progress, and Event, in Europe, Asia, Africa, and America. And Exhibiting the State of the Belligerent Powers at the Commencement of the War; Their Interests and Objects in It's Continuation; and Remarks on the Measures, Which Led Great Britain to Victory and Conquest. Interspersed with the Characters of the Able and Disinterested Statesmen, to Whose Wisdom and Integrity, and of the Heroes, to Whose Courage and Conduct, We Are Indebted for That Naval and Military Success, Which Is Not to Be Equalled in the Annals of This, or of Any Other Nation. And with Accurate Descriptions of the Seat of War, the Nature and Importance of Our Conquests, and of the Most Remarkable Battles by Sea and Land. Illustrated with a Variety of Heads, Plans, Maps, and Charts, Designed and Engraved by the Best Artists. . . . By the Rev. John Entick, M.A. And Other Gentlemen,* Vol. 5. London: Printed for Edward Dilly and John Millan, 1764.

Forrest, Thomas. *A Voyage to New Guinea, and the Moluccas, from Balambangan: Including an Account of Magindano, Sooloo, and Other Islands; and Illustrated with Thirty Copperplates. Performed in the Tartar Galley, Belonging to the Honourable East India Company, During the Years 1774, 1775, and 1776, by Captain Thomas Forrest. To Which Is Added, a Vocabulary of the Magindano Tongue.* 2nd ed. Edinburgh: Printed by G. Scott, 1780.

Hurtado de Corquera, Sebastian. *Relación del levantamiento de los sangleyes en las islas Philipinas. Su castigo, y pacificacion este año de 1640. Por Don Sebastian Hurtado de Corquera, cauallero del Orden de Alcantara, gouernador, y capitan general de ellas: cuyo magnanimo esfuerco, y prudencia militar, ha hecho mas respetables, y famosas en aquellas partes las armas de su magestad.* Mexico: Por Francisco Robledo impressor y mercader de libros, en la calle de San Francisco, 1640.

Londoño, Sancho de. *Discurso sobre la forma de reducir la disciplina militar a mejor y antiguo estado.* Madrid: por Luys Sanchez, 1593.

Lozano, Pedro. *Historia de la Compañia de Jesús en la provincia del Paraguay escrita por el Padre Pedro Lozano de la misma Compañia.* Madrid: en la Imprenta de la Viuda de Manuel Fernandez, 1754.

Martínez de Arizala, Pedro de la Santísima Trinidad. *Carta pastoral del illmo. y rmo. señor arzobispo de Manila,* Manila, 1754.

Martinez de Zuñiga, Joaquín. *An Historical View of the Philippine Islands: Exhibiting Their Discovery, Population, Language, Government, Manners, Customs, Productions and Commerce.* Translated by John Maver. Vol. 1, 2nd ed. 2 vols. London: Black, Parry, and Co., 1814.

Murillo Velarde, Pedro. *Historia de la provincia de Philipinas de la Compañia de Jesús: segunda parte, que comprende los progresos de esta provincia desde el año de 1616 hasta el de 1716.* Manila: En la Imprenta de la Compañia de Jesús, por D. Nicolas de la Cruz Bagay, 1749.

Murillo Velarde, Pedro, and Nicolás de la Cruz Bagay. "Carta hydrographica y chorographica de las yslas filipinas." 1734.

Ovando y Solis, Francisco Jose de. *Manifiesto, en que succintamente se exponen los motivos, y feliz éxito de la embajada á la isla, y corte de Borney, despachada desde esta capital de manila en 8. de abril de 1752.* [Manila?] 1752.

San Augustin, Gaspar de. *Conquistas de las islas Philipinas: la temporal, por las armas del señor Don Phelipe Segundo el prudente: y la espiritval, por los religiosos del Orden de nuestro padre San Augustin: fvndacion, y progressos de sv provincia del Santissimo Nombre de Jesus: parte primera.* Madrid: en la Imprenta de Manuel Ruí de Morga, 1698.

Tanner, Mathias. *Societas Jesu usque ad sanguinis et vitae profusionem militans, in Europa, Africa, Asia, et America, Contra gentiles, Mahometanos, Judaeos, haereticos, impios, pro Deo, fide, Ecclesia, pietate, sive, Vita, et mors eorum, qui ex Societate Jesu in causa fidei, & virtutis propugnatae, violentâ morte toto orbe sublati sunt.* Prague: Typis Universitatis Carolo-Ferdinandeae, in Collegio Societatis Jesu ad S. Clementem, per Joannem Nicolaum Hampel Factorem, 1675.

Torrubia, José. *Dissertación histórico-política, y en mucha parte geográfica, de las Islas Philipinas, extensión del mahometismo en ellas.* Madrid: en la Imprenta de Alonso Balvás, 1736.

———. *Dissertación histórico-política, y en mucha parte geográfica, de las islas philipinas, extensión del mahometismo en ellas.* Madrid: Imprenta de A. de Gordejuela y Sierra, 1753.

Zurita, Diego, Tomás Adriano, and Pedro de Ire. *Oracion panegyrico moral en la solemne fiesta, qve la provincia del Ssmo. Rosario, Orden de Predicadores en Las Islas Philipinas, consagró a Maria Santissima en su prodigiosa thaumaturga imagen del rosario venerada en la iglesia del patriarcha Señor Santo Domingo de la M. N. y L. C de Manila.* Manila: Collegio y Universidad de Santo Thomas, por Thomas Adriano Tipo de Documento, 1764.

Secondary Works and Edited Collections of Primary Sources

Aguilar-Cariño, Maria Luisa. "The Igorot as Other: Four Discourses from the Colonial Period." *Philippines Studies* 42 (1994): 194–209.

Alip, Eufronio M. *Political and Cultural History of the Philippines*. Manila: Alip & Sons, 1964.

Alonso Álvarez, Luís. *El costo del imperio Asiático. La formación colonial de las Islas Filipinas bajo dominio español 1565–1800*. México, D.F.: Instituto Mora, Universidade da Coruña, 2009.

Álvarez, Luis Alonso. "Caminos sobre la mar. Las expediciones a las Islas de la Especiería después de Magallanes, 1525–1564." *Historia Mexicana* 72 (2022): 539–614.

Andaya, Barbara. *A History of Early Modern Southeast Asia, 1400–1830*. Cambridge, UK: Cambridge University Press, 2015.

Andaya, Barbara, and Yoneo Ishii. "Religious Developments in Southeast Asia C. 1500–1800." In *The Cambridge History of Southeast Asia*, edited by Nicholas Tarling, 508–571. Cambridge, UK: Cambridge University Press, 1993.

Anderson, Clare, Niklas Frykman, Lex Heerma Van Voss, and Marcus Rediker. "Mutiny and Maritime Radicalism in the Age of Revolution: An Introduction." *International Review of Social History*. Special issue, 21 (2014): 1–14.

Anderson, Fred. *Crucible of War: The Seven Years' War and the Fate of Empire in British North America, 1754–1766*. New York: Alfred A. Knopf, 2000.

———. *A People's Army: Massachusetts Soldiers and Society in the Seven Years' War*. Chapel Hill: University of North Carolina Press, 1984.

Andrade, Tonio. "A Chinese Farmer, Two African Boys, and a Warlord: Toward a Global Microhistory." *Journal of World History* 21, no. 4 (2010): 573–591.

———. *How Taiwan Became Chinese: Dutch, Spanish, and Han Colonization in the Seventeenth Century*. New York: Columbia University Press, 2008.

Andrade, Tonio, and Xing Hang. "Introduction: The East Asian Maritime Realm in Global History, 1500–1700." In *Sea Rovers, Silver, and Samurai: Maritime East Asia in Global History, 1550–1700*, 1–27. Honolulu: University of Hawai'i Press, 2016.

Angeles, Jose Amiel. "The Battle of Mactan and the Indigenous Discourse on War." *Philippine Studies* 55, no. 1 (2007): 3–52.

Antony, Robert J. "Bloodthirsty Pirates? Violence and Terror on the South China Sea in Early Modern Times." *Journal of Early Modern History*, 16, no. 6 (2012): 481–502.

———. *Like Froth Floating on the Sea: The World of Pirates and Seafarers in Late Imperial South China*. Berkeley, CA: Institute of East Asian Studies, 2003.

———. "Piracy on the South China Coast Through Modern Times." In *Piracy and Maritime Crime: Historical and Modern Case Studies*, edited by Bruce A. Elleman, Andrew Forbes, and David Rosenberg, 35–51. Newport, RI: Naval War College Press, 2010.

Arcilla, José S. "The Pangasinan Uprising, 1762–1765." *Philippine Historical Review* 4 (1971): 35–52.

Argensola, Bartolomé Leonardo. *Conquista de las Islas Malucas: al Rey Felipe Tercero, nuestro señor*. Zaragoza, Spain: Imprenta del Hospicio Provincial, 1891.

Aslanian, Sebouh David. *From the Indian Ocean to the Mediterranean. The Global Trade Networks of Armenian Merchants from New Julfa*. Berkeley: University of California Press, 2011.

Baena Zapatero, Alberto. "Intercambios culturales y globalización a través del galeón de Manila: comercio y producción de biombos." In *La nao de China, 1565–1815*, edited by Salvador Bernabéu Albert, 213–244. Sevilla: Universidad de Sevilla, 2013.

———. "Regalos de Filipinas a Cádiz en los barcos de la armada (1765–1784)." *Anuario de Estudios Americanos* 74, no. 2 (2017): 491–523.

Baena Zapatero, Alberto, and Xabier Lamikiz. "Presencia de una diáspora global: comerciantes armenios y comercio intercultural en Manila, C. 1660–1800." *Revista de Indias* 74, no. 262 (2014): 693–722.

Bakewell, Peter. *Miners of the Red Mountain: Indian Labor in Potosi, 1545–1650.* Albuquerque: University of New Mexico Press, 1984.

Barco Ortega, José. "El gobierno de Manuel Antonio Rojo, Filipinas 1761–1764." PhD thesis, Universidad de Navarra, 1997.

Barragán, Rossana. "Working Silver for the World: Mining Labor and Popular Economy in Colonial Potosi." *Hispanic American Historical Review* 97, no. 2 (2017): 193–222.

Barrio Muñoz, José Ángel del. *Vientos de reforma ilustrada en Filipinas. el gobernador Fernando Valdés Tamón (1729–1739).* Madrid: Consejo Superior de Investigaciones Científicas, 2012.

Bassi, Ernesto. *An Aqueous Territory: Sailor Geographies and New Granada's Transimperial Greater Caribbean World.* Chapel Hill, NC: Duke University Press, 2017.

Baugh, Daniel. *The Global Seven Years War, 1754–1763.* London: Pearson, 2011.

Bayly, C. A. *The Birth of the Modern World, 1780–1914: Global Connections and Comparisons* Malden, MA: Blackwell, 2004.

Beauchesne, Kim. "Trans-Pacific Connections: Cultural Contacts Through the Lens of Miguel López de Legazpi's Representation of the Philippines and Its Relationship with the Early Accounts of the New World." *Asian Journal of Latin American Studies* 28, no. 4 (2015): 1–28.

Bell, David A. *The First Total War: Napoleon's Europe and the Birth of Warfare as We Know It.* New York: Houghton Mifflin Harcourt, 2007.

Bernad, Miguel A. "Father Ducos and the Muslim Wars, 1753–1759." *Philippine Studies* 16, no. 4 (1968): 690–728.

Bhattacharya, Bhaswati. "Making Money at the Blessed Place of Manila: Armenians in the Madras–Manila Trade in the Eighteenth Century." *Journal of Global History* 3, no. 1 (2008): 1–20.

Biedermann, Zoltán. *(Dis)Connected Empires: Imperial Portugal, Sri Lankan Diplomacy, and the Making of a Habsburg Conquest in Asia.* Oxford: Oxford University Press, 2019.

Blair, Emma Helen, and James Alexander Robertson, eds. *The Philippine Islands, 1493–1898.* 55 vols. Cleveland: Arthur H. Clark, 1909–1915.

Blanco Andrés, Roberto. "El 'Padre Capitán' Julián Bermejo y la defensa contra la piratería mora en Cebu." *Archivo Agustiniano* 101, no. 219 (2017): 7–54.

———. *Entre frailes y clérigos. Las claves de la cuestión clerical en Filipinas (1776–1872).* Madrid: CSIC, 2012.

———. "La revuelta de Ilocos de 1807." *Archivo Agustiniano* 96, no. 214 (2012): 43–72.

Blanco, John D. "Presumptions of Empire: Relapses, Reboots, and Reversions in the Transpacific Networks of Iberian Globalization." In *The Routledge Hispanic Studies Companion to Colonial Latin America and the Caribbean (1492–1898)*, edited by Yolanda Martínez-San Miguel and Santa Arias, 199–214. New York: Routledge, 2021.

Blussé, Leonard. *Visible Cities: Canton, Nagasaki, and Batavia and the Coming of the Americans*. Cambridge, MA: Harvard University Press, 2008.

Borao, José Eugenio. "The Massacre of 1603: Chinese Perception of the Spaniards in the Philippines." *Itinerario* 22, no. 1 (1998): 22–39.

———. "Contextualizing the Pampangos (and Gagayano) Soldiers in the Spanish Fortress in Taiwan (1626–1642)/Soldados Pampangos (y Cagayanos) de la fortaleza española de Taiwan, en su contexto." *Anuario de Estudios Americanos* 70, no. 2 (2013): 581–605.

Borchgrevink, Axel. "Ideas of Power in the Philippines: Amulets and Sacrifice." *Cultural Dynamics* 15, no. 1 (2003): 41–69.

Borschberg, Peter. "Chinese Merchants, Catholic Clerics and Spanish Colonists in British-Occupied Manila, 1762–1764." In *Maritime China in Transition 1750 - 1850*, edited by Wang Gungwu and Ng Chin-keong, 355–372. Wiesbaden: Harrassowitz Verlag, 2004.

Böttcher, Nikolaus, Bernd Hausberger, and Max S. Hering Torres. "Introducción." In *El peso de la sangre: limpios, mestizos y nobles en el mundo hispánico*, edited by Nikolaus Böttcher, Bernd Hausberger, and Max S. Hering Torres, 9–28. México, D.F.: El Colegio de México, 2011.

Brading, David. *Mexican Phoenix: Our Lady of Guadalupe, Image and Tradition Across Five Centuries*. Cambridge, UK: Cambridge University Press, 2002.

Brewer, Carolyn. *Shamanism, Catholicism and Gender Relations in Colonial Philippines, 1521–1685*. Aldershot, UK: Hants Ashgate, 2004.

Brockey, Liam Mathew. "Conquests of Memory: Franciscan Chronicles of the East Asian Church in the Early Modern Period." *Culture & History Digital Journal* 5, no. 2 (2016): 1–15.

———. "The First China Hands: The Forgotten Iberian Origins of Sinology." In *Western Visions of the Far East in a Transpacific Age, 1522-1657*, edited by Christina H. Lee, 69–84. Burlington, VT: Ashgate, 2016.

———. *Journey to the East: The Jesuit Mission to China, 1579-1724*. Cambridge, MA: Belknap Press, 2007.

Brook, Timothy. *The Troubled Empire: China in the Yuan and Ming Dynasties*. Cambridge, MA: Harvard University Press, 2010.

Brooks, James. *Captives & Cousins: Slavery, Kinship, and Community in the Southwest Borderlands*. Chapel Hill: University of North Carolina Press, 2002.

Brown, Vincent. *Tacky's Revolt: The Story of an Atlantic Slave War*. Cambridge, MA: Belknap Press, 2022.

Burrus, Ernest J. "A Diary of Exiled Philippine Jesuits." *Archivum Historicum Societatis Iesu* 20 (1951): 269–299.

Buschmann, Rainer F., Edward R. Slack, and James B. Tueller. *Navigating the Spanish Lake: The Pacific in the Iberian World, 1521-1898*. Honolulu: University of Hawai'i Press, 2014.

Busquets, Anna. "Three Manila-Fujian Diplomatic Encounters: Different Aims and Different Embassies in the Seventeenth Century." *Journal of Early Modern History* 23, no. 5 (2019): 442–457.

Cáceres Menéndez, Beatriz, and Robert W. Patch. "«Gente de Mal Vivir»: Families and Incorrigible Sons in New Spain, 1721-1729." *Revista de Indias* 66, no. 237 (2006): 363–392.

Callanta, Cesar V. *The Limahong Invasion*. Quezon City: New Day, 1989.

Calloway, Colin G. *The Scratch of a Pen: 1763 and the Transformation of North America*. Oxford, UK: Oxford University Press, 2006.

Camacho, Julia María Schiavone. *Chinese Mexicans: Transpacific Migration and the Search for a Homeland, 1910–1960*. Chapel Hill: University of North Carolina Press, 2012.

Cañeque, Alejandro. *The King's Living Image: The Culture and Politics of Viceregal Power in Colonial Mexico*. New York: Routledge, 2004.

Canialo, Michael Armand P. "Isles of Garrisons: Remote Sensing Ijangs in Northern Philippines." *GeoJournal: Spatially Integrated Social Sciences and Humanities* (2018). https://doi .org/10.1007/s10708-018-9921-0.

Cañizares-Esguerra, Jorge. "The Devil in the New World: A Transnational Perspective." In *The Atlantic in Global History, 1500–2000*, edited by Jorge Cañizares-Esguerra and Erik R. Seeman, 22–40. Upper Saddle River, NJ: Pearson Prentice Hall, 2007.

Cano García, María Gloria. "La construcción del pasado español en Filipinas según la historiografía imperialista norteamericana. The Philippine Islands 1493–1898, el proyecto imperialista más ambicioso." In *De Tartessos a Manila: siete estudios coloniales y poscoloniales*, 209–239. Publicacions de la Universitat de València, 2008.

———. "The "Spanish Colonial Past" in the Construction of Modern Philippine History: A Critical Inquiry into the (Mis)Use of Spanish Sources." PhD thesis, National University of Singapore, 2005.

Castro y Amuedo, Agustín María. "Relación sucinta, clara y verídica de la toma de Manila por la escuadra inglesa, escrita por el p. Fr. Agustín María De Castro y Amuedo, natural de la Villa De Bañeza, agustino calzado. año de 1770." In *Documentos indispensables para la verdadera historia de Filipinas*, edited by Eduardo Navarro, 46–92. Madrid: Imprenta el asilo de Huérfanos, 1908.

Cevera, José Antonio. *Cartas del Parián: los chinos de Manila a finales del siglo XVI a través de los ojos de Juan Cobo y Domingo de Salazar*. México, D.F.: Palabra de Clío, 2015.

Chakraborty, Titas, and Matthias Van Rossum. "Slave Trade and Slavery in Asia—New Perspectives." *Journal of Social History* 54 (2020): 1–14.

Chang, Jason Oliver. *Chino: Anti-Chinese Racism in Mexico, 1880–1940*. Champaign: University of Illinois Press, 2017.

———. "Four Centuries of Imperial Succession in the Comprador Pacific." *Pacific Historical Review* 86, no. 2 (2017): 193–227.

Charbonneau, Oliver. *Civilizational Imperatives: Americans, Moros, and the Colonial World*. Ithaca, NY: Cornell University Press, 2021.

Chaves, Jonathan. *The Columbia Book of Later Chinese Poetry: Yuan, Ming, and Ch'ing Dynasties (1279–1911)*. New York, Columbia University Press, 1988.

Chen, Boyi. "The Hokkiens in Early Modern Hoi An, Batavia, and Manila: Political Agendas and Selective Adaptations." *Journal of Southeast Asian Studies* 52 (2021): 67–89.

Cheng, Weichung. *War, Trade and Piracy in the China Seas (1622–1683)*. Leiden: Brill, 2013.

Chet, Guy. *The Ocean Is a Wilderness: Atlantic Piracy and the Limits of State Authority, 1688–1856*. Amherst: University of Massachusetts Press, 2014.

Chia, Lucille. "The Butcher, the Baker, and the Carpenter: Chinese Sojourners in the Spanish Philippines and Their Impact on Southern Fujian." *Journal of the Economic and Social History of the Orient* 44, no. 4 (2006): 509–544.

Childs, Matt D. *The 1812 Aponte Rebellion in Cuba and the Struggle Against Atlantic Slavery*. Chapel Hill: University of North Carolina Press, 2006.

Chiquín, Selvin. "Administración y gasto de las cajas de comunidad en la audiencia de Guatemala: el Corregimiento de Quetzaltenango, 1790–1820." *Estudios de Cultura Maya* 57 (2021): 215–244.

Chu, Richard. *Chinese and Chinese Mestizos of Manila: Family, Identity, and Culture, 1860s–1930s.* Leiden: Brill, 2010.

Clossey, Luke. *Salvation and Globalization in the Early Jesuit Missions.* New York: Cambridge University Press, 2008.

Coakley, John. "'The Piracies of Some Little Privateers': Language, Law and Maritime Violence in the Seventeenth-Century Caribbean." *Britain and the World* 13, no. 1 (2020): 6–26.

Coballes, Jake, and Harold S. de la Cruz. "An Ethnography of Ibanag Warfare and Weaponry Based on Spanish Colonial Records." *Tala* 4, no. 1 (2021): 78–140.

Coello de la Rosa, Alexandre. *Jesuits at the Margins: Missions and Missionaries in the Marianas (1668–1769).* New York: Routledge, 2016.

———. "Políticas geo-estratégicas y misionales en el sur de Filipinas: el caso de Mindanao y Joló (siglo XVIII)." *Revista de Indias* 79, no. 277 (2019): 729–763.

Cohen Suarez, Ananda. *Heaven, Hell, and Everything in Between: Murals of the Colonial Andes.* Austin: University of Texas Press, 2016.

Colín Sales, Ostwald. "La escasez de soldados en las Filipinas de la primera mitad del siglo XVIII." In *Estudios sobre Amércia: siglos XVI-XX,* Sevilla: Asociación Española de Americanístas, 2005.

Conrad, Sebastian. "Enlightenment in Global History: A Historiographical Critique." *American Historical Review* 117, no. 4 (2012): 999–1027.

Constantino, Renato. *A History of the Philippines: From the Spanish Colonization to the Second World War.* New York: Monthly Review Press, 1975.

———. "Identity and Consciousness: The Philippine Experience." *Journal of Contemporary Asia* 6 (1976): 5–28.

———. *The Philippines: A Past Revisited from the Spanish Colonization to the Second World War.* 2nd ed. Manila, 1984.

Cook, Karoline P. *Forbidden Passages: Muslims and Moriscos in Colonial Spanish America.* Philadelphia: University of Pennsylvania Press, 2016.

Cooper, Frederick. *Colonialism in Question: Theory, Knowledge, History.* Berkeley: University of California Press, 2005.

Cope, Robert Douglas. *The Limits of Racial Domination: Plebeian Society in Colonial Mexico City, 1660–1720.* Madison: University of Wisconsin Press, 1994.

Corpuz, O. D. *The Roots of the Filipino Nation.* Vol. 1. Quezon City: University of the Philippines Press, 2005.

Costa, Horacio de la. "The Development of the Native Clergy in the Philippines." *Theological Studies* 8, no. 2 (1947): 219–250.

Costa, Horacio de la, Francis Jourdan, A. Dalrymple, and Vizentio de Azivledo. "Muhammad Alimuddin I, Sultan of Sulu, 1735–1773." *Journal of the Malaysian Branch of the Royal Asiatic Society* 38, no. 1 (1965): 43–76.

Covey, Alan R. *Inca Apocalypse: The Spanish Conquest and the Transformation of the Andean World.* New York: Oxford University Press, 2020.

Crailsheim, Eberhard. "The Baptism of Sultan Azim Ud-Din of Sulu: Festivities for the Consolidation of Spanish Power in the Philippines in Middle of the Eighteenth Century." In

Image—Object—Performance, edited by Eberhard Crailsheim and Astrid Windus, 93–120. Munster: Waxmann Verlag, 2013.

Crewe, Ryan Dominic. "Occult Cosmopolitanism: Convivencia and Ethno-Religious Exclusion in Manila, 1590–1650." In *Philippine Confluence: Iberian, Chinese and Islamic Currents, C. 1500–1800*, edited by Jos Gommans and Ariel Cusi Lopez, 55–74. Leiden: Leiden University Press, 2020.

———. "Pacific Purgatory: Spanish Dominicans, Chinese Sangleys, and the Entanglement of Mission and Commerce in Manila, 1580–1620." *Journal of Early Modern History* 19 (2015): 337–365.

———. "Transpacific Mestizo: Religion and Caste in the Worlds of a Moluccan Prisoner of the Mexican Inquisition." *Itinerario* 39, no. 3 (2016): 463–485.

Cruikshank, Bruce. "The British Occupation of Manila, 1762–1764, Through Franciscan Eyes." 2015. Unpublished manuscript, https://www.academia.edu/12429534/The_British_Occupation_of_Manila_1762_1764_through_Franciscan_Eyes.

———. "Silver in the Provinces: A Critique of the Classic View of Philippine Economic History in the Seventeenth and Eighteenth Centuries." *Philippine Quarterly of Culture and Society* 36, no. 3 (2008): 124–151.

Cuadriello, Jaime. *Las glorias de la república de Tlaxcala: o la conciencia como imagen sublime*. México, D.F.: Instituto de Investigaciones Estéticas, 2004.

Cushner, Nicholas P. *Documents Illustrating the British Conquest of Manila, 1762–1763*. London: Royal Historical Society, 1971.

———. "Meysapan: The Formation and Social Effects of a Landed Estate in the Philippines." *Journal of Asian History* 7, no. 1 (1973): 23–53.

———. "A Note on HM 4101 and the Expulsion of the Jesuits from the Philippines." *Huntington Library Quarterly* 29 (1965): 83–88.

———. *Spain in the Philippines: From Conquest to Revolution*. Quezon City: Ateneo de Manila University, 1977.

CuUnjieng Aboitiz, Nicole. *Asian Place, Filipino Nation*. New York: Columbia University Press, 2020.

Day, Iyko, Juliana Hu Pegues, Malissa Phung, Dean Itsuji Saranillio, and Danika Medak-Saltzman. "Settler Colonial Studies, Asian Diasporic Questions." *Verge: Studies in Global Asias* 5, no. 1 (2019): 1–45.

Dean, Carolyn. *Inka Bodies and the Body of Christ*. Durham, NC: Duke University Press, 1999.

Dean, Kenneth. *Taoist Ritual and Popular Cults of Southeast China*. Princeton, NJ: Princeton University Press, 1993.

Deloira, Philip J. "What Is the Middle Ground, Anyway?" *William and Mary Quarterly* 63, no. 1 (2006): 15–22.

Díaz-Trechuelo, María Lourdes. "Eighteenth Century Philippine Economy: Commerce." *Philippine Quarterly of Culture and Society* 14, no. 2 (1966): 253–279.

———. "Religiosidad popular en Filipinas: hermanedades y cofradias (siglos XVI-XVIII)." *Hispania Sacra* 53 (2001): 345–366.

Dodds Pennock, Caroline. *On Savage Shores: How Indigenous Americans Discovered Europe*. New York: Alfred A. Knopf, 2023.

Donoso, Isaac. "The Hispanic Moros y Cristianos and the Philippine Komedya." *Philippine Humanities Review* 11/12 (2009): 87–120.

———. "The Philippines and Al-Andalus: Linking the Edges of the Classical Islamic World." *Philippine Studies* 63, no. 2 (2015): 247–273.

———. "El Islam en Filipinas (siglos X-XIX)." PhD thesis, Universidad de Alicante, 2011.

Dreaper, James. *Pitt's Gallant Conquerer*. London: I. B. Tauris & Co., 2006.

East India Company. *Manilha Consultations*. 9 vols. Madras: Superintendent of Government Press, 1940–1946.

Echeverri, Marcela. *Indian and Slave Royalists in the Age of Revolution: Reform, Revolution, and Royalism in the Northern Andes, 1780–1825*. New York: Cambridge University Press, 2016.

Ehlers, Benjamin. "The Spanish Encounter with Islam." In *The Early Modern Hispanic World: Transnational and Interdisciplinary Approaches*, edited by Kimberly Lynn and Erin Kathleen Rowe, 153–173. Cambridge, UK: Cambridge University Press, 2017.

Eklöf Amirell, Stefan. *Pirates of Empire: Colonisation and Maritime Violence in Southeast Asia*. Cambridge, UK: Cambridge University Press, 2019.

Elliott, J. H. *Empires of the Atlantic World: Britain and Spain in America 1492-1830*. New Haven, CT: Yale University Press, 2006.

Ennis, Daniel James. *Enter the Press-Gang: Naval Impressment in Eighteenth-Century British Literature*. Newark: University of Delaware Press, 2002.

Escoto, Salvador P. "Expulsion of the Chinese and Readmission to the Philippines: 1764–1779." *Philippine Studies* 47, no. 1 (1999): 48–76.

———. "Haidar Alí: un intento frustrado de relación comercial entre Mysore y Filipinas, 1773–1779." *Revista Española del Pacífico* 10 (1999).

———. "A Spaniards's Diary of Mangalore, 1776–1777." *Asian Studies* 28 (1980): 121–135.

———. "A Supplement to the Expulsion of the Chinese from the Philippines: 1764–1779." *Philippine Studies* 48, no. 2 (2000): 209–234.

Exbalin, Arnaud. "Riot in Mexico City: A Challenge to the Colonial Order?" *Urban History* 43, no. 2 (2016): 215–231.

Fernandez, Doreen G. "Princesa Miramar and Principe Leandro: Text and Context in a Philippine Komedya." *Philippine Studies* 39, no. 4 (1991): 413–442.

Fernandez, Erwin S. "Towards an Early History of Pangasinan: Preliminary Notes and Observations." *Philippine Quarterly of Culture and Society* 38, no. 2 (2010): 174–198.

Fernández Palacios, José María. "El papel activo de los indígenas en la conquista y defensa de las islas filipinas: las compañias pampangas en el siglo XVII." In *Un mar de islas, un mar de gentes*, edited by Marta Manchado López and Miguel Luque Talaván, 101–126. Cordoba: Universidad de Cordoba, 2014.

Ferrando, Juan, and Joaquin Fonseca. *Historia de los pp. Dominicos en las Islas Filipinas y en sus misiones del Japon, China, Tung-Kin y Formosa, que comprende los sucesos principales de la historia general de este archipiélago, desde el descubrimiento y conquista de estas islas por las flotas españolas, hasta el año de 1840*. Vol. 5. Madrid: M. Rivadeneyra, 1871.

Fish, Shirley. *When Britain Ruled the Philippines*. Bloomington, IN: First Books, 2003.

Fisher, Andrew B., and Matthew D. O'Hara. "Introduction: Racial Identities and Their Interpreters in Colonial Latin America." In *Imperial Subjects: Race and Identity in Colonial Latin America*, edited by Andrew B. Fisher, Matthew D. O'Hara, Walter D. Mignolo, Irene Silverblatt, and Sonia Saldívar-Hull, 1–38. Chapel Hill, NC: Duke University Press, 2009.

Flannery, Kristie Patricia. "Can the Devil Cross the Deep Blue Sea? Imagining the Spanish Pacific and Vast Early America from Below." *William and Mary Quarterly* 79, no. 1 (2022): 31–60.

———. "Prohibited Games, Prohibited People: Race and Gambling and Segregation in Early Modern Manila." *Newberry Essays in Medieval and Early Modern Studies* 8 (2014): 81–92.

———. "The Trans-Imperial Biography of César Falliet: A Life Between Global Cities." *Urban History* 48, no. 3 (August 2021): 479–497.

Flannery, Kristie Patricia, and Guillermo Ruiz-Stovel. "The Loyal Foreign Merchant Captain: Thomé Gaspar de León and the Making of Manila's Intra-Asian Connections." *Vegueta. Anuario de la Facultad de Geografía e Historia* 20 (2020): 189–215.

Flint, Richard, and Shirley Cushing Flint. "Guido de Lavezaris: The Life of a Financier of the Coronado and Villalobos Expeditions." *New Mexico Historical Review* 86 (2011): 1–19.

Flores, Emil Francis M. "Up in the Sky, Feet on the Ground: Cultural Identity in Filipino Superhero Komiks." In *Cultural Excavation and Formal Expression in the Graphic Novel*, edited by Jonathan C. Evans and Thomas Giddens, 73–86. Leiden: Brill, 2013.

Flynn, Dennis O., and Arturo Giráldez. "Cycles of Silver: Globalization as Historical Process." *World Economics* 3, no. 2 (2002): 1–16.

Folger, Robert. *Writing as Poaching: Interpellation and Self-Fashioning in Colonial Relaciones de Méritos Y Servicios*. Leiden: Brill, 2011.

Foreman, John. *The Philippine Islands. A Political, Geographical, Ethnographical, Social and Commercial History of the Philippine Archipelago and Its Political Dependencies, Embracing the Whole Period of Spanish Rule*. New York: C. Scribner's Sons, 1899.

Fradera, Josep M. *Filipinas, la colonia más peculiar: la hacienda pública en la definición e la política colonial, 1762–1868*. Madrid: CSIC, 1999.

———. *Colonias para despues de un imperio*. Barcelona: Bellaterra, 2005.

Francisco, Leeann. "Flipping the Script: Gabriela Silang's Legacy through Stagecraft." Senior thesis, Dominican University of California, 2020.

Frank, Andre Gunder. "The World Economic System in Asia before European Hegemony." *The Historian* 56 (1994): 259–276.

Fuchs, Barbara. *Mimesis and Empire. The New World, Islam, and European Identities*. New York: Cambridge University Press, 2001.

———. "Virtual Spaniards. The Moriscos and the Fictions of Spanish Identity." *Journal of Spanish Cultural Studies* 2 (2001): 13–26.

Gabbert, Wolfgang. *Violence and the Caste War of Yucatán*. Cambridge, UK: Cambridge University Press, 2019.

Gallup-Díaz, Ignacio. "A Legacy of Strife: Rebellious Slaves in Sixteenth-Century Panamá." *Colonial Latin American Review* 19, no. 10 (2010): 391–412.

Ganson, Barbara. *The Guaraní Under Spanish Rule in the Río de La Plata*. Stanford, CA: Stanford University Press, 2003.

García-Abásalo, Antonio. "Los Chinos y el modelo colonial español en Filipinas." *Cuadernos de Historia Moderna* (2011): 223–242.

Gebhardt, Jonathan. "Microhistory and Microcosm: Chinese Migrants, Spanish Empire, and Globalization in Early Modern Manila." *Journal of Medieval and Early Modern Studies* 47, no. 1 (2017): 167–192.

Gharala, Norah H. *Taxing Blackness: Free Afromexican Tribute in Bourbon New Spain*. Tuscaloosa: University of Alabama Press, 2019.

Gil, Juan. *Los chinos en Manila: siglos XVI y XVII*. Lisbon: Centro Científico e Cultural de Macau, 2011.

Giráldez, Arturo. *The Age of Trade: The Manila Galleons and the Dawn of the Global Economy*. London: Rowman and Littlefield, 2015.

Go, Bon Juan. "Ma'I in Chinese Records—Mindoro or Bai? An Examination of a Historical Puzzle." *Philippine Studies* 53, no. 1 (2005): 119–138

Go, Bon Juan, and Joaquin Sy. *The Philippines in Ancient Chinese Maps*. Manila: Kaisa Para Sa Kaunlaran, 2000.

Gomez Platero, Eusebio. *Catálogo biográfico de los religiosos franciscanos de la provincia de San Gregorio Magno de Filipinas desde 1577 en que llegaron los primeros á Manila hasta los de nuestros días*. Manila: Manila Press of the Royal College of Sto. Tomas, 1880.

Gómez-Centurión, Carlos. "Treasures Fit for a King: King Charles III of Spain's Indian Elephants." *Journal of the History of Collections* 22 (2009): 29–44.

Gómez-Centurión Jiménez, Carlos. "Curiosidades vivas. Los animales de América y Filipinas en la ménagerie real durante el siglo XVIII." *Anuario de Estudios Americanos* 66, no. 2 (2009): 181–211.

Gonzalves, Theodore S. "When the Walls Speak a Nation: Contemporary Murals and the Narration of Filipina/O America." *Journal of Asian American Studies* 1 (1998): 31–63.

Grafe, Regina, and Alejandra Irigoin. "Bargaining for Absolutism: A Spanish Path to Nation-State and Empire Building." *Hispanic American Historical Review* 88, no. 2 (2008): 173–2019.

Güereca Durán, Raquel Eréndira. *Milicias indígenas en Nueva España: Reflexiones del derecho indiano sobre los derechos de guerra*. México, D.F.: Universidad Nacional Autónoma de México, Instituto de Investigaciones Jurídicas, 2016.

———. "Un profeta Otomí en tiempos de crisis: Diego Agustín y el movimiento religioso de la Sierra de Tutotepec, 1769." *Nuevo Mundo Mundos Nuevos* (2012).https://doi.org/10.4000/nuevomundo.63669.

Guingona, Phillip B. "A Ghost and His Apparition Roam the South China Sea: Limahong and the Dream of a Hokkien Nation (南中國海上陰魂不散的鬼魅及其幻影：林鳳和一個閩南民族的夢)." *Translocal Chinese: East Asian Perspectives* 11, no. 1 (2017): 90–124.

Hämäläinen, Pekka. *The Comanche Empire*. New Haven, CT: Yale University Press, 2008.

Hang, Xing. *Conflict and Commerce in Maritime East Asia: The Zheng Family and the Shaping of the Modern World, C.1620–1720*. Cambridge, UK: Cambridge University Press, 2015.

———. "A Question of Hairdos and Fashion." *Oriens Extremus* 47 (2008): 246–280.

Hanna, Mark G. *Pirate Nests and the Rise of the British Empire, 1570–1740*. Chapel Hill: University of North Carolina Press, 2015.

Harvey, L. P. *Muslims in Spain, 1500 to 1614*. Chicago: University of Chicago Press, 2005.

Hau, Caroline. "Transregional Southeast Asia: Perspectives from an Outlier." *Philippine Studies* 68, no. 1 (2020): 3–28.

Heng, Geraldine. *The Invention of Race in the European Middle Ages*. New York: Cambridge University Press, 2018.

Hernández Lefranc, Harold. "El trayecto de Santiago Apóstol de Europa Al Perú." *Investigaciones Sociales* 10, no. 16 (2006): 51–92.

Hershenzon, Daniel. *The Captive Sea: Slavery, Communication, and Commerce in Early Modern Spain and the Mediterranean*. Philadelphia: University of Pennsylvania Press, 2018.

Herzog, Tamar. "¡Viva el rey, muera el mal gobierno! y la administración de justicia quiteña, siglos XVII-XVIII." In *Dinámicas de antiguo régimen y orden constitucional: representación, justicia y administración en Iberoamérica, siglos XVIII-XIX*, edited by Marco Bellingeri, 77-96. Turín: Otto Editore, 2000.

Hezel, Francis X., and Marjorie C. Driver. "From Conquest to Colonisation: Spain in the Mariana Islands 1690-1740." *Journal of Pacific History* 23, no. 2 (1988): 137-155.

Hidalgo Nuchera, Patricio. "La encomienda en Filipinas." In *España y el Pacífico: Legazpi* edited by Leoncio Cabrero Fernández, 465-484. Madrid: Sociedad Estatal de Conmemoraciones Culturales, 2004.

———. "La entrada de los gobernadores en Manila: el ceremonial y sus costes." *Revista de Indias* 75, no. 265 (2015): 615-644.

Hu-DeHart, Evelyn. "Indispensable Enemy or Convenient Scapegoat? A Critical Examination of Sinophobia in Latin America and the Caribbean, 1870s to 1930s." In *The Chinese in Latin America and the Caribbean*, edited by Walton Look Lai and Chee-Beng Tan. Boston: Brill, 2010.

Hu-DeHart, Evelyn, and Kathleen López. "Asian Diasporas in Latin America and the Caribbean: An Historical Overview." *Afro-Hispanic Review* 27, no. 1 (2008): 9-21.

Iglesias, Lucila. "Moros en la costa (del Pacífco). Imágenes e ideas sobre el muslmán en el virreinato del Perú." *Diálogo Andino* 45 (2014): 5-15.

Ileto, Reynaldo Clemeña. *Pasyon and Revolution: Popular Movements in the Philippines, 1840-1910*. Quezon City: Ateneo de Manila University Press, 1979.

Ireton, Chloe. "Africans' Freedom Litigation Suits to Define Just War and Just Slavery in the Early Spanish Empire." *Renaissance Quarterly* 73, no. 4 (2020): 1277-1319.

Irving, D. R. M. *Colonial Counterpoint: Music in Early Modern Manila*. New York: Oxford University Press, 2010.

Jackson, R. H. *Regional Conflict and Demographic Patterns on the Jesuit Missions among the Guaraní in the Seventeenth and Eighteenth Centuries*. Leiden: Brill, 2018.

Javellana, René. *Fortress of Empire: Spanish Colonial Fortifications in the Philippines 1565-1898*. Makati City: Bookmark, 1997.

Jonas, Raymond Anthony. *France and the Cult of the Sacred Heart: An Epic Tale for Modern Times*. Berkeley: University of California Press, 2000.

Jones, Russell. "The Chiangchew Hokkiens, the True Pioneers in the Nanyang." *Journal of the Malaysian Branch of the Royal Asiatic Society* 82 (2009): 39-66.

Junker, Laura Lee. *Raiding, Trading, and Feasting: The Political Economy of Philippine Chiefdoms*. Honolulu: University of Hawai'i Press, 1999.

———. "Trade Competition, Conflict, and Political Transformations in Sixth- to Sixteenth-Century Philippine Chiefdoms." *Asian Perspectives* 33, no. 2 (1994): 230-260.

Kars, Marjoleine. *Blood on the River: A Chronicle of Mutiny and Freedom on the Wild Coast*. New York: The New Press, 2020.

———. "Dodging Rebellion. Politics and Gender in the Berbice Slave Uprising." *American Historical Review* 121, no. 1 (February 2016): 39-69.

Kenji, Igawa. "At the Crossroads: Limahon and Wakō in Sixteenth-Century Philippines." In *Elusive Pirates, Pervasive Smugglers: Violence and Clandestine Trade in the Greater China Seas*, edited by Robert J. Antony, 73-84. Hong Kong: Hong Kong University Press, 2011.

Kinkel, Sarah. *Disciplining the Empire: Politics, Governance, and the Rise of the British Navy* Cambridge, MA: Harvard University Press, 2018.

Klooster, Wim. *Revolutions in the Atlantic World, New Edition: A Comparative History*. 2nd ed. New York: New York University Press, 2018.

Kramer, Paul A. *The Blood of Government. Race, Empire, the United States, and the Philippines*. Chapel Hill: University of North Carolina Press, 2006.

Kreike, Emmanuel. *Scorched Earth: Environmental Warfare as a Crime Against Humanity and Nature*. Princeton, NJ: Princeton University Press, 2021.

Kroupa, Sebestian. "Reading Beneath the Skin: Indigenous Tattooing in the Early Spanish Philippines, ca. 1520–1720." *American Historical Review* 127, no. 3 (2022): 1252–1287.

Kueh, Joshua Eng Sin. "Adaptive Strategies of Parián Chinese: Fictive Kinship and Credit in Seventeenth-Century Manila." *Philippine Studies* 61, no. 3 (2013): 362–384.

———. "The Manila Chinese: Community, Trade and Empire, C. 1570–C. 1770." PhD diss., Georgetown University, 2014.

Kuethe, Allan, and Kenneth J. Andrien. *The Spanish Atlantic World in the Eighteenth Century: War and the Bourbon Reforms 1713–1796*. New York: Cambridge University Press, 2014.

Laarhoven, Ruurdje. "The Chinese at Maguindanao in the Seventeenth Century." *Philippines Studies* 35, no. 1 (1987): 31–50.

Lane, Kris. *Pillaging the Empire: Global Piracy on the High Seas, 1500–1750*. Armonk, NY: M. E. Sharpe, 1998.

Lara, Jaime. *City, Temple, Stage: Eschatological Architecture and Liturgical Theatrics New Spain*. Notre Dame, IN: University of Notre Dame Press, 2004.

Larkin, John A. *The Pampangans: Colonial Society in a Philippine Province*. Berkeley: University of California Press, 1972.

Le Gentil, Guillaume Joseph Hyacinthe Jean Baptiste. *A Voyage to the Indian Seas by Guillaume Joseph Hyacinthe Jean Baptiste Le Gentil de La Galaisière*. Translated by Frederick C. Fischer. Manila: Filipiniana Book Guild, 1964.

Lee, Christina H. "The Chinese Problem in the Early Modern Missionary Project of the Spanish Philippines." *Laberinto* 9 (2016): 5–32.

———. *Saints of Resistance. Devotions in the Philippines Under Early Spanish Rule*. New York: Oxford University Press, 2021.

Lee, Erika. *The Making of Asian America: A History*. New York: Simon & Schuster, 2015.

Legarda, Benito. *After the Galleons: Foreign Trade, Economic Change & Entrepreneurship in the Nineteenth Century Philippines*. Quezon City: Ateneo de Manila University Press, 1999.

Leibsohn, Dana. "'Dentro y fuera de los muros': Manila, Ethnicity, and Colonial Cartography." *Ethnohistory* 61, no. 2 (2014): 229–251.

Lemarchand, René. "Introduction." In *Forgotten Genocides: Oblivion, Denial, and Memory*, edited by René Lemarchand, 1–19. Philadelphia: University of Pennsylvania Press, 2013.

León Portilla, Miguel. "La embajada de los japoneses en México, 1614: el testimonio en náhuatl del cronista Chimalpahin." *Estudios de Asia yÁfrica* 16, no. 2 (1981): 215–242.

Lesser, Jeffrey, Evelyn Hu-Dehart, and Ignacio López-Calvo. "Why Asia and Latin America?" *Verge: Studies in Global Asias* 3 (2017): 1–16.

Liu, Yonghua. *Confucian Rituals and Chinese Villagers: Ritual Change and Social Transformation in a Southeastern Chinese Community, 1368–1949*. Leiden: Brill, 2013.

Llanes, Ferdinand C. "Dropping Artillery, Loading Rice and Elephants: A Spanish Ambassador in the Court of Ayudhya in 1718." *New Zealand Journal of Asian Studies* 11, no. 1 (2009): 60–74.

Llobet, Ruth de. "Chinese Mestizo and Natives' Disputes in Manila and the 1812 Constitution: Old Privileges and New Political Realities (1813–15)." *Journal of Southeast Asian Studies* 45, no. 2 (2014): 214–235.

Lockhart, James Martin. *The Men of Cajamarca: A Social and Biographical Study of the First Conquerors of Peru.* Austin: University of Texas Press, 1972.

Lopez, Ariel Cusi. "An Exploration into the Political Background of the Maguindanao 'Piracy' in the Early Eighteenth Century." In *Piracy and Surreptitious Activities in the Malay Archipelago and Adjacent Seas, 1600–1840,* edited by Y. H. Teddy Sim, 105–120. Singapore: Springer Singapore, 2014.

López Lázaro, Fabio. *The Misfortunes of Alonso Ramírez: The True Adventures of a Spanish-American with 17th-Century Pirates.* Austin: University of Texas Press, 2011.

Lüdtke, Alf. "Explaining Forced Migration." In *Removing Peoples. Forced Removal in the Modern World,* edited by Richard Bessell and Claudia B. Haake, 13–32. Oxford, UK: Oxford University Press, 2009.

Luengo Gutiérrez, Pedro. "European Architecture in Southeast Asia During the 18th Century: Between Tradition and Hybridization." In *New Worlds: Frontiers, Inclusion, Utopias,* edited by Claudia Mattos Avolese and Roberto Conduru, 254–270. Campinas: Comitê Brasileiro de História da Arte, 2017.

——. "Fortificaciones musulmanes en Joló: Resistencia, adaptación, y reinterpretación de la guerra moderna occidental." *Revista Aldaba* 40 (2015): 197–213.

——. "La fortificación del archipiélago Filipino en el siglo XVIII: La defensa integral ante lo local y lo global." *Revista de Indias* 77, no. 271 (2017): 727–758.

——. *Manila, plaza fuerte (1762–1788): Ingenieros militares entre Asia, América y Europa.* Madrid: Consejo Superior de Investigaciones Científicas: Ministerio de Defensa, 2013.

——. "Military Engineering in Eighteenth-Century Havana and Manila: The Experience of the Seven Years War." *War in History* 24, no. 1 (2017): 4–27.

Luis, Diego. "The Armed *Chino*: Licensing Fear in New Spain." *Journal of Colonialism and Colonial History* 20, no. 1 (2019). https://doi.org/10.1353/cch.2019.0000.

Lynch, John. "The Expulsion of the Jesuits and the Late Colonial Period." In *The Cambridge History of Religions in Latin America,* edited by Virginia Garrard-Burnett, 220–230. Cambridge, UK: Cambridge University Press, 2016.

Macdougall, Philip. "British Seapower and the Mysore Wars of the Eighteenth Century." *Mariner's Mirror* 97, no. 4 (2013): 299–314.

——. *Naval Resistance to Britain's Growing Power in India, 1660–1800: The Saffron Banner and the Tiger of Mysore.* Martlesham, UK: Boydell & Brewer, 2014.

Machado, Pedro. "A Forgotten Corner of the Indian Ocean: Gujarati Merchants, Portuguese India and the Mozambique Slave-Trade, C. 1730–1830." *Slavery & Abolition: A Journal of Slave and Post-Slave Studies* 28, no. 2 (2008): 17–32.

Majul, Cesar Adib. "The Moro Struggle in the Philippines." *Third World Quarterly* 10 (1988): 897–922.

——. *Muslims in the Philippines.* Quezon City: University of the Philippines Press, 1999.

Mallari, Francisco, S. J. "The Eighteenth Century Tirones." *Philippine Studies* 46, no. 3 (1998): 293–312.

Manchado López, Marta María. "Las relaciones entre la autoridad civil y las órdenes religiosas en filipinas durante el gobierno de Don Pedro Manuel de Arandía." *Anuario de Estudios Americanos* 53, no. 1 (1996): 37–52.

———. "El proyecto de convento para mestizas de Santa Rosa de Lima, en Filipinas." *Anuario de estudios americanos* 56, no. 2 (1999): 485–512.

———. "Religiosidad femenina y educación de la mujer indígena en Filipinas. El beaterio-colegio de la Madre Paula de La Santísima Trinidad." *Revista de Indias* 59, no. 215 (1999): 171–202.

Mancini, J. M. *Art and War in the Pacific World: Making, Breaking, and Taking from Anson's Voyage to the Philippine-American War*. Berkeley: University of California Press, 2018.

———. "Siege Mentalities: Objects in Motion, British Imperial Expansion, and the Pacific Turn." *Winterthur Portfolio* 45, no. 2/3 (2011): 125–140.

Mapp, Paul. *The Elusive West and the Contest for Empire, 1713–1763*. Chapel Hill: University of North Carolina Press, 2011.

Marichal, Carlos. *Bankruptcy of Empire: Mexican Silver and the Wars Between Spain, Britain and France, 1760–1810*. Cambridge, UK: Cambridge University Press, 2007.

———. "Rethinking Negotiation and Coercion in an Imperial State." *Hispanic American Historical Review* 88, no. 2 (2008): 211–218.

Marshall, P. J. *The Making and Unmaking of Empires: Britain, India, and America, C.1750–1783*. Oxford: Oxford University Press, 2005.

Martens, Pieter. "Siege Warfare (Early Modern)." In *The Encyclopedia of War*, edited by Gordon Martel, 1987–1994. Oxford: Wiley-Blackwell, 2012.

Martin, Meredith, and Gillian Weiss. *The Sun King at Sea: Maritime Art and Galley Slavery in Louis XIV's France*. Los Angeles: Getty Publications, 2022.

Martínez de Zuñiga, Joaquín. *Estadismo de las Islas Filipinas, o mis viajes por este país / por el padre Fr. Joaquín Martínez de Zúñiga; publica esta obra por primera vez extensamente anotada, W.E. Retana*. Vol. 2. Madrid: Imprenta de la Viuda de M. Minuesa de los Ríos, 1893.

Martínez, María Elena. "The Black Blood of New Spain: Limpieza de Sangre, Racial Violence, and Gendered Power in Early Colonial Mexico." *William and Mary Quarterly* 61, no. 3 (2004): 479–520.

———. *Genealogical Fictions. Limpieza de Sangre, Religion, and Gender in Colonial Mexico*. Stanford, CA: Stanford University Press, 2008.

Martínez, Miguel. "Manila's Sangleys and a Chinese Wedding (1625)." In *The Spanish Pacific, 1521–1815: A Reader of Primary Sources*, edited by Christina H. Lee and Ricardo Padrón, 73–89. Amsterdam: Amsterdam University Press, 2020.

Matthew, Laura E., and Michel R. Oudijk. *Indian Conquistadors: Indigenous Allies in the Conquest of Mesoamerica*. Norman: University of Oklahoma Press, 2007.

Mawani, Renisa. "Law, Settler Colonialism, and 'the Forgotten Space' of Maritime Worlds." *Annual Review of Law and Social Science* 12 (2016): 107–131.

Mawson, Stephanie. "Philippine Indios in the Service of Empire: Indigenous Soldiers and Contingent Loyalty, 1600–1700." *Ethnohistory* 63, no. 2 (2016): 381–413.

———. "Slavery, Conflict, and Empire in the Seventeenth-Century Philippines." In *Slavery and Bonded Labor in Asia, 1250–1900*, edited by Richard Allen, 256–283. Leiden: Brill, 2021.

———. "Unruly Plebeians and the Forzado System: Convict Transportation Between New Spain and the Philippines During the Seventeenth Century." *Revista de Indias* 73, no. 259 (2013): 693–730.

Mayshle, Peter. "Walled 'Memoria': Presencing Memory Sites in Intramuros, Manila." PhD diss., University of Wisconsin–Madison, 2014.

McDonnell, Michael. *Masters of Empire: Great Lakes Indians and the Making of America*. New York: Hill and Wang, 2015.

McEnroe, Sean F. "A Sleeping Army: The Military Origins of Interethnic Civic Structures on Mexico's Colonial Frontier." *Ethnohistory* 59, no. 1 (2011): 109–139.

McManus, Stuart M., and Dana Leibsohn. "Eloquence and Ethnohistory: Indigenous Loyalty and the Making of a Tagalog *Letrado*." *Colonial Latin American Review* 27, no. 4 (2019): 522–574.

Mehl, Eva Maria. *Forced Migration in the Spanish Pacific World: From Mexico to the Philippines, 1765–1811*. Cambridge, UK: Cambridge University Press, 2016.

Mendoza Cortes, Rosario. *Pangasinan, 1572–1800*. Quezon City: University of the Philippines Press, 1974.

Miles, Steven. *Chinese Diasporas: A Social History of Global Migration*. Cambridge, UK: Cambridge University Press, 2020.

Minamiki, George. *The Chinese Rites Controversy: From Its Beginning to Modern Times*. Chicago: Loyola University Press, 1985.

Mínguez, Víctor. "Iconografía de Lepanto. Arte, propaganda y representación simbólica de una monarquía universal y católica." *Obradoiro de Historia Moderna* 20 (2011): 251–280.

Mojares, Resil B. "Lapulapu in Folk Tradition." *Philippine Quarterly of Culture and Society* 7, no. 1/2 (1979): 59–68.

Mojarro Romero, Jorge. "Notas en torno a tres crónicas eclesiásticas hispanofilipinas del siglo XVIII." *Transmodernity: Journal of Peripheral Cultural Production of the Luso-Hispanic World* 4, no. 1 (2014): 100–110.

Montanez Sanabria, Elizabeth Del Pilar. "Challenging the Pacific Spanish Empire: Pirates in the Viceroyalty of Peru, 1570–1750." PhD diss., University of California, Davis, 2014.

Montero y Vidal, José. *Historia general de Filipinas desde el descubrimiento de dichas islas hasta nuestros días*. Vol. 2. Madrid: Impresor de cámara de S. M. c. de San Francisco, 4, 1894.

More, Anna. "The Colonial Latin American Archive: Dispossession, Ruins, Reinvention." In *The Routledge Hispanic Studies Companion to Colonial Latin America and the Caribbean (1492–1898)*, edited by Yolanda Martínez-San Miguel and Santa Arias, 295–308. New York: Routledge, 2021.

Morga, Antonio de. *The Philippine Islands, Moluccas, Siam, Cambodia, Japan, and China*. edited by Henry E. J. Stanley. Farnham, England: Ashgate, 2010.

———. *Sucesos de Las Islas Filipinas*. Madrid: V. Suárez, 1909.

Morley, Ian. *Cities and Nationhood: American Imperialism and Urban Design in the Philippines, 1898–1916*. Honolulu: University of Hawai'i Press, 2018.

Mulich, Jeppe. "Maritime Marronage in Colonial Borderlands." In *A World at Sea: Maritime Practices and Global History*, edited by Lauren Benton and Nathan Perl-Rosenthal, 133–148. Philadelphia: University of Pennsylvania Press, 2020.

Mundy, Barbara E. *The Death of Aztec Tenochtitlan, the Life of Mexico City*. Austin: University of Texas Press, 2015.

Muñoz, Juan Bautista, and Francisco Ignacio Alcina. *The Muñoz Text of Alcina's History of the Bisayan Islands (1668)*. Vol. 3. Chicago: University of Chicago 1962.

Murakami, Ei. "Trade and Crisis: China's Hinterlands in the Eighteenth Century." In *Hinterlands and Commodities: Place, Space, Time and the Political Economic Development of Asia over the Long Eighteenth Century*, edited by Tsukasa Mizushima, George Bryan Souza, and Dennis O. Flynn, 215–234. Leiden: Brill, 2015.

Nawab, Mohamed, and Mohamed Osman. "Understanding Islamophobia in Southeast Asia." In *The Routledge International Handbook of Islamophobia*, edited by Irene Zempi and Imran Awan, 286–297. New York: Routledge, 2019.

Neri, L. M., A. M. M. Ragragio, E. C. R. Robles, and A. J. Carlos. "The Archeology of Initao, Misamis Oriental." *Philippine Quarterly of Culture and Society* 37, no. 2/3 (2009): 173–187.

Newson, Linda A. *Conquest and Pestilence in the Early Spanish Philippines*. Honolulu: University of Hawai'i Press, 2009.

Ngai, Mae. *The Chinese Question: The Gold Rushes and Global Politics*. New York: W. W. Norton, 2021.

Nicolas, Arsenio. "Gongs, Bells, and Cymbals: The Archaeological Record in Maritime Asia from the Ninth to the Seventeenth Centuries." *Yearbook for Traditional Music* 41 (2009): 62–93.

Nightingale, Carl H. "Before Race Mattered: Geographies of the Color Line in Early Colonial Madras and New York." *American Historical Review* 113, no. 1 (2008): 48–71.

Nutini, Hugo G. "Syncretism and Acculturation: The Historical Development of the Cult of the Patron Saint in Tlaxcala, Mexico (1519–1670)." *Ethnology* 15, no. 3 (1976): 301–321

Osorio, Alejandra B. "Of National Boundaries and Imperial Geographies: A New Radical History of the Spanish Habsburg Empire." *Radical History Review*, 2018, no. 130 (2018): 100–130.

Owens, Sarah E. *Nuns Navigating the Spanish Empire*. Albuquerque: University of New Mexico Press, 2017.

Owensby, Brian P. *Empire of Law and Indian Justice in Colonial Mexico*. Stanford, CA: Stanford University Press, 2008.

Padrón, Ricardo. *The Indies of the Setting Sun: How Early Modern Spain Mapped the Far East as the Transpacific West* Chicago: University of Chicago Press, 2020.

Palanco Aguado, Fernando. "The Tagalog Revolts of 1745 According to Spanish Primary Sources." *Philippine Studies* 8, no. 1–2 (2010): 45–77.

Palanco, Fernando, and José S. Arcilla. "Diego Silang's Revolt: A New Approach." *Philippine Studies* 50, no. 4 (2002): 522–537.

Paquette, Gabriel. "The Image of Imperial Spain in British Political Thought, 1750–1800." *Bulletin of Spanish Studies* 81, no. 2 (2004): 187–214.

———. *Enlightenment, Governance, and Reform in Spain and Its Empire 1759–1808*. New York: Palgrave Macmillan, 2008.

Paredes, Oona. "Fringe Histories: Re-Placing Imperial Spaces in Southeast Asia Within an Indigenous Context." Friday Forum Lecture Series, Center for Southeast Asian Studies, University of Wisconsin–Madison, 2022.

———. *A Mountain of Difference: The Lumad in Early Colonial Mindanao*. Ithaca, NY: Southeast Asia Program Publications, Cornell University, 2013.

———. "Rivers of Memory and Oceans of Difference in the Lumad World of Mindanao." *TRaNS: Trans-Regional and National Studies of Southeast Asia* 4, no. 2 (2016): 324–349.

Parker, Geoffrey. "Crisis and Catastrophe: The Global Crisis of the Seventeenth Century Reconsidered." *American Historical Review* 113, no. 4 (2008): 1053–1079.

Pérez-Mallaína Bueno, Pablo Emilio. *Spain's Men of the Sea: Daily Life on the Indies Fleets in the Sixteenth Century*. Translated by Carla Rahn Phillips. Baltimore: Johns Hopkins University Press, 1998.

Permanyer Ugartemendia, Ander. "Beyond the Galleons: China Trade, Colonial Agenda and Regional Integration in the Eighteenth-Century Philippines." In *Philippine Confluence: Iberian, Chinese and Islamic Currents, C. 1500-1800*, edited by Jos Gommans and Ariel Cusi Lopez, 115-136. Leiden: Leiden University Press, 2020.

Phelan, John Leddy. *The Hispanization of the Philippines: Spanish Aims and Filipino Responses, 1565-1700*. Madison: University of Wisconsin Press, 1959.

———. *The People and the King: The Comunero Revolution in Colombia, 1781*. Madison: University of Wisconsin Press, 1978.

Phillips, Carla Rahn. *Six Galleons for the King of Spain: Imperial Defense in the Early Seventeenth Century*. Baltimore: Johns Hopkins University Press, 1986.

Pinzón Ríos, Guadalupe. *Acciones y reacciones en los puertos del mar del sur: desarrollo portuario del Pacífico Novohispano a Partir de Sus Políticas Defensivas, 1713-1789*. México, D.F.: Universidad Nacional Autónoma de México, 2012.

———. "En pos de nuevos botines. expediciones inglesas en el Pacífico Novohispano (1680-1763)." *Estudios de historia novohispana* 44 (2011): 45-76.

Po-Chia Hsia, Ronnie. "Imperial China and the Christian Mission." In *A Companion to the Early Modern Catholic Global Mission*, 344-364. Leiden: Brill, 2018.

———. "Introduction." In *A Companion to the Early Modern Catholic Global Missions*, edited by Ronnie Po-Chia Hsia, 1-14. Leiden: Brill, 2018.

Pollack, Aaron. "Hacia una historia social del tributo de indios y castas en Hispanoamérica. Notas en torno a su creación, desarrollo y abolición." *Historia Mexicana* 66, no. 1 (2016): 65-160.

Prange, Sebastian R. *Monsoon Islam: Trade and Faith on the Medieval Malabar Coast*. Cambridge, UK: Cambridge University Press, 2018.

———. "A Trade of No Dishonor: Piracy, Commerce, and Community in the Western Indian Ocean, Twelfth to Sixteenth Century." *American Historical Review* 116 (2011): 1269-1293.

Prange, Sebastian R., and Robert J. Antony. "Piracy in Asian Waters Part 2: Piracy, Sovereignty, and the Early Modern Asian State—an Introduction." *Journal of Early Modern History* 17 (2013): 1-7.

Pratt, Mary Louise. *Planetary Longings*. Durham, NC: Duke University Press, 2022.

Premo, Bianca. *Children of the Father King: Youth, Authority, & Legal Minority in Colonial Lima* Chapel Hill: University of North Carolina Press, 2005.

———. "Familiar: Thinking Beyond Lineage and across Race in Spanish Atlantic Family History." *William and Mary Quarterly* 70, no. 2 (2013): 295-316.

Prieto, Andrés I. "The Perils of Accommodation: Jesuit Missionary Strategies in the Early Modern World." *Journal of Jesuit Studies* 4, no. 3 (2017): 395-414.

Prieto Lucena, Ana María. *Filipinas durante el gobierno de Manrique de Lara, 1653-1663*. Seville: CSIC, 1984.

Priyadarshini, Meha. *Chinese Porcelain in Colonial Mexico: The Material Worlds of an Early Modern Trade*. Cham: Springer International Publishing, 2018.

Puente Luna, José Carlos de la. *Andean Cosmopolitans: Seeking Justice and Reward at the Spanish Royal Court*. Austin: University of Texas Press, 2018.

Quiason, Serafin D. *English "Country Trade" with the Philippines, 1644-1765*. Quezon City: University of the Philippines Press, 1966.

Rafael, Vincente L. *Contracting Colonialism: Translation and Christian Conversion in Tagalog Society Under Early Spanish Rule*. Ithaca: Cornell University Press, 1988.

———. "From Mardicas to Filipinos: Ternate, Cavite, in Philippine History." *Philippine Studies* 26, no. 4 (1978): 343–362.

Rai K., Mohankrishna. "Portuguese Hegemony over Mangalore." *Proceedings of the Indian History Congress* 64 (2003): 614–621.

Ramos, Frances L. *Identity, Ritual, and Power in Colonial Puebla.* Tucson: University of Arizona Press, 2012.

Ramos, Gabriela. "Conversion of Indigenous People in the Peruvian Andes: Politics and Historical Understanding." *History Compass* 14, no. 8 (2016). https://doi.org/10.1111/hic3.12323

Redden, Andrew. "Priestly Violence, Martyrdom, and Jesuits: The Case of Diego De Alfaro." In *Exploring Jesuit Distinctiveness: Interdisciplinary Perspectives on Ways of Proceeding within the Society of Jesus,* edited by Robert Aleksander Maryks, 81–113. Leiden: Brill, 2016.

Rediker, Marcus. *Between the Devil and the Deep Blue Sea: Merchant Seamen, Pirates and the Anglo-American Maritime World, 1700–1750.* Cambridge, UK: Cambridge University Press, 1989.

Rediker, Marcus, and Peter Linebaugh. *The Many-Headed Hydra: Sailors, Slaves, Commoners, and the Hidden History of the Revolutionary Atlantic* Boston: Beacon Press, 2000.

Reid, Anthony. "Entrepreneurial Minorities, Nationalism, and the State." In *Essential Outsiders: Chinese and Jews in the Modern Transformation of Southeast Asia and Central Europe,* 33–72. Seattle: University of Washington Press, 1997.

Reid-Vazquez, Michele. *The Year of the Lash: Free People of Color in Cuba and the Nineteenth-Century Atlantic World.* Athens: University of Georgia Press, 2011.

Reséndez, Andrés. *Conquering the Pacific: An Unknown Mariner and the Final Great Voyage of the Age of Discovery.* New York: Houghton Mifflin Harcourt, 2021.

Restall, Matthew. *Seven Myths of the Spanish Conquest: Updated Edition.* New York: Oxford University Press, 2021.

Reyes, Melba Falck, and Héctor Palacios. *El Japonés que conquistó Guadalajara. La historia de Juan de Páez en la Guadalajara del siglo XVIII.* Guadalajara, Jalisco, México: Universidad de Guadalajara, Biblioteca Pública del Estado de Jalisco Juan José Arreola, 2009.

Reyes, Raquel A. G. "Flaunting It: How the Galleon Trade Made Manila, Circa 1571–1800." *Early American Studies* 15, no. 4 (2017): 683–713.

Reyes y Florentino, Isabelo de los. *Historia de Ilocos.* Vol. 2. Manila: Establecimiento tipográfico La Opinión, 1890.

Risso, Patricia. "Cross-Cultural Perceptions of Piracy: Maritime Violence in the Western Indian Ocean and Persian Gulf Region During a Long Eighteenth Century." *Journal of World History* 12, no. 2 (2001): 293–319.

Rixhon, Gerard. *Voices from Sulu: A Collection of Tausug Oral Traditions.* Quezon City: Ateneo de Manila University Press, 2010.

Rizal, José. *El Filibusterismo.* Barcelona: F. Granada y Cª, 1911.

———. *Noli Me Tangere.* Caracas: Biblioteca Ayacucho, 1976.

Rodríguez Moya, Inmaculada. "El renacimiento del águila hispánica. La emblemática en los festejos por los nacimientos de príncipes españoles en Milán." *Revista Goya* 364 (2019): 210–234.

Roman y Zamora, Jerónimo. *Repúblicas de Indias: idolatrias y gobierno en México y Perú antes de la conquista.* Vol. 2. Madrid: V. Suárez, 1897.

Romero Mesaque, Carlos José. "Los comienzos de la cofradía de Nuestra Señora Del Rosario de Manila (1594–1650). Notas históricas de una institución colonial de la Orden de Predicadores." *Archivo Dominicao* 37 (2016): 391–413.

Routledge, David. *Diego Silang and the Origins of Philippine Nationalism*. Quezon City: Philippine Center for Advanced Studies, University of the Philippines, 1979.

Ruitenbeek, Klass. "Mazu, the Patroness of Sailors, in Chinese Pictorial Art." *Artibus Asiae* 58, no. 3/4 (1999): 281–289.

Ruíz Gutiérrez, Ana. "De indomables a almas temerosas: percepciones de los indígenas de la Cordillera de Luzón: los Igorrotes," In *En compañía de salvajes: el sujeto indígena en la construcción del otro*, edited by Alberto Baena Zapatero and Izaskun Alvarez Cuartero, 227–261. Madrid: Iberoamericana Editorial Vervuert, 2021.

———. "El Parián de Manila: Origen y evolución de la Alcaicería de los sangleyes." Paper presented at the Mirando a Clío. El arte español espejo de su historia, Santiago de Compostela, 2010.

Ruiz-Stovel, Guillermo. "Chinese Shipping and Merchant Networks at the Edge of the Spanish Pacific: The Minnan-Manila Trade, 1680–1840." PhD diss., UCLA, 2019.

Ryan, Lyndall. "Digital Map of Colonial Frontier Massacres in Australia 1788–1930." *Teaching History* 54, no. 3 (2020): 13–20.

Sala-Boza, Astrid. "The Genealogy of Hari'tupas: An Ethnohistory of Chiefly Power and Heirarchy in Sugbu as a Protostate." *Philippine Quarterly of Culture and Society* 34, no. 3 (2006): 253–311.

Salas y Rodriguez, F. J. *Coleccíon de documentos inéditos relativos al descubrimiento, conquista y organización de las antiguas posesiones españolas de ultramar*. Vol. 2–3. Madrid: Est. Tipográfico, 1887.

Salazar Carreño, Robinson. "El compadrazgo de esclavos en el siglo XVIII en la parroquia de Nuestra Señora del Socorro (Nuevo Reino de Granada)." *Anuario de Estudios Americanos* 76, no. 2 (2019): 467–494.

Saleeby, Najeeb M. *The History of Sulu*. Manila: Bureau of Science, 1908.

Santiago, Luciano P. R. "The First Filipino Doctors of Ecclesiastical Sciences (1772–1796)." *Philippine Quarterly of Culture and Society* 12, no. 4 (1984): 257–270.

———. *The Hidden Light: The First Filipino Priests*. Quezon City: New Day Publishers, 1987.

Sartorius, David. *Ever Faithful: Race, Loyalty, and the Ends of Empire in Spanish Cuba*. Durham, NC: Duke University Press, 2013.

Scammell, G. V. "European Exiles, Renegades and Outlaws and the Maritime Economy of Asia C.1500–1750." *Modern Asian Studies* 26, no. 4 (1992): 641–661.

Schneider, Elena Andrea. *The Occupation of Havana: War, Trade, and Slavery in the Atlantic World*. Chapel Hill: University of North Carolina Press, 2018.

Schreurs, Peter. "The Royal Fort at Tandag (1609–1823)." *Philippine Quarterly of Culture and Society* 11, no. 2/3 (1983): 107–122.

Schultz, Travis. "Limahong's Pirates, Ming Mariners, and Early Sino-Spanish Relations. The Pangasinan Campaign of 1575 and Global History from Below." *Philippine Studies* 67, no. 3/4 (2019): 315–342.

Schurz, William Lytle. *The Manila Galleon*. New York: E. P. Dutton, 1939.

Schwaller, Robert. "'For Honor and Defense': Race and the Right to Bear Arms in Early Colonial Mexico." *Colonial Latin American Review* 21, no. 2 (2012): 239–266.

Scott, James C. *The Art of Not Being Governed: An Anarchist History of Upland Southeast Asia*. New Haven: Yale University Press, 2009.

———. *Domination and the Arts of Resistance: Hidden Transcripts*. New Haven: Yale University Press, 1990.

Scott, Julius S. *The Common Wind: Afro-American Currents in the Age of the Haitian Revolution*. London: Verso, 2018.

Scott, William Henry. *Barangay: Sixteenth-Century Philippine Culture and Society*. Quezon City: Ateneo de Manila University Press, 1994.

———. *Cracks in the Parchment Curtain and Other Essays in Philippine History*. Quezon City: New Day Publishers, 1985.

———. *The Discovery of the Igorots: Spanish Contacts with the Pagans of Northern Luzon*. Quezon City: New Day Press, 1974.

———. "Filipino Class Structure in the Sixteenth Century." *Philippine Studies* 28, no. 2 (1980): 142–175.

———. *Slavery in the Spanish Philippines*. Manila: De La Salle Press, 1991.

Seijas, Tatiana. *Asian Slaves in Colonial Mexico: From Chinos to Indians*. Cambridge, UK: Cambridge University Press 2014.

———. "Indios Chinos in Eighteenth-Century Mexico." In *To Be Indio in Colonial Spanish America*, edited by Mónica Díaz, 123–140. Albuquerque: University of New Mexico Press, 2017.

Sen, Sudipta, and May Joseph. "Introduction." In *Terra Aqua: The Amphibious Lifeworlds of Coastal and Maritime South Asia*, edited by Sudipta Sen and May Joseph, 1–12. New York: Routledge, 2022.

Serulnikov, Sergio. *Revolution in the Andes: The Age of Túpac Amaru*. Translated by David Frye. Durham, NC: Duke University Press, 2013.

Siu, Lok C. D. *Memories of a Future Home: Diasporic Citizenship of Chinese in Panama*. Stanford, CA: Stanford University Press, 2005.

Sivasundaram, Sujit. *Waves Across the South: A New History of Revolution and Empire*. London: William Collins, 2020.

Skemer, Don C. "An Arabic Book Before the Spanish Inquisition." *Princeton University Library Chronicle* 64 (2002): 107–120.

Slack, Edward R. "New Perspectives on Manila's Chinese Community at the Turn of the Eighteenth Century. The Forgotten Case of Pedro Barredo, Alcalde Mayor of the Parián 1701–1704." *Journal of Chinese Overseas* 17 (2021): 111–146.

So, Kwan-Wai. *Japanese Piracy in Ming China During the 16th Century*. East Lansing: Michigan State University Press, 1975.

Souza, George Bryan, and Jeffrey Scott Turley. *The Boxer Codex: Transcription and Translation of an Illustrated Late Sixteenth-Century Spanish Manuscript Concerning the Geography, History and Ethnography of the Pacific, South-East and East Asia*. Leiden: Brill, 2016.

Soyer, Francois. "The Public Baptism of Muslims in Early Modern Spain and Portugal: Forging Communal Identity through Collective Emotional Display." *Journal of Religious History* 39, no. 4 (2015): 506–523.

Stanyukovich, Maria V. "Peacemaking Ideology in a Headhunting Society: Hudhud, Women's Epic of the Ifugao." In *Hunters and Gatherers in the Modern World. Conflict, Resistance, and Self-Determination*, edited by Peter P. Schweitzer, Megan Biesele, and Robert Hitchcock, 399–409. New York: Berghahn Books, 2000.

Stark, David. "Ties That Bind: Baptismal Sponsorship of Slaves in Eighteenth-Century Puerto Rico." *Slavery & Abolition* 36, no. 1 (2015): 84–110.

Stoler, Ann Laura. "Rethinking Colonial Categories: European Communities and the Boundaries of Rule." *Comparative Studies in Society and History* 31, no. 1 (1989): 134–161.

Sutherland, Heather. "The Sulu Zone Revisited." *Journal of Southeast Asian Studies* 35, no. 1 (2004): 133–157.

Tan, Antonio S. "The Chinese Mestizos and the Formation of the Filipino Nationality." *Archipel* 32 (1986): 141–162.

Tardieu, Jean-Pierre. *Cimarrones de Panamá: la forja de una identidad afroamericana en el siglo XVI*. Frankfurt am Main: Vervuert Verlagsgesellschaft, 2009.

Taylor, William B. *Drinking, Homicide & Rebellion in Colonial Mexican Villages*. Stanford, CA: Stanford University Press, 1979.

———. *Magistrates of the Sacred: Priests and Parishioners in Eighteenth-Century Mexico*. Stanford, CA: Stanford University Press, 1996.

Thomas, Megan C. "Proclaiming Sovereignty: Reflections from the Eighteenth-Century Philippines." In *Comparative Political Theory in Time and Place*, edited by Daniel J. Kapust and Helen M. Kinsella, 79–104. New York: Palgrave, 2017.

———. "Securing Trade: The Military Labor of the British Occupation of Manila, 1762–1764." *International Review of Social History* 64, no. 27 (2019): 125–147.

Ting, Michael Teodoro G., Jr., Augencio Bagsic, Mylene M. Eguilos, Ryan Jaen, Maria Loudes P. Respicio, and Christopher Ryan T. Tan. "Modernity Vs. Culture: Protecting the Indigenous Peoples of the Philippines." *European Journal of Economic and Political Studies* 1 (2008): 77–98.

Tiongson, Nicanor G. *Komedya*. Diliman, Quezon City: University of the Philippines Press, 1999.

Tracy, Nicholas. "The British Expedition to Manila." In *The Seven Year's War: Global Views*, edited by Mark H. Danley and Patrick J. Speelman, 461–486. Leiden: Brill, 2012.

———. *Manila Ransomed: The British Assault on Manila in the Seven Years War*. Exeter, UK: University of Exeter Press, 1995.

Tremml, Birgit Magdalena. "The Global and the Local: Problematic Dynamics of the Triangular Trade in Early Modern Manila." *Journal of World History* 23, no. 3 (2012): 555–588.

———. *Spain, China and Japan in Manila, 1571–1644: Local Comparisons and Global Connections*. Amsterdam: Amsterdam University Press, 2015.

———. "When Political Economies Meet: Spain, China and Japan in Manila, ca. 1571–1644." PhD diss., University of Vienna, 2012.

———. "Marginal Players and Intra-Network Connections: New Perspectives on the Manila Trade, C. 1640–1780." *Journal of Social Sciences and Philosophy* 29, no. 4 (2017): 599–626.

Trota Jose, Regalado. "Imaging Our Lady in Sixteenth-Century Manila: Nuestra Señora Del Rosario de La Naval." *Diagonal: Journal of the Center for Iberian and Latin American Music* (2008). https://cilam.ucr.edu/diagonal/issues/2008/TrotaJose2.pdf.

Tueller, James B. "The Moriscos Who Stayed Behind or Returned: Post-1609." In *The Expulsion of the Moriscos from Spain: A Mediterranean Diaspora*, 197–215. Leiden: Brill, 2014.

Twinam, Ann. *Purchasing Whiteness: Pardos, Mulattos, and the Quest for Social Mobility in the Spanish Indies*. Stanford, CA: Stanford University Press, 2015.

U.S. Philippine Commission. *Report of the Philippine Commission, Part 1*. Washington, DC: Government Printing Office, 1995.

Valenzuela-Márquez, Jaime. "Los indios *cuzcos* de Chile colonial: estrategias semánticas, usos de la memoria y gestión de identidades entre inmigrantes andinos (siglos XVI-XVII)." *Nuevo Mundo Mundos Nuevos* (2010). https://journals.openedition.org/nuevomun do/60271.

van Deusen, Nancy E. "Seeing Indios in Sixteenth Century Castile." *William and Mary Quarterly* 69, no. 2 (2012): 205–234.

van Duijnen, Michel. "'Sacrificed to the Madness of the Bloodthirsty Sabre': Violence and the Great Turkish War in the Work of De Hooghe." In *A Global History of Early Modern Violence*, edited by Erica M. Charters, Marie Houllemare, and Peter Wilson, 179–200. Manchester, UK: Manchester University Press, 2020.

Van Young, Eric. *The Other Rebellion: Popular Violence, Ideology, and the Mexican Struggle for Independence, 1810-18*. Stanford, CA: Stanford University Press, 2001.

Vanoli, Alessandro. "Between Absence and Presence: New Paths in the Historiography of Islam in the New World." *Journal of Medieval Iberian Studies* 2 (2010): 77–91.

Vaughn, James M. "The Ideological Origins of Illiberal Imperialism: Metropolitan Politics and the Post-1763 Transformation of the British Empire." In *Envisioning Empire: The New British World from 1763 to 1773*, edited by James M. Vaughn and Robert A. Olwell, 27–55, London: Bloomsbury Academic, 2020.

Viana, Francisco Leandro de. "Diario del sitio de la plaza de Manila por los ingleses." In *Documentos indispensables para la verdadera historia de Filipinas*, edited by P. Eduardo Navarro, 329–514. Madrid: Imprenta del Asilo de Huérfanos, 1908.

Victoria, Fr. José, and Fr. Manuel Rebollo. "Documento inédito." In *Documentos indispensables para la verdadera historia de Filipinas: 1762-1763*, edited by P. Eduardo Navarro, 11–45. Madrid: Imprenta del Asilo del Huérfanos, 1908.

Vicuña Guengerich, Sara. "A Royalist Cacica: Doña Teresa Choquehuanca and the Postrebellion Natives of the Peruvian Highlands." In *Cacicas: The Indigenous Women Leaders of Spanish America, 1492-1825*, edited by Margarita R. Ochoa and Sara Vicuña Guengerich, 215–239. Norman: University of Oklahoma Press, 2021.

Vila Miranda, Carlos. "Toma de Manila por los ingleses en 1762." *Anuario de Estudios Atlánticos* 53 (2007): 167–219.

Valerio. Miguel. *Sovereign Joy: Afro-Mexican Kings and Queens, 1539-1640*. Cambridge, UK: Cambridge University Press, 2002.

Villarroel, Fidel. *A History of the University of Santo Tomas: Four Centuries of Higher Education in the Philippines, 1611-2011*. Quezon City: University of Santo Tomas Publishing House, 2012.

Vinson III, Ben. *Bearing Arms for His Majesty: The Free-Colored Militia in Colonial Mexico* Stanford, CA: Stanford University Press, 2001.

Vivar, Pedro del, "Relación de los alzamientos de la ciudad de Vigán, cabecera de la provincia de Ilocos, en los años de 1762 y 1763." In *Biblioteca Histórica Filipina*, edited by Juan de Medina, 281–489. Manila: Chofré y Comp, 1893.

Voigt, Lisa. *Spectacular Wealth: The Festivals of Colonial South American Mining Towns*. Austin: University of Texas Press, 2016.

Walker, Charles F. *The Tupac Amaru Rebellion*. Cambridge, MA: Belknap Press, 2014.

Walravens, Meia. "Multiple Audiences of a History from Sixteenth-Century Malabar: Zayn Al-Din Al-Maʿbarī's Gift of the Strugglers for Jihad." *South Asian Studies* 35, no. 2 (2019): 226–236.

Wang, Wensheng. *White Lotus Rebels and South China Pirates: Crisis and Reform in the Qing Empire.* Cambridge, MA: Harvard University Press, 2014.

Wang, Yuanfei. *Writing Pirates: Vernacular Fiction and Oceans in Late Ming China.* Ann Arbor: University of Michigan Press, 2021.

Wang, Yueying. ""The Ancient Rites of China': Yan Mo on Ancestral Rites During the Chinese Rites Controversy." *Journal of World Christianity* 12, no. 1 (2022): 90–112.

Ward, Kerry. *Networks of Empire: Forced Migration in the Dutch East India Company.* Cambridge, UK: Cambridge University Press, 2009.

Warren, James Francis. "Balambangan and the Rise of the Sulu Sultanate, 1772–1775." *Journal of the Malaysian Branch of the Royal Asiatic Society* 50, no. 1 (1977): 73–93.

———. "The Iranun and Balangingi Slaving Voyage: Middle Passages in the Sulu Zone." In *Many Middle Passages: Forced Migration and the Making of the Modern World*, edited by Emma Christopher, Cassandra Pybus, and Marcus Rediker, 52–71. Berkeley: University of California Press, 2007.

———. *Iranun and Balangingi: Globalization, Maritime Raiding, and the Birth of Ethnicity.* Singapore: NUS Press, 2002.

———. *The Sulu Zone, 1768–1898: The Dynamics of External Trade, Slavery and Ethnicity in the Transformation of a Southeast Asian Maritime State.* 2nd ed. Singapore: NUS Press, 2007.

———. "Volcanoes, Refugees, and Raiders: The 1765 Macaturin Eruption and the Rise of the Iranun." In *Bondage and the Environment in the Indian Ocean World*, edited by Gwyn Campbell, 79–100. London: Palgrave Macmillan, 2018.

Way, Peter. "Rebellion of the Regulars: Working Soldiers and the Mutiny of 1763–1764." *William and Mary Quarterly* 57, no. 4 (2000): 761–792.

Weber, David J. *Bárbaros: Spaniards and Their Savages in the Age of Enlightenment.* New Haven, CT: Yale University Press, 2005.

White, Richard. *The Middle Ground: Indians, Empires, and Republics in the Great Lakes Region, 1650–1815.* Cambridge, UK: Cambridge University Press, 1991.

Wickberg, Edgar. *The Chinese in Philippine Life, 1850–1898.* New Haven, CT: Yale University Press, 1965.

———. "The Chinese Mestizo in Philippine History." *Journal of Southeast Asian History* 5 (1964): 62–100.

Wilson, Kathleen. *The Sense of the People: Politics, Culture, and Imperialism in England, 1715–1785.* Cambridge, UK: Cambridge University Press, 1995.

Yannakakis, Yanna. *The Art of Being In-Between: Native Intermediaries, Indian Identity, and Local Rule in Colonial Oaxaca.* Durham, NC: Duke University Press, 2008.

Yun Hui, Tsu "Between Heaven and the Deep Sea: The Religious Practice of Chinese Seafarers from the Eleventh to the Mid-Nineteenth Century." *East Asian History* 23 (2002): 69–86.

Yuste López, Carmen. *Emporios transpacíficos: comerciantes mexicanos en Manila, 1710–1815.* Mexico City: Universidad Nacional Autónoma de México, Instituto de Historia 2007.

Zires, Margarita. "Los mitos de la Virgen de Guadalupe. Su proceso de construcción y reinterpretación en el México pasado y contemporáneo." *Mexican Studies / Estudios Mexicanos* 10, no. 2 (1994): 281–313.

INDEX

bakers, 65, 74, 76, 79, 143, 144
Balaba (island), 41
Balooy, 50–51
bandala system, 33, 123, 157, 223
banditry, 92, 93, 95, 143
Bantay, 119, 159, 160, 232
Bantilan (brother of Azim ud-Din), 36, 41
Barangay, 8, 12, 26, 45, 55, 90, 91, 112, 122,
    132, 136, 138
Basco y Vargas, José (governor), 195
Basilan, 40
Batac, 116, 122, 124, 127
Batad, 92, 213
Batavia, 10, 27, 35, 63, 105, 147, 171, 188, 213.
    See also Dutch empire
battles, 1, 23, 43–47, 52–55, 73, 75–76, 80, 86,
    89, 91–93, 97–99, 108, 110, 112, 119–121, 125,
    127, 129, 131, 134, 136, 138, 139, 141, 147,
    148–152, 154, 159–161, 1163, 178, 203, 204
Bayambang, 127, 161
Bayúg, 34
beaterios, as prisons, 109, 229; Beaterio de
    Santa Cathalina de Sena, 196
Becbec, Pedro, 158, 159, 238
Bell, David A., 122, 160
Bible, 40, 67, 150
Binalatongan, 115, 116, 117, 118, 160, 161,
    163, 230
Binmaley, 116, 230
Binondo, 37, 88, 90, 139, 143, 179, 182, 190,
    191, 215
black legend of Spanish colonial rule,
    100, 226
Blanco, John D., 197
blockades, 27, 82, 152, 200
Bohol, 30, 34, 46, 48, 56, 107, 120, 136, 174;
    rebellion, 56–57, 58, 107, 203
Bonaparte, Napoleon, 4, 205
Borderlands and frontier zones: Philippines,
    11–12, 14, 20–24, 28–29, 31–34, 47, 49,
    57–58, 84, 99, 135, 201–202; in China, 73;
    in the Americas, 28–29, 33, 52, 134, 168,
    193. *See also* presidios
Borneo, 10, 24, 27, 34, 36, 41, 172, 213, 215
Bourbon monarchy, 170–171, 239, 240;
    Bourbon reforms, 4, 168, 171, 195–196,
    205–206
British empire, 164, 171, 200; British East
    India Company, 5, 16, 96, 99, 101, 107, 108,
    141, 146, 162, 172, 200, 213, 214; Manila

Council, 107, 129, 146, 151, 153, 156,
    228–229; British Royal Navy, 5, 16, 55, 96,
    101, 130, 145, 162, 200, 217
bronze, 118, 132, 164, 191, 200, 203
Bulacan: town, 103, 106, 109, 110, 134, 136,
    143, 180, 181; province, 103, 106, 139, 172,
    175, 192
burials, 46, 56, 99, 114
Bustos Lent, Mariano José, (Spanish
    general), 140, 164
Butuan, 28

cabecilla de los Sangleyes, 81, 89, 90, 176,
    187–188, 191
cabezas de barangay, 55, 79, 90, 91, 106,
    112, 136
Cabugao, 159
Cadíz, 201
Cagayan, 98, 119, 124, 127, 129, 136, 138,
    149, 161, 230, Cagayan river, 119, upris-
    ing, 119
Calamba, 75
Calasiao, 150, 160, 161
Calderón, Pedro, 191–193, 243
Calicut (Kozhikode), 24, 199
Camarines, 51, 135, 148
Canleong, Domingo, 174, 195, 244
cannibalism, 154, 237
Canton, 188, 189
Caraballo mountains, 119
Caraga, 51, 174
Caribbean, 7, 9, 176, 240. *See also* Cuba
casicasi (blood-mixing ceremony), 1
Casten, Francisco, 188–189
Castro y Amuedo, Fray Pedro Andrés de,
    114, 122, 134, 135, 141, 145, 146, 150, 152
Catbalogan, 51, 186
Catholic churches: fortified, 11, 21, 29–32, 57,
    100, 102, 116, 120–121, 128, 134–135, 136,
    160; destruction of, 20–21, 26, 67, 76, 81,
    99–101, 104–105, 122, 128, 151, 161, 163,
    167–168, 181–183; royal chapel in
    Intramuros, 46; Santo Domingo, 87, 102
Catholic masses, 33, 46, 86, 87, 116, 125, 158,
    164, 179–180, 191, 194
Catholic sacraments: anointing of the sick,
    155, 186; baptism, 24, 33, 37–40, 57, 64, 67,
    73–75, 78–87, 89, 94, 149, 155, 158, 167,
    170–175, 182, 185–187, 192, 193, 218, 220,
    221, 224, 240, 242; confession (penance),

ACKNOWLEDGMENTS

I was raised in Botany Bay (Kamay), the birthplace of the British empire in Australia, on the stolen land of the Kamaygal people. My interest in the history of my settler ancestors' contributions to genocide and dispossession in this country grew into a curiosity about colonialism and its afterlives in other parts of the world. The questions that I have asked about Spanish colonial rule in the Philippines, and that I have attempted to answer in this book, are the questions that I initially asked of the British empire. How did a small European nation establish a global empire? How did diverse imperial subjects experience colonial rule? In what ways did subalterns resist, support, escape from, and shape colonial politics and culture? And why did empire endure for so long? How should we write histories of empire? And how do we confront the weight of its legacies and afterlives? Thinking with the Spanish empire has given me an appreciation for the multiple possible trajectories that empires could have taken; there was nothing predetermined or inevitable about the emergence of the modern world as we know it. I hope this book speaks to readers with interests across Area Studies' artificial boundaries. To truly understand the history of colonialism, we need to look beyond near and familiar pasts.

My path to history began when I was an undergraduate student at the University of Sydney. As the first person in my family to go to university, I needed and benefited from the support of smart and enthusiastic historian teachers, including Emma Christopher, Clare Corbould, and Mike McDonnell. I am grateful for their friendship and willingness to provide all kinds of advice many years after graduation. Thank you, too, to Mum and Dad, Daniel and Bianka, and my Sydney tribe, including the Dinner Club caucus, Maria Catanzariti, Jenifer Luby, and Ashlie Hartigan, who have cheered me on over the years and have always welcomed me home with open arms.

Chasing knowledge about the past took me far from home, and I incurred many debts on this journey. I completed much of the research for this book as a doctoral student at the University of Texas at Austin. My advisor, Jorge Cañizares-Esguerra, encouraged me to take my dissertation project in different and exciting directions, along roads and across seas less traveled, and supported me to balance writing with parenting after my baby Oliver was born during my studies. I am grateful to my wonderful dissertation committee: Susan Deans-Smith, David R. M. Irving, Philippa Levine, and James Vaughn. Faculty members including Lina del Castillo, Julie Hardwick, Alison Frazier, and Joan Neuberger went above and beyond to provide valuable learning opportunities and cultivate a supportive community on campus. I benefited from the collegiality and friendships offered by a smart, supportive, and fun group of PhD students including Chloe Ireton, Adrian Masters, and Elizabeth O'Brien who accompanied me on research trips, as well as Maria José Afanador-Llach, Dharitri Bhattacharjee, Ben Breen, Sherry Chanis, Sandy Chang, Jesse Cromwell, Marcelo José Domingos, Luritta DuBois, Brittany Erwin, Nicolás Alejandro González Quintero, Julia Gossard, Christopher Heaney, Emily Kinney, Jack Loveridge, Jimena Perry, Nicholas Roland, Danielle Sanchez, Eddie Shore, Angela Sonquo Tapia, Christina Villarreal, Eyal Weinberg, and Susan Zacaib. Gulia Straw, Arup Chakraborty, Michael Diamond, Florencia Robledo, and Altina Hoti also made our Austin years happy ones.

Guadalupe Pinzón Rios was a generous mentor in Mexico City. Charlie kindly opened his home to me. Susan Zacaib and Kenny Moss helped me to navigate the archives and the city. In Pasadena I was hosted by Carolyn Sykes and her cats. Juan Gómez, Grace Egan, and Nicola Kirkby looked after me at the Huntington Library. The (then) junior faculty and alumni of the History Department at the University of the Philippines gave me a warm welcome in Manila and Quezon City were Kerby Alvarez, Alvin Camba, Grace Concepción, Ros Costello, Kristoffer Esquejo, Jely Galang, Kristyl Obispado, Mark Marvin Lagos, Aaron Mallari, Janet Reguindin-Estella, Nicholas Sy, and Rhoda Wani-Obias. Mam Rose Mendoza and Sir Ricky Trota shared their expert knowledge of the city's archives. Jorge Mojarro, Ambeth Ocampo, Ramón Sunico, and Guillermo Ramos were kind hosts.

Sebastian Prange brought me to the University of British Columbia's Department of History as a postdoctoral fellow and has been a kind and generous mentor ever since. Vancouver colleagues and friends who helped me set up in a new city and weather the pandemic include Jessica Hanser, Ben Bryce, Anna Casas Aguilar, Gabriel, Billy Coleman, Kerrin Bell, Clementine, Leonora Angeles, Mikki Stelder, Erika Doucette, Renisa Mawani, and Alexia Valdéz. The stunning forests and coastlines of Musqueam land provided calm and comfort when the world shut down.

I also want to thank other interlocutors who have shared ideas about history, empire, the early modern world, and the often mysterious mechanisms of academia: Matthew Champion, Eberhard Crailsheim, Heather Dalton, Mariana Dantas, Ashleigh Dean, Josep Fradera, Eliga Gould, Emma Hart, the late and missed Philippa Hetherington, Christina Juan, Samia Khatun, Dana Liebsohn, Cristina Lee, Ruth de Llobet, Sophie Loy Wilson, Adrian de Leon, Fabio López Lázaro, Jane Mangan, Stephanie Mawson, Una McIlvenna, Eva Mehl, Isobelle Barrett Meyering, Oona Paredes, Ander Permanyer, Vicente Rafael, Carla Rahn Phillips, Marcus Rediker, Elena Schneider, Tatiana Seijas, Lila Shahani, Jenny Spinks, and Miguel Valerio. A special thank you is owed to Guillermo Ruiz Stovel, who shared access to his entire digital archive, and Esther González, who assisted with some of the research for this book.

I finished writing this book in Naarm Melbourne on Wurundjeri land. I am grateful to Joy Damousi, Kate Fullagar, and Kathryn Perez for bringing me to Australia in the middle of a global pandemic. It is a privilege to be part of a vibrant community of researchers at the Institute for Humanities and Social Sciences at Australian Catholic University. I'm also grateful to Bob Lockhart at Penn Press for his excitement about this book and his patience with a first-time author. Norah Gharala and Robert Antony were generous in their feedback on an earlier version of the manuscript.

Special thanks to my little family—Alex, Oliver, and Leila—for accompanying me on this adventure.

A number of small and large grants enabled me to travel to archives to carry out research. At the University of Texas at Austin I received funding from the History Department, the Edward A. Clark Center for Australian and New Zealand Studies, the Teresa Lozano Long Institute of Latin American Studies (LLILAS), the College of Liberal Arts, and the Graduate School. I also received grants from the Newberry Library, the Huntington Library, the Lilly Library, the American Historical Association, the Manuscript Society, the American Society for Eighteenth-Century Studies, the Conference on Latin American History, the Fideicomiso Teixidor, the University of Sydney, Cornell University, and the Joint Center for History and

Economics at Harvard University and the University of Cambridge. A Killam postdoctoral fellowship at the University of British Columbia and funding from Australian Catholic University helped me to transform my dissertation into this book. In addition, I received funding from the Australian Academy of the Humanities Publication Subsidy Scheme.

Printed in the USA
CPSIA information can be obtained
at www.ICGtesting.com
JSHW021339130524
63050JS00002B/3

9 781512 825749